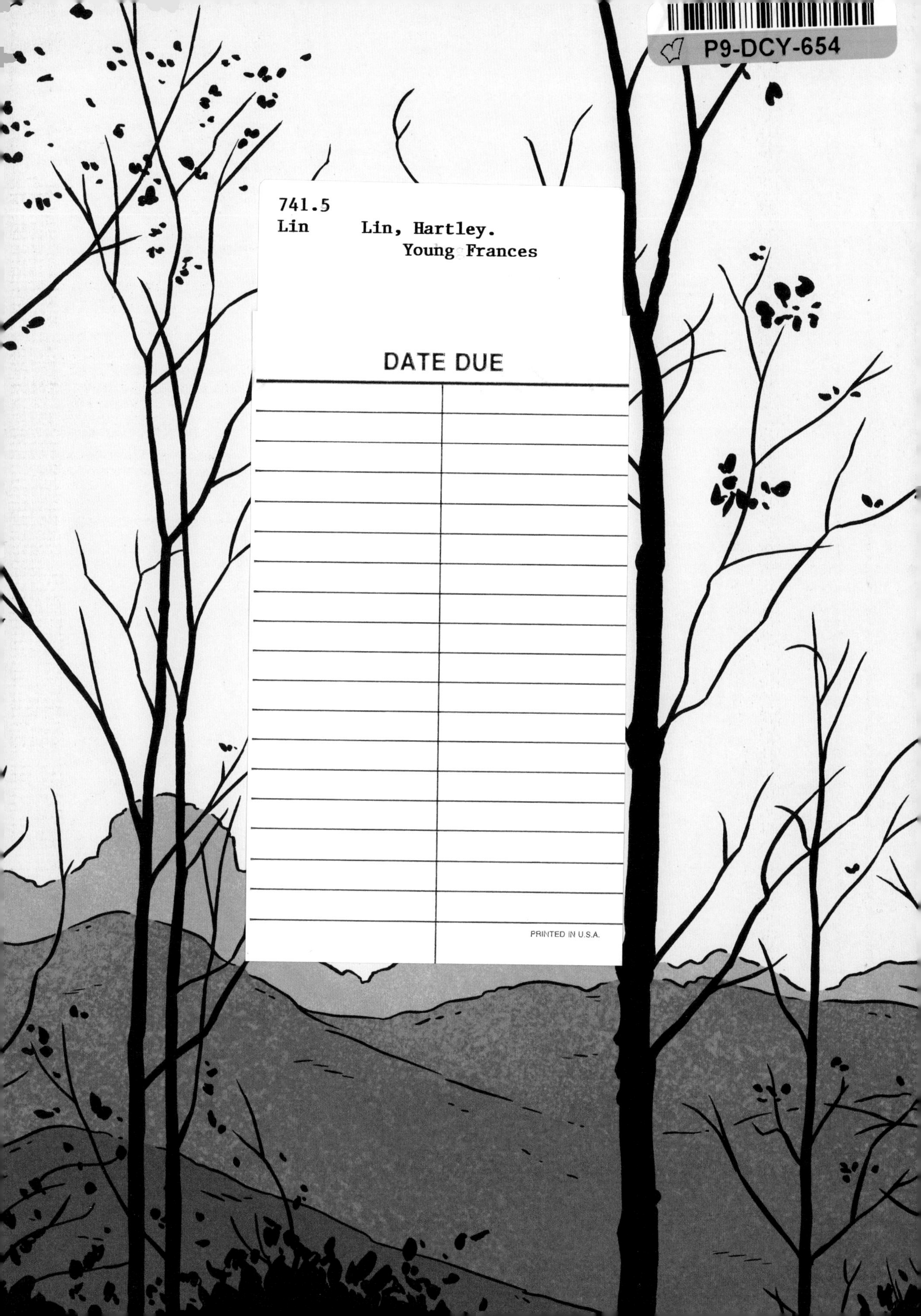

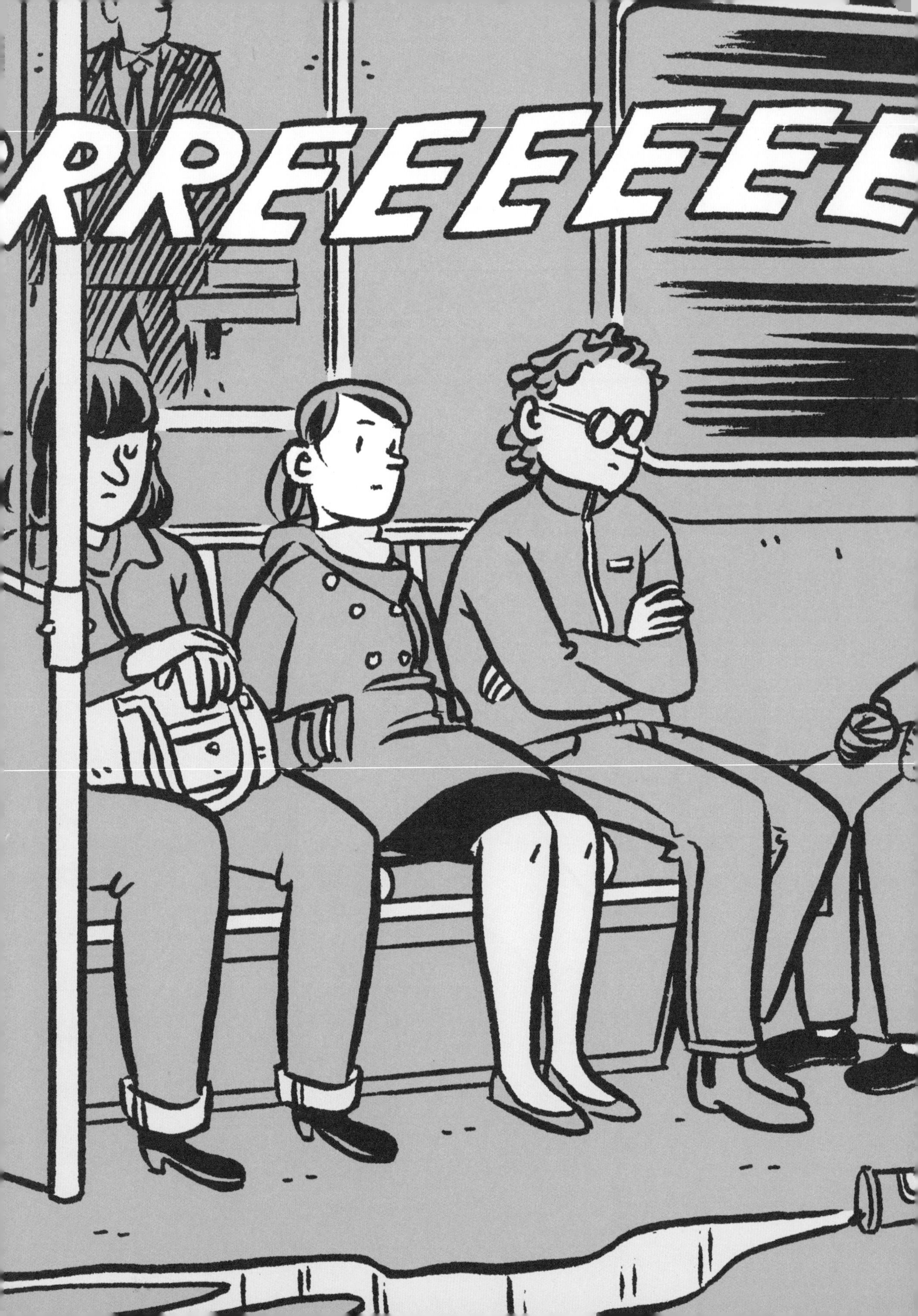
RREEEEEEE

YOUNG FRANCES

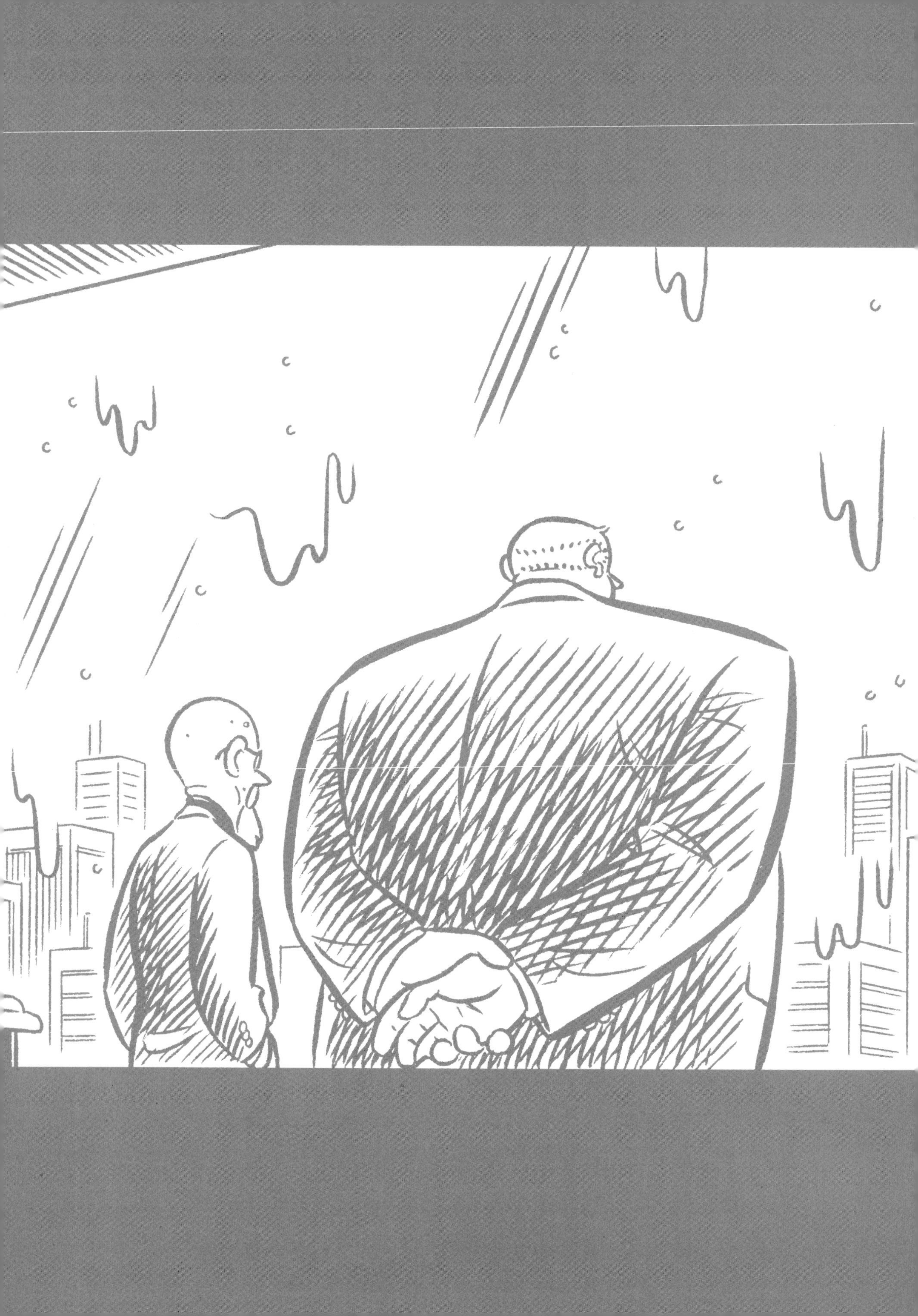

YOUNG FRANCES

HARTLEY LIN

South Sioux City Public Library
2121 Dakota Avenue
South Sioux City, NE 68776

ADHOUSE BOOKS
RICHMOND, VA

YOUNG FRANCES
COPYRIGHT © HARTLEY LIN, 2018

SECOND PRINTING, MAY 2018

ADHOUSE BOOKS
CHRIS PITZER, PUBLISHER
3905 BROOK ROAD, RICHMOND, VIRGINIA 23227
WWW.ADHOUSEBOOKS.COM

ADHOUSE LOGO IS COPYRIGHT © 2018 ADHOUSE BOOKS

DESIGN: LIN + PITZER

ALL RIGHTS RESERVED. EXCEPT FOR SMALL PORTIONS FOR REVIEW PURPOSES, THE USE OF ANY PART
OF THIS PUBLICATION REPRODUCED OR TRANSMITTED IN ANY FORM OR BY ANY MEANS ELECTRONIC,
MECHANICAL, PHOTOCOPYING, RECORDING OR OTHERWISE, OR STORED IN A RETRIEVAL SYSTEM WITHOUT
THE PRIOR WRITTEN CONSENT OF THE AUTHOR OR PUBLISHER, IS AN INFRINGEMENT OF THE COPYRIGHT LAW.

LIBRARY OF CONGRESS CONTROL NUMBER: 2017957353
ISBN: 978-1-935233-42-8
         1-935233-42-4

PRINTED AND BOUND IN CHINA

YOUNG FRANCES WAS ORIGINALLY SERIALIZED IN ISSUES 2, 3, AND 5 OF THE COMIC BOOK *POPE HATS*.
THIS IS A WORK OF FICTION. NAMES, CHARACTERS, PLACES AND INCIDENTS ARE PRODUCTS OF THE AUTHOR'S
IMAGINATION OR ARE USED FICTITIOUSLY. ANY RESEMBLANCE TO ACTUAL EVENTS OR LOCALES OR PERSONS,
LIVING OR DEAD, IS ENTIRELY COINCIDENTAL.

THE AUTHOR WISHES TO ACKNOWLEDGE THE SUPPORT OF THE CANADA COUNCIL FOR THE ARTS.

10 9 8 7 6 5 4 3 2

Canada Council   Conseil des arts
for the Arts   du Canada

FOR LAURA
AND HER LAUGHTER

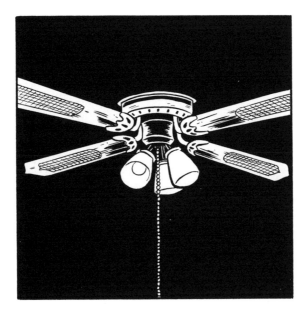

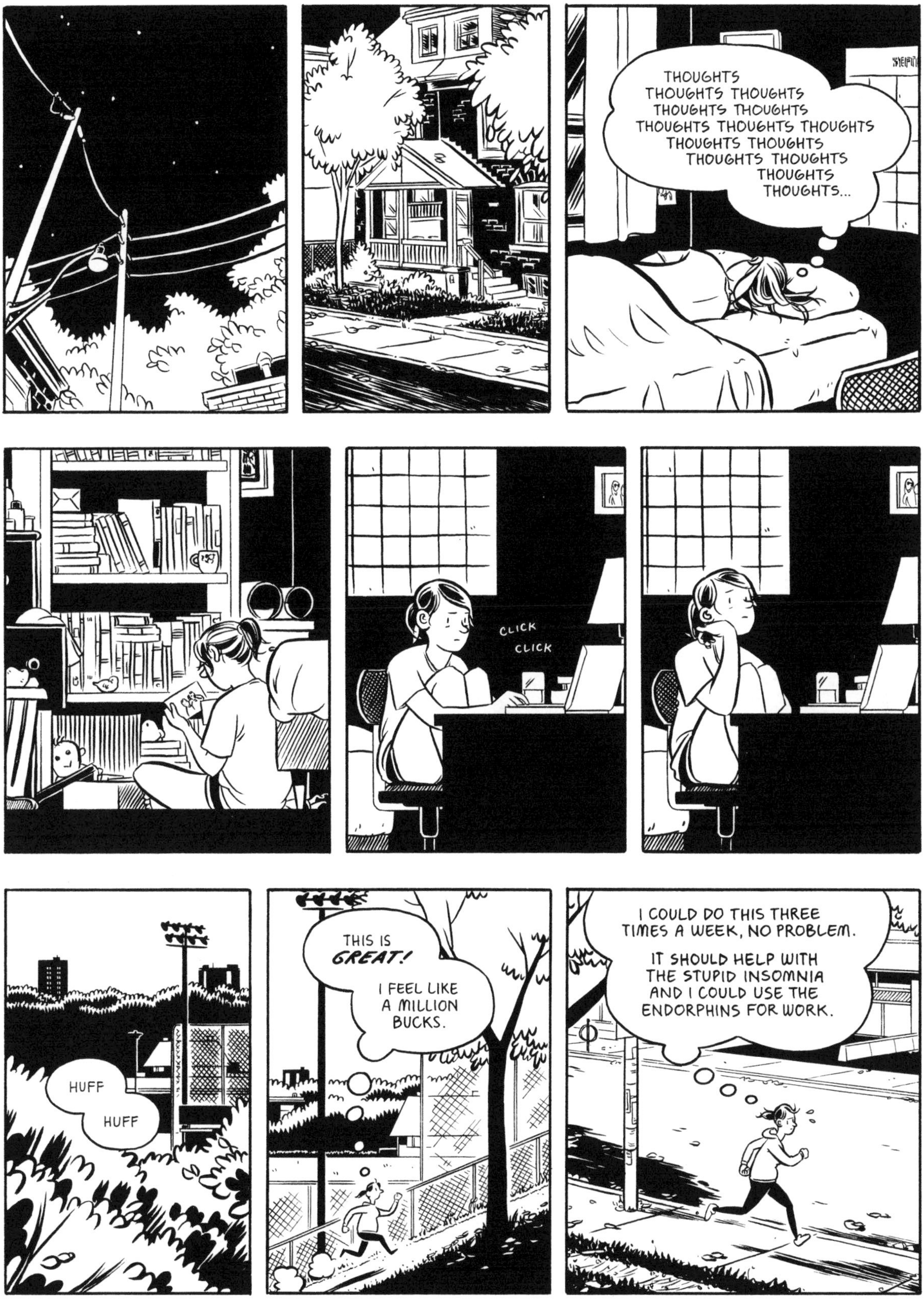
THOUGHTS THOUGHTS THOUGHTS THOUGHTS THOUGHTS THOUGHTS THOUGHTS THOUGHTS THOUGHTS THOUGHTS THOUGHTS THOUGHTS THOUGHTS...
CLICK
CLICK
HUFF
HUFF
THIS IS GREAT!
I FEEL LIKE A MILLION BUCKS.
I COULD DO THIS THREE TIMES A WEEK, NO PROBLEM.
IT SHOULD HELP WITH THE STUPID INSOMNIA AND I COULD USE THE ENDORPHINS FOR WORK.

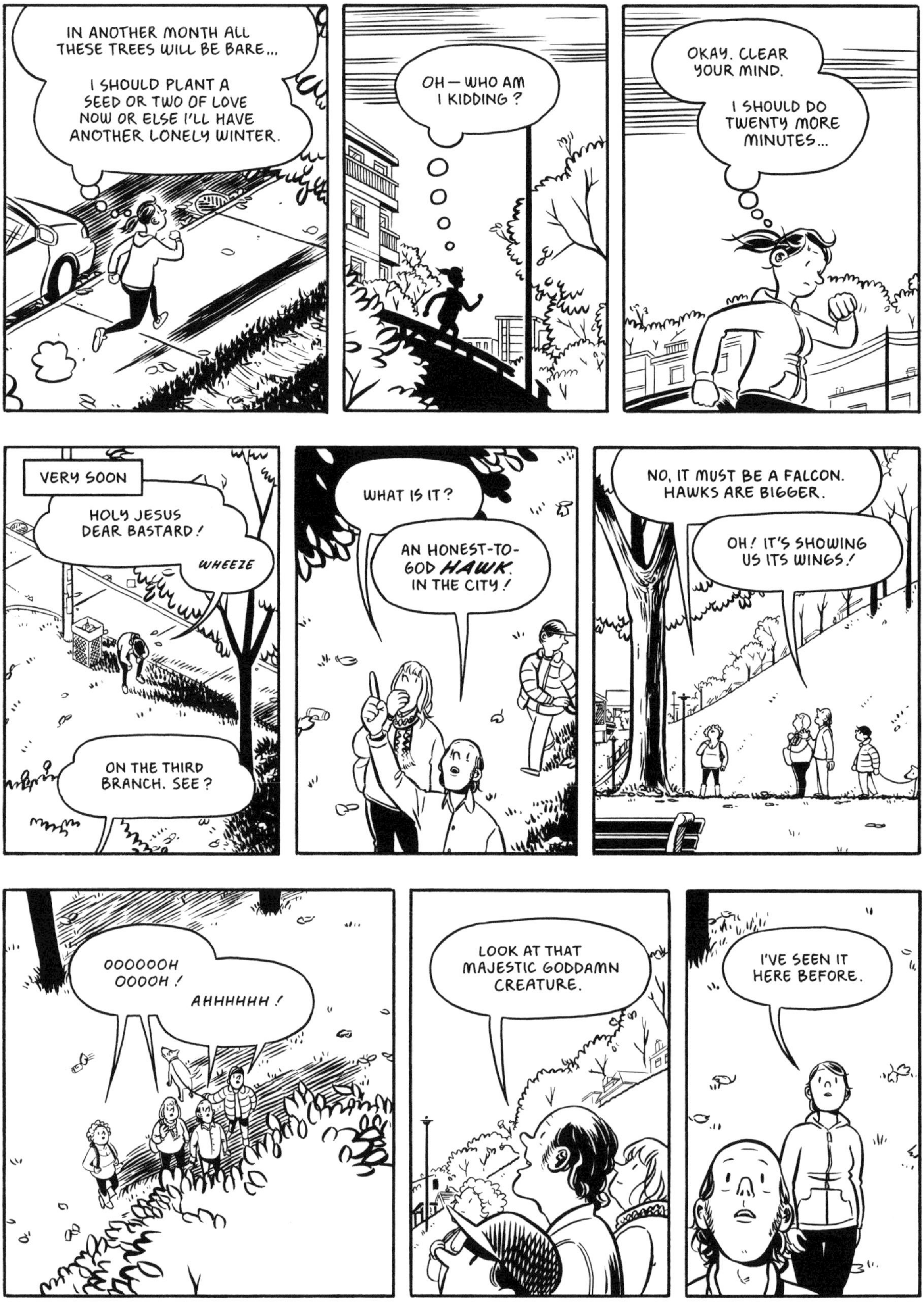
IN ANOTHER MONTH ALL THESE TREES WILL BE BARE...
I SHOULD PLANT A SEED OR TWO OF LOVE NOW OR ELSE I'LL HAVE ANOTHER LONELY WINTER.
OH — WHO AM I KIDDING?
OKAY. CLEAR YOUR MIND.
I SHOULD DO TWENTY MORE MINUTES...
VERY SOON
HOLY JESUS DEAR BASTARD!
WHEEZE
ON THE THIRD BRANCH. SEE?
WHAT IS IT?
AN HONEST-TO-GOD HAWK IN THE CITY!
NO, IT MUST BE A FALCON. HAWKS ARE BIGGER.
OH! IT'S SHOWING US ITS WINGS!
OOOOOOH OOOOH!
AHHHHHH!
LOOK AT THAT MAJESTIC GODDAMN CREATURE.
I'VE SEEN IT HERE BEFORE.

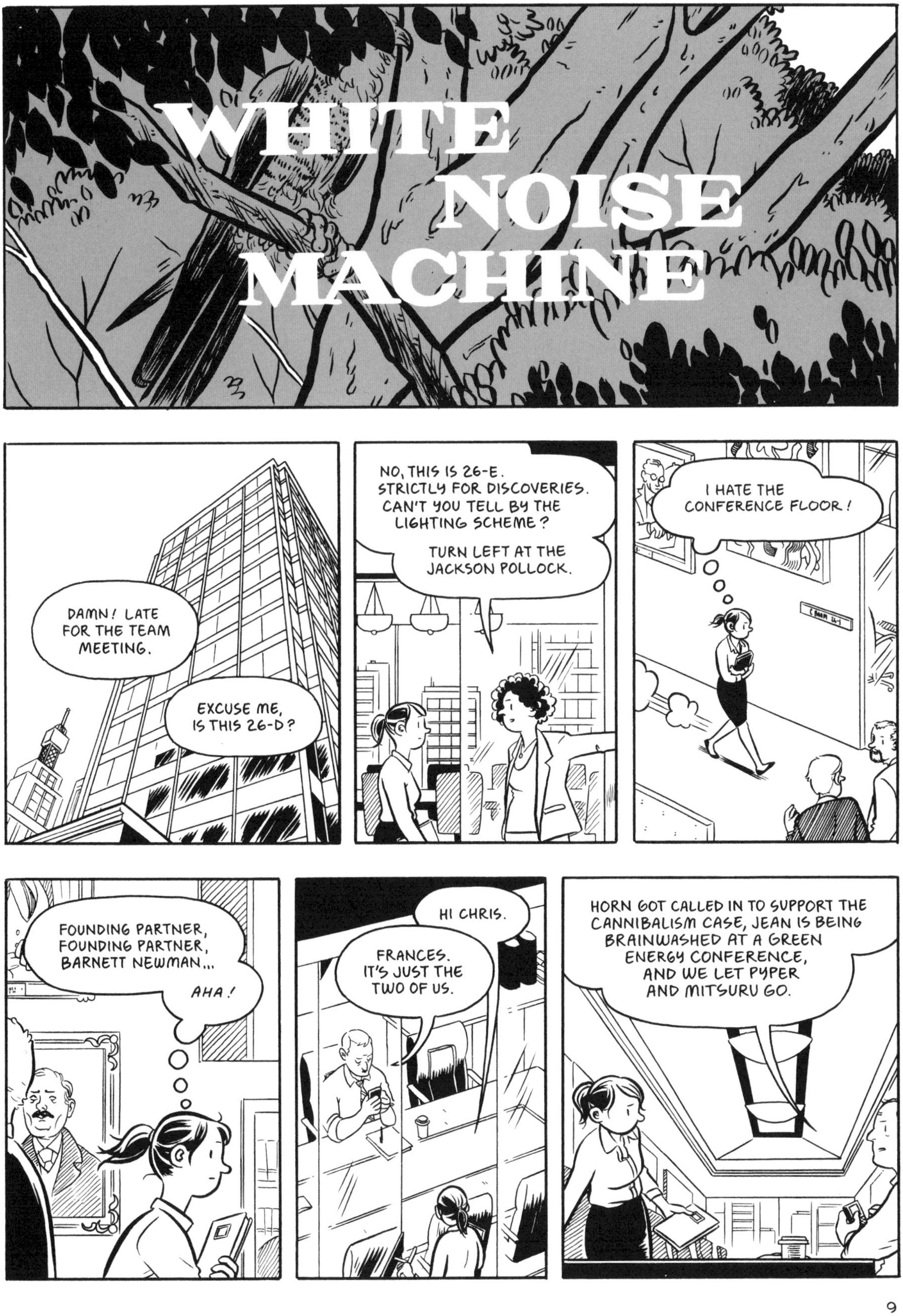
WHITE NOISE MACHINE
DAMN! LATE FOR THE TEAM MEETING.
EXCUSE ME, IS THIS 26-D?
NO, THIS IS 26-E. STRICTLY FOR DISCOVERIES. CAN'T YOU TELL BY THE LIGHTING SCHEME?
TURN LEFT AT THE JACKSON POLLOCK.
I HATE THE CONFERENCE FLOOR!
FOUNDING PARTNER, FOUNDING PARTNER, BARNETT NEWMAN...
AHA!
HI CHRIS.
FRANCES. IT'S JUST THE TWO OF US.
HORN GOT CALLED IN TO SUPPORT THE CANNIBALISM CASE, JEAN IS BEING BRAINWASHED AT A GREEN ENERGY CONFERENCE, AND WE LET PYPER AND MITSURU GO.

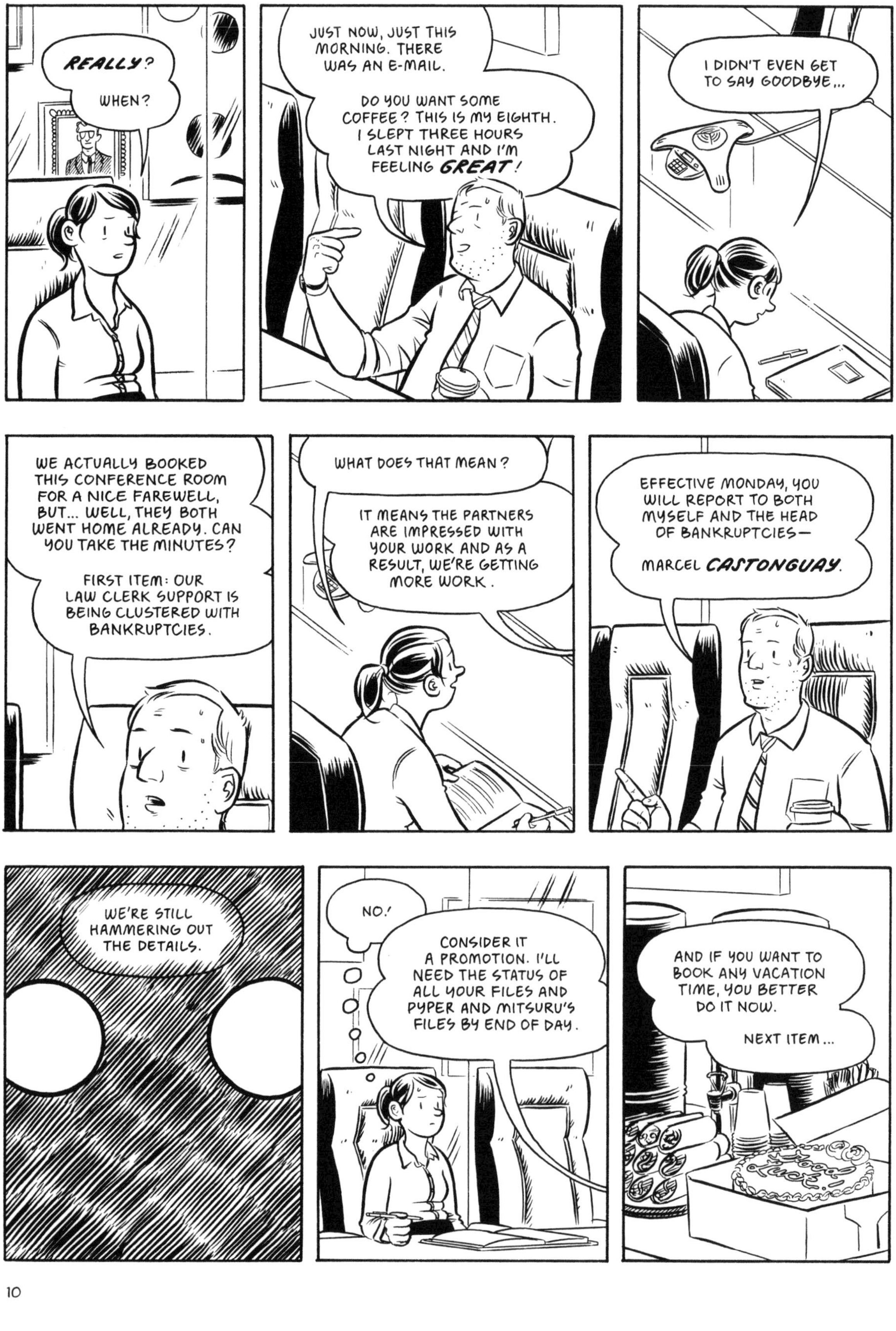
REALLY? WHEN?
JUST NOW, JUST THIS MORNING. THERE WAS AN E-MAIL.
DO YOU WANT SOME COFFEE? THIS IS MY EIGHTH. I SLEPT THREE HOURS LAST NIGHT AND I'M FEELING GREAT!
I DIDN'T EVEN GET TO SAY GOODBYE...
WE ACTUALLY BOOKED THIS CONFERENCE ROOM FOR A NICE FAREWELL, BUT... WELL, THEY BOTH WENT HOME ALREADY. CAN YOU TAKE THE MINUTES?
FIRST ITEM: OUR LAW CLERK SUPPORT IS BEING CLUSTERED WITH BANKRUPTCIES.
WHAT DOES THAT MEAN?
IT MEANS THE PARTNERS ARE IMPRESSED WITH YOUR WORK AND AS A RESULT, WE'RE GETTING MORE WORK.
EFFECTIVE MONDAY, YOU WILL REPORT TO BOTH MYSELF AND THE HEAD OF BANKRUPTCIES—
MARCEL CASTONGUAY.
WE'RE STILL HAMMERING OUT THE DETAILS.
NO.!
CONSIDER IT A PROMOTION. I'LL NEED THE STATUS OF ALL YOUR FILES AND PYPER AND MITSURU'S FILES BY END OF DAY.
AND IF YOU WANT TO BOOK ANY VACATION TIME, YOU BETTER DO IT NOW.
NEXT ITEM...

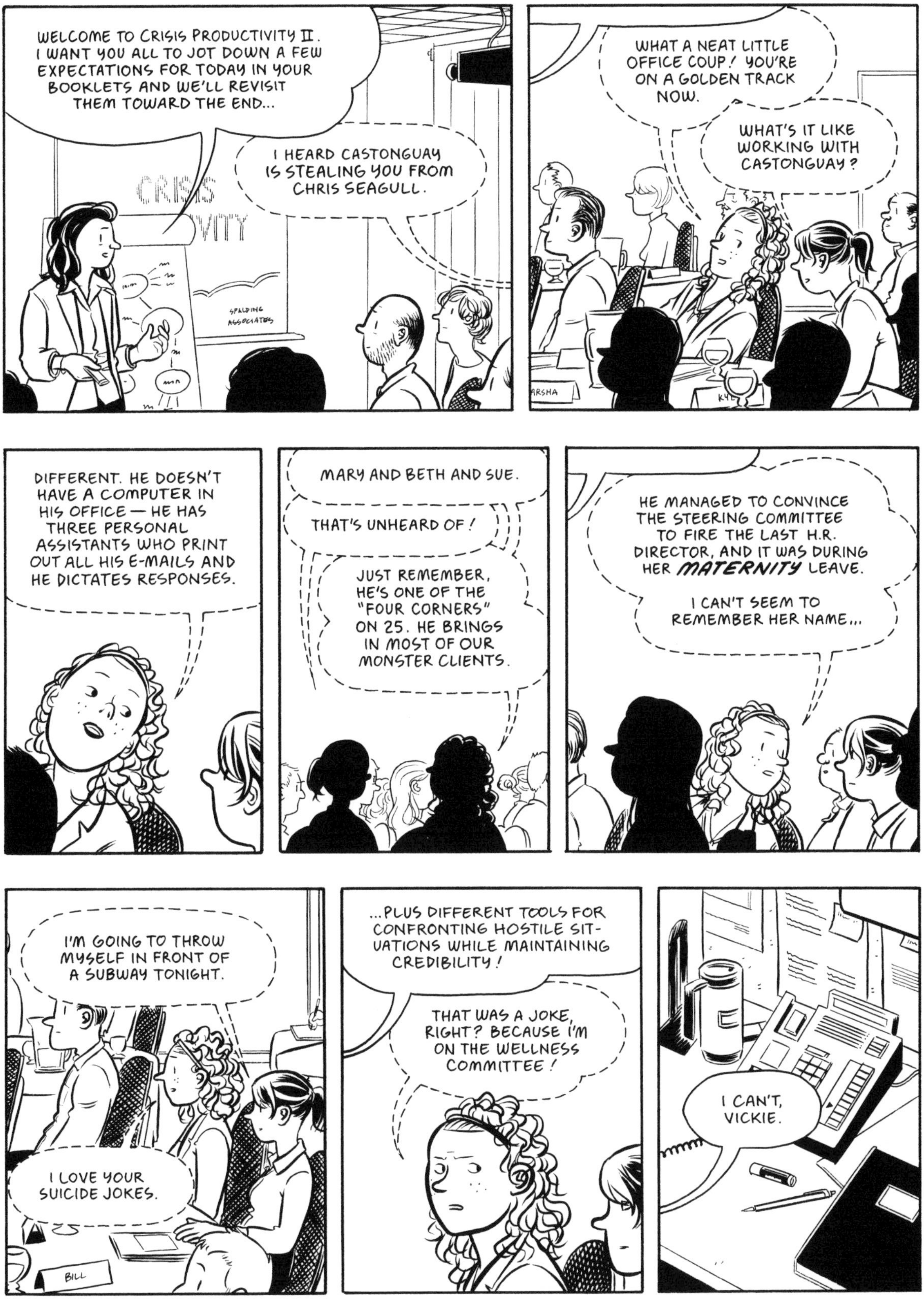
WELCOME TO CRISIS PRODUCTIVITY II. I WANT YOU ALL TO JOT DOWN A FEW EXPECTATIONS FOR TODAY IN YOUR BOOKLETS AND WE'LL REVISIT THEM TOWARD THE END...
SPALDING ASSOCIATES
I HEARD CASTONGUAY IS STEALING YOU FROM CHRIS SEAGULL.
WHAT A NEAT LITTLE OFFICE COUP! YOU'RE ON A GOLDEN TRACK NOW.
WHAT'S IT LIKE WORKING WITH CASTONGUAY?
DIFFERENT. HE DOESN'T HAVE A COMPUTER IN HIS OFFICE — HE HAS THREE PERSONAL ASSISTANTS WHO PRINT OUT ALL HIS E-MAILS AND HE DICTATES RESPONSES.
MARY AND BETH AND SUE.
THAT'S UNHEARD OF!
JUST REMEMBER, HE'S ONE OF THE "FOUR CORNERS" ON 25. HE BRINGS IN MOST OF OUR MONSTER CLIENTS.
HE MANAGED TO CONVINCE THE STEERING COMMITTEE TO FIRE THE LAST H.R. DIRECTOR, AND IT WAS DURING HER MATERNITY LEAVE.
I CAN'T SEEM TO REMEMBER HER NAME...
I'M GOING TO THROW MYSELF IN FRONT OF A SUBWAY TONIGHT.
I LOVE YOUR SUICIDE JOKES.
BILL
...PLUS DIFFERENT TOOLS FOR CONFRONTING HOSTILE SIT-UATIONS WHILE MAINTAINING CREDIBILITY!
THAT WAS A JOKE, RIGHT? BECAUSE I'M ON THE WELLNESS COMMITTEE!
I CAN'T, VICKIE.

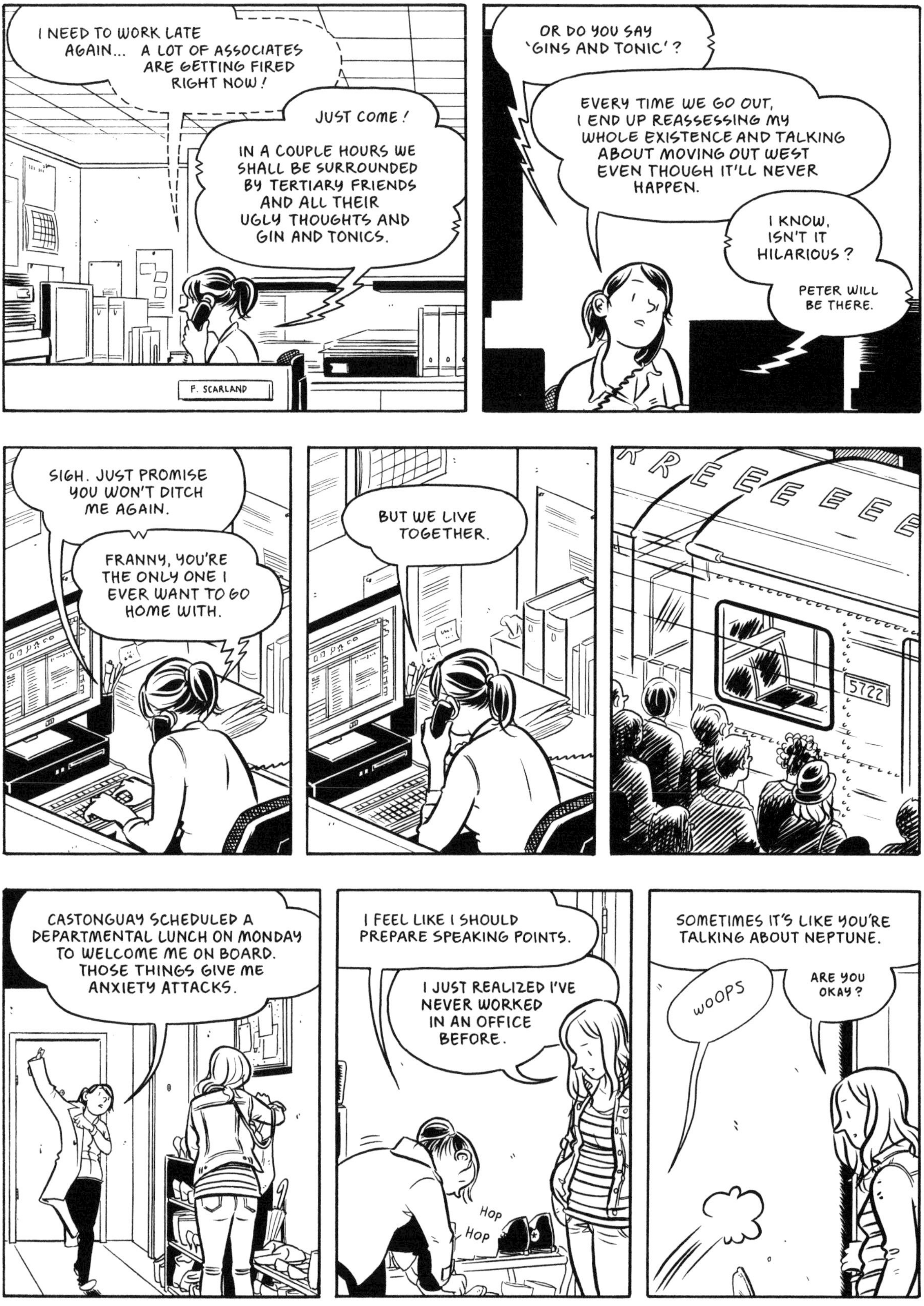
I NEED TO WORK LATE AGAIN... A LOT OF ASSOCIATES ARE GETTING FIRED RIGHT NOW!
JUST COME!
IN A COUPLE HOURS WE SHALL BE SURROUNDED BY TERTIARY FRIENDS AND ALL THEIR UGLY THOUGHTS AND GIN AND TONICS.
F. SCARLAND
OR DO YOU SAY 'GINS AND TONIC'?
EVERY TIME WE GO OUT, I END UP REASSESSING MY WHOLE EXISTENCE AND TALKING ABOUT MOVING OUT WEST EVEN THOUGH IT'LL NEVER HAPPEN.
I KNOW, ISN'T IT HILARIOUS?
PETER WILL BE THERE.
SIGH. JUST PROMISE YOU WON'T DITCH ME AGAIN.
FRANNY, YOU'RE THE ONLY ONE I EVER WANT TO GO HOME WITH.
BUT WE LIVE TOGETHER.
RREEEEEE
5722
CASTONGUAY SCHEDULED A DEPARTMENTAL LUNCH ON MONDAY TO WELCOME ME ON BOARD. THOSE THINGS GIVE ME ANXIETY ATTACKS.
I FEEL LIKE I SHOULD PREPARE SPEAKING POINTS.
I JUST REALIZED I'VE NEVER WORKED IN AN OFFICE BEFORE.
Hop
Hop
SOMETIMES IT'S LIKE YOU'RE TALKING ABOUT NEPTUNE.
WOOPS
ARE YOU OKAY?

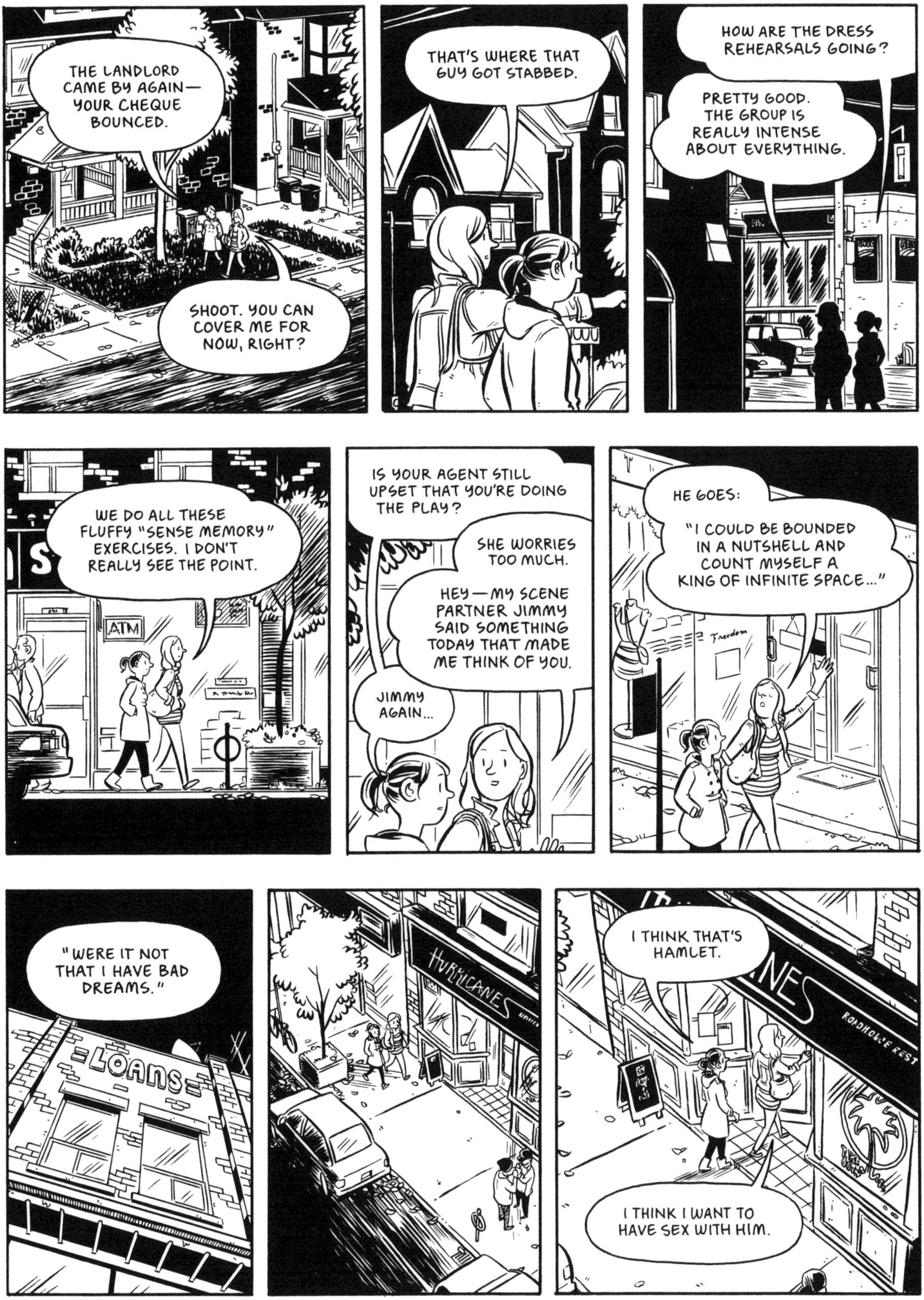

THE LANDLORD CAME BY AGAIN— YOUR CHEQUE BOUNCED.
SHOOT. YOU CAN COVER ME FOR NOW, RIGHT?
THAT'S WHERE THAT GUY GOT STABBED.
HOW ARE THE DRESS REHEARSALS GOING?
PRETTY GOOD. THE GROUP IS REALLY INTENSE ABOUT EVERYTHING.
WE DO ALL THESE FLUFFY "SENSE MEMORY" EXERCISES. I DON'T REALLY SEE THE POINT.
ATM
IS YOUR AGENT STILL UPSET THAT YOU'RE DOING THE PLAY?
SHE WORRIES TOO MUCH.
HEY—MY SCENE PARTNER JIMMY SAID SOMETHING TODAY THAT MADE ME THINK OF YOU.
JIMMY AGAIN...
HE GOES:
"I COULD BE BOUNDED IN A NUTSHELL AND COUNT MYSELF A KING OF INFINITE SPACE..."
"WERE IT NOT THAT I HAVE BAD DREAMS."
LOANS
HURRICANES
I THINK THAT'S HAMLET.
ROADHOUSE REST
I THINK I WANT TO HAVE SEX WITH HIM.

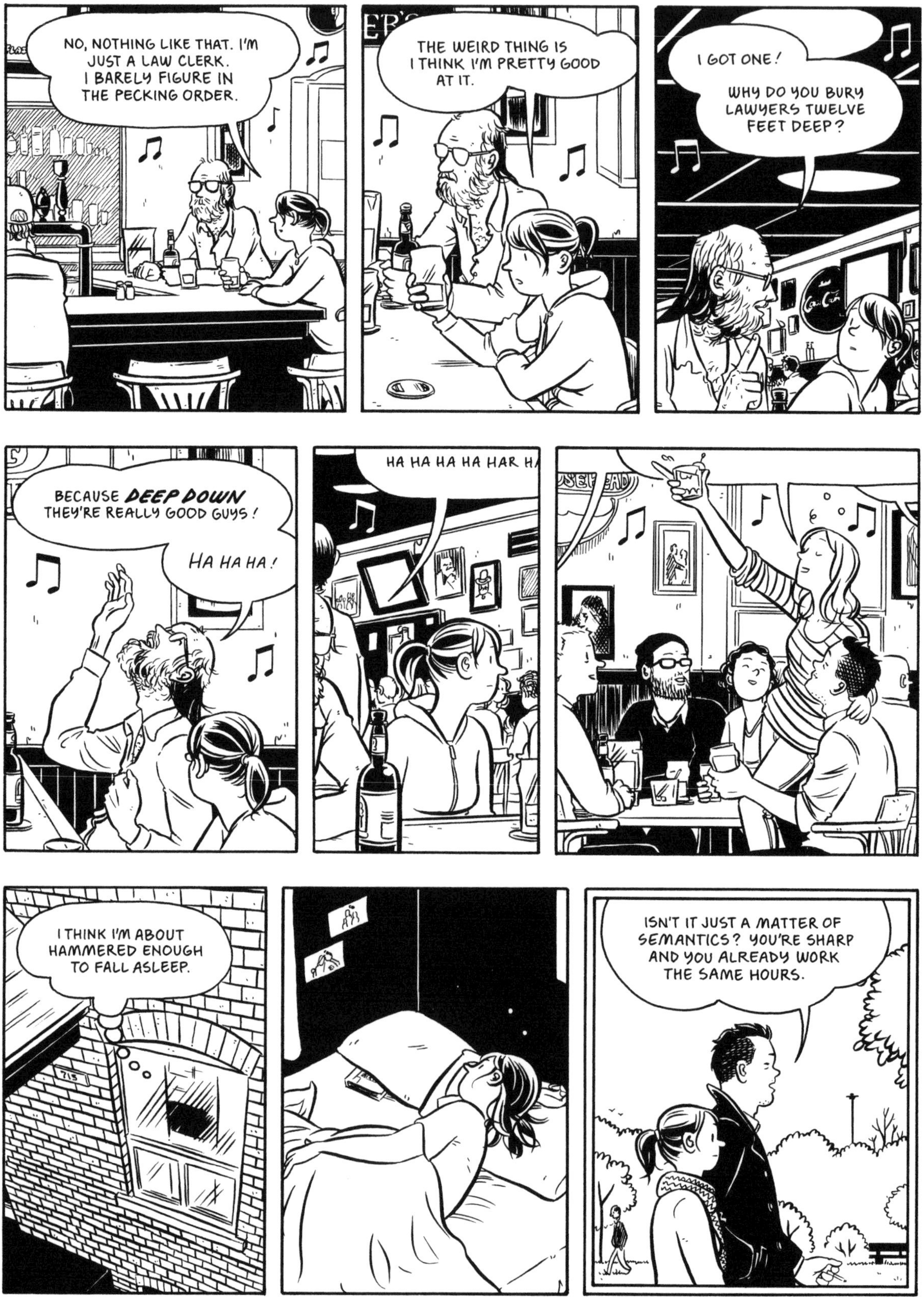
NO, NOTHING LIKE THAT. I'M JUST A LAW CLERK. I BARELY FIGURE IN THE PECKING ORDER.
THE WEIRD THING IS I THINK I'M PRETTY GOOD AT IT.
I GOT ONE!
WHY DO YOU BURY LAWYERS TWELVE FEET DEEP?
BECAUSE **DEEP DOWN** THEY'RE REALLY GOOD GUYS!
HA HA HA!
HA HA HA HA HAR
I THINK I'M ABOUT HAMMERED ENOUGH TO FALL ASLEEP.
ISN'T IT JUST A MATTER OF SEMANTICS? YOU'RE SHARP AND YOU ALREADY WORK THE SAME HOURS.

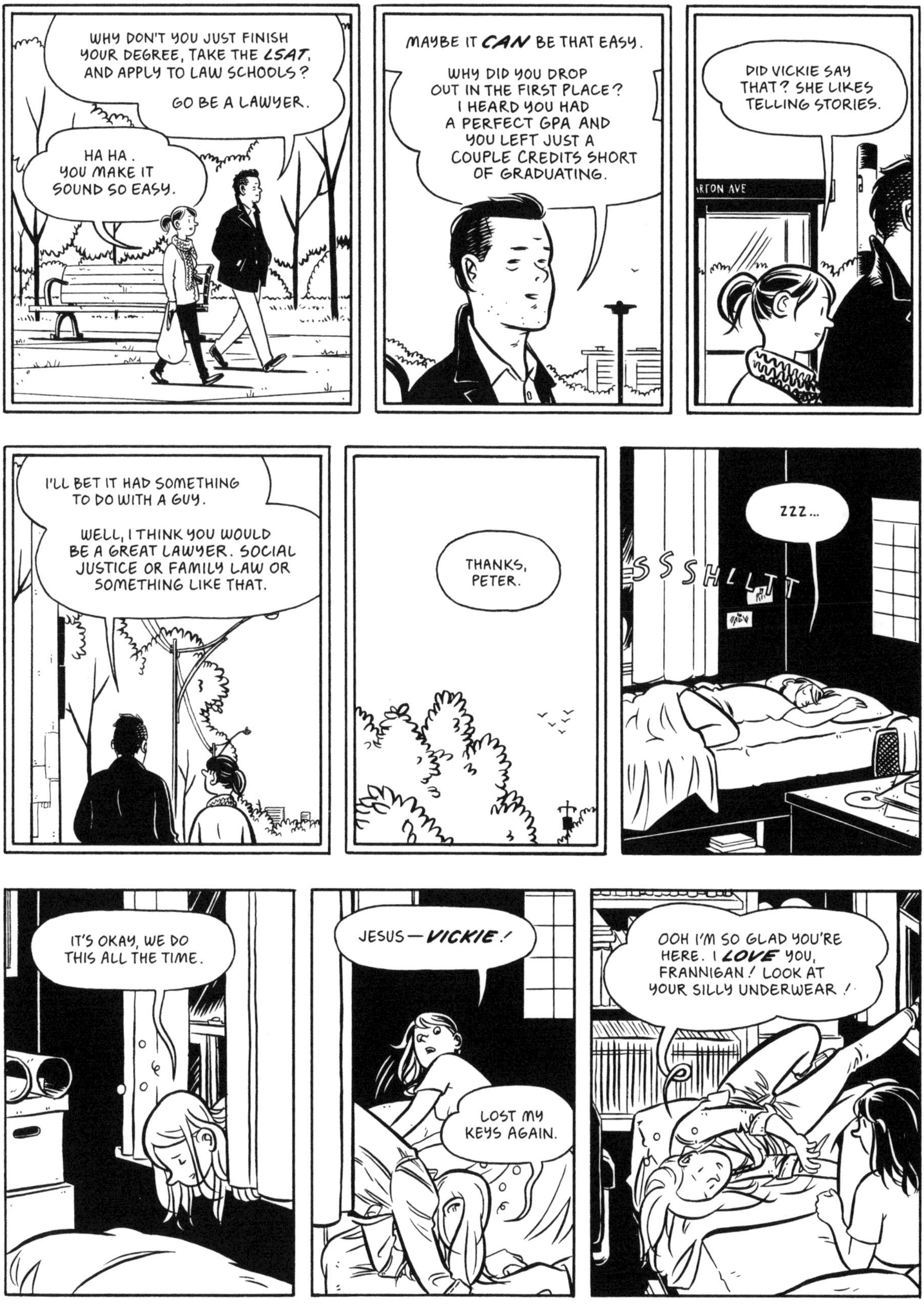
WHY DON'T YOU JUST FINISH YOUR DEGREE, TAKE THE LSAT, AND APPLY TO LAW SCHOOLS?
GO BE A LAWYER.
HA HA. YOU MAKE IT SOUND SO EASY.
MAYBE IT CAN BE THAT EASY.
WHY DID YOU DROP OUT IN THE FIRST PLACE? I HEARD YOU HAD A PERFECT GPA AND YOU LEFT JUST A COUPLE CREDITS SHORT OF GRADUATING.
DID VICKIE SAY THAT? SHE LIKES TELLING STORIES.
ARTON AVE
I'LL BET IT HAD SOMETHING TO DO WITH A GUY.
WELL, I THINK YOU WOULD BE A GREAT LAWYER. SOCIAL JUSTICE OR FAMILY LAW OR SOMETHING LIKE THAT.
THANKS, PETER.
ZZZ...
SSSHLLTT
IT'S OKAY, WE DO THIS ALL THE TIME.
JESUS—VICKIE!
LOST MY KEYS AGAIN.
OOH I'M SO GLAD YOU'RE HERE. I LOVE YOU, FRANNIGAN! LOOK AT YOUR SILLY UNDERWEAR!

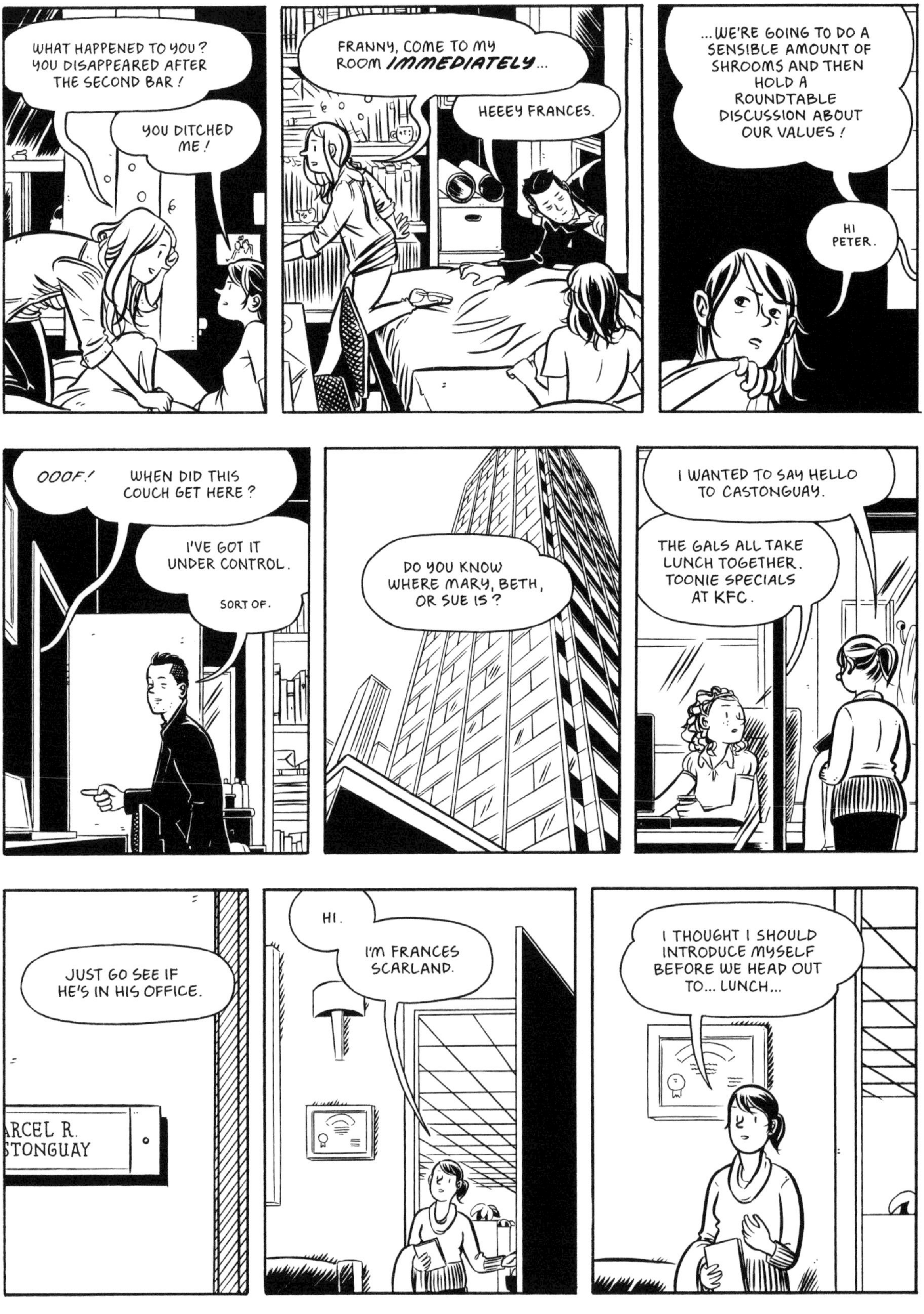
WHAT HAPPENED TO YOU? YOU DISAPPEARED AFTER THE SECOND BAR!
YOU DITCHED ME!
FRANNY, COME TO MY ROOM IMMEDIATELY...
HEEEY FRANCES.
...WE'RE GOING TO DO A SENSIBLE AMOUNT OF SHROOMS AND THEN HOLD A ROUNDTABLE DISCUSSION ABOUT OUR VALUES!
HI PETER.
OOOF!
WHEN DID THIS COUCH GET HERE?
I'VE GOT IT UNDER CONTROL.
SORT OF.
DO YOU KNOW WHERE MARY, BETH, OR SUE IS?
I WANTED TO SAY HELLO TO CASTONGUAY.
THE GALS ALL TAKE LUNCH TOGETHER. TOONIE SPECIALS AT KFC.
JUST GO SEE IF HE'S IN HIS OFFICE.
ARCEL R.
STONGUAY
HI.
I'M FRANCES SCARLAND.
I THOUGHT I SHOULD INTRODUCE MYSELF BEFORE WE HEAD OUT TO... LUNCH...

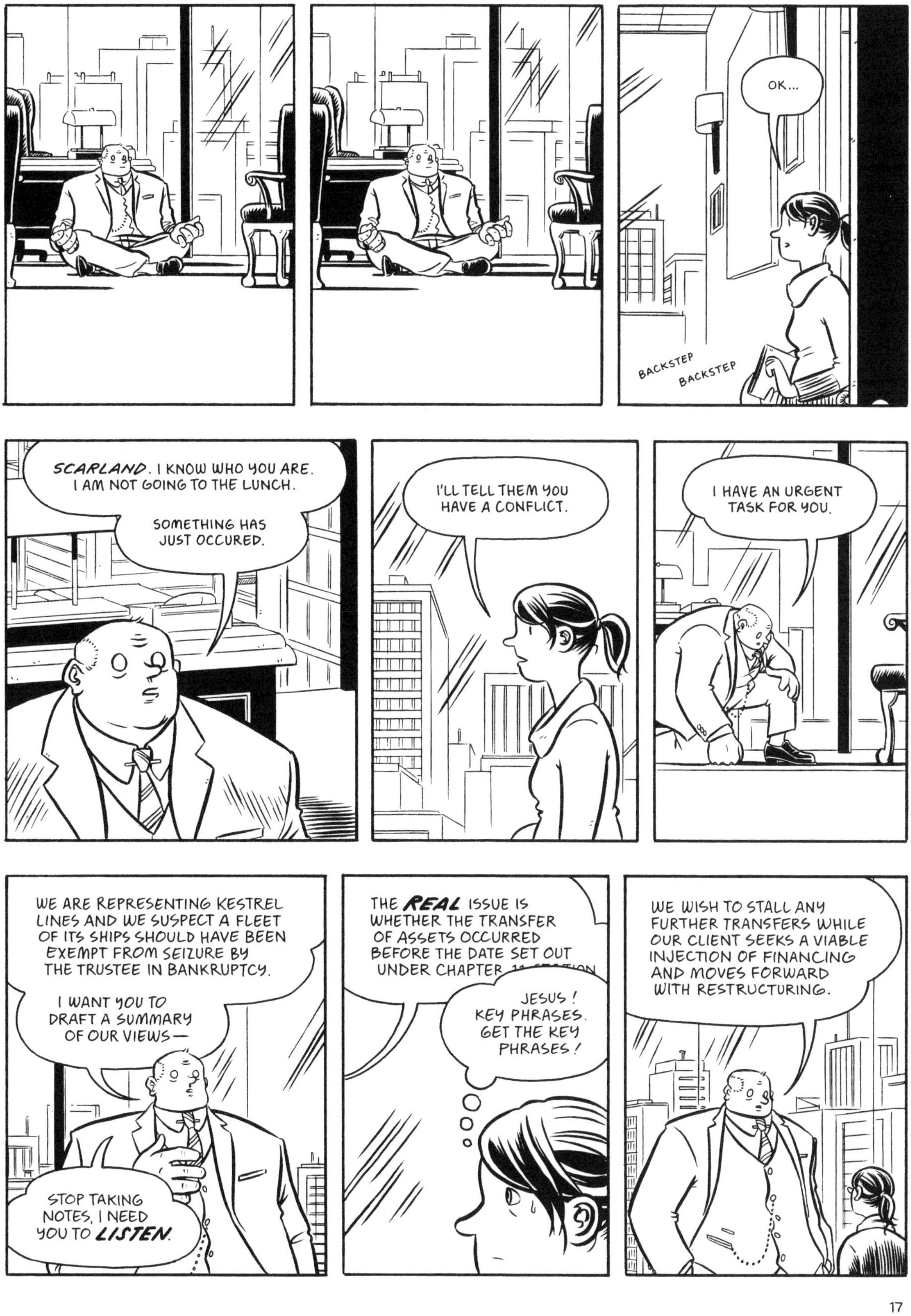
OK...
BACKSTEP
BACKSTEP
SCARLAND. I KNOW WHO YOU ARE. I AM NOT GOING TO THE LUNCH.
SOMETHING HAS JUST OCCURED.
I'LL TELL THEM YOU HAVE A CONFLICT.
I HAVE AN URGENT TASK FOR YOU.
WE ARE REPRESENTING KESTREL LINES AND WE SUSPECT A FLEET OF ITS SHIPS SHOULD HAVE BEEN EXEMPT FROM SEIZURE BY THE TRUSTEE IN BANKRUPTCY.
I WANT YOU TO DRAFT A SUMMARY OF OUR VIEWS—
STOP TAKING NOTES, I NEED YOU TO LISTEN.
THE REAL ISSUE IS WHETHER THE TRANSFER OF ASSETS OCCURRED BEFORE THE DATE SET OUT UNDER CHAPTER
JESUS! KEY PHRASES. GET THE KEY PHRASES!
WE WISH TO STALL ANY FURTHER TRANSFERS WHILE OUR CLIENT SEEKS A VIABLE INJECTION OF FINANCING AND MOVES FORWARD WITH RESTRUCTURING.

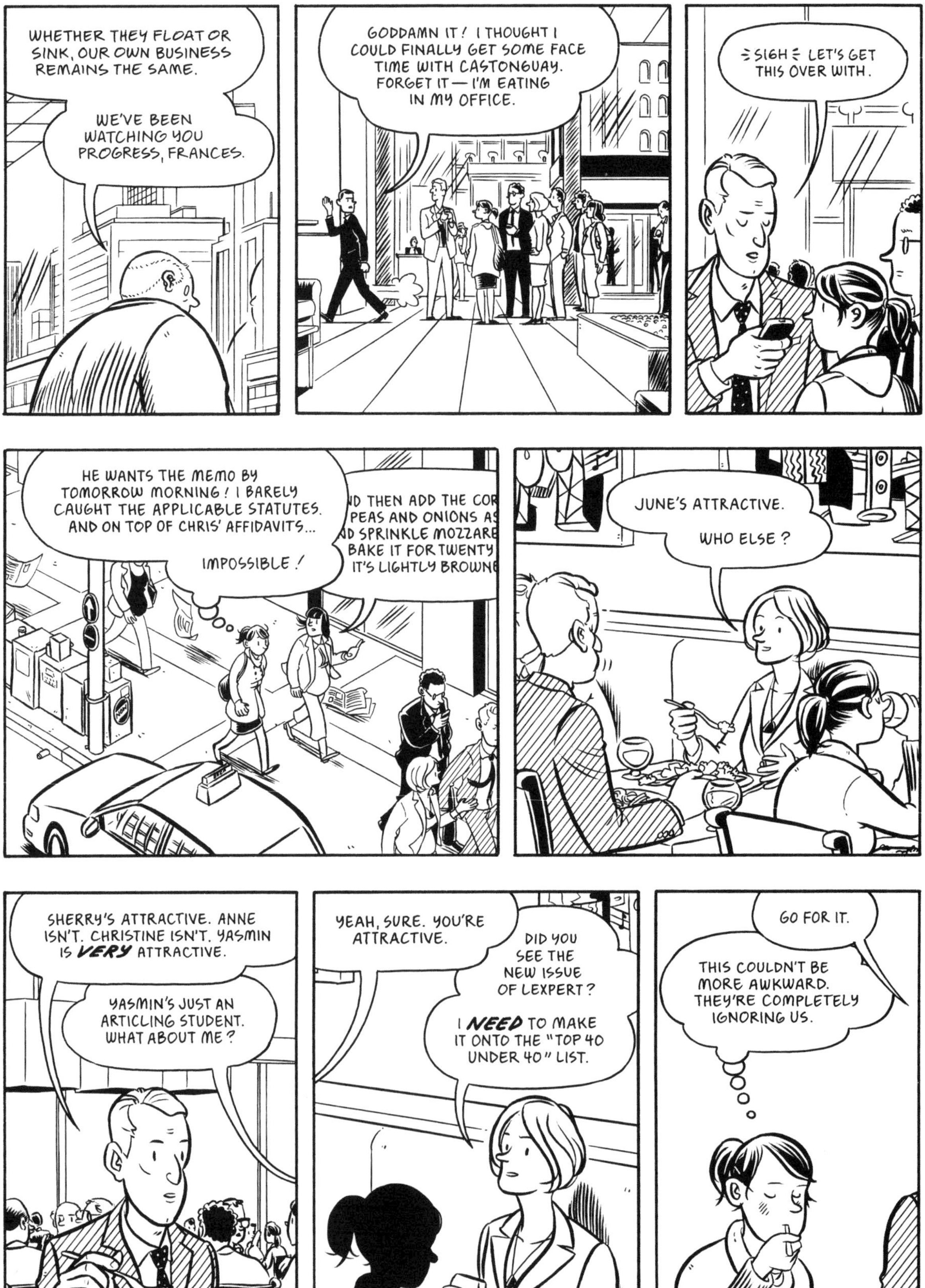
WHETHER THEY FLOAT OR SINK, OUR OWN BUSINESS REMAINS THE SAME.
WE'VE BEEN WATCHING YOU PROGRESS, FRANCES.
GODDAMN IT! I THOUGHT I COULD FINALLY GET SOME FACE TIME WITH CASTONGUAY. FORGET IT — I'M EATING IN MY OFFICE.
SIGH LET'S GET THIS OVER WITH.
HE WANTS THE MEMO BY TOMORROW MORNING! I BARELY CAUGHT THE APPLICABLE STATUTES. AND ON TOP OF CHRIS' AFFIDAVITS...
IMPOSSIBLE!
ND THEN ADD THE COR PEAS AND ONIONS AS ND SPRINKLE MOZZARE BAKE IT FOR TWENTY IT'S LIGHTLY BROWNE
JUNE'S ATTRACTIVE.
WHO ELSE?
SHERRY'S ATTRACTIVE. ANNE ISN'T. CHRISTINE ISN'T. YASMIN IS VERY ATTRACTIVE.
YASMIN'S JUST AN ARTICLING STUDENT. WHAT ABOUT ME?
YEAH, SURE. YOU'RE ATTRACTIVE.
DID YOU SEE THE NEW ISSUE OF LEXPERT?
I NEED TO MAKE IT ONTO THE "TOP 40 UNDER 40" LIST.
GO FOR IT.
THIS COULDN'T BE MORE AWKWARD. THEY'RE COMPLETELY IGNORING US.

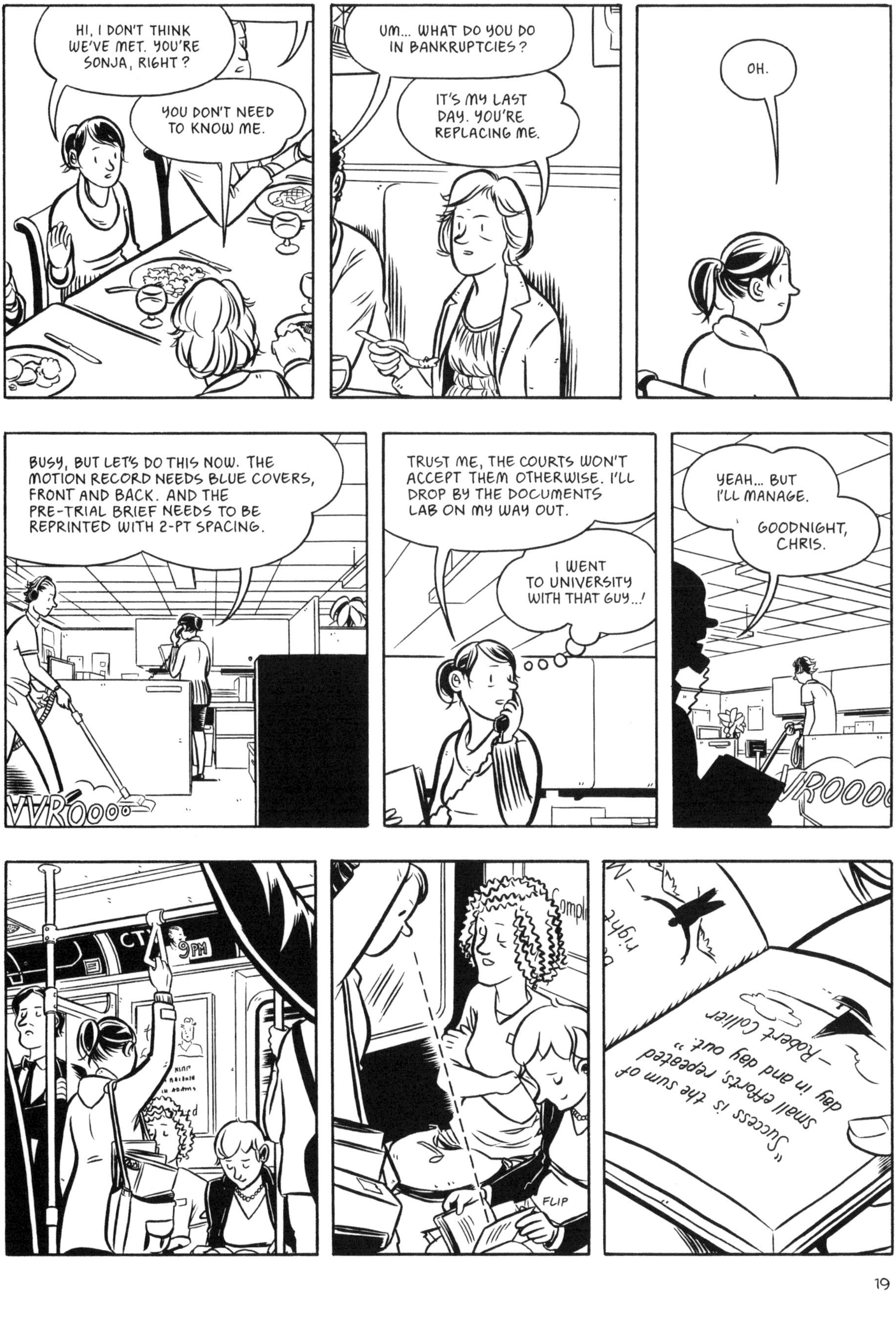
HI, I DON'T THINK WE'VE MET. YOU'RE SONJA, RIGHT?
YOU DON'T NEED TO KNOW ME.
UM... WHAT DO YOU DO IN BANKRUPTCIES?
IT'S MY LAST DAY. YOU'RE REPLACING ME.
OH.
BUSY, BUT LET'S DO THIS NOW. THE MOTION RECORD NEEDS BLUE COVERS, FRONT AND BACK. AND THE PRE-TRIAL BRIEF NEEDS TO BE REPRINTED WITH 2-PT SPACING.
VVROoooo
TRUST ME, THE COURTS WON'T ACCEPT THEM OTHERWISE. I'LL DROP BY THE DOCUMENTS LAB ON MY WAY OUT.
I WENT TO UNIVERSITY WITH THAT GUY...!
YEAH... BUT I'LL MANAGE.
GOODNIGHT, CHRIS.
VROOOO
9PM
FLIP
"Success is the sum of small efforts, repeated day in and day out."
—Robert Collier

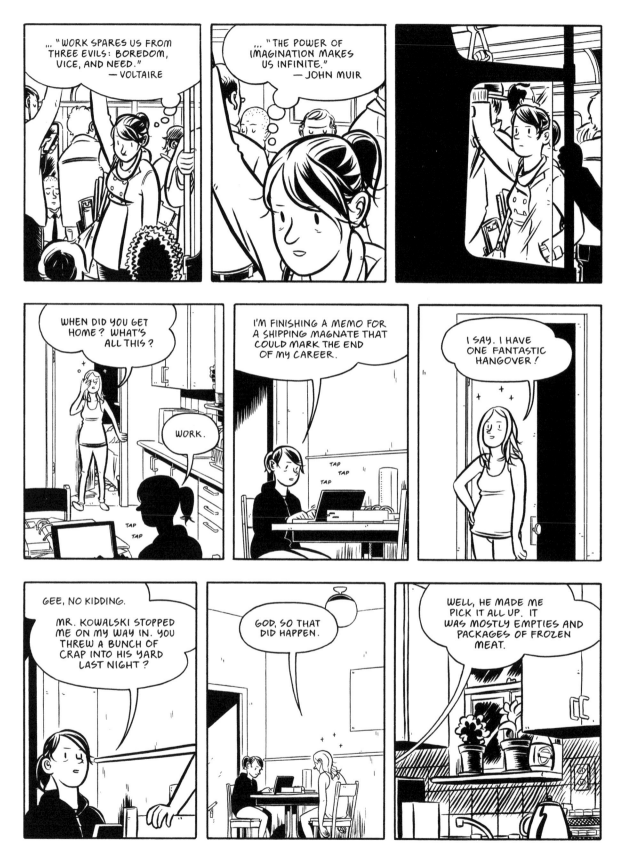

... "WORK SPARES US FROM THREE EVILS: BOREDOM, VICE, AND NEED."
— VOLTAIRE

... "THE POWER OF IMAGINATION MAKES US INFINITE."
— JOHN MUIR

WHEN DID YOU GET HOME? WHAT'S ALL THIS?

WORK.

I'M FINISHING A MEMO FOR A SHIPPING MAGNATE THAT COULD MARK THE END OF MY CAREER.

TAP TAP TAP

I SAY. I HAVE ONE FANTASTIC HANGOVER!

GEE, NO KIDDING.

MR. KOWALSKI STOPPED ME ON MY WAY IN. YOU THREW A BUNCH OF CRAP INTO HIS YARD LAST NIGHT?

GOD, SO THAT DID HAPPEN.

WELL, HE MADE ME PICK IT ALL UP. IT WAS MOSTLY EMPTIES AND PACKAGES OF FROZEN MEAT.

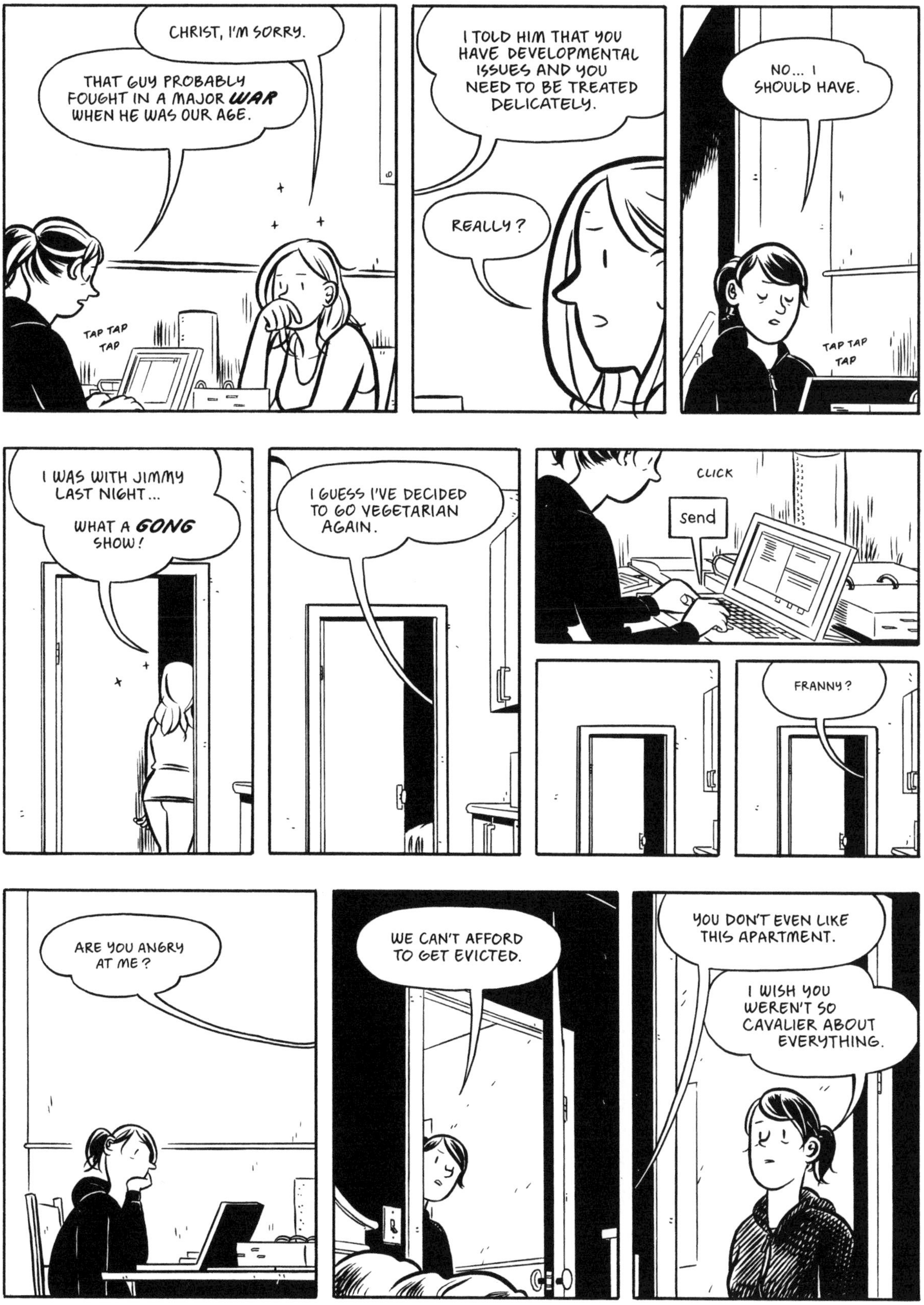

THAT GUY PROBABLY FOUGHT IN A MAJOR WAR WHEN HE WAS OUR AGE.
CHRIST, I'M SORRY.
TAP TAP TAP
I TOLD HIM THAT YOU HAVE DEVELOPMENTAL ISSUES AND YOU NEED TO BE TREATED DELICATELY.
REALLY?
NO... I SHOULD HAVE.
TAP TAP TAP
I WAS WITH JIMMY LAST NIGHT...
WHAT A GONG SHOW!
I GUESS I'VE DECIDED TO GO VEGETARIAN AGAIN.
CLICK
send
FRANNY?
ARE YOU ANGRY AT ME?
WE CAN'T AFFORD TO GET EVICTED.
YOU DON'T EVEN LIKE THIS APARTMENT.
I WISH YOU WEREN'T SO CAVALIER ABOUT EVERYTHING.

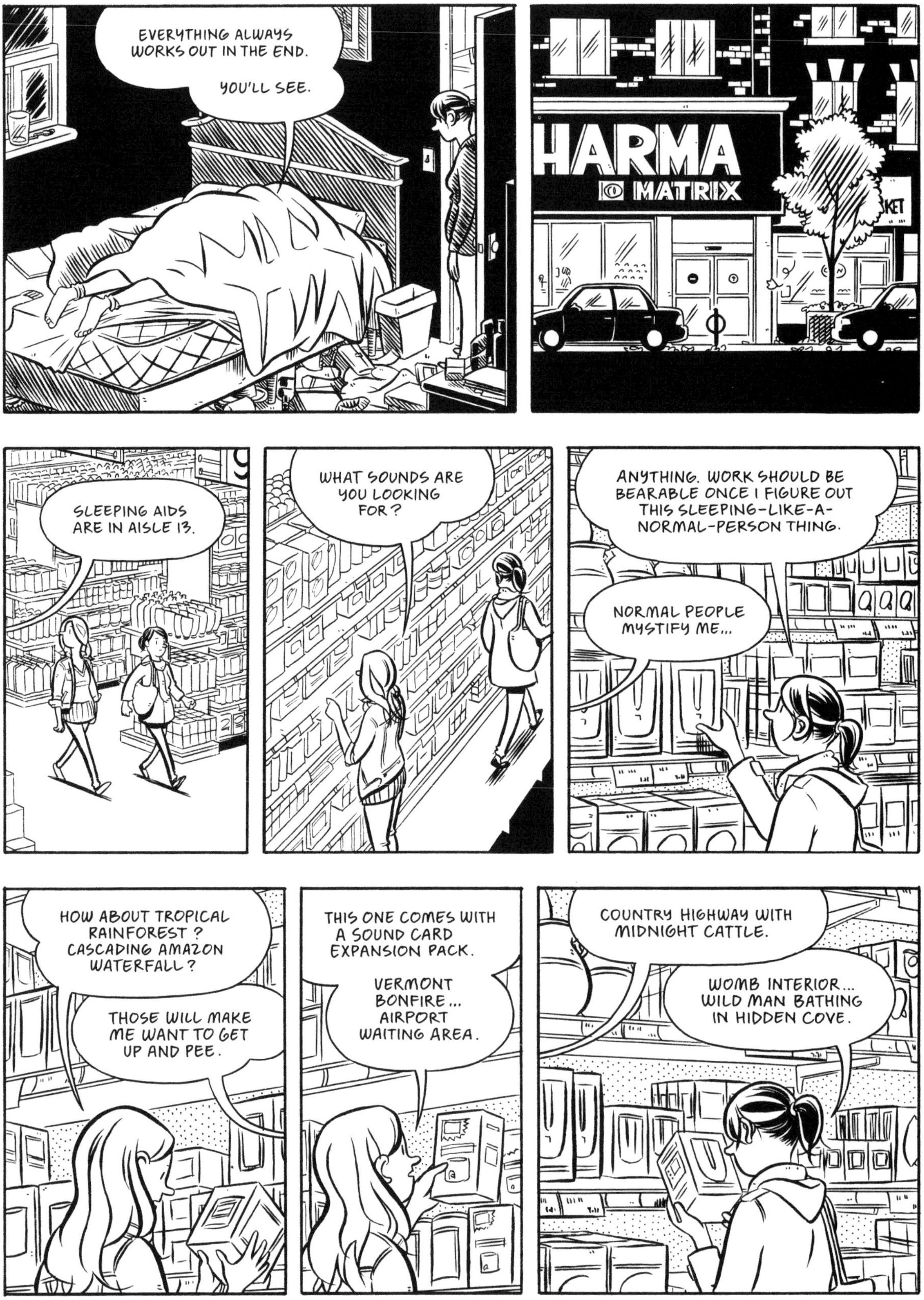
EVERYTHING ALWAYS WORKS OUT IN THE END.
YOU'LL SEE.
HARMA
MATRIX
SLEEPING AIDS ARE IN AISLE 13.
WHAT SOUNDS ARE YOU LOOKING FOR?
ANYTHING. WORK SHOULD BE BEARABLE ONCE I FIGURE OUT THIS SLEEPING-LIKE-A-NORMAL-PERSON THING.
NORMAL PEOPLE MYSTIFY ME...
HOW ABOUT TROPICAL RAINFOREST? CASCADING AMAZON WATERFALL?
THOSE WILL MAKE ME WANT TO GET UP AND PEE.
THIS ONE COMES WITH A SOUND CARD EXPANSION PACK.
VERMONT BONFIRE... AIRPORT WAITING AREA.
COUNTRY HIGHWAY WITH MIDNIGHT CATTLE.
WOMB INTERIOR... WILD MAN BATHING IN HIDDEN COVE.

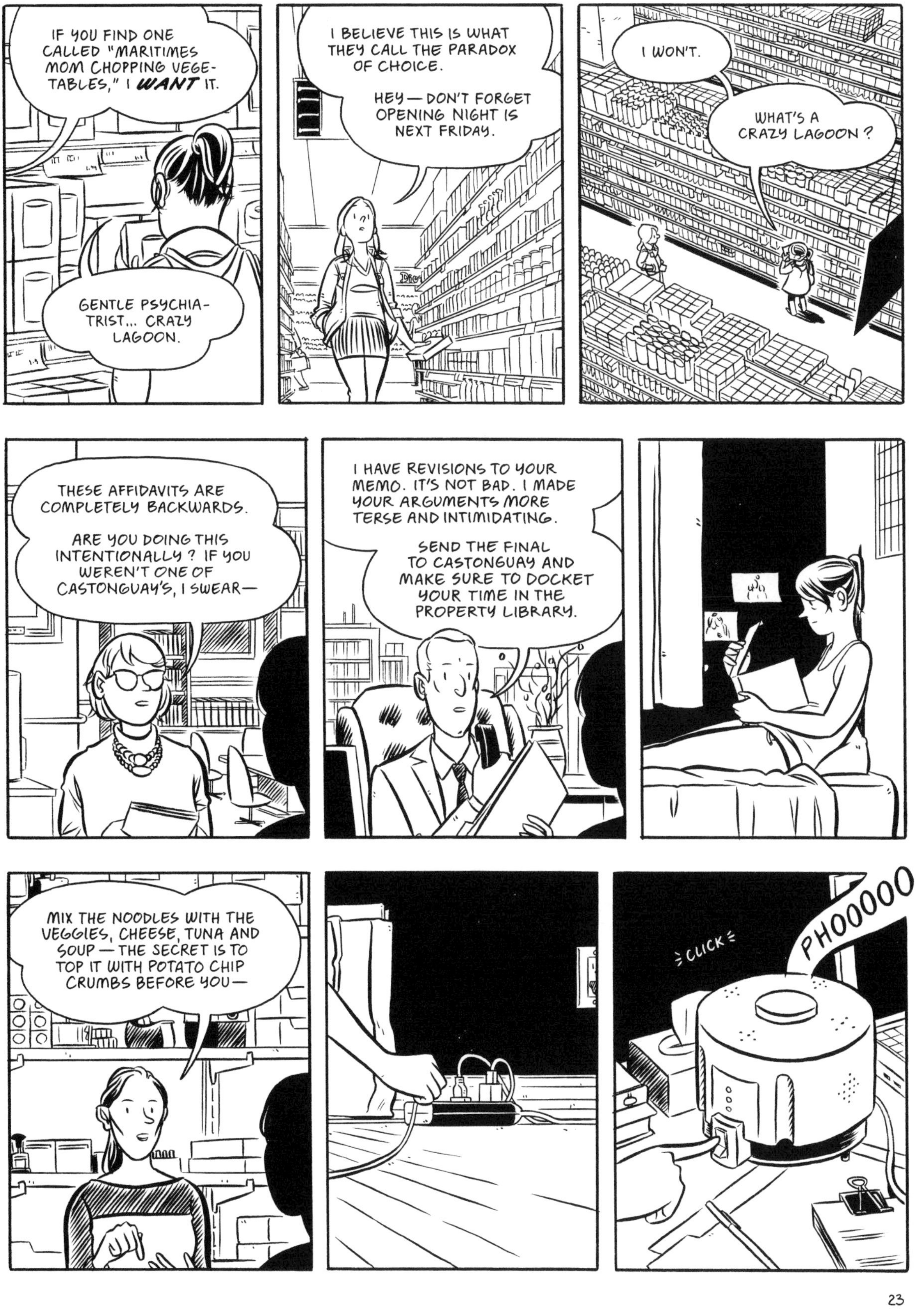
IF YOU FIND ONE CALLED "MARITIMES MOM CHOPPING VEGE-TABLES," I *WANT* IT.
GENTLE PSYCHIA-TRIST... CRAZY LAGOON.
I BELIEVE THIS IS WHAT THEY CALL THE PARADOX OF CHOICE.
HEY — DON'T FORGET OPENING NIGHT IS NEXT FRIDAY.
I WON'T.
WHAT'S A CRAZY LAGOON ?
THESE AFFIDAVITS ARE COMPLETELY BACKWARDS.
ARE YOU DOING THIS INTENTIONALLY ? IF YOU WEREN'T ONE OF CASTONGUAY'S, I SWEAR—
I HAVE REVISIONS TO YOUR MEMO. IT'S NOT BAD. I MADE YOUR ARGUMENTS MORE TERSE AND INTIMIDATING.
SEND THE FINAL TO CASTONGUAY AND MAKE SURE TO DOCKET YOUR TIME IN THE PROPERTY LIBRARY.
MIX THE NOODLES WITH THE VEGGIES, CHEESE, TUNA AND SOUP — THE SECRET IS TO TOP IT WITH POTATO CHIP CRUMBS BEFORE YOU—
CLICK
PHOOOOO

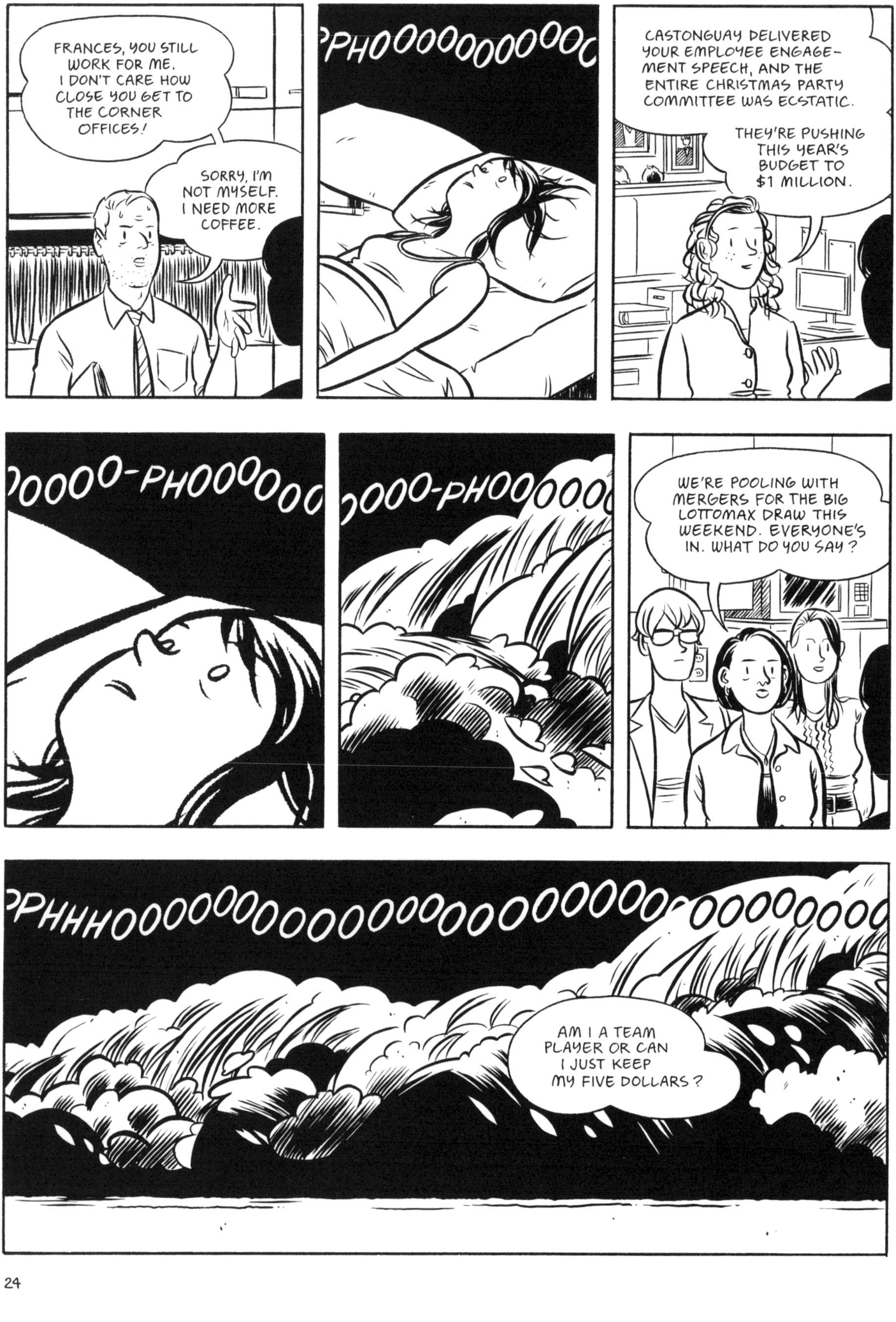
FRANCES, YOU STILL WORK FOR ME. I DON'T CARE HOW CLOSE YOU GET TO THE CORNER OFFICES!
SORRY, I'M NOT MYSELF. I NEED MORE COFFEE.
PHOOOOOOOOOOO
CASTONGUAY DELIVERED YOUR EMPLOYEE ENGAGE-MENT SPEECH, AND THE ENTIRE CHRISTMAS PARTY COMMITTEE WAS ECSTATIC.
THEY'RE PUSHING THIS YEAR'S BUDGET TO $1 MILLION.
OOOOO-PHOOOOOOO
OOOO-PHOOOOOO
WE'RE POOLING WITH MERGERS FOR THE BIG LOTTOMAX DRAW THIS WEEKEND. EVERYONE'S IN. WHAT DO YOU SAY?
PHHHOOOOOOOOOOOOOOOOOOOOOOOOOOOOOO
AM I A TEAM PLAYER OR CAN I JUST KEEP MY FIVE DOLLARS?

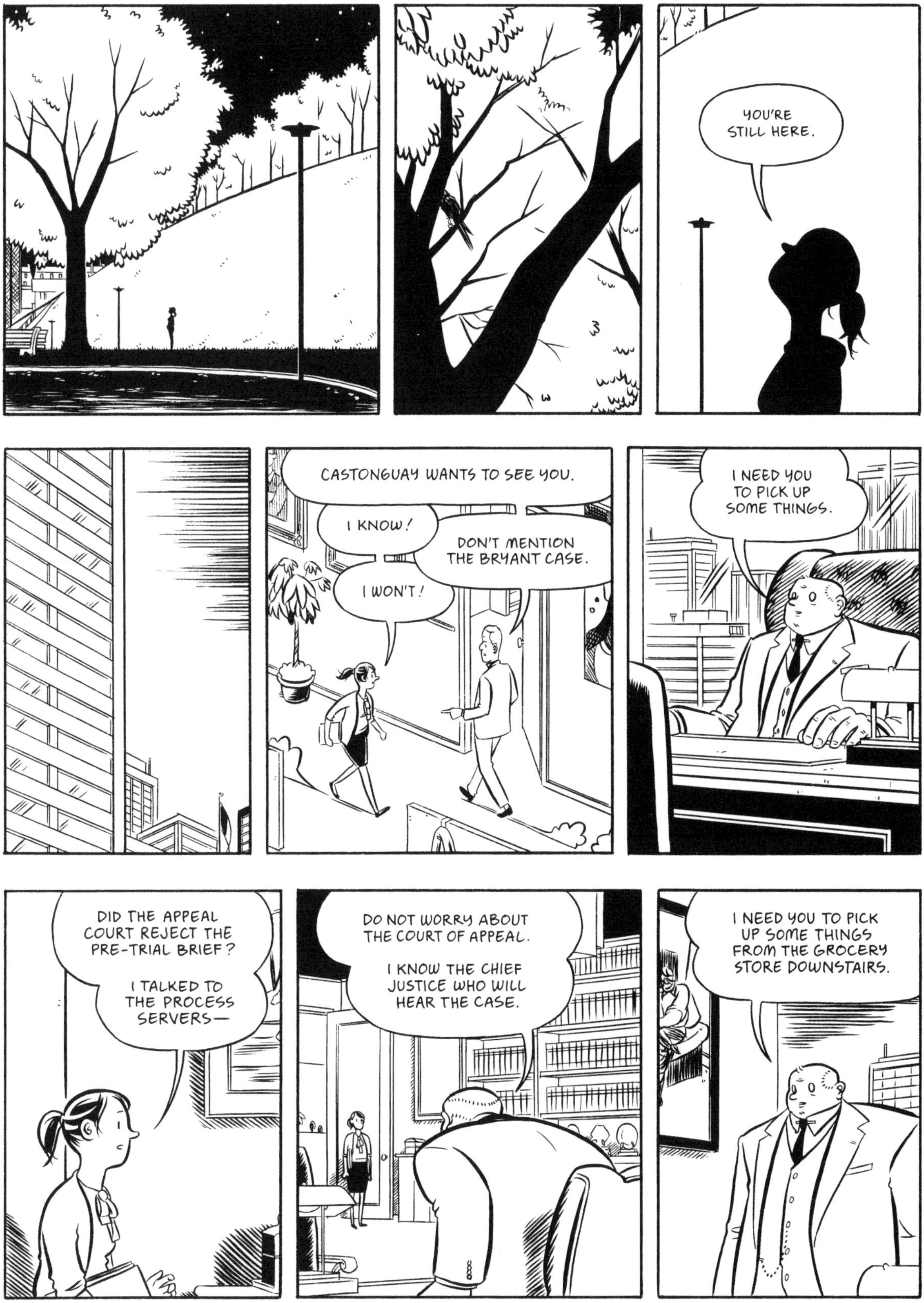
YOU'RE STILL HERE.
CASTONGUAY WANTS TO SEE YOU.
I KNOW!
DON'T MENTION THE BRYANT CASE.
I WON'T!
I NEED YOU TO PICK UP SOME THINGS.
DID THE APPEAL COURT REJECT THE PRE-TRIAL BRIEF?
I TALKED TO THE PROCESS SERVERS—
DO NOT WORRY ABOUT THE COURT OF APPEAL.
I KNOW THE CHIEF JUSTICE WHO WILL HEAR THE CASE.
I NEED YOU TO PICK UP SOME THINGS FROM THE GROCERY STORE DOWNSTAIRS.

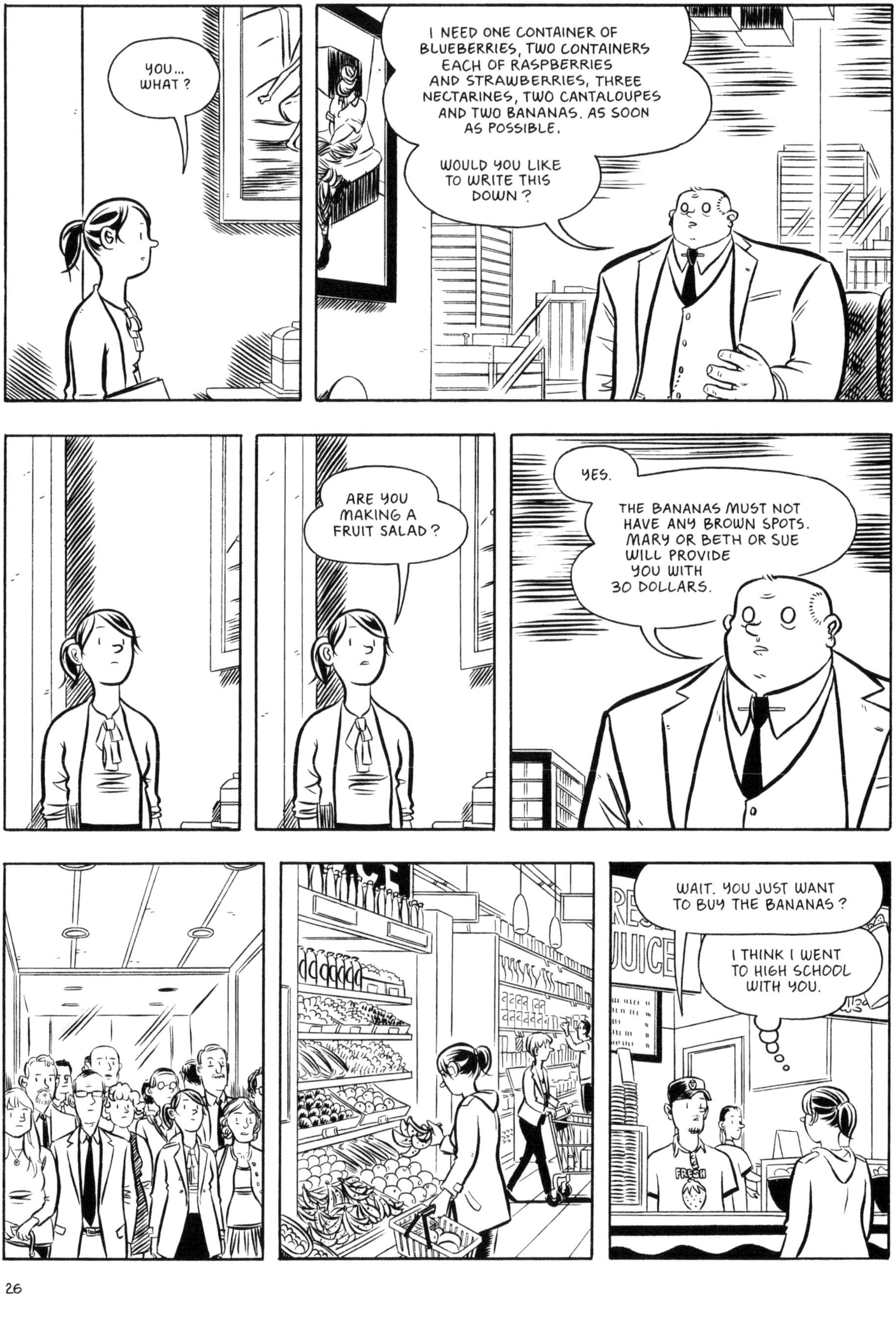
YOU... WHAT?
I NEED ONE CONTAINER OF BLUEBERRIES, TWO CONTAINERS EACH OF RASPBERRIES AND STRAWBERRIES, THREE NECTARINES, TWO CANTALOUPES AND TWO BANANAS. AS SOON AS POSSIBLE.
WOULD YOU LIKE TO WRITE THIS DOWN?
ARE YOU MAKING A FRUIT SALAD?
YES.
THE BANANAS MUST NOT HAVE ANY BROWN SPOTS. MARY OR BETH OR SUE WILL PROVIDE YOU WITH 30 DOLLARS.
FRESH
WAIT. YOU JUST WANT TO BUY THE BANANAS?
I THINK I WENT TO HIGH SCHOOL WITH YOU.

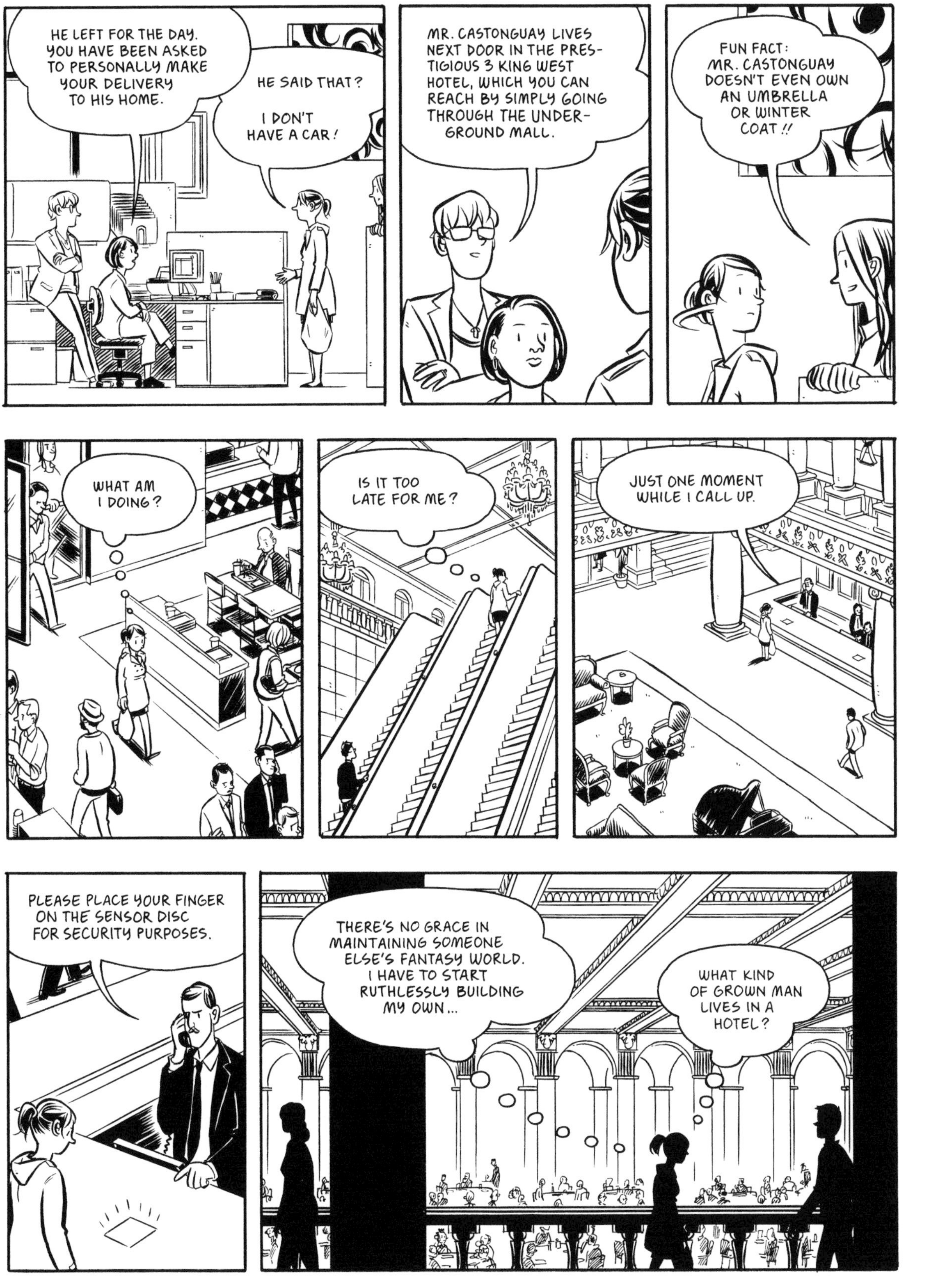
HE LEFT FOR THE DAY. YOU HAVE BEEN ASKED TO PERSONALLY MAKE YOUR DELIVERY TO HIS HOME.
HE SAID THAT?
I DON'T HAVE A CAR!
MR. CASTONGUAY LIVES NEXT DOOR IN THE PRESTIGIOUS 3 KING WEST HOTEL, WHICH YOU CAN REACH BY SIMPLY GOING THROUGH THE UNDERGROUND MALL.
FUN FACT: MR. CASTONGUAY DOESN'T EVEN OWN AN UMBRELLA OR WINTER COAT!!
WHAT AM I DOING?
IS IT TOO LATE FOR ME?
JUST ONE MOMENT WHILE I CALL UP.
PLEASE PLACE YOUR FINGER ON THE SENSOR DISC FOR SECURITY PURPOSES.
THERE'S NO GRACE IN MAINTAINING SOMEONE ELSE'S FANTASY WORLD. I HAVE TO START RUTHLESSLY BUILDING MY OWN...
WHAT KIND OF GROWN MAN LIVES IN A HOTEL?

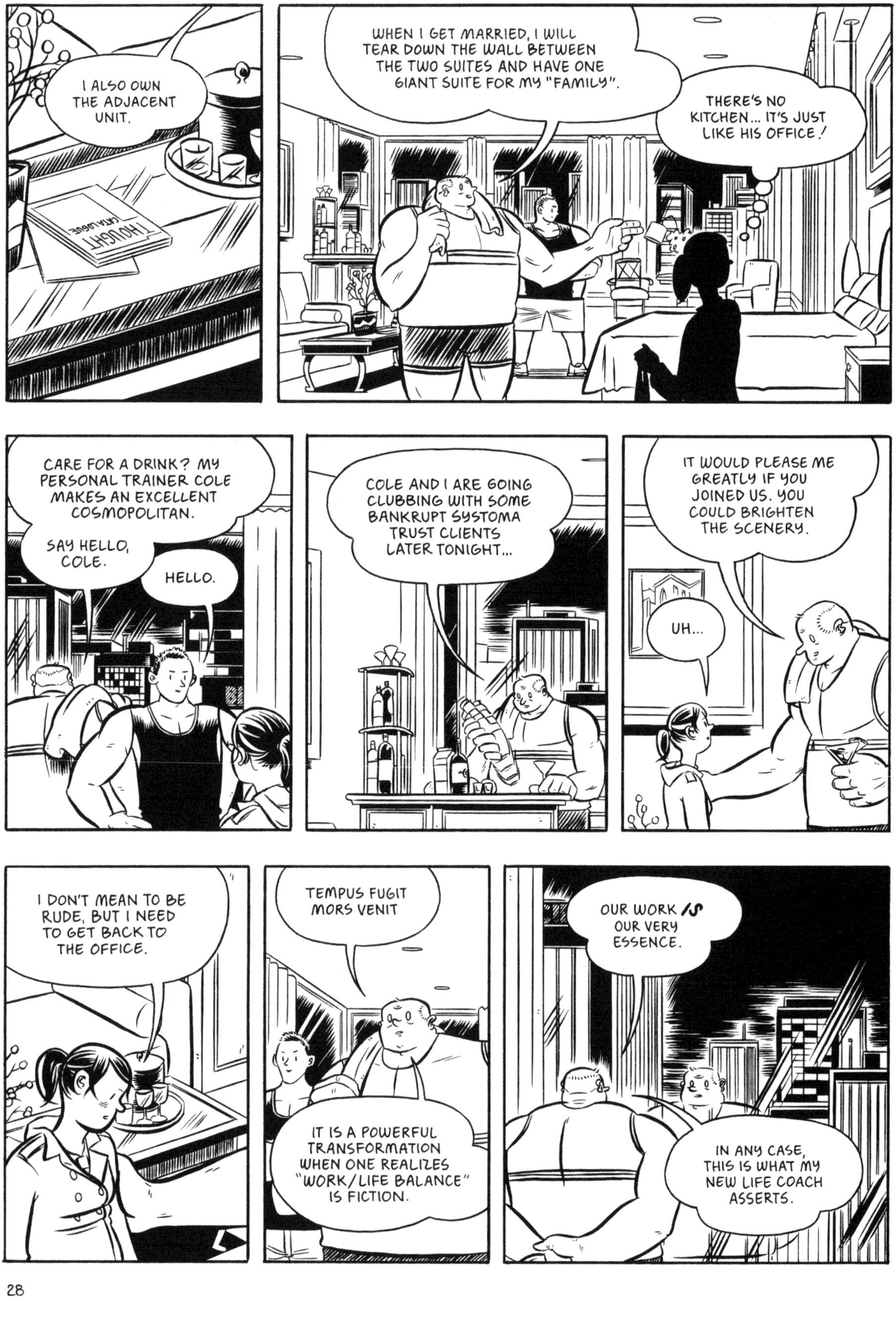
I ALSO OWN THE ADJACENT UNIT.
THOUGHT CATALOGUE
WHEN I GET MARRIED, I WILL TEAR DOWN THE WALL BETWEEN THE TWO SUITES AND HAVE ONE GIANT SUITE FOR MY "FAMILY".
THERE'S NO KITCHEN... IT'S JUST LIKE HIS OFFICE!
CARE FOR A DRINK? MY PERSONAL TRAINER COLE MAKES AN EXCELLENT COSMOPOLITAN.
SAY HELLO, COLE.
HELLO.
COLE AND I ARE GOING CLUBBING WITH SOME BANKRUPT SYSTOMA TRUST CLIENTS LATER TONIGHT...
IT WOULD PLEASE ME GREATLY IF YOU JOINED US. YOU COULD BRIGHTEN THE SCENERY.
UH...
I DON'T MEAN TO BE RUDE, BUT I NEED TO GET BACK TO THE OFFICE.
TEMPUS FUGIT MORS VENIT
IT IS A POWERFUL TRANSFORMATION WHEN ONE REALIZES "WORK/LIFE BALANCE" IS FICTION.
OUR WORK IS OUR VERY ESSENCE.
IN ANY CASE, THIS IS WHAT MY NEW LIFE COACH ASSERTS.

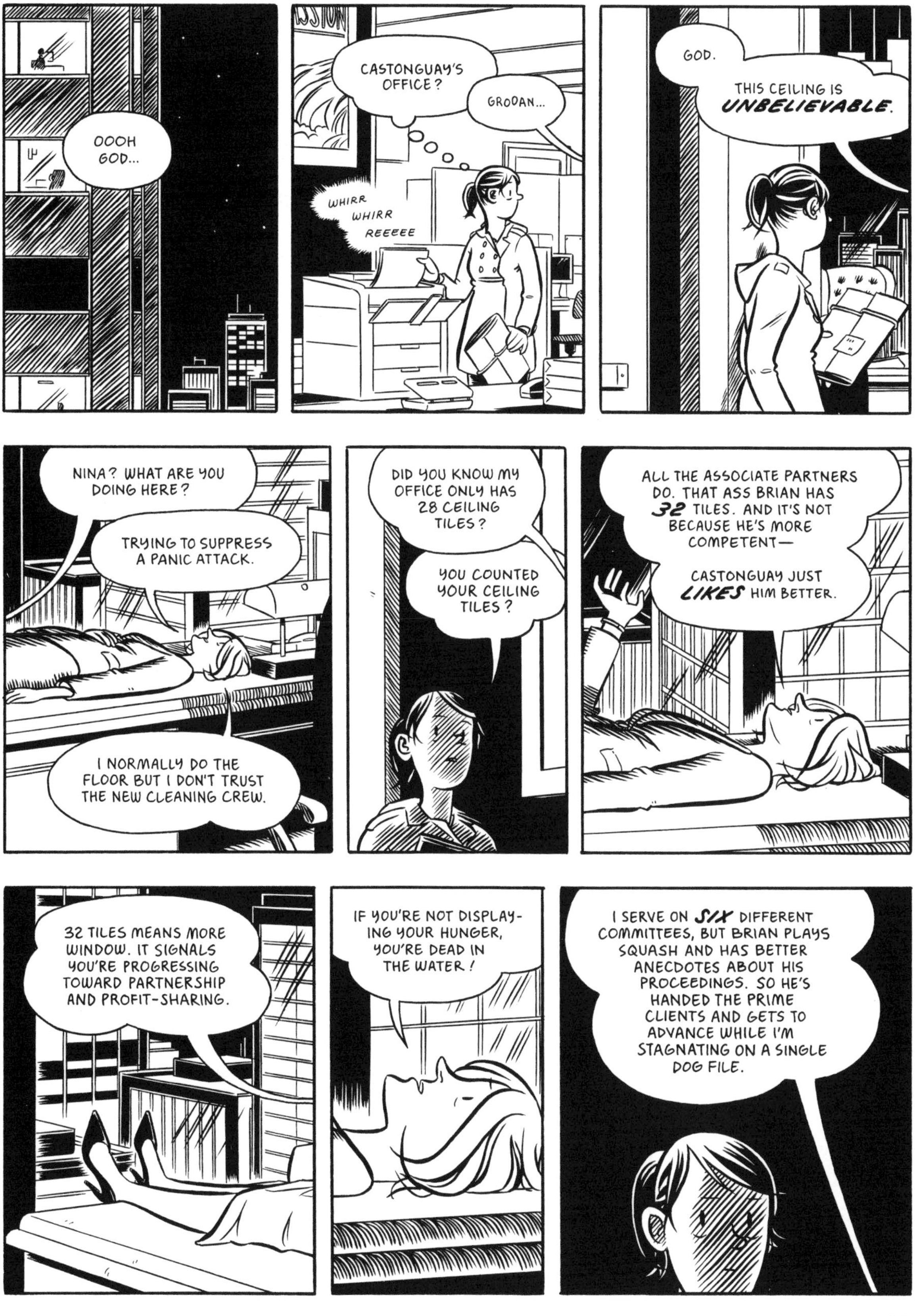
OOOH GOD...
CASTONGUAY'S OFFICE?
GRODAN...
WHIRR WHIRR REEEEE
GOD.
THIS CEILING IS UNBELIEVABLE.
NINA? WHAT ARE YOU DOING HERE?
TRYING TO SUPPRESS A PANIC ATTACK.
I NORMALLY DO THE FLOOR BUT I DON'T TRUST THE NEW CLEANING CREW.
DID YOU KNOW MY OFFICE ONLY HAS 28 CEILING TILES?
YOU COUNTED YOUR CEILING TILES?
ALL THE ASSOCIATE PARTNERS DO. THAT ASS BRIAN HAS 32 TILES. AND IT'S NOT BECAUSE HE'S MORE COMPETENT—
CASTONGUAY JUST LIKES HIM BETTER.
32 TILES MEANS MORE WINDOW. IT SIGNALS YOU'RE PROGRESSING TOWARD PARTNERSHIP AND PROFIT-SHARING.
IF YOU'RE NOT DISPLAYING YOUR HUNGER, YOU'RE DEAD IN THE WATER!
I SERVE ON SIX DIFFERENT COMMITTEES, BUT BRIAN PLAYS SQUASH AND HAS BETTER ANECDOTES ABOUT HIS PROCEEDINGS. SO HE'S HANDED THE PRIME CLIENTS AND GETS TO ADVANCE WHILE I'M STAGNATING ON A SINGLE DOG FILE.

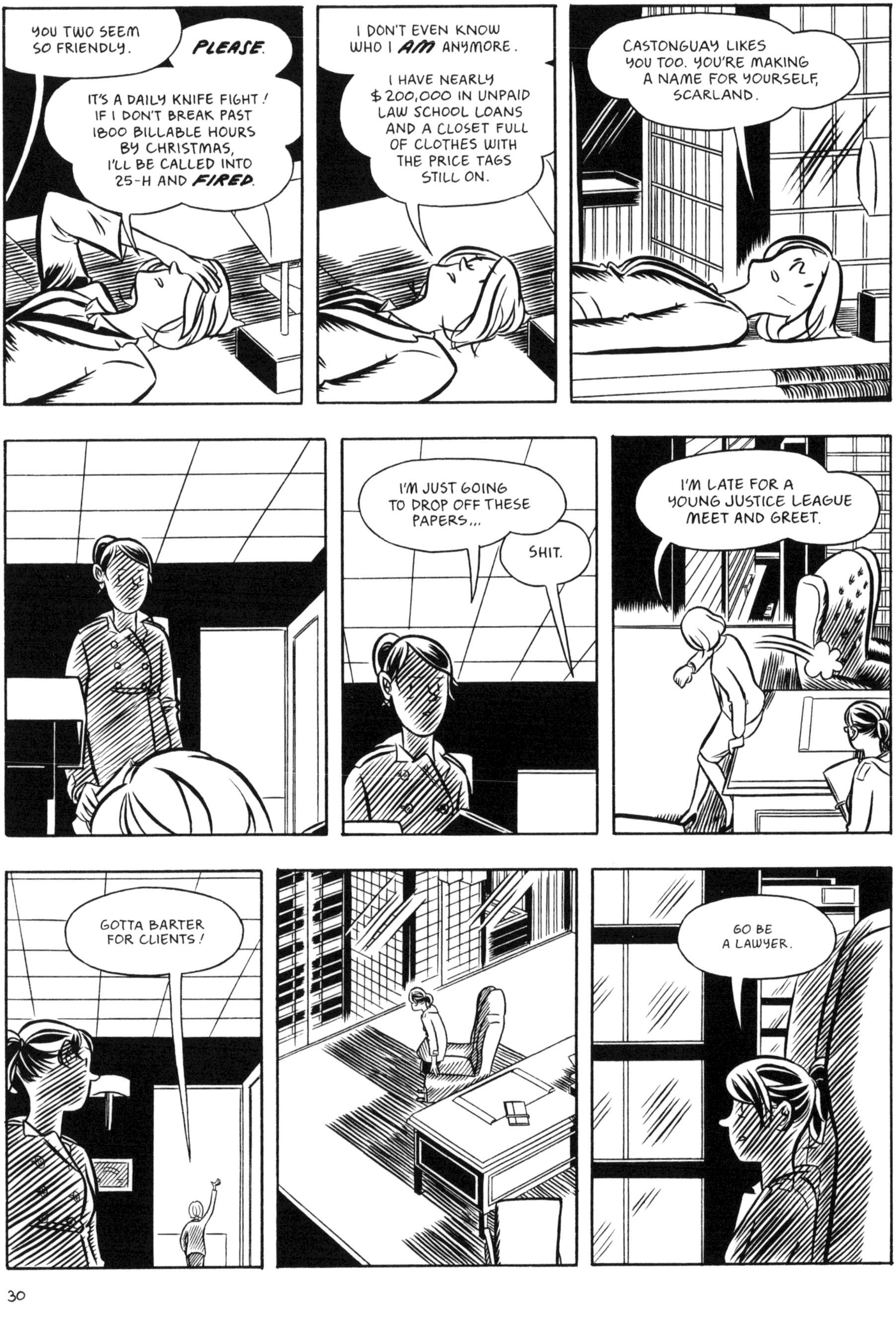
YOU TWO SEEM SO FRIENDLY.
PLEASE.
IT'S A DAILY KNIFE FIGHT! IF I DON'T BREAK PAST 1800 BILLABLE HOURS BY CHRISTMAS, I'LL BE CALLED INTO 25-H AND FIRED.
I DON'T EVEN KNOW WHO I AM ANYMORE.
I HAVE NEARLY $200,000 IN UNPAID LAW SCHOOL LOANS AND A CLOSET FULL OF CLOTHES WITH THE PRICE TAGS STILL ON.
CASTONGUAY LIKES YOU TOO. YOU'RE MAKING A NAME FOR YOURSELF, SCARLAND.
I'M JUST GOING TO DROP OFF THESE PAPERS...
SHIT.
I'M LATE FOR A YOUNG JUSTICE LEAGUE MEET AND GREET.
GOTTA BARTER FOR CLIENTS!
GO BE A LAWYER.

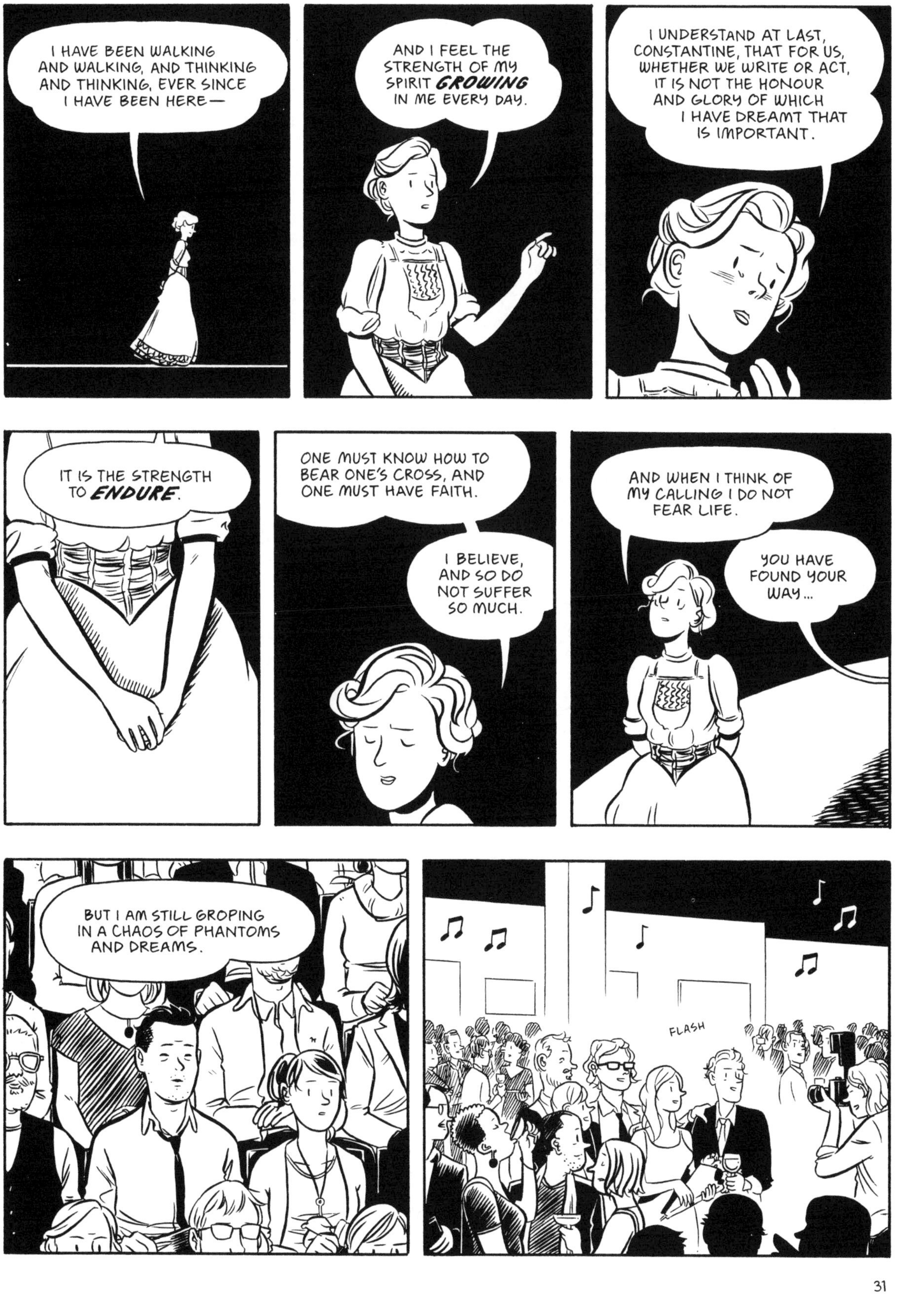
I HAVE BEEN WALKING AND WALKING, AND THINKING AND THINKING, EVER SINCE I HAVE BEEN HERE—
AND I FEEL THE STRENGTH OF MY SPIRIT **GROWING** IN ME EVERY DAY.
I UNDERSTAND AT LAST, CONSTANTINE, THAT FOR US, WHETHER WE WRITE OR ACT, IT IS NOT THE HONOUR AND GLORY OF WHICH I HAVE DREAMT THAT IS IMPORTANT.
IT IS THE STRENGTH TO **ENDURE**.
ONE MUST KNOW HOW TO BEAR ONE'S CROSS, AND ONE MUST HAVE FAITH.
I BELIEVE, AND SO DO NOT SUFFER SO MUCH.
AND WHEN I THINK OF MY CALLING I DO NOT FEAR LIFE.
YOU HAVE FOUND YOUR WAY...
BUT I AM STILL GROPING IN A CHAOS OF PHANTOMS AND DREAMS.
FLASH

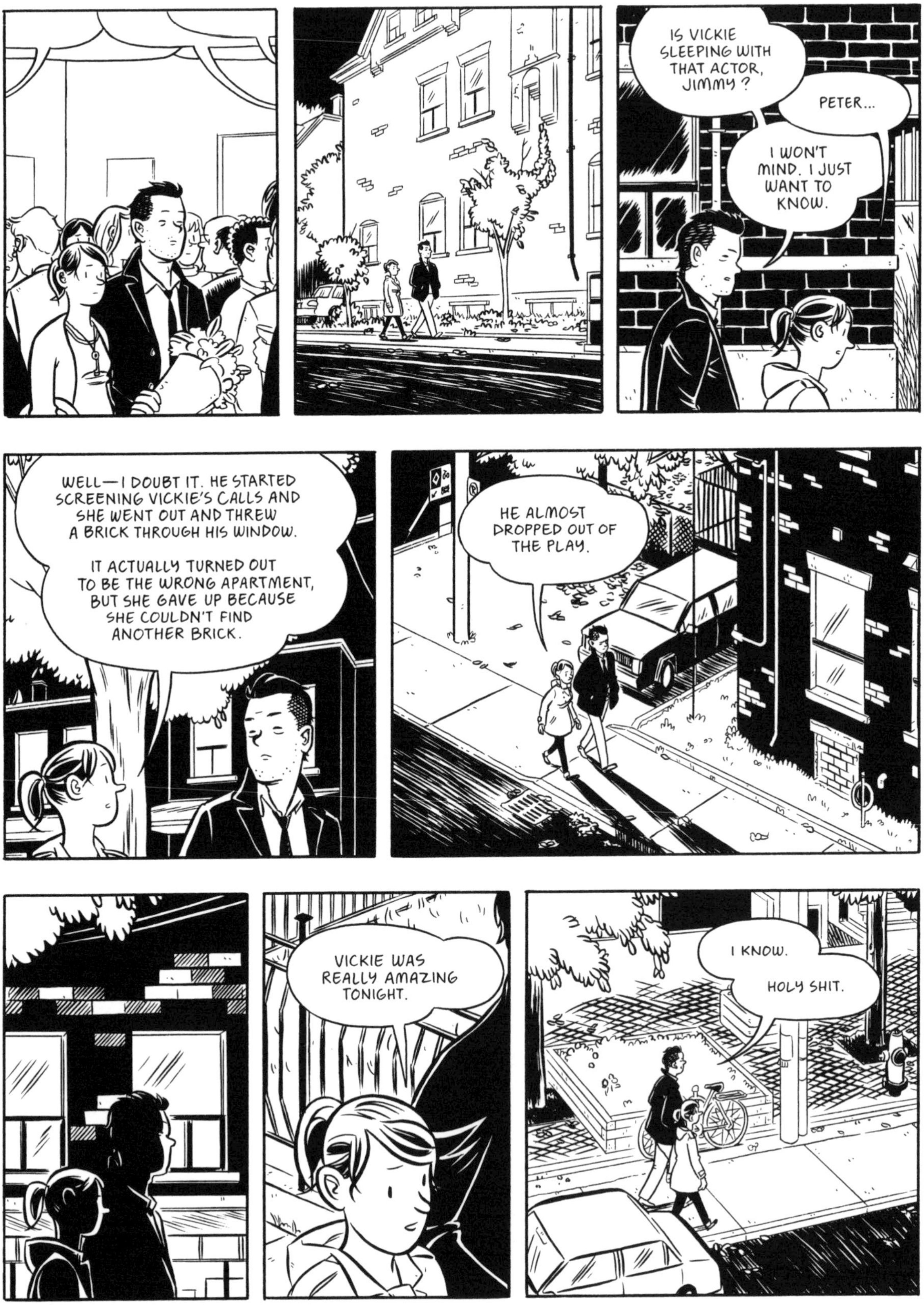
IS VICKIE SLEEPING WITH THAT ACTOR, JIMMY?
PETER...
I WON'T MIND. I JUST WANT TO KNOW.
WELL—I DOUBT IT. HE STARTED SCREENING VICKIE'S CALLS AND SHE WENT OUT AND THREW A BRICK THROUGH HIS WINDOW.
IT ACTUALLY TURNED OUT TO BE THE WRONG APARTMENT, BUT SHE GAVE UP BECAUSE SHE COULDN'T FIND ANOTHER BRICK.
HE ALMOST DROPPED OUT OF THE PLAY.
VICKIE WAS REALLY AMAZING TONIGHT.
I KNOW.
HOLY SHIT.

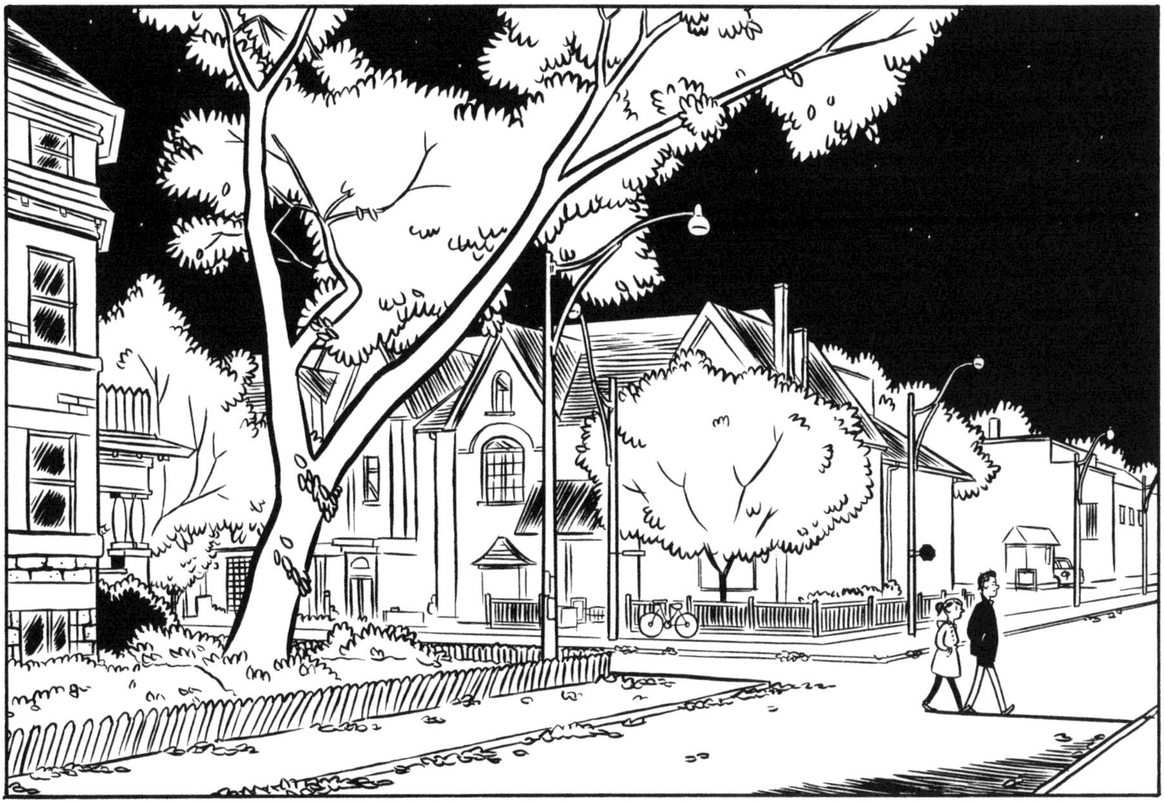

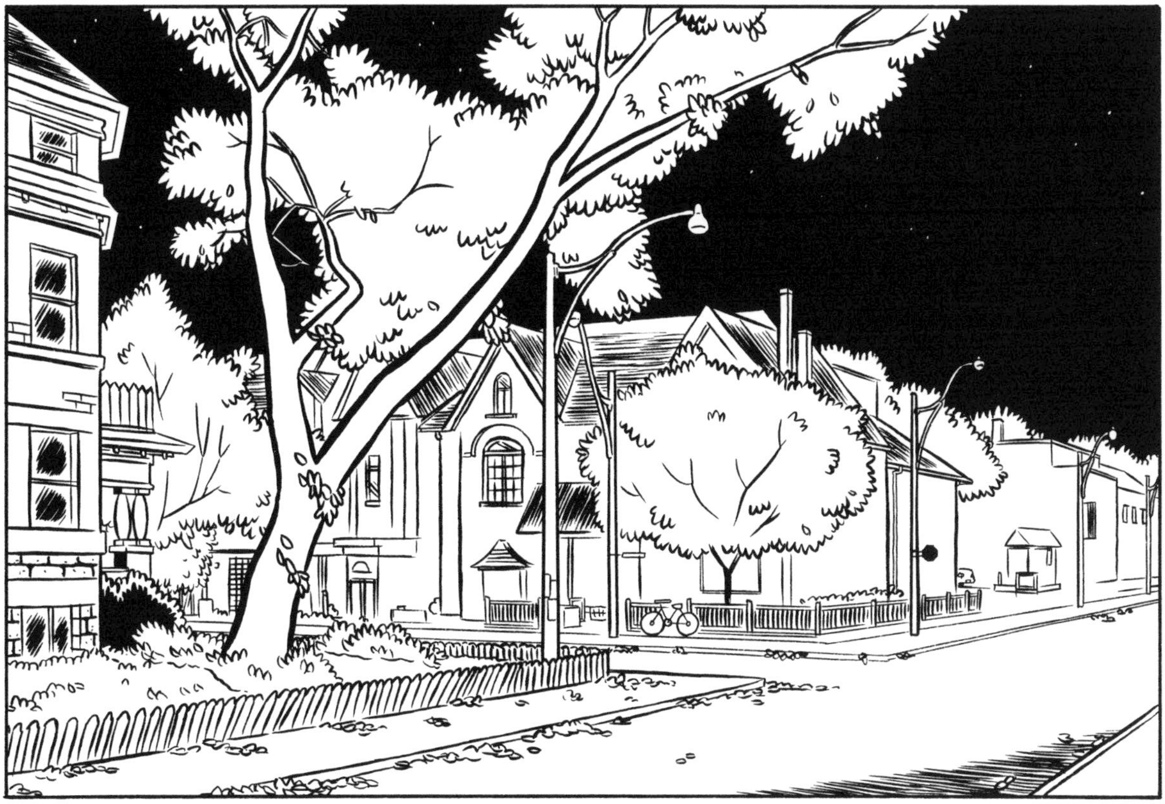

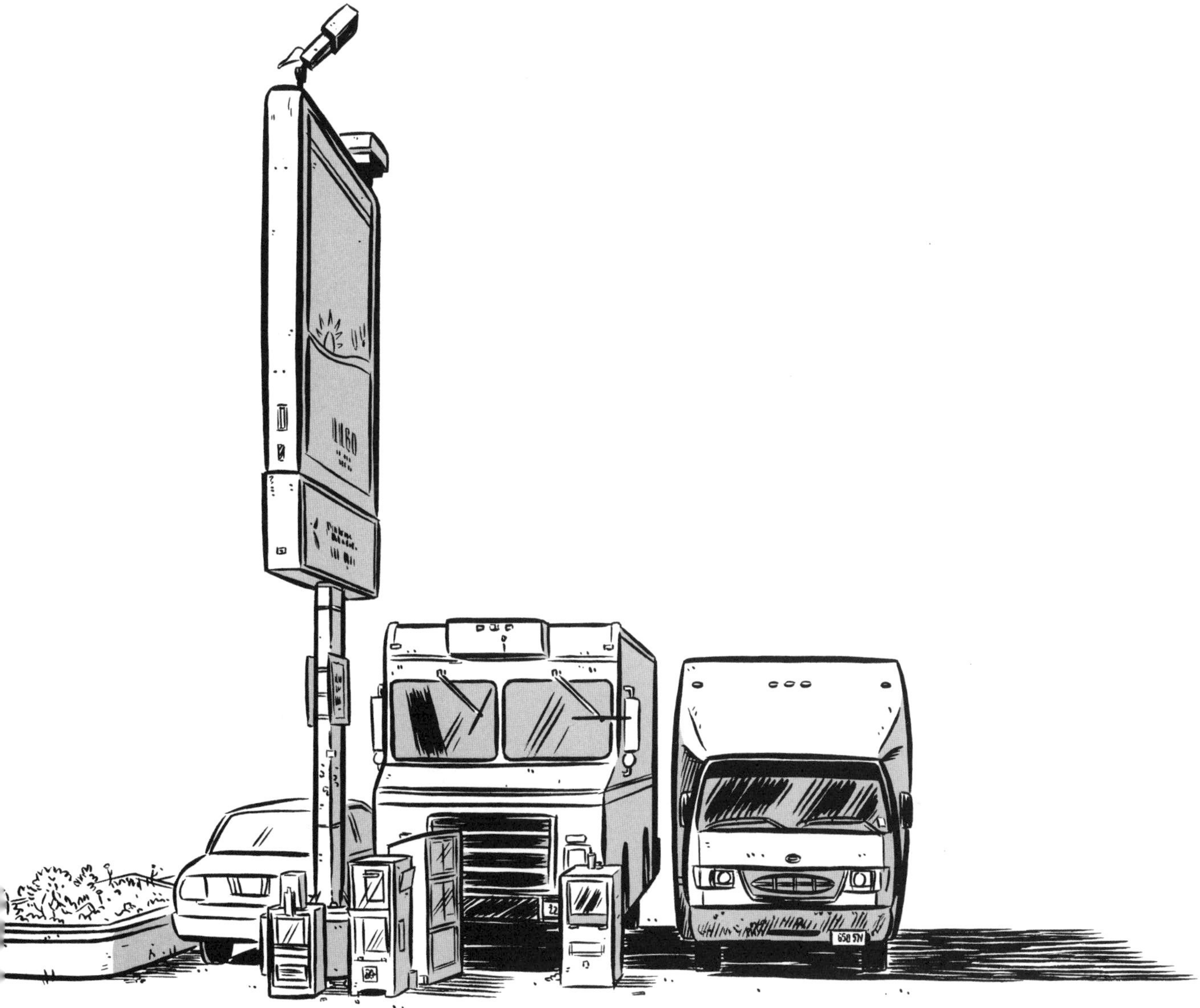

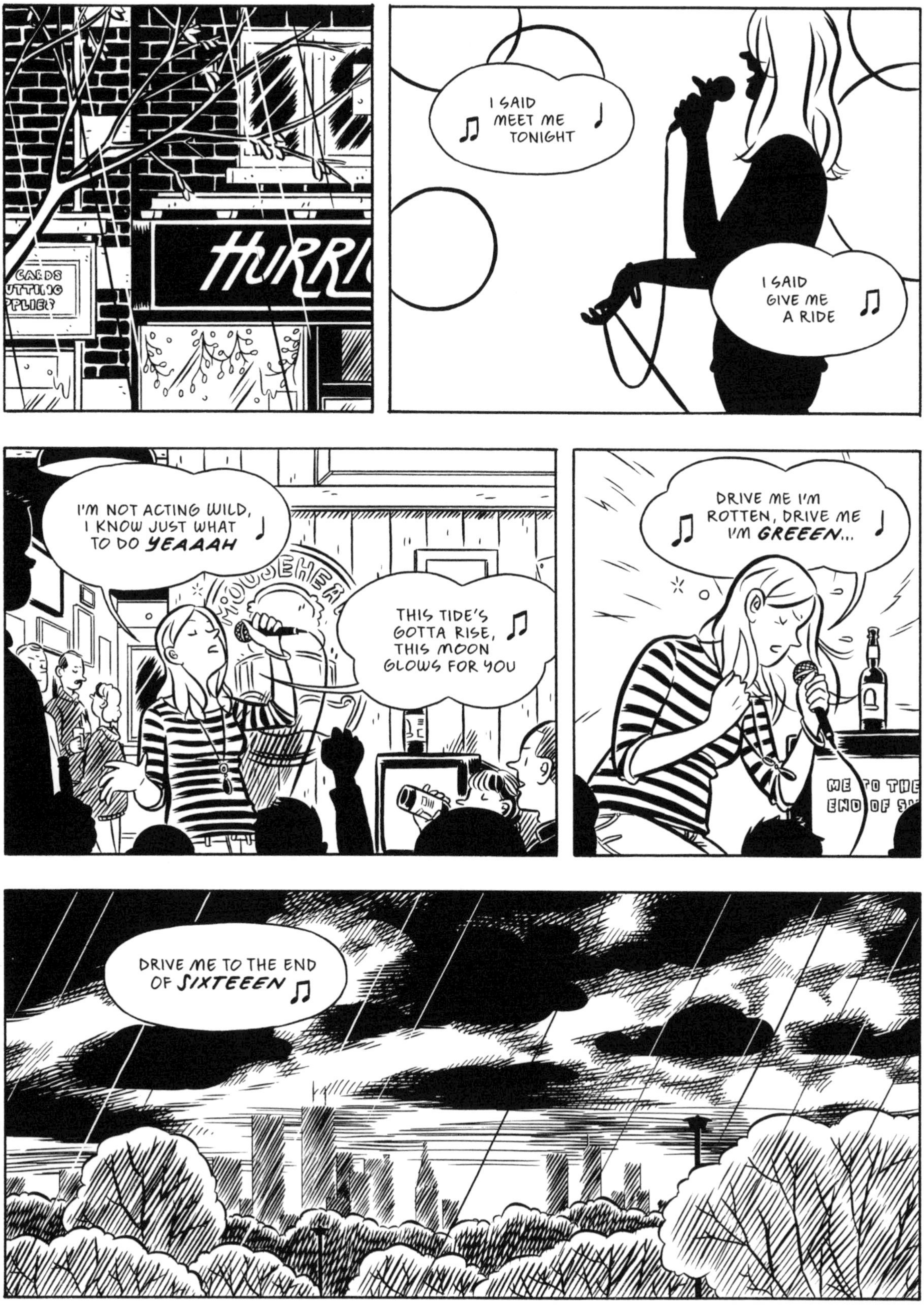
I SAID MEET ME TONIGHT
I SAID GIVE ME A RIDE
I'M NOT ACTING WILD, I KNOW JUST WHAT TO DO **YEAAAH**
THIS TIDE'S GOTTA RISE, THIS MOON GLOWS FOR YOU
DRIVE ME I'M ROTTEN, DRIVE ME I'M **GREEEN**...
DRIVE ME TO THE END OF **SIXTEEEN**

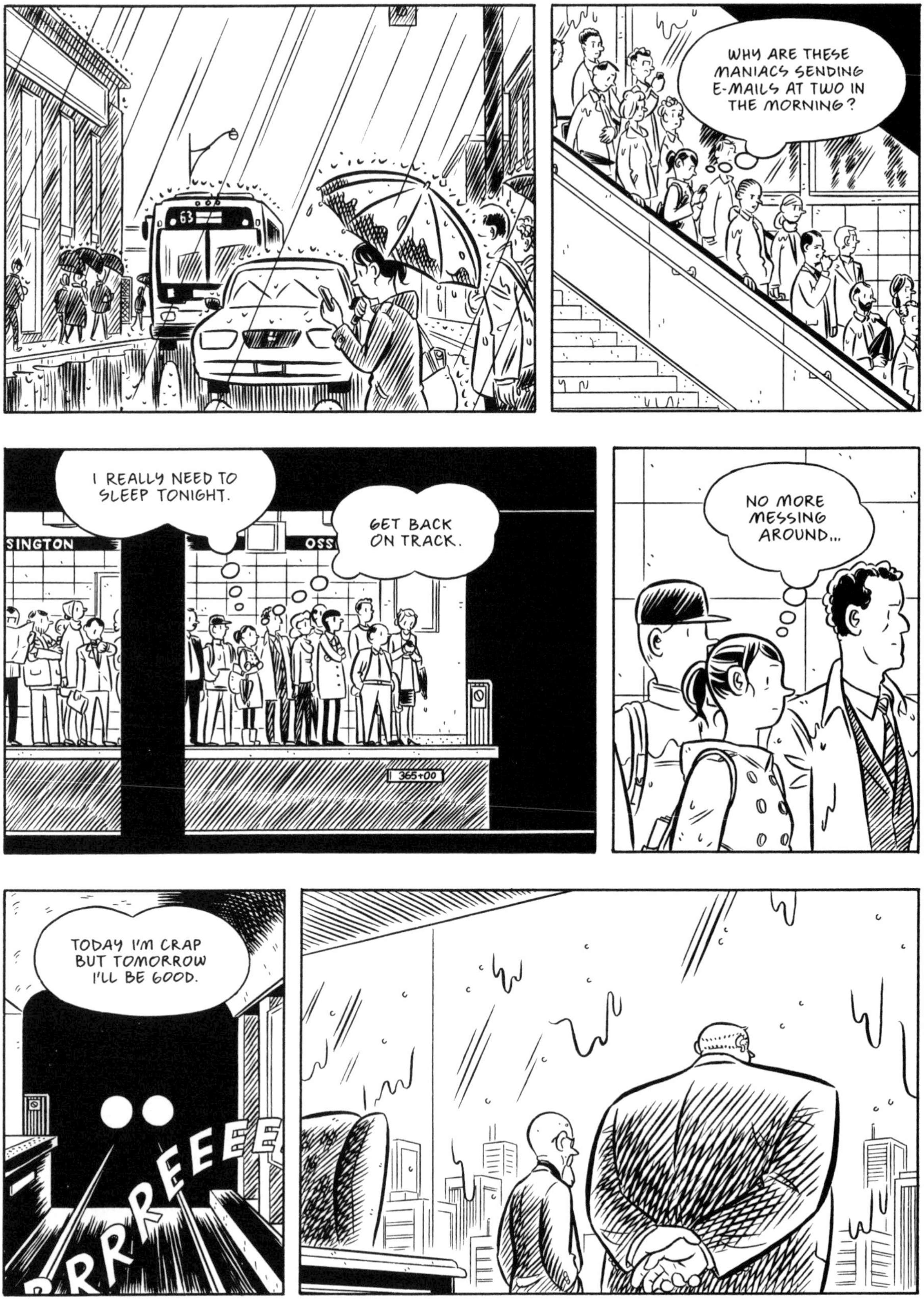
63
WHY ARE THESE MANIACS SENDING E-MAILS AT TWO IN THE MORNING?
I REALLY NEED TO SLEEP TONIGHT.
SINGTON
OSS
GET BACK ON TRACK.
365+00
NO MORE MESSING AROUND...
TODAY I'M CRAP BUT TOMORROW I'LL BE GOOD.
RRRREEEE

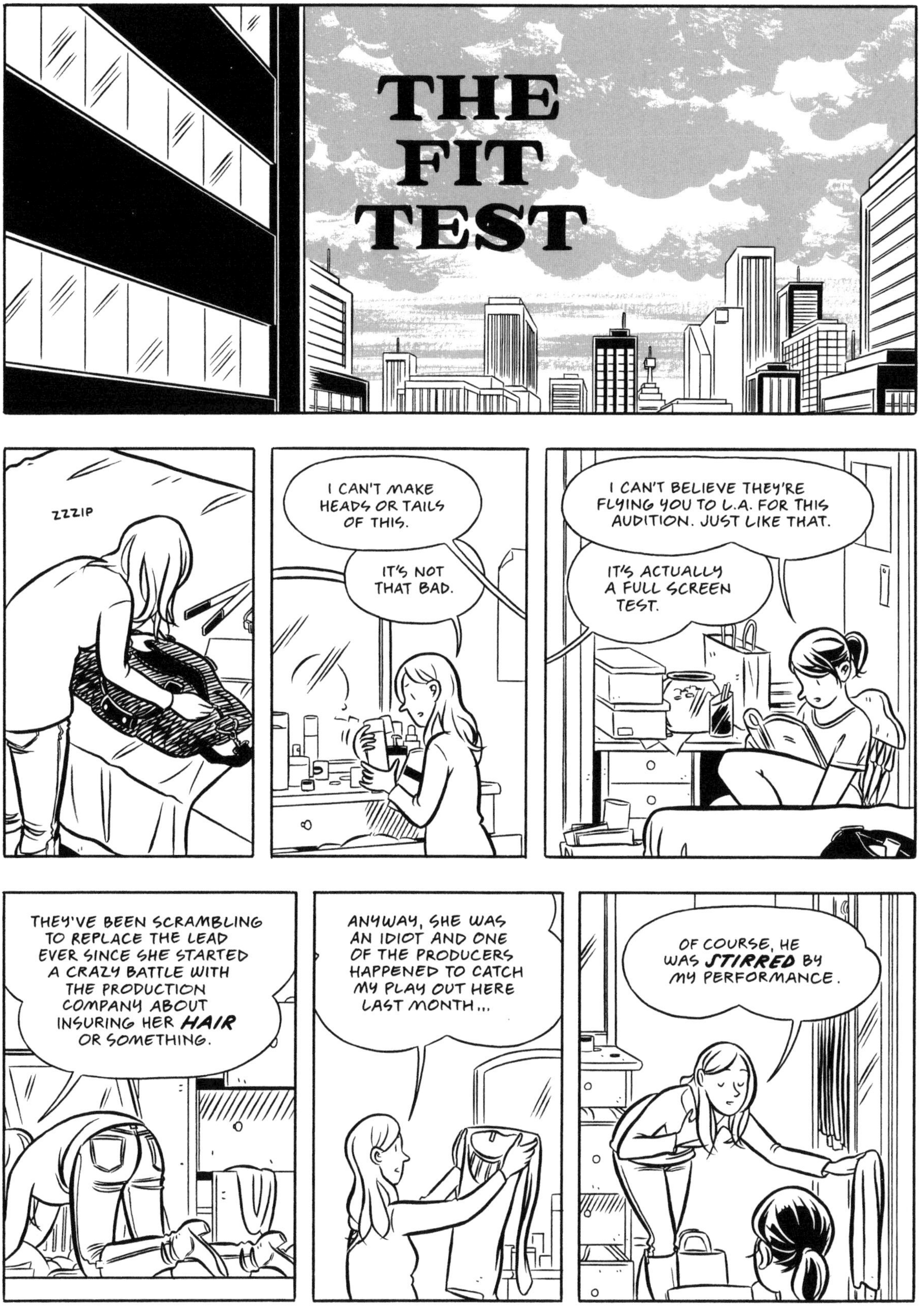
THE FIT TEST
ZZZIP
I CAN'T MAKE HEADS OR TAILS OF THIS.
IT'S NOT THAT BAD.
I CAN'T BELIEVE THEY'RE FLYING YOU TO L.A. FOR THIS AUDITION. JUST LIKE THAT.
IT'S ACTUALLY A FULL SCREEN TEST.
THEY'VE BEEN SCRAMBLING TO REPLACE THE LEAD EVER SINCE SHE STARTED A CRAZY BATTLE WITH THE PRODUCTION COMPANY ABOUT INSURING HER ***HAIR*** OR SOMETHING.
ANYWAY, SHE WAS AN IDIOT AND ONE OF THE PRODUCERS HAPPENED TO CATCH MY PLAY OUT HERE LAST MONTH...
OF COURSE, HE WAS ***STIRRED*** BY MY PERFORMANCE.

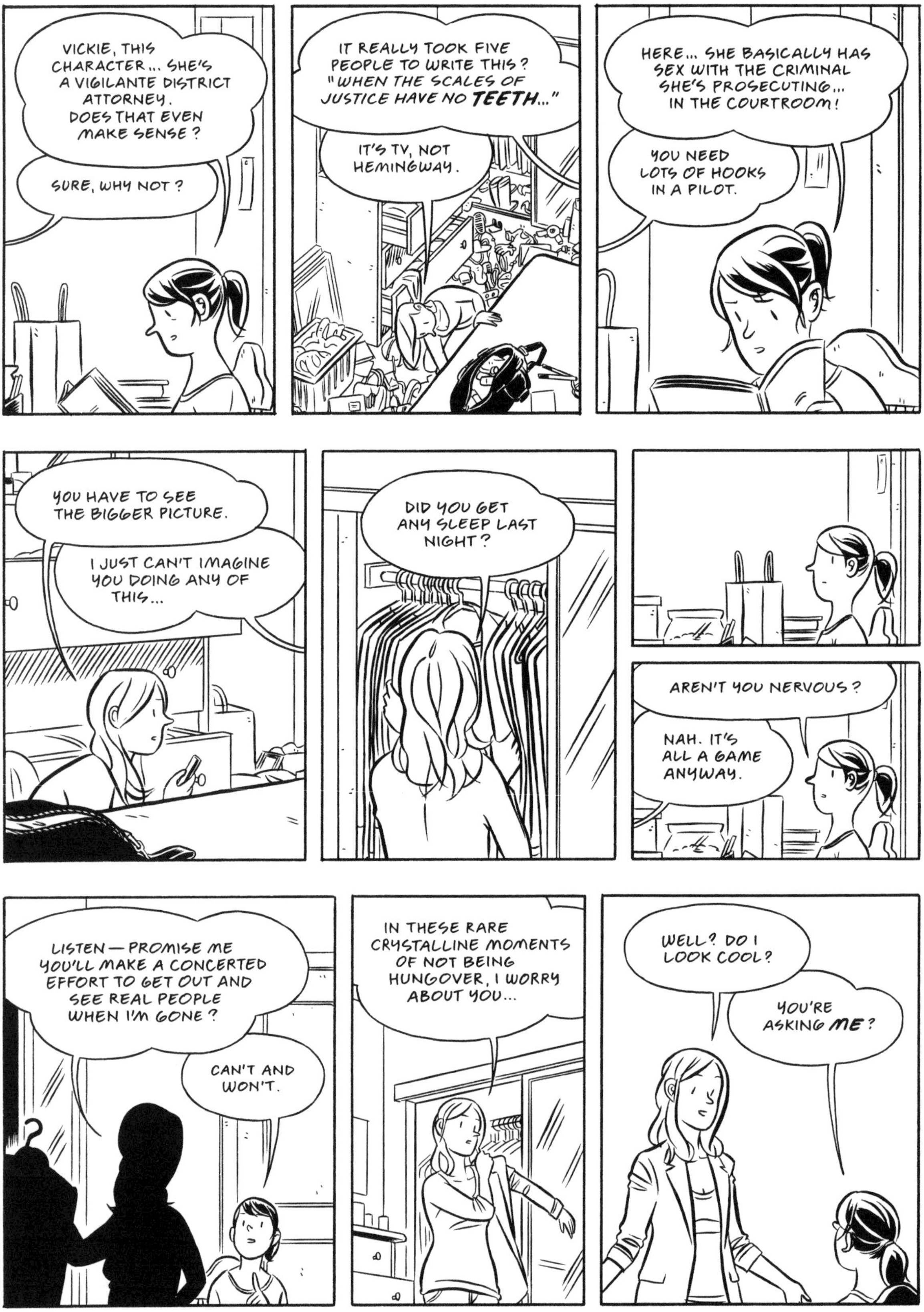
VICKIE, THIS CHARACTER... SHE'S A VIGILANTE DISTRICT ATTORNEY. DOES THAT EVEN MAKE SENSE?
SURE, WHY NOT?
IT REALLY TOOK FIVE PEOPLE TO WRITE THIS? "WHEN THE SCALES OF JUSTICE HAVE NO **TEETH**..."
IT'S TV, NOT HEMINGWAY.
HERE... SHE BASICALLY HAS SEX WITH THE CRIMINAL SHE'S PROSECUTING... IN THE COURTROOM!
YOU NEED LOTS OF HOOKS IN A PILOT.
YOU HAVE TO SEE THE BIGGER PICTURE.
I JUST CAN'T IMAGINE YOU DOING ANY OF THIS...
DID YOU GET ANY SLEEP LAST NIGHT?
AREN'T YOU NERVOUS?
NAH. IT'S ALL A GAME ANYWAY.
LISTEN — PROMISE ME YOU'LL MAKE A CONCERTED EFFORT TO GET OUT AND SEE REAL PEOPLE WHEN I'M GONE?
CAN'T AND WON'T.
IN THESE RARE CRYSTALLINE MOMENTS OF NOT BEING HUNGOVER, I WORRY ABOUT YOU...
WELL? DO I LOOK COOL?
YOU'RE ASKING **ME**?

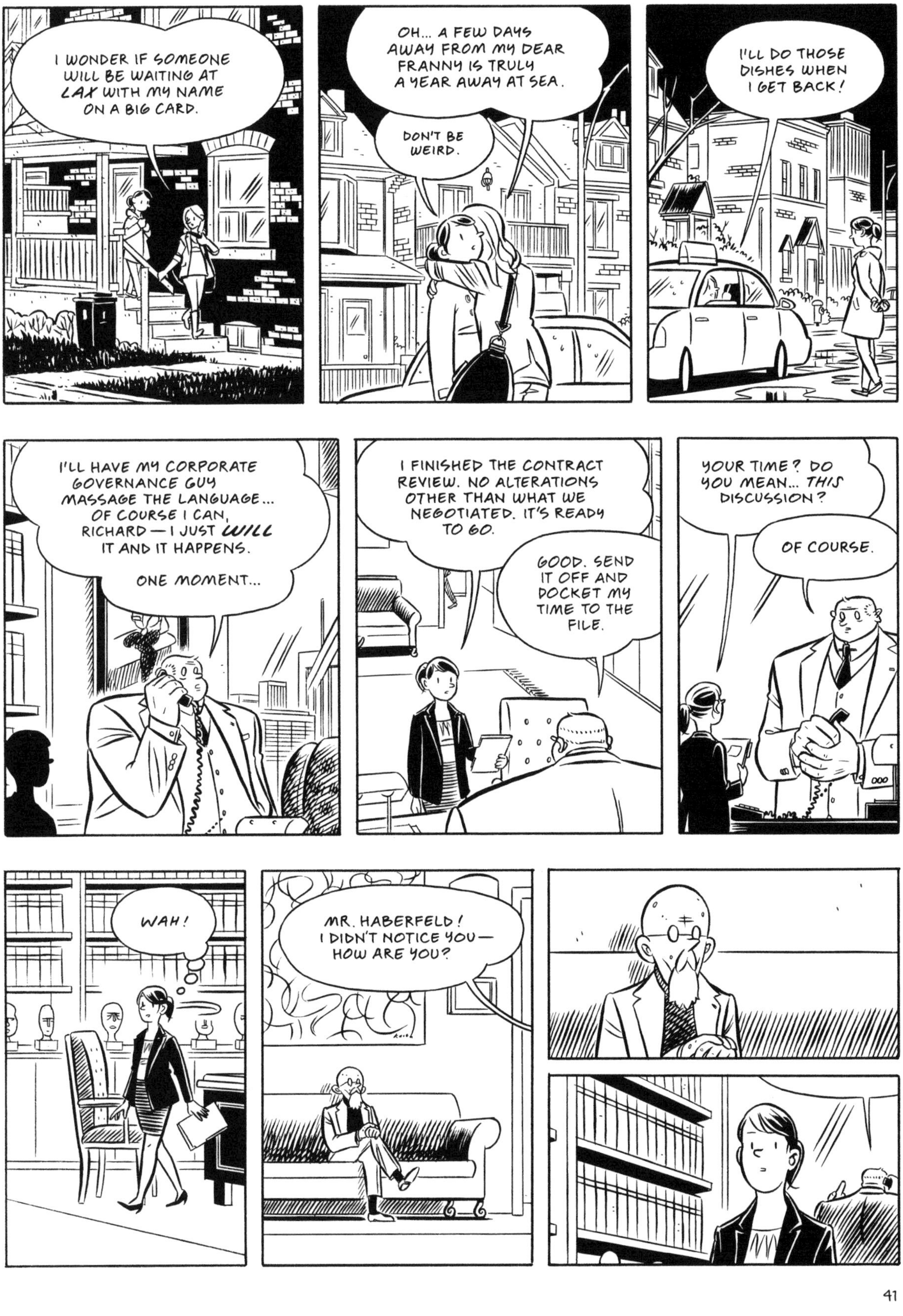
I WONDER IF SOMEONE WILL BE WAITING AT LAX WITH MY NAME ON A BIG CARD.
OH... A FEW DAYS AWAY FROM MY DEAR FRANNY IS TRULY A YEAR AWAY AT SEA.
DON'T BE WEIRD.
I'LL DO THOSE DISHES WHEN I GET BACK!
I'LL HAVE MY CORPORATE GOVERNANCE GUY MASSAGE THE LANGUAGE... OF COURSE I CAN, RICHARD — I JUST WILL IT AND IT HAPPENS.
ONE MOMENT...
I FINISHED THE CONTRACT REVIEW. NO ALTERATIONS OTHER THAN WHAT WE NEGOTIATED. IT'S READY TO GO.
GOOD. SEND IT OFF AND DOCKET MY TIME TO THE FILE.
YOUR TIME? DO YOU MEAN... THIS DISCUSSION?
OF COURSE.
WAH!
MR. HABERFELD! I DIDN'T NOTICE YOU— HOW ARE YOU?

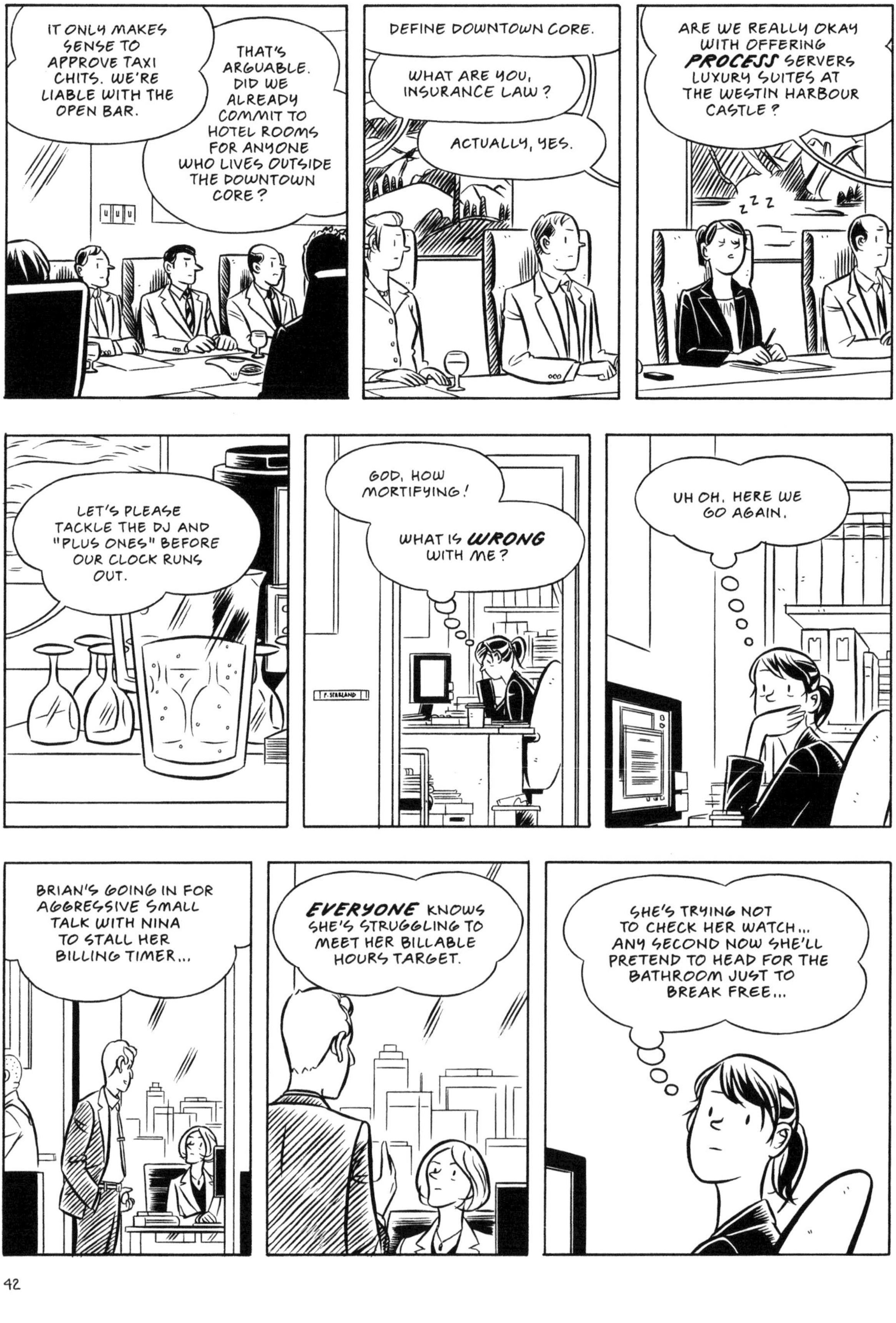
IT ONLY MAKES SENSE TO APPROVE TAXI CHITS. WE'RE LIABLE WITH THE OPEN BAR.
THAT'S ARGUABLE. DID WE ALREADY COMMIT TO HOTEL ROOMS FOR ANYONE WHO LIVES OUTSIDE THE DOWNTOWN CORE?
DEFINE DOWNTOWN CORE.
WHAT ARE YOU, INSURANCE LAW?
ACTUALLY, YES.
ARE WE REALLY OKAY WITH OFFERING PROCESS SERVERS LUXURY SUITES AT THE WESTIN HARBOUR CASTLE?
Z Z Z
LET'S PLEASE TACKLE THE DJ AND "PLUS ONES" BEFORE OUR CLOCK RUNS OUT.
GOD, HOW MORTIFYING!
WHAT IS WRONG WITH ME?
UH OH. HERE WE GO AGAIN.
BRIAN'S GOING IN FOR AGGRESSIVE SMALL TALK WITH NINA TO STALL HER BILLING TIMER...
EVERYONE KNOWS SHE'S STRUGGLING TO MEET HER BILLABLE HOURS TARGET.
SHE'S TRYING NOT TO CHECK HER WATCH... ANY SECOND NOW SHE'LL PRETEND TO HEAD FOR THE BATHROOM JUST TO BREAK FREE...

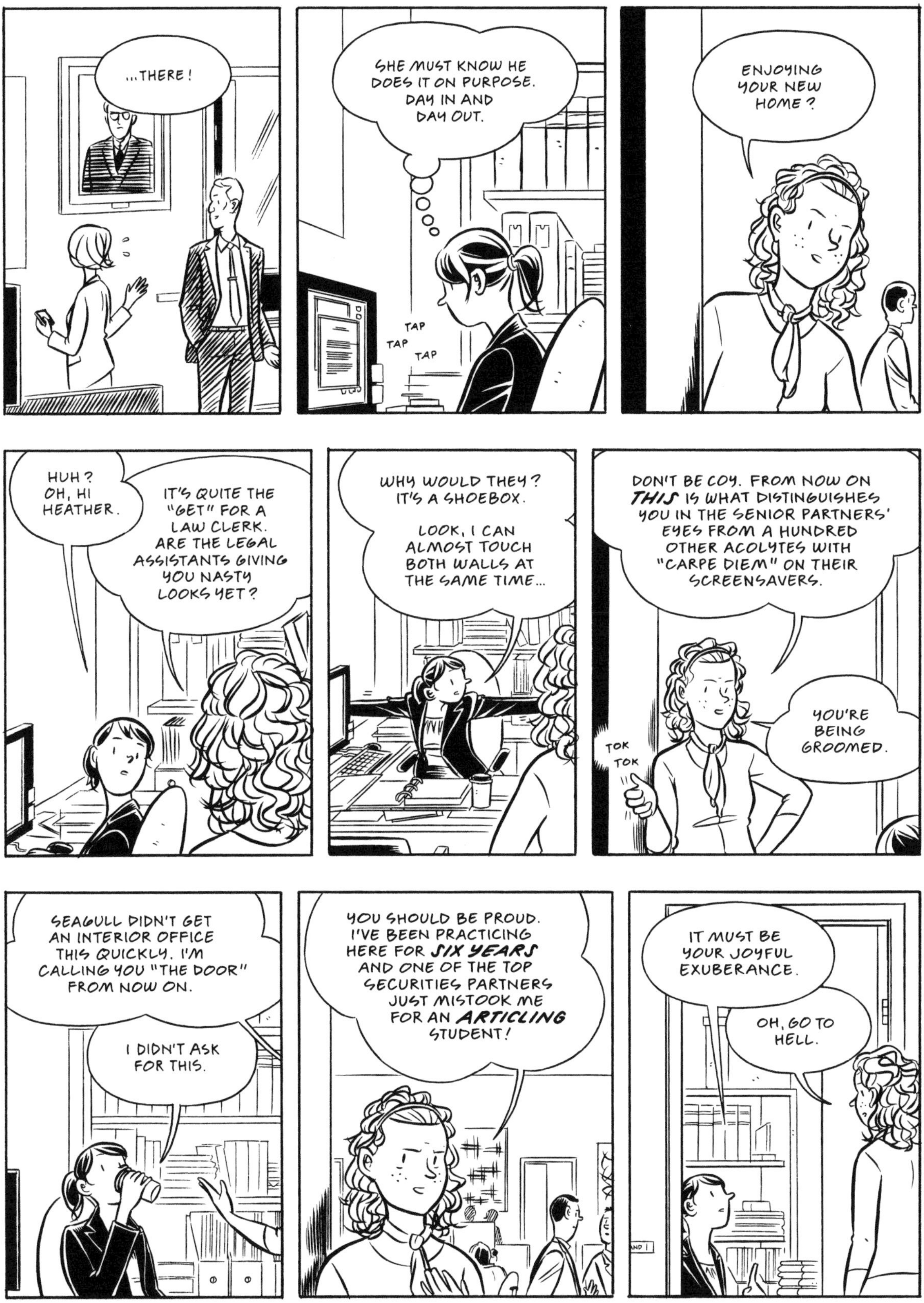
...THERE!
SHE MUST KNOW HE DOES IT ON PURPOSE. DAY IN AND DAY OUT.
TAP TAP TAP
ENJOYING YOUR NEW HOME?
HUH? OH, HI HEATHER.
IT'S QUITE THE "GET" FOR A LAW CLERK. ARE THE LEGAL ASSISTANTS GIVING YOU NASTY LOOKS YET?
WHY WOULD THEY? IT'S A SHOEBOX.
LOOK, I CAN ALMOST TOUCH BOTH WALLS AT THE SAME TIME...
DON'T BE COY. FROM NOW ON THIS IS WHAT DISTINGUISHES YOU IN THE SENIOR PARTNERS' EYES FROM A HUNDRED OTHER ACOLYTES WITH "CARPE DIEM" ON THEIR SCREENSAVERS.
TOK TOK
YOU'RE BEING GROOMED.
SEAGULL DIDN'T GET AN INTERIOR OFFICE THIS QUICKLY. I'M CALLING YOU "THE DOOR" FROM NOW ON.
I DIDN'T ASK FOR THIS.
YOU SHOULD BE PROUD. I'VE BEEN PRACTICING HERE FOR SIX YEARS AND ONE OF THE TOP SECURITIES PARTNERS JUST MISTOOK ME FOR AN ARTICLING STUDENT!
IT MUST BE YOUR JOYFUL EXUBERANCE.
OH, GO TO HELL.

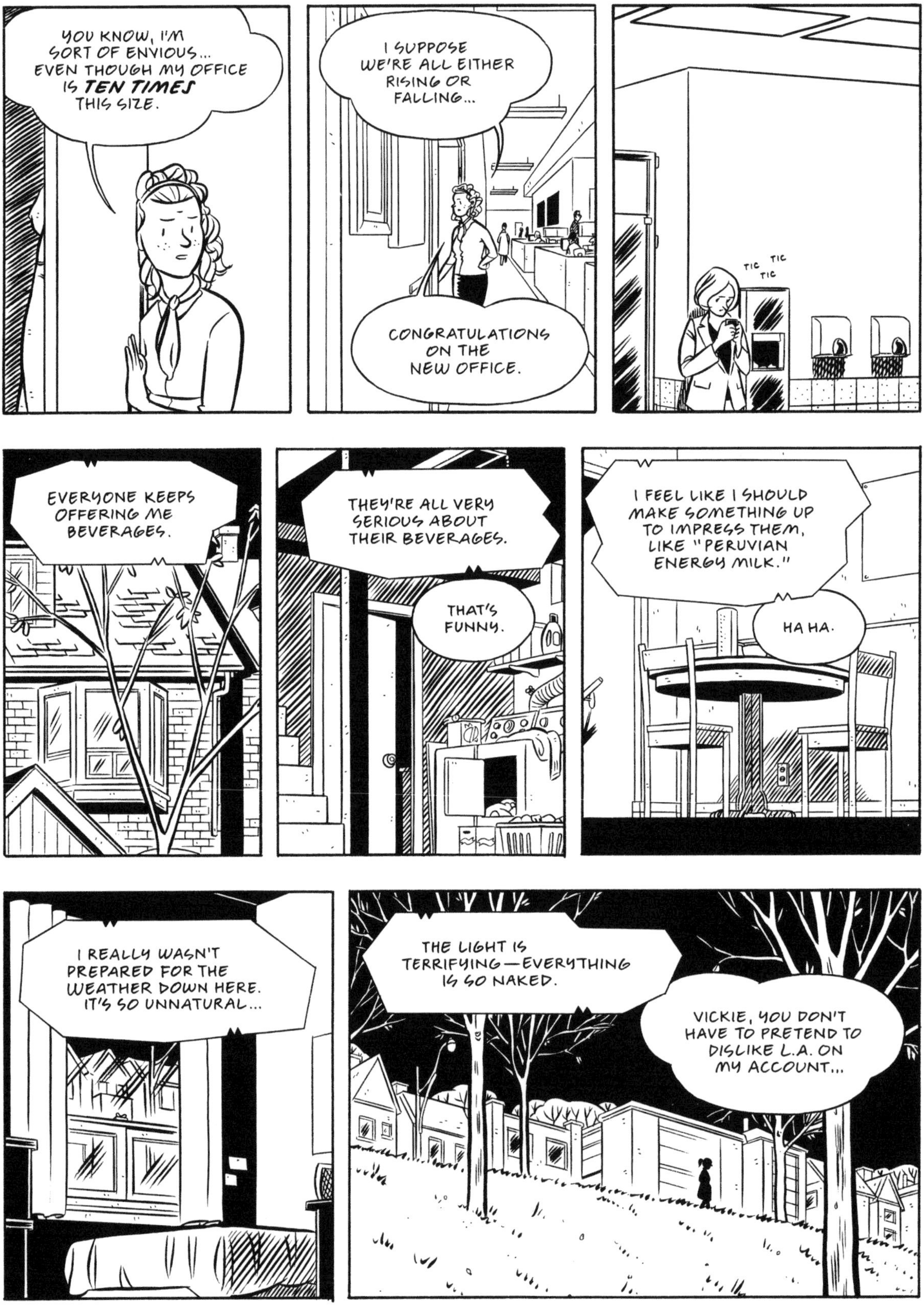
YOU KNOW, I'M SORT OF ENVIOUS... EVEN THOUGH MY OFFICE IS **TEN TIMES** THIS SIZE.
I SUPPOSE WE'RE ALL EITHER RISING OR FALLING...
CONGRATULATIONS ON THE NEW OFFICE.
TIC TIC TIC
EVERYONE KEEPS OFFERING ME BEVERAGES.
THEY'RE ALL VERY SERIOUS ABOUT THEIR BEVERAGES.
THAT'S FUNNY.
I FEEL LIKE I SHOULD MAKE SOMETHING UP TO IMPRESS THEM, LIKE "PERUVIAN ENERGY MILK."
HA HA.
I REALLY WASN'T PREPARED FOR THE WEATHER DOWN HERE. IT'S SO UNNATURAL...
THE LIGHT IS TERRIFYING—EVERYTHING IS SO NAKED.
VICKIE, YOU DON'T HAVE TO PRETEND TO DISLIKE L.A. ON MY ACCOUNT...

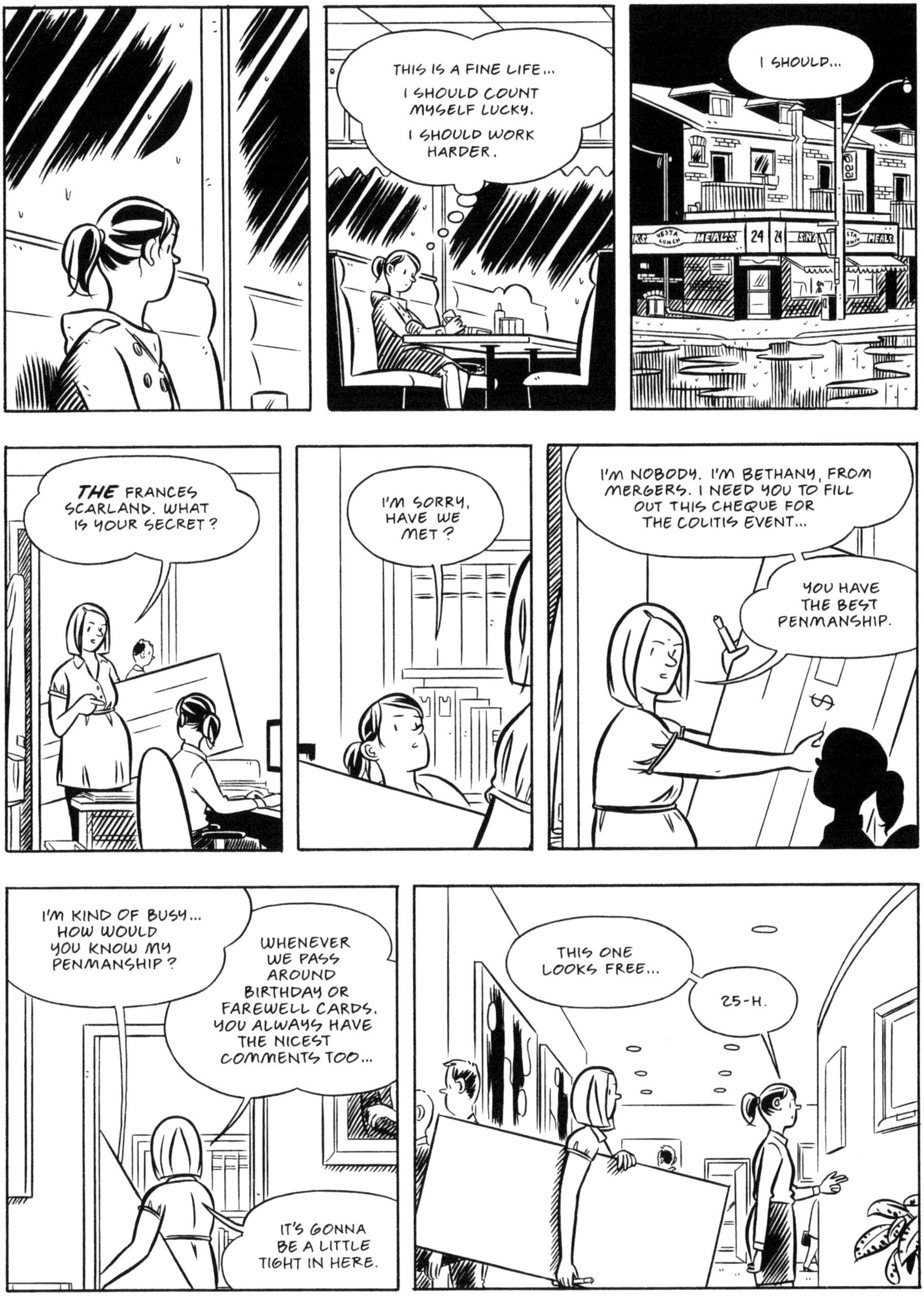
THIS IS A FINE LIFE...
I SHOULD COUNT MYSELF LUCKY.
I SHOULD WORK HARDER.
I SHOULD...
VESTA LUNCH
MEALS
24
24
THE FRANCES SCARLAND. WHAT IS YOUR SECRET?
I'M SORRY, HAVE WE MET?
I'M NOBODY. I'M BETHANY, FROM MERGERS. I NEED YOU TO FILL OUT THIS CHEQUE FOR THE COLITIS EVENT...
YOU HAVE THE BEST PENMANSHIP.
$
I'M KIND OF BUSY... HOW WOULD YOU KNOW MY PENMANSHIP?
WHENEVER WE PASS AROUND BIRTHDAY OR FAREWELL CARDS. YOU ALWAYS HAVE THE NICEST COMMENTS TOO...
IT'S GONNA BE A LITTLE TIGHT IN HERE.
THIS ONE LOOKS FREE...
25-H.

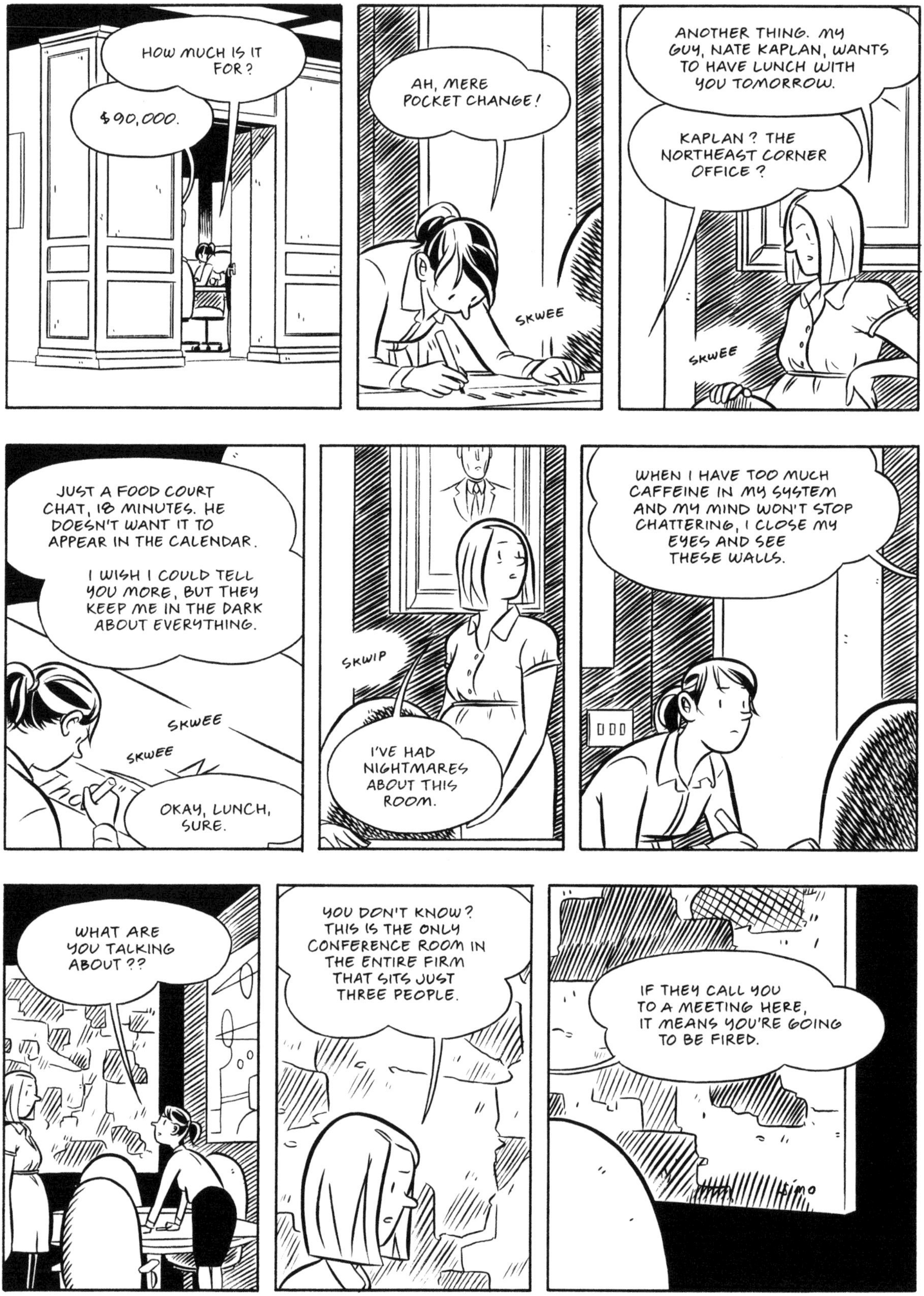
HOW MUCH IS IT FOR?
$90,000.
AH, MERE POCKET CHANGE!
SKWEE
ANOTHER THING. MY GUY, NATE KAPLAN, WANTS TO HAVE LUNCH WITH YOU TOMORROW.
KAPLAN? THE NORTHEAST CORNER OFFICE?
SKWEE
JUST A FOOD COURT CHAT, 18 MINUTES. HE DOESN'T WANT IT TO APPEAR IN THE CALENDAR.
I WISH I COULD TELL YOU MORE, BUT THEY KEEP ME IN THE DARK ABOUT EVERYTHING.
SKWEE
SKWEE
OKAY, LUNCH, SURE.
SKWIP
I'VE HAD NIGHTMARES ABOUT THIS ROOM.
WHEN I HAVE TOO MUCH CAFFEINE IN MY SYSTEM AND MY MIND WON'T STOP CHATTERING, I CLOSE MY EYES AND SEE THESE WALLS.
WHAT ARE YOU TALKING ABOUT??
YOU DON'T KNOW? THIS IS THE ONLY CONFERENCE ROOM IN THE ENTIRE FIRM THAT SITS JUST THREE PEOPLE.
IF THEY CALL YOU TO A MEETING HERE, IT MEANS YOU'RE GOING TO BE FIRED.

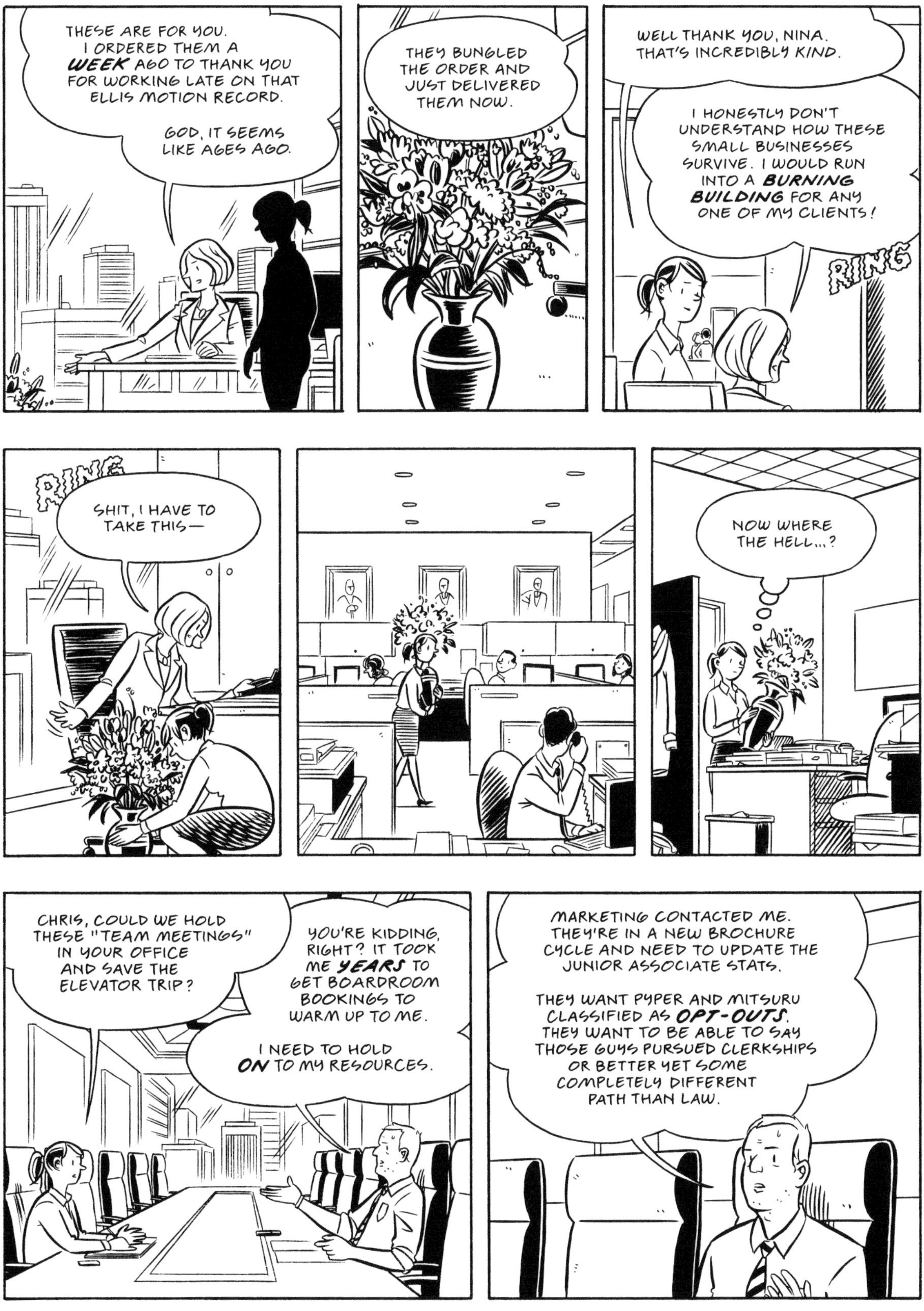
THESE ARE FOR YOU. I ORDERED THEM A WEEK AGO TO THANK YOU FOR WORKING LATE ON THAT ELLIS MOTION RECORD.
GOD, IT SEEMS LIKE AGES AGO.
THEY BUNGLED THE ORDER AND JUST DELIVERED THEM NOW.
WELL THANK YOU, NINA. THAT'S INCREDIBLY KIND.
I HONESTLY DON'T UNDERSTAND HOW THESE SMALL BUSINESSES SURVIVE. I WOULD RUN INTO A BURNING BUILDING FOR ANY ONE OF MY CLIENTS!
RING
RING
SHIT, I HAVE TO TAKE THIS—
NOW WHERE THE HELL...?
CHRIS, COULD WE HOLD THESE "TEAM MEETINGS" IN YOUR OFFICE AND SAVE THE ELEVATOR TRIP?
YOU'RE KIDDING, RIGHT? IT TOOK ME YEARS TO GET BOARDROOM BOOKINGS TO WARM UP TO ME.
I NEED TO HOLD ON TO MY RESOURCES.
MARKETING CONTACTED ME. THEY'RE IN A NEW BROCHURE CYCLE AND NEED TO UPDATE THE JUNIOR ASSOCIATE STATS.
THEY WANT PYPER AND MITSURU CLASSIFIED AS OPT-OUTS. THEY WANT TO BE ABLE TO SAY THOSE GUYS PURSUED CLERKSHIPS OR BETTER YET SOME COMPLETELY DIFFERENT PATH THAN LAW.

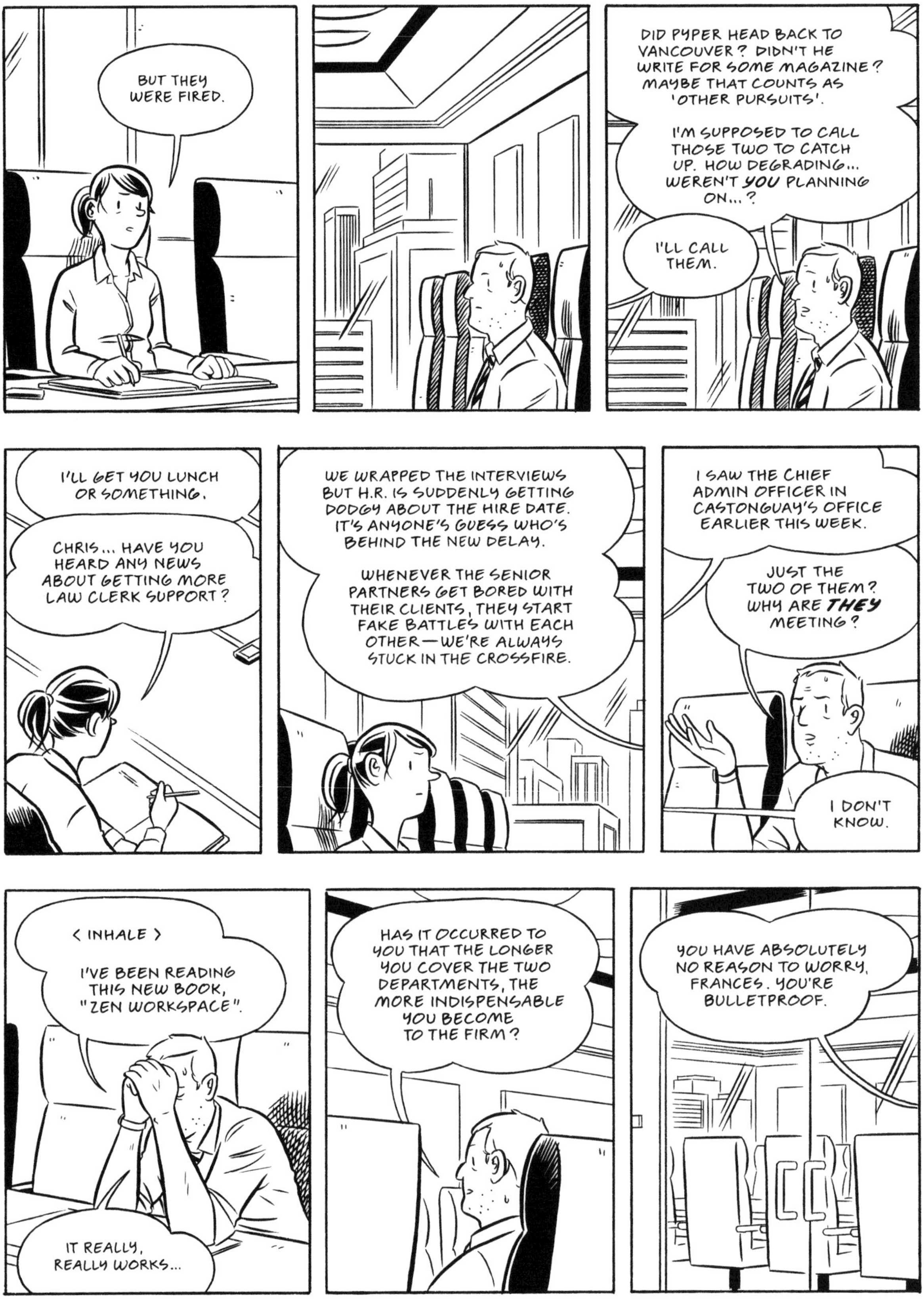
BUT THEY WERE FIRED.
DID PYPER HEAD BACK TO VANCOUVER? DIDN'T HE WRITE FOR SOME MAGAZINE? MAYBE THAT COUNTS AS 'OTHER PURSUITS'.
I'M SUPPOSED TO CALL THOSE TWO TO CATCH UP. HOW DEGRADING... WEREN'T YOU PLANNING ON...?
I'LL CALL THEM.
I'LL GET YOU LUNCH OR SOMETHING.
CHRIS... HAVE YOU HEARD ANY NEWS ABOUT GETTING MORE LAW CLERK SUPPORT?
WE WRAPPED THE INTERVIEWS BUT H.R. IS SUDDENLY GETTING DODGY ABOUT THE HIRE DATE. IT'S ANYONE'S GUESS WHO'S BEHIND THE NEW DELAY.
WHENEVER THE SENIOR PARTNERS GET BORED WITH THEIR CLIENTS, THEY START FAKE BATTLES WITH EACH OTHER—WE'RE ALWAYS STUCK IN THE CROSSFIRE.
I SAW THE CHIEF ADMIN OFFICER IN CASTONGUAY'S OFFICE EARLIER THIS WEEK.
JUST THE TWO OF THEM? WHY ARE THEY MEETING?
I DON'T KNOW.
< INHALE >
I'VE BEEN READING THIS NEW BOOK, "ZEN WORKSPACE".
IT REALLY, REALLY WORKS...
HAS IT OCCURRED TO YOU THAT THE LONGER YOU COVER THE TWO DEPARTMENTS, THE MORE INDISPENSABLE YOU BECOME TO THE FIRM?
YOU HAVE ABSOLUTELY NO REASON TO WORRY, FRANCES. YOU'RE BULLETPROOF.

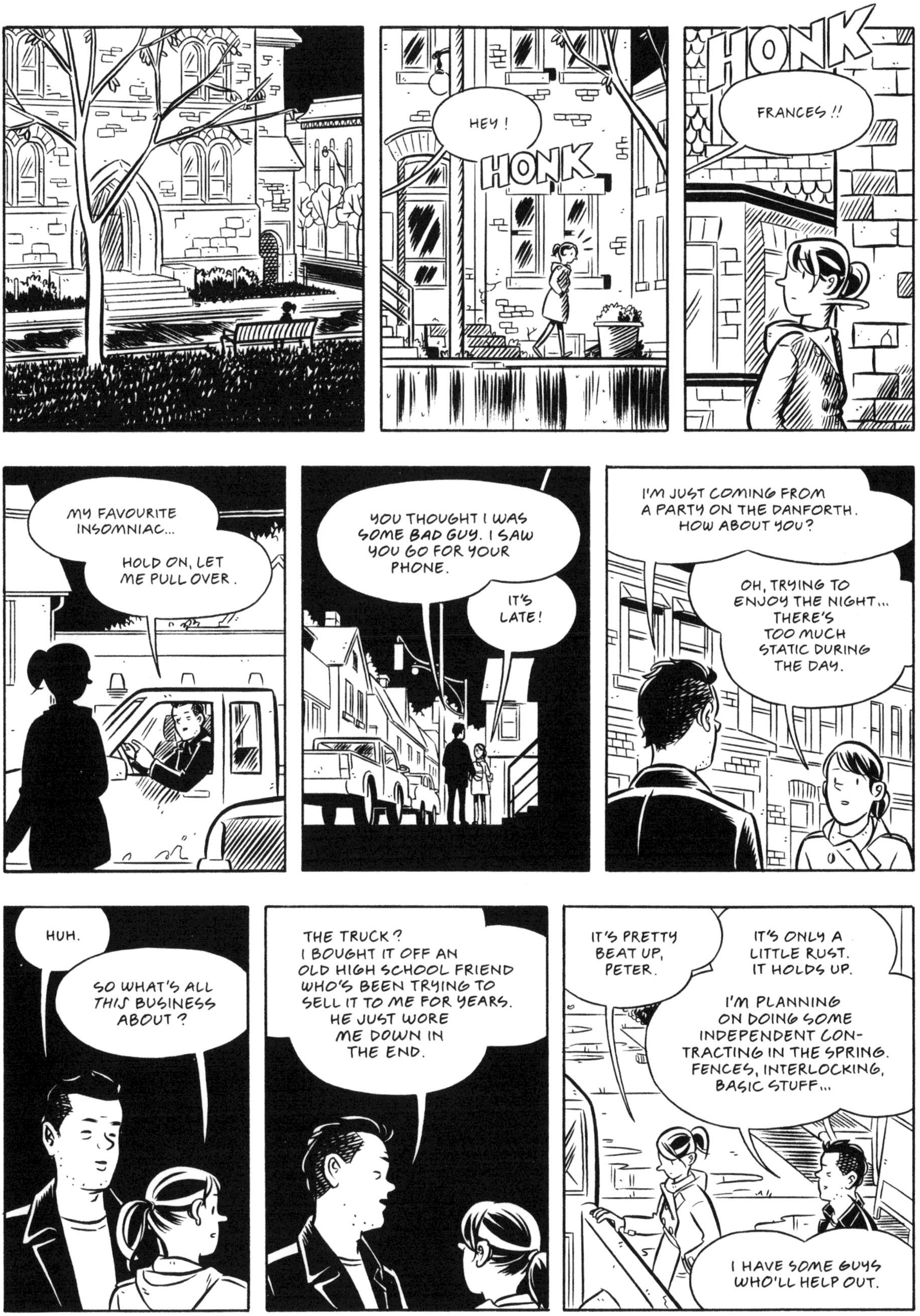
HONK
HEY !
HONK
FRANCES !!
MY FAVOURITE INSOMNIAC...
HOLD ON, LET ME PULL OVER.
YOU THOUGHT I WAS SOME BAD GUY. I SAW YOU GO FOR YOUR PHONE.
IT'S LATE!
I'M JUST COMING FROM A PARTY ON THE DANFORTH. HOW ABOUT YOU?
OH, TRYING TO ENJOY THE NIGHT... THERE'S TOO MUCH STATIC DURING THE DAY.
HUH.
SO WHAT'S ALL THIS BUSINESS ABOUT ?
THE TRUCK? I BOUGHT IT OFF AN OLD HIGH SCHOOL FRIEND WHO'S BEEN TRYING TO SELL IT TO ME FOR YEARS. HE JUST WORE ME DOWN IN THE END.
IT'S PRETTY BEAT UP, PETER.
IT'S ONLY A LITTLE RUST. IT HOLDS UP.
I'M PLANNING ON DOING SOME INDEPENDENT CONTRACTING IN THE SPRING. FENCES, INTERLOCKING, BASIC STUFF...
I HAVE SOME GUYS WHO'LL HELP OUT.

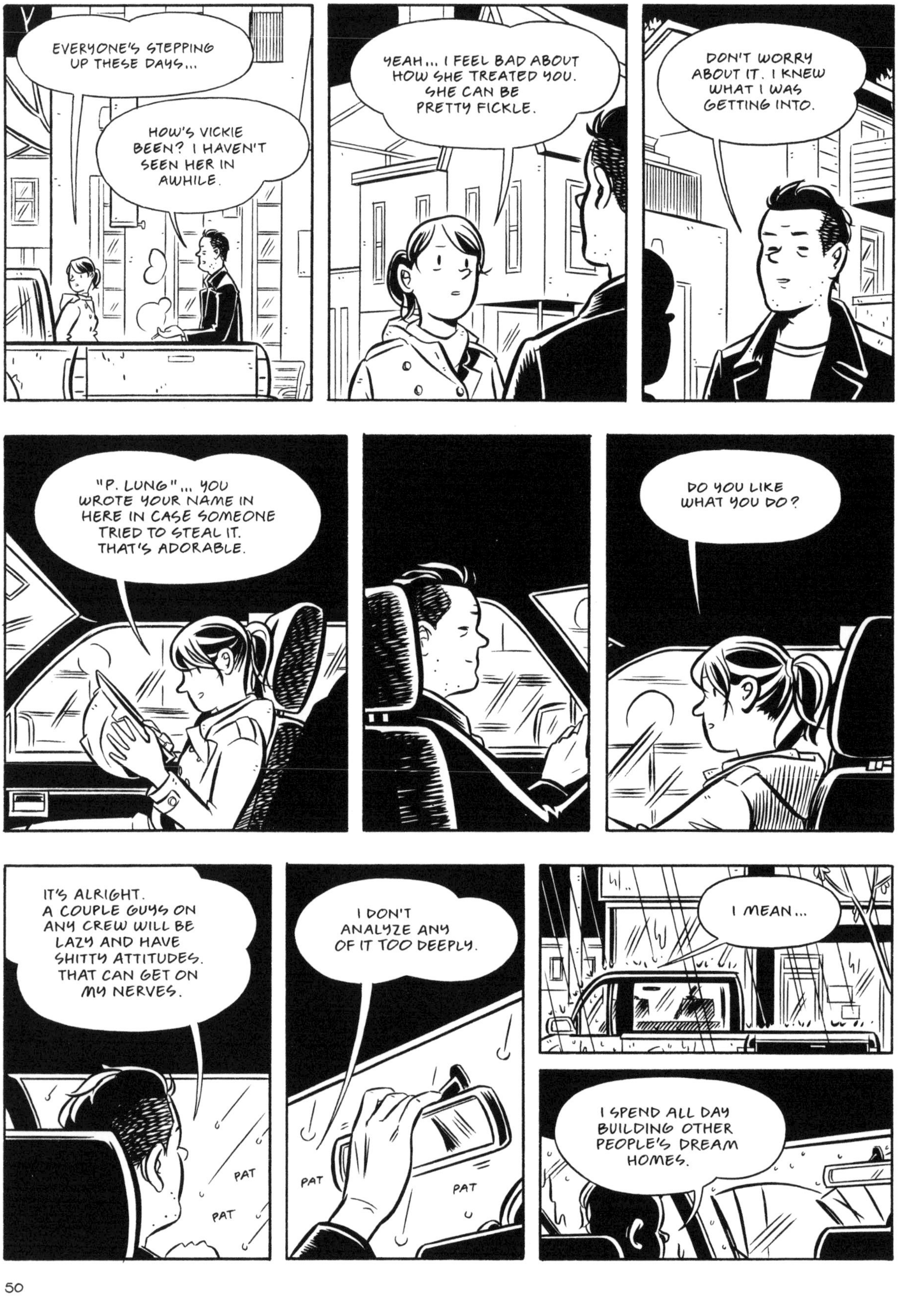
EVERYONE'S STEPPING UP THESE DAYS...
HOW'S VICKIE BEEN? I HAVEN'T SEEN HER IN AWHILE.
YEAH... I FEEL BAD ABOUT HOW SHE TREATED YOU. SHE CAN BE PRETTY FICKLE.
DON'T WORRY ABOUT IT. I KNEW WHAT I WAS GETTING INTO.
"P. LUNG"... YOU WROTE YOUR NAME IN HERE IN CASE SOMEONE TRIED TO STEAL IT. THAT'S ADORABLE.
DO YOU LIKE WHAT YOU DO?
IT'S ALRIGHT. A COUPLE GUYS ON ANY CREW WILL BE LAZY AND HAVE SHITTY ATTITUDES. THAT CAN GET ON MY NERVES.
PAT
PAT
I DON'T ANALYZE ANY OF IT TOO DEEPLY.
PAT
PAT
I MEAN...
I SPEND ALL DAY BUILDING OTHER PEOPLE'S DREAM HOMES.

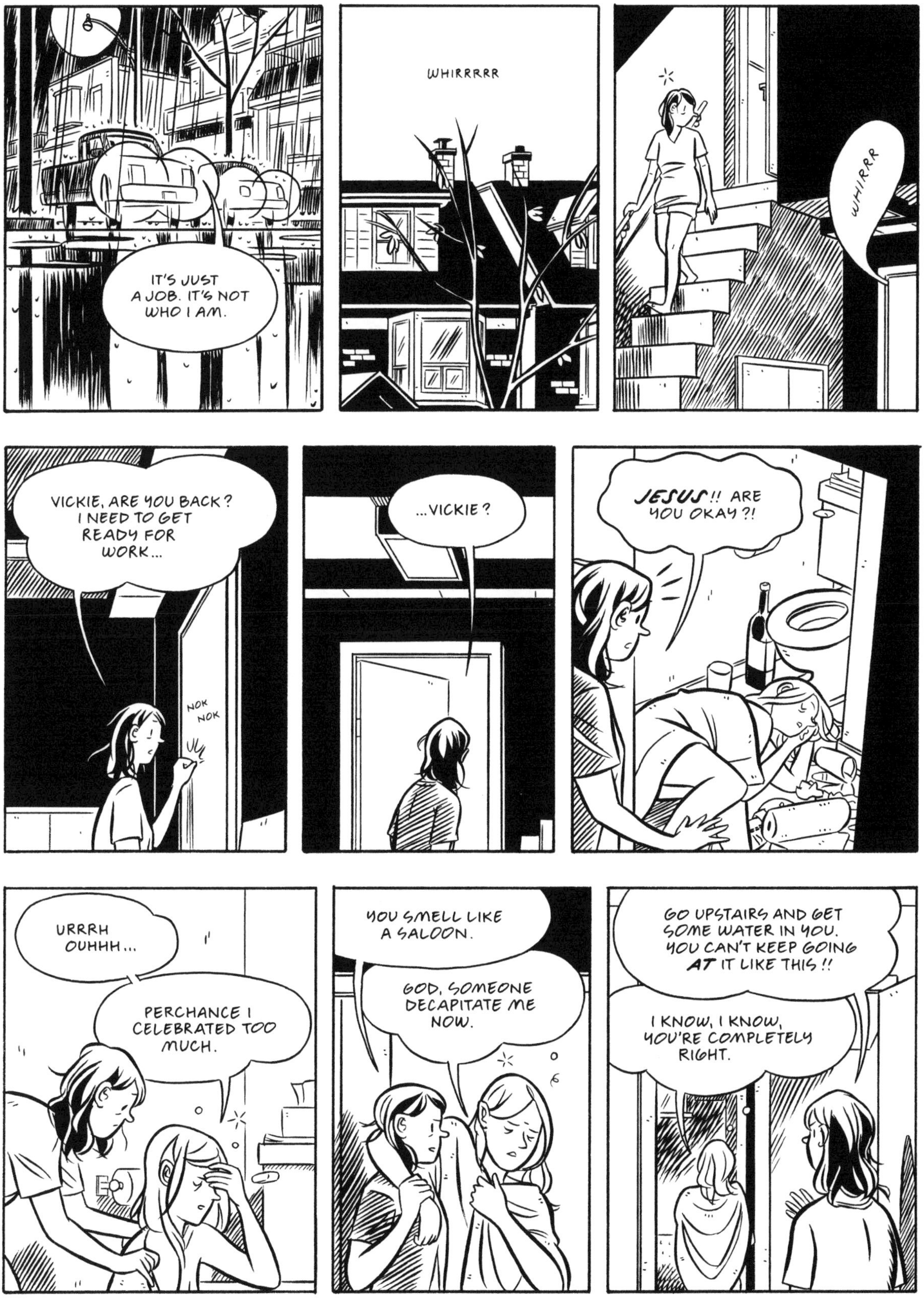
IT'S JUST A JOB. IT'S NOT WHO I AM.
WHIRRRRR
WHIRRR
VICKIE, ARE YOU BACK? I NEED TO GET READY FOR WORK...
NOK NOK
...VICKIE?
JESUS!! ARE YOU OKAY?!
URRRH OUHHH...
PERCHANCE I CELEBRATED TOO MUCH.
YOU SMELL LIKE A SALOON.
GOD, SOMEONE DECAPITATE ME NOW.
GO UPSTAIRS AND GET SOME WATER IN YOU. YOU CAN'T KEEP GOING AT IT LIKE THIS!!
I KNOW, I KNOW, YOU'RE COMPLETELY RIGHT.

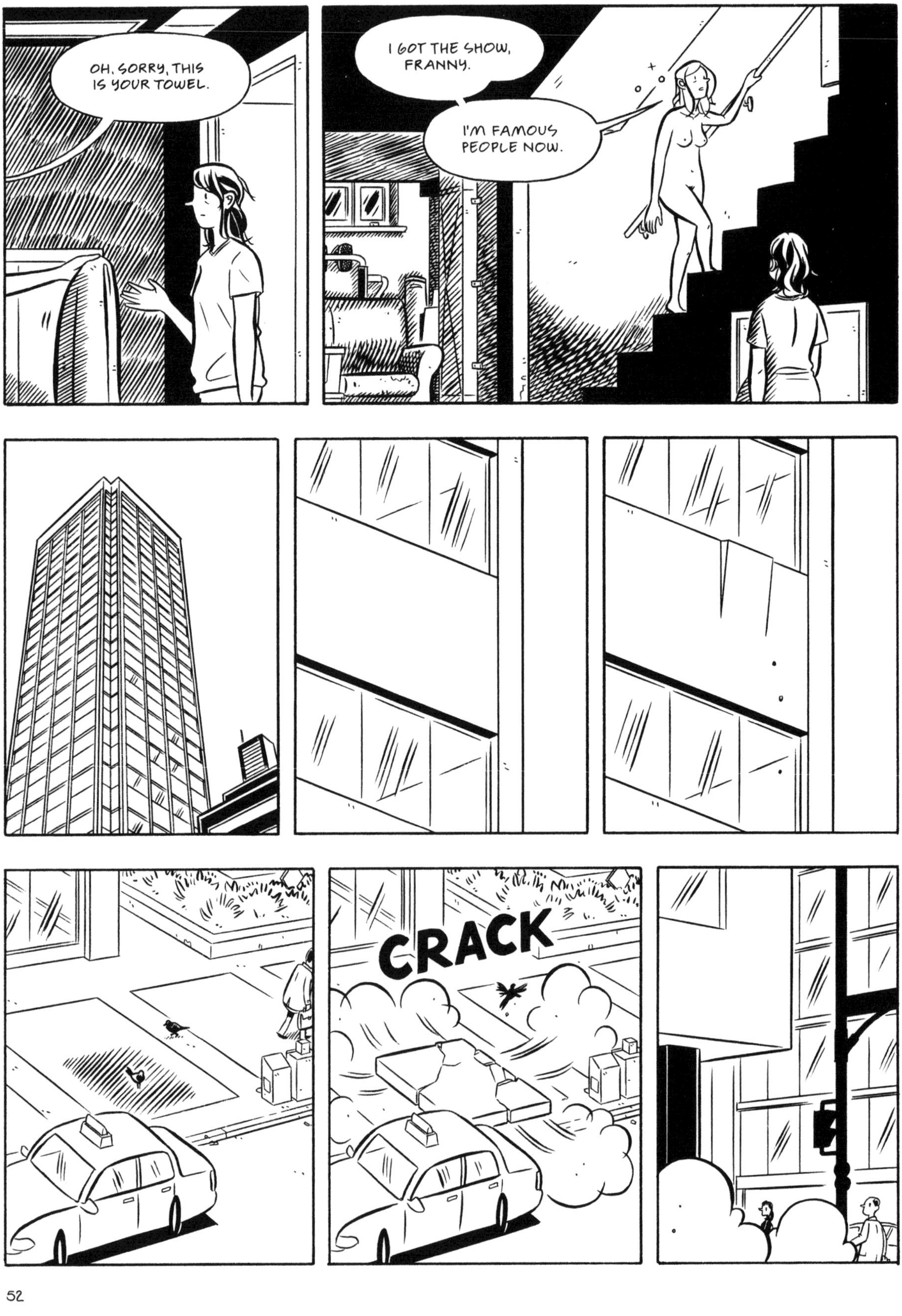
OH, SORRY, THIS IS YOUR TOWEL.
I GOT THE SHOW, FRANNY.
I'M FAMOUS PEOPLE NOW.
CRACK

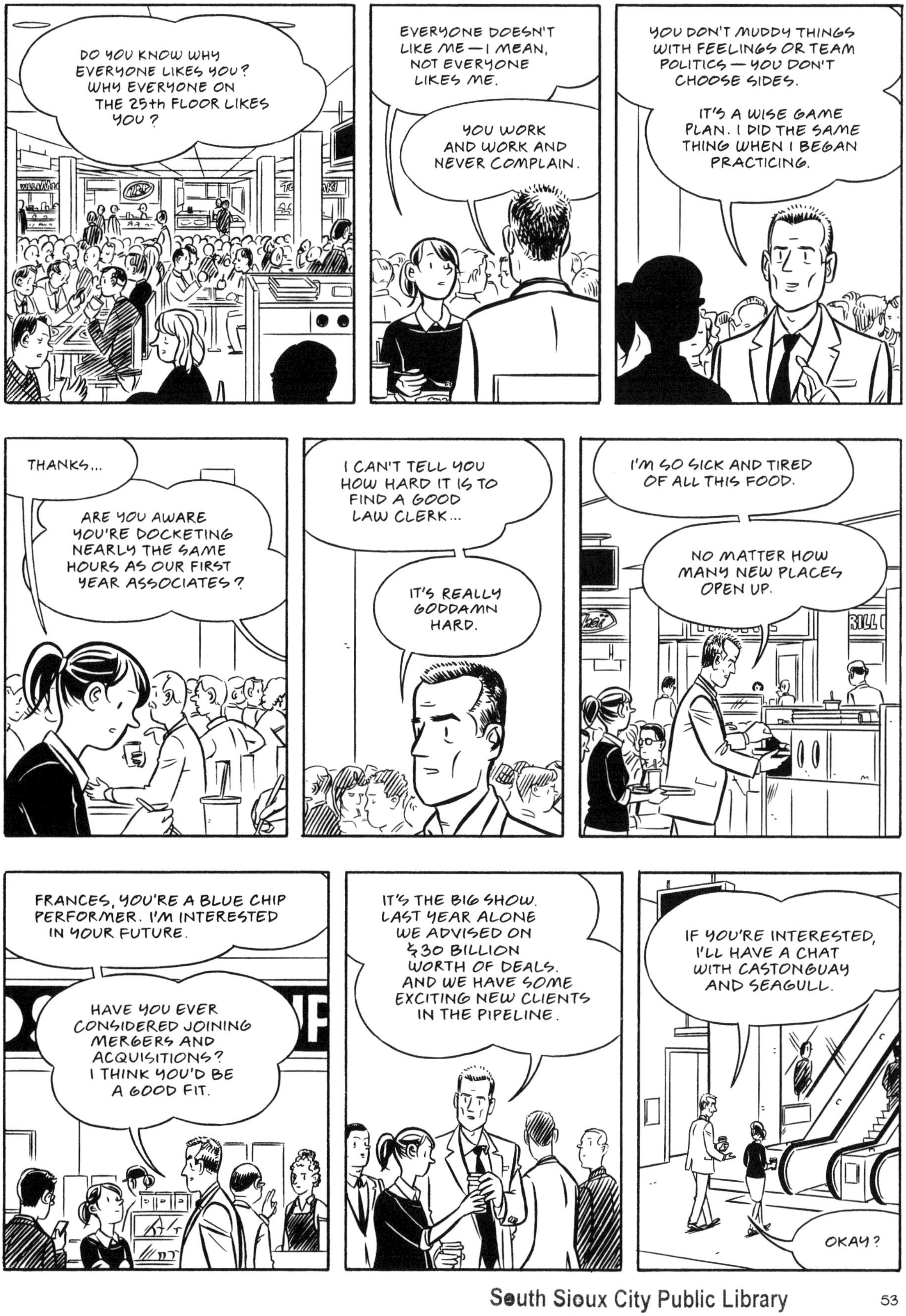
DO YOU KNOW WHY EVERYONE LIKES YOU? WHY EVERYONE ON THE 25th FLOOR LIKES YOU?
EVERYONE DOESN'T LIKE ME — I MEAN, NOT EVERYONE LIKES ME.
YOU WORK AND WORK AND NEVER COMPLAIN.
YOU DON'T MUDDY THINGS WITH FEELINGS OR TEAM POLITICS — YOU DON'T CHOOSE SIDES.
IT'S A WISE GAME PLAN. I DID THE SAME THING WHEN I BEGAN PRACTICING.
THANKS...
ARE YOU AWARE YOU'RE DOCKETING NEARLY THE SAME HOURS AS OUR FIRST YEAR ASSOCIATES?
I CAN'T TELL YOU HOW HARD IT IS TO FIND A GOOD LAW CLERK...
IT'S REALLY GODDAMN HARD.
I'M SO SICK AND TIRED OF ALL THIS FOOD.
NO MATTER HOW MANY NEW PLACES OPEN UP.
FRANCES, YOU'RE A BLUE CHIP PERFORMER. I'M INTERESTED IN YOUR FUTURE.
HAVE YOU EVER CONSIDERED JOINING MERGERS AND ACQUISITIONS? I THINK YOU'D BE A GOOD FIT.
IT'S THE BIG SHOW. LAST YEAR ALONE WE ADVISED ON $30 BILLION WORTH OF DEALS. AND WE HAVE SOME EXCITING NEW CLIENTS IN THE PIPELINE.
IF YOU'RE INTERESTED, I'LL HAVE A CHAT WITH CASTONGUAY AND SEAGULL.
OKAY?

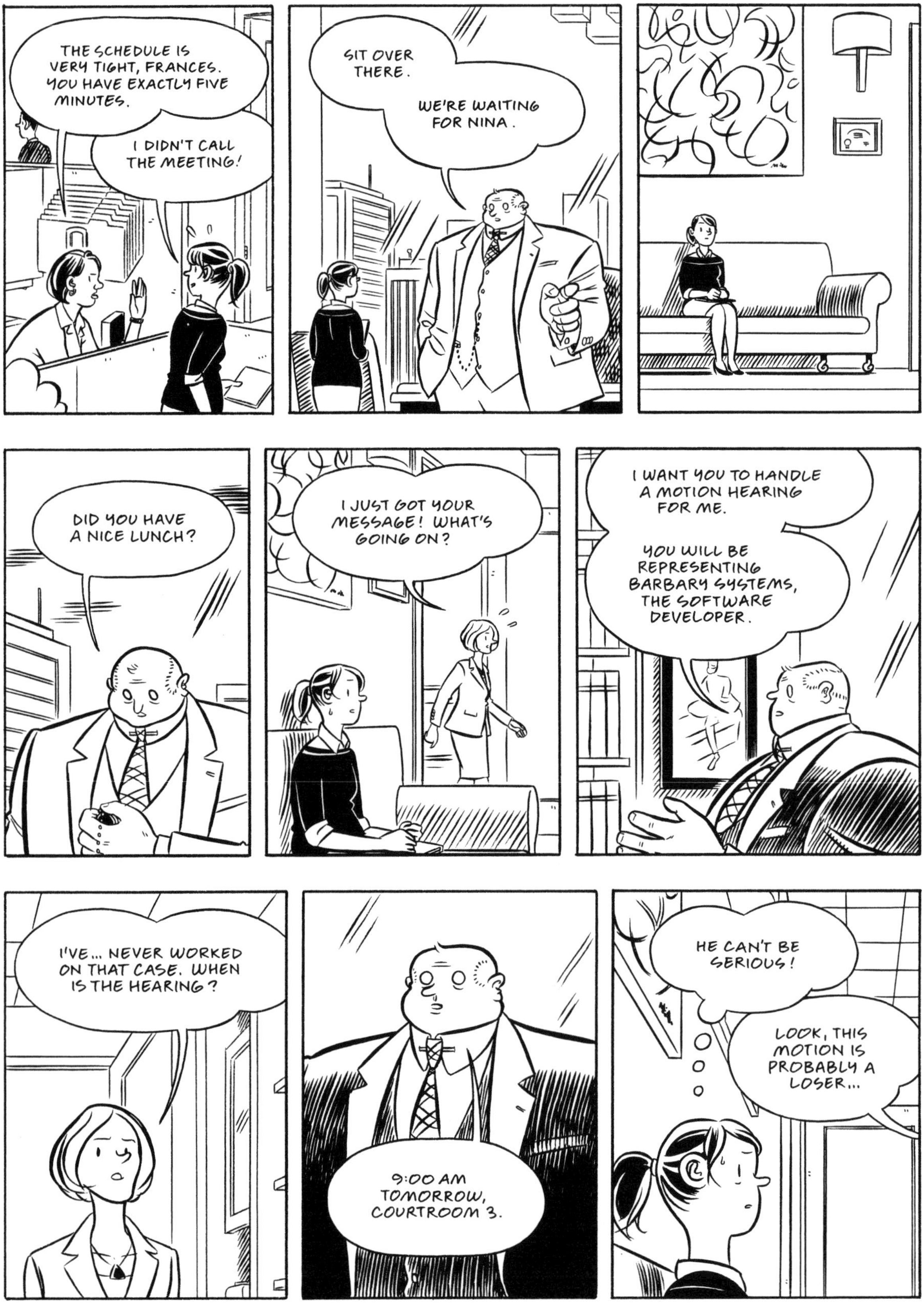
THE SCHEDULE IS VERY TIGHT, FRANCES. YOU HAVE EXACTLY FIVE MINUTES.
I DIDN'T CALL THE MEETING!
SIT OVER THERE.
WE'RE WAITING FOR NINA.
DID YOU HAVE A NICE LUNCH?
I JUST GOT YOUR MESSAGE! WHAT'S GOING ON?
I WANT YOU TO HANDLE A MOTION HEARING FOR ME.
YOU WILL BE REPRESENTING BARBARY SYSTEMS, THE SOFTWARE DEVELOPER.
I'VE... NEVER WORKED ON THAT CASE. WHEN IS THE HEARING?
9:00 AM TOMORROW, COURTROOM 3.
HE CAN'T BE SERIOUS!
LOOK, THIS MOTION IS PROBABLY A LOSER...

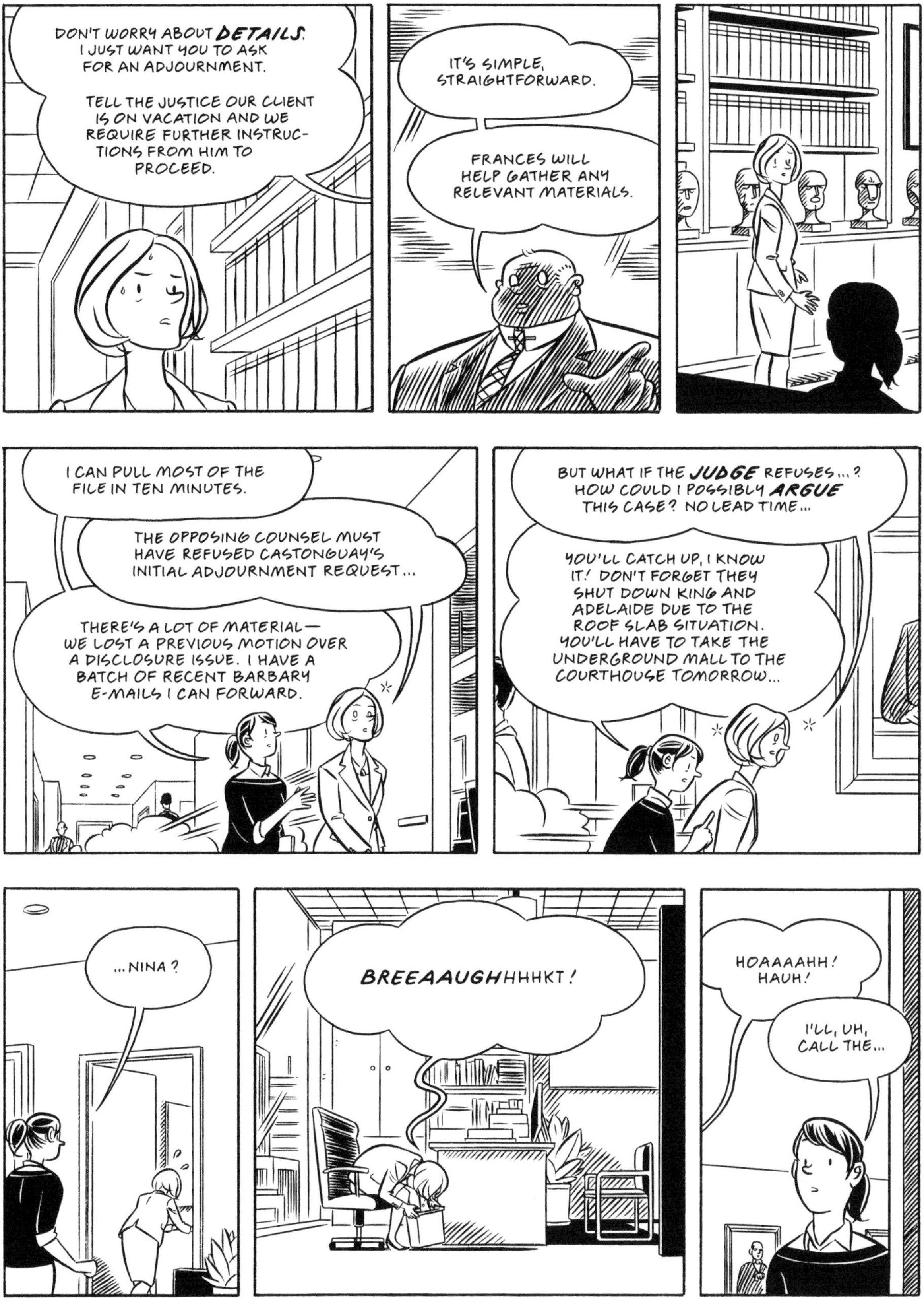
DON'T WORRY ABOUT DETAILS. I JUST WANT YOU TO ASK FOR AN ADJOURNMENT.
TELL THE JUSTICE OUR CLIENT IS ON VACATION AND WE REQUIRE FURTHER INSTRUCTIONS FROM HIM TO PROCEED.
IT'S SIMPLE, STRAIGHTFORWARD.
FRANCES WILL HELP GATHER ANY RELEVANT MATERIALS.
I CAN PULL MOST OF THE FILE IN TEN MINUTES.
THE OPPOSING COUNSEL MUST HAVE REFUSED CASTONGUAY'S INITIAL ADJOURNMENT REQUEST...
THERE'S A LOT OF MATERIAL— WE LOST A PREVIOUS MOTION OVER A DISCLOSURE ISSUE. I HAVE A BATCH OF RECENT BARBARY E-MAILS I CAN FORWARD.
BUT WHAT IF THE JUDGE REFUSES...? HOW COULD I POSSIBLY ARGUE THIS CASE? NO LEAD TIME...
YOU'LL CATCH UP, I KNOW IT! DON'T FORGET THEY SHUT DOWN KING AND ADELAIDE DUE TO THE ROOF SLAB SITUATION. YOU'LL HAVE TO TAKE THE UNDERGROUND MALL TO THE COURTHOUSE TOMORROW...
...NINA?
BREEAAUGHHHHKT!
HOAAAAHH! HAUH!
I'LL, UH, CALL THE...

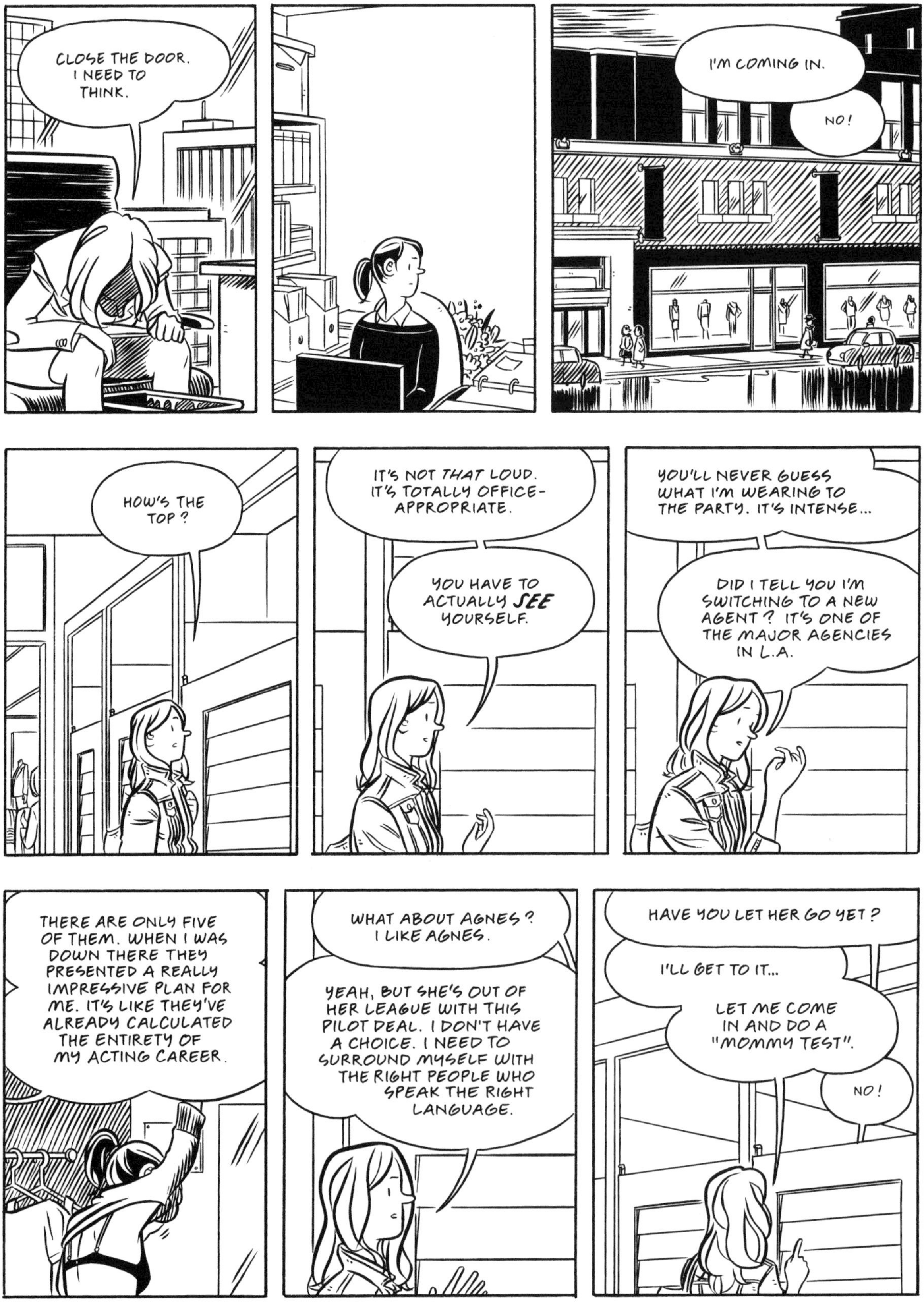

CLOSE THE DOOR. I NEED TO THINK.
I'M COMING IN.
NO!
HOW'S THE TOP?
IT'S NOT *THAT* LOUD. IT'S TOTALLY OFFICE-APPROPRIATE.
YOU HAVE TO ACTUALLY ***SEE*** YOURSELF.
YOU'LL NEVER GUESS WHAT I'M WEARING TO THE PARTY. IT'S INTENSE...
DID I TELL YOU I'M SWITCHING TO A NEW AGENT? IT'S ONE OF THE MAJOR AGENCIES IN L.A.
THERE ARE ONLY FIVE OF THEM. WHEN I WAS DOWN THERE THEY PRESENTED A REALLY IMPRESSIVE PLAN FOR ME. IT'S LIKE THEY'VE ALREADY CALCULATED THE ENTIRETY OF MY ACTING CAREER.
WHAT ABOUT AGNES? I LIKE AGNES.
YEAH, BUT SHE'S OUT OF HER LEAGUE WITH THIS PILOT DEAL. I DON'T HAVE A CHOICE. I NEED TO SURROUND MYSELF WITH THE RIGHT PEOPLE WHO SPEAK THE RIGHT LANGUAGE.
HAVE YOU LET HER GO YET?
I'LL GET TO IT...
LET ME COME IN AND DO A "MOMMY TEST".
NO!

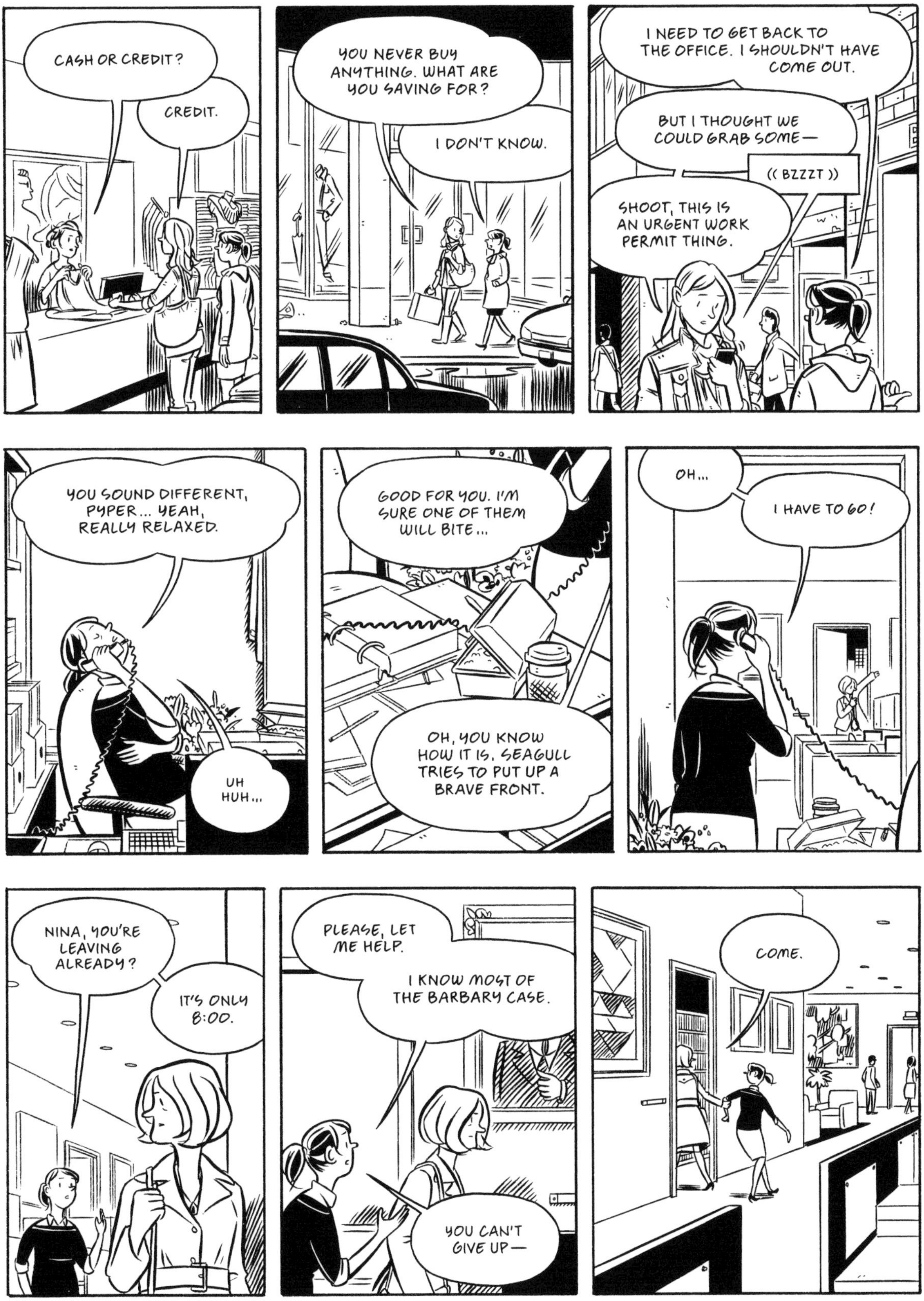
CASH OR CREDIT?
CREDIT.
YOU NEVER BUY ANYTHING. WHAT ARE YOU SAVING FOR?
I DON'T KNOW.
I NEED TO GET BACK TO THE OFFICE. I SHOULDN'T HAVE COME OUT.
BUT I THOUGHT WE COULD GRAB SOME—
((BZZZT))
SHOOT, THIS IS AN URGENT WORK PERMIT THING.
YOU SOUND DIFFERENT, PYPER... YEAH, REALLY RELAXED.
UH HUH...
GOOD FOR YOU. I'M SURE ONE OF THEM WILL BITE...
OH, YOU KNOW HOW IT IS. SEAGULL TRIES TO PUT UP A BRAVE FRONT.
OH...
I HAVE TO GO!
NINA, YOU'RE LEAVING ALREADY?
IT'S ONLY 8:00.
PLEASE, LET ME HELP.
I KNOW MOST OF THE BARBARY CASE.
YOU CAN'T GIVE UP—
COME.

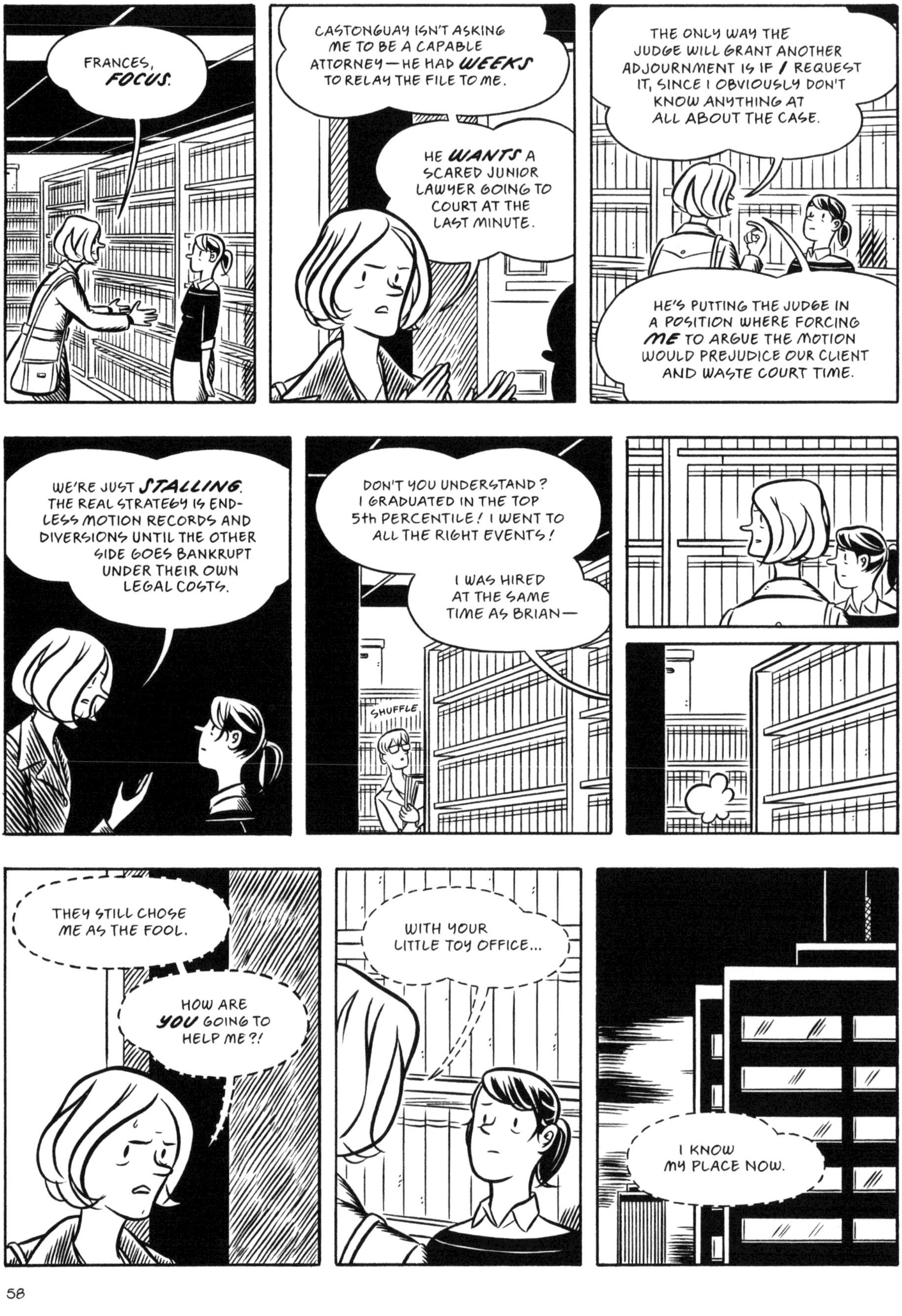
FRANCES, FOCUS.
CASTONGUAY ISN'T ASKING ME TO BE A CAPABLE ATTORNEY—HE HAD WEEKS TO RELAY THE FILE TO ME.
HE WANTS A SCARED JUNIOR LAWYER GOING TO COURT AT THE LAST MINUTE.
THE ONLY WAY THE JUDGE WILL GRANT ANOTHER ADJOURNMENT IS IF I REQUEST IT, SINCE I OBVIOUSLY DON'T KNOW ANYTHING AT ALL ABOUT THE CASE.
HE'S PUTTING THE JUDGE IN A POSITION WHERE FORCING ME TO ARGUE THE MOTION WOULD PREJUDICE OUR CLIENT AND WASTE COURT TIME.
WE'RE JUST STALLING. THE REAL STRATEGY IS ENDLESS MOTION RECORDS AND DIVERSIONS UNTIL THE OTHER SIDE GOES BANKRUPT UNDER THEIR OWN LEGAL COSTS.
DON'T YOU UNDERSTAND? I GRADUATED IN THE TOP 5th PERCENTILE! I WENT TO ALL THE RIGHT EVENTS!
I WAS HIRED AT THE SAME TIME AS BRIAN—
SHUFFLE
THEY STILL CHOSE ME AS THE FOOL.
HOW ARE YOU GOING TO HELP ME?!
WITH YOUR LITTLE TOY OFFICE...
I KNOW MY PLACE NOW.

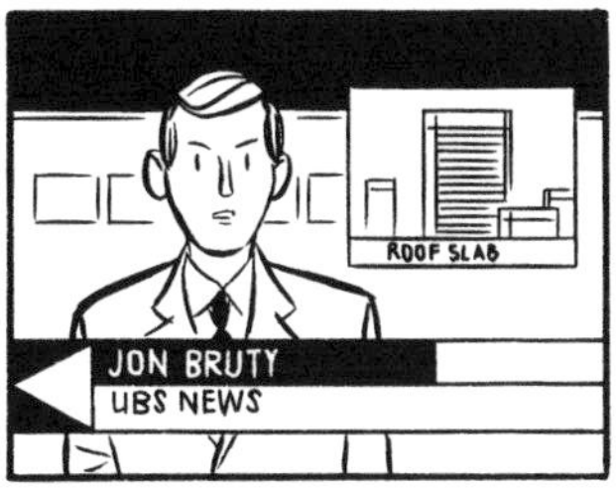
ROOF SLAB
JON BRUTY
UBS NEWS

...AND SURROUNDING STREETS REMAIN CLOSED.

WE ARE NOW JOINED BY ARCHITECT HERB STINSON...

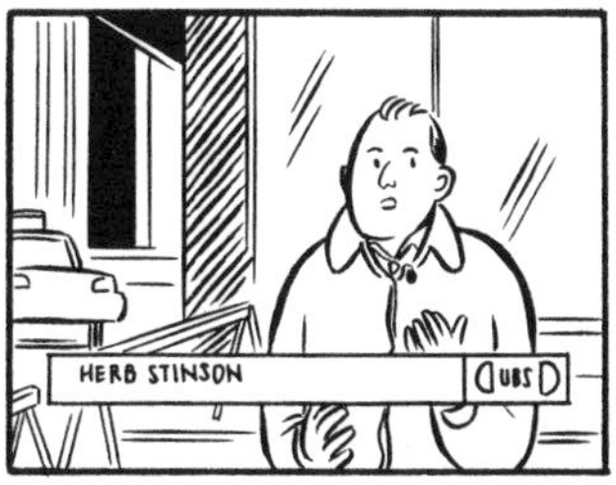
HERB STINSON
UBS

...HERB, WHAT CAN YOU TELL US ABOUT THE STRUCTURE ?

THE ENTIRE CLADDING IS WHITE CARRARA MARBLE. IT LOOKS GREAT BUT IT'S *POROUS*.

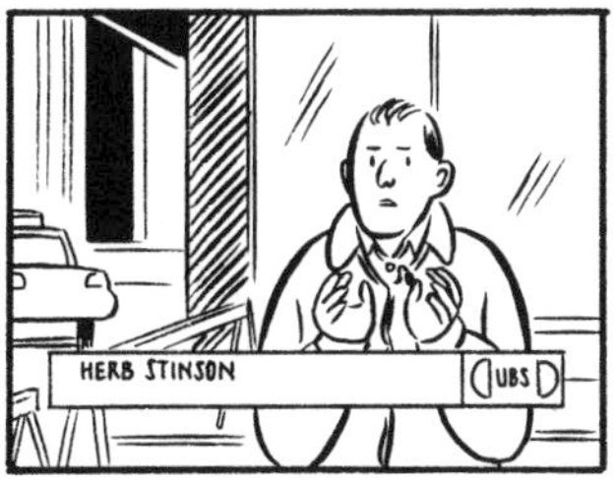
HERB STINSON
UBS

MOISTURE CAN PENETRATE THE STONE, WHICH CAN LEAD TO DISINTEGRATION AND WARPING.

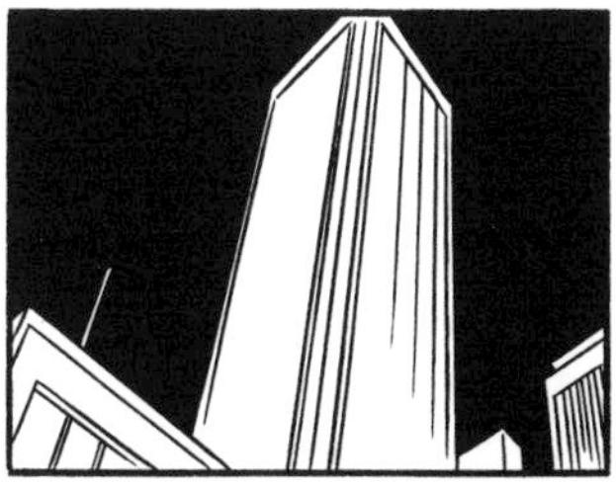

EACH OF THOSE PANELS UP THERE WEIGHS 300 POUNDS.

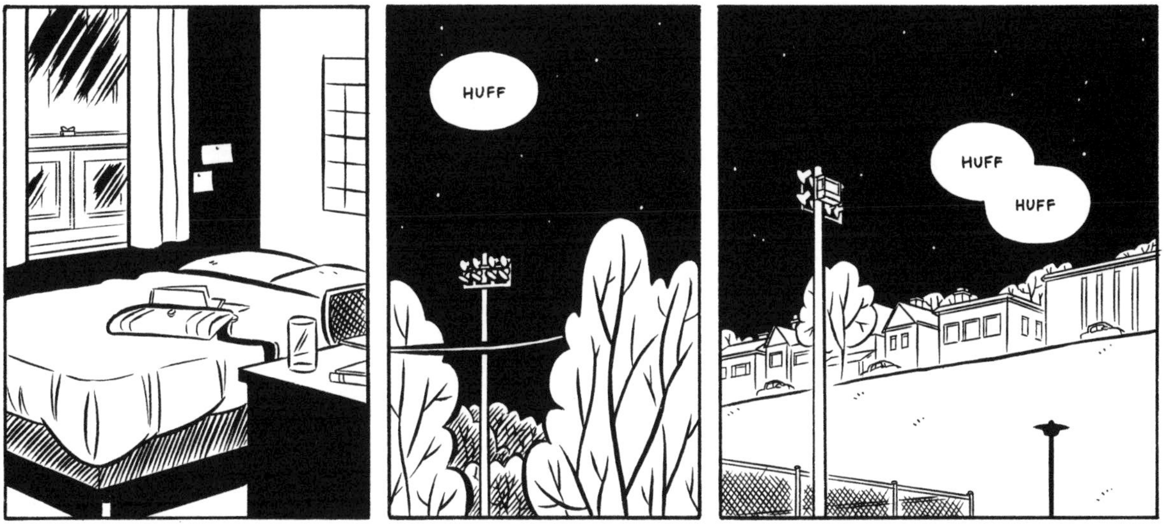
HUFF
HUFF
HUFF

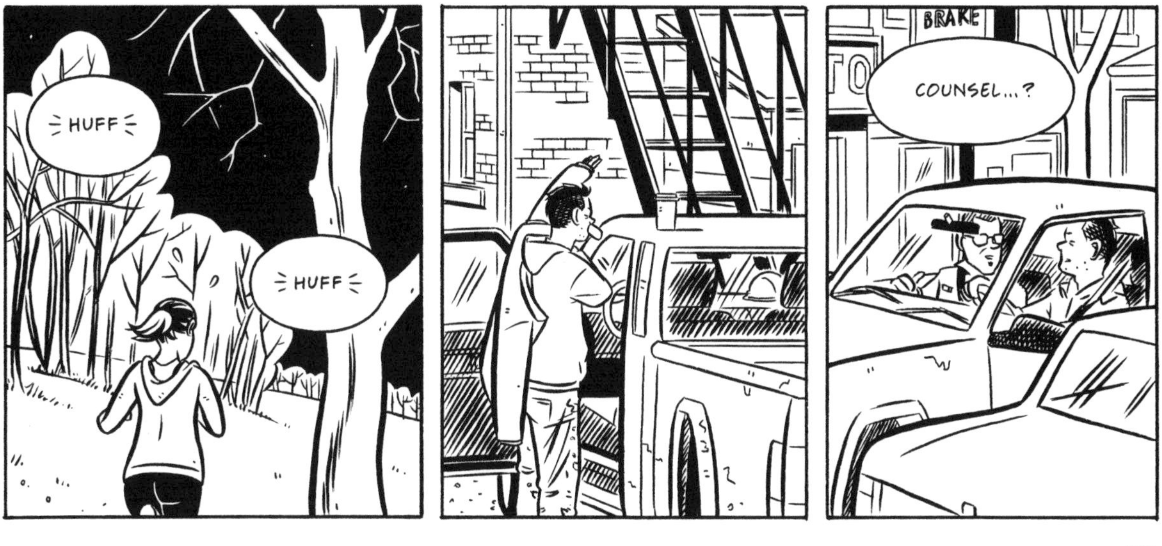
HUFF
HUFF
BRAKE
COUNSEL...?

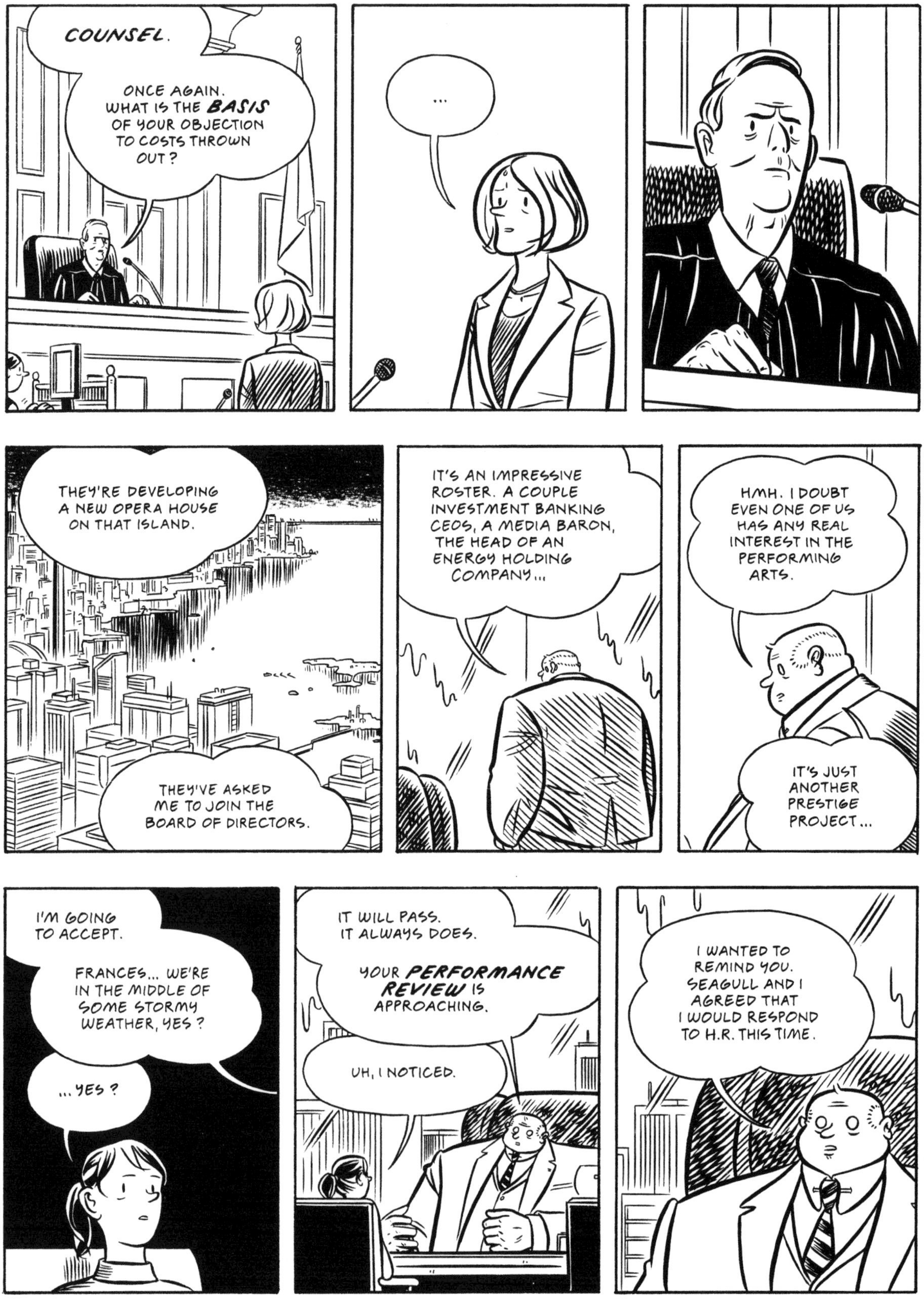
COUNSEL.
ONCE AGAIN. WHAT IS THE BASIS OF YOUR OBJECTION TO COSTS THROWN OUT?
...
THEY'RE DEVELOPING A NEW OPERA HOUSE ON THAT ISLAND.
THEY'VE ASKED ME TO JOIN THE BOARD OF DIRECTORS.
IT'S AN IMPRESSIVE ROSTER. A COUPLE INVESTMENT BANKING CEOS, A MEDIA BARON, THE HEAD OF AN ENERGY HOLDING COMPANY...
HMH. I DOUBT EVEN ONE OF US HAS ANY REAL INTEREST IN THE PERFORMING ARTS.
IT'S JUST ANOTHER PRESTIGE PROJECT...
I'M GOING TO ACCEPT.
FRANCES... WE'RE IN THE MIDDLE OF SOME STORMY WEATHER, YES?
...YES?
IT WILL PASS. IT ALWAYS DOES.
YOUR PERFORMANCE REVIEW IS APPROACHING.
UH, I NOTICED.
I WANTED TO REMIND YOU. SEAGULL AND I AGREED THAT I WOULD RESPOND TO H.R. THIS TIME.

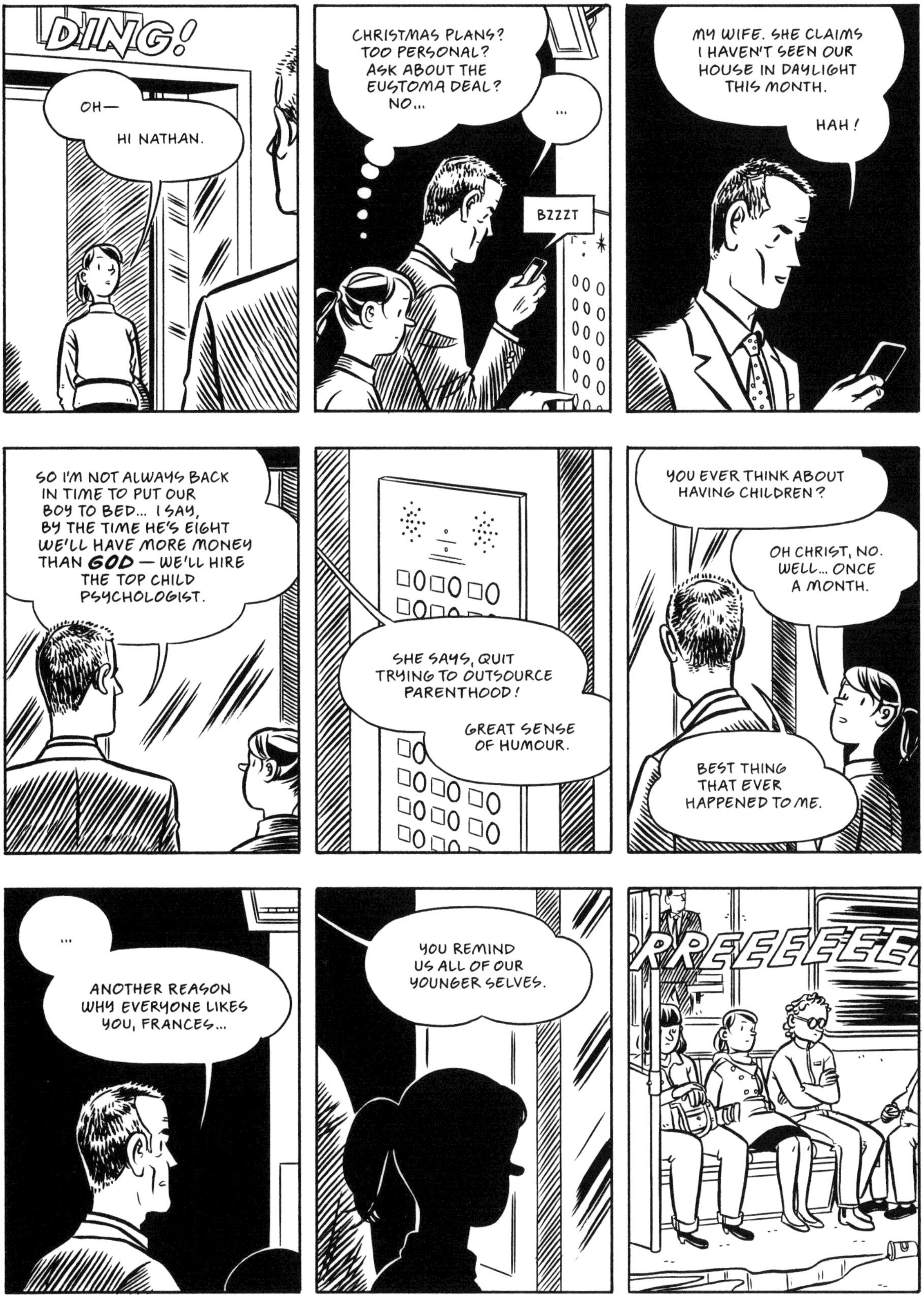
DING!
OH—
HI NATHAN.
CHRISTMAS PLANS? TOO PERSONAL? ASK ABOUT THE EUSTOMA DEAL? NO...
...
BZZZT
MY WIFE. SHE CLAIMS I HAVEN'T SEEN OUR HOUSE IN DAYLIGHT THIS MONTH.
HAH!
SO I'M NOT ALWAYS BACK IN TIME TO PUT OUR BOY TO BED... I SAY, BY THE TIME HE'S EIGHT WE'LL HAVE MORE MONEY THAN GOD — WE'LL HIRE THE TOP CHILD PSYCHOLOGIST.
SHE SAYS, QUIT TRYING TO OUTSOURCE PARENTHOOD!
GREAT SENSE OF HUMOUR.
YOU EVER THINK ABOUT HAVING CHILDREN?
OH CHRIST, NO. WELL... ONCE A MONTH.
BEST THING THAT EVER HAPPENED TO ME.
...
ANOTHER REASON WHY EVERYONE LIKES YOU, FRANCES...
YOU REMIND US ALL OF OUR YOUNGER SELVES.
RREEEEEEE

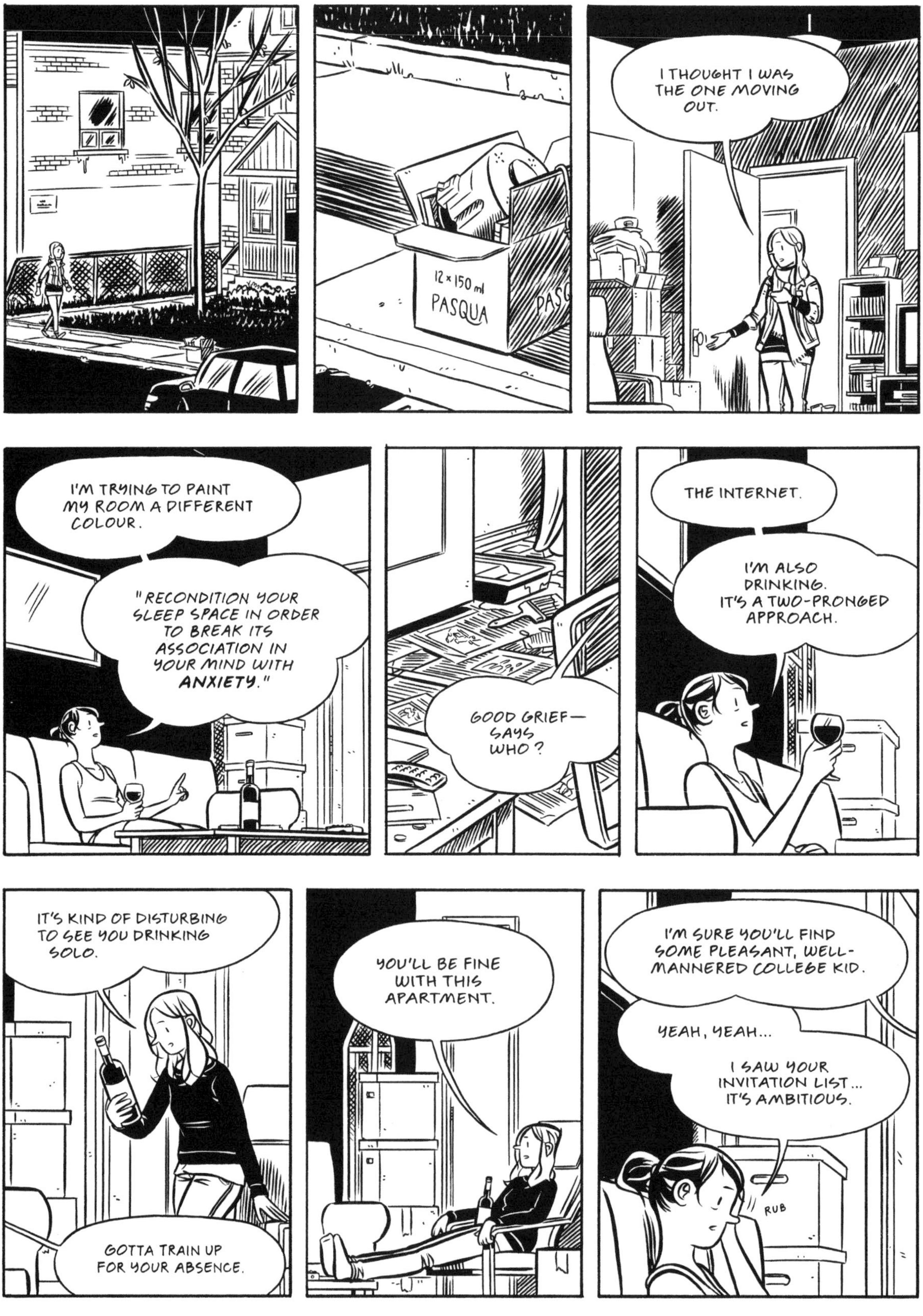
12 × 150 ml
PASQUA
PASQ
I THOUGHT I WAS THE ONE MOVING OUT.
I'M TRYING TO PAINT MY ROOM A DIFFERENT COLOUR.
"RECONDITION YOUR SLEEP SPACE IN ORDER TO BREAK ITS ASSOCIATION IN YOUR MIND WITH **ANXIETY**."
GOOD GRIEF— SAYS WHO?
THE INTERNET.
I'M ALSO DRINKING. IT'S A TWO-PRONGED APPROACH.
IT'S KIND OF DISTURBING TO SEE YOU DRINKING SOLO.
GOTTA TRAIN UP FOR YOUR ABSENCE.
YOU'LL BE FINE WITH THIS APARTMENT.
I'M SURE YOU'LL FIND SOME PLEASANT, WELL-MANNERED COLLEGE KID.
YEAH, YEAH...
I SAW YOUR INVITATION LIST... IT'S AMBITIOUS.
RUB

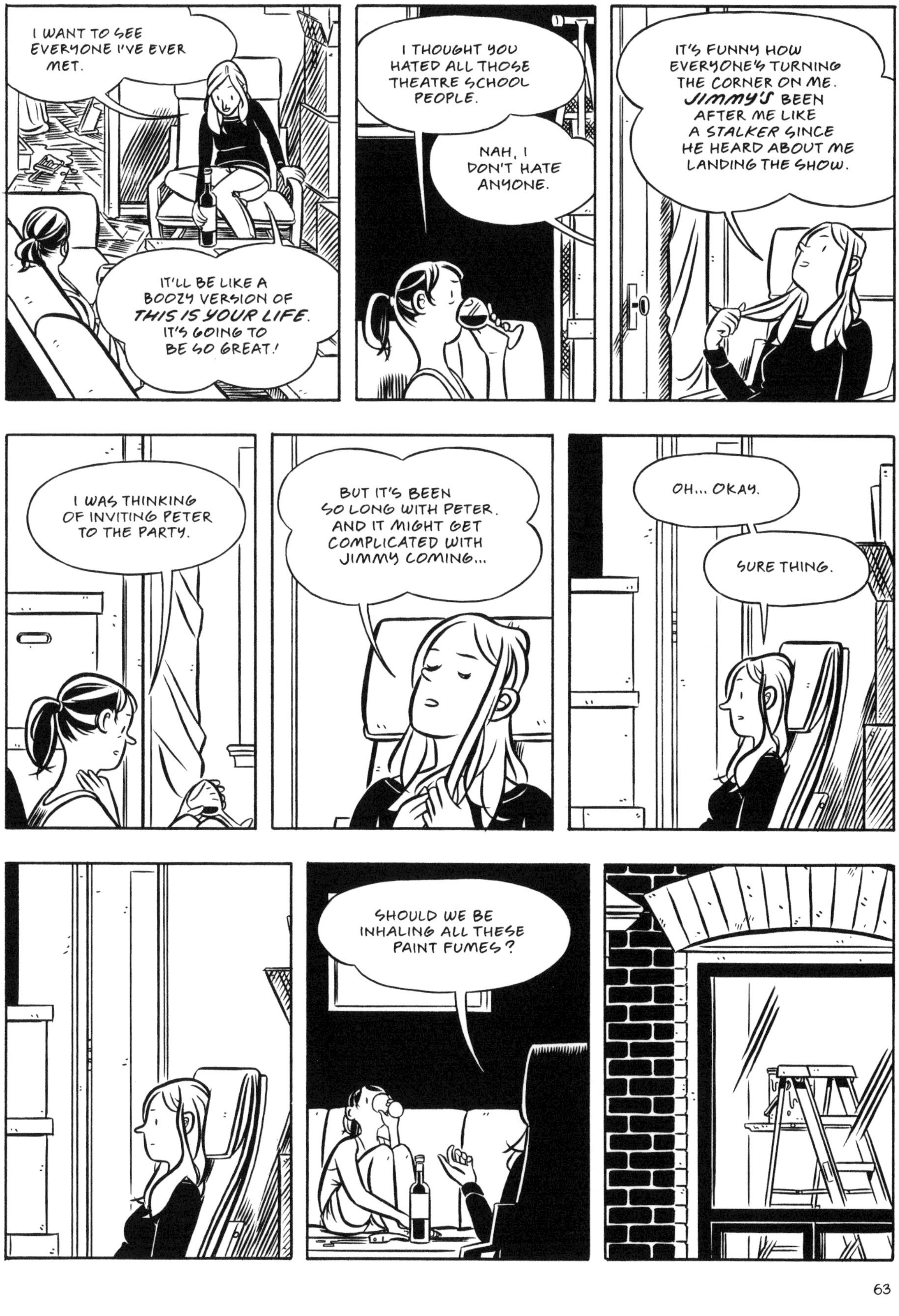
I WANT TO SEE EVERYONE I'VE EVER MET.
IT'LL BE LIKE A BOOZY VERSION OF *THIS IS YOUR LIFE*. IT'S GOING TO BE SO GREAT!
I THOUGHT YOU HATED ALL THOSE THEATRE SCHOOL PEOPLE.
NAH, I DON'T HATE ANYONE.
IT'S FUNNY HOW EVERYONE'S TURNING THE CORNER ON ME. *JIMMY'S* BEEN AFTER ME LIKE A *STALKER* SINCE HE HEARD ABOUT ME LANDING THE SHOW.
I WAS THINKING OF INVITING PETER TO THE PARTY.
BUT IT'S BEEN SO LONG WITH PETER. AND IT MIGHT GET COMPLICATED WITH JIMMY COMING...
OH... OKAY.
SURE THING.
SHOULD WE BE INHALING ALL THESE PAINT FUMES?

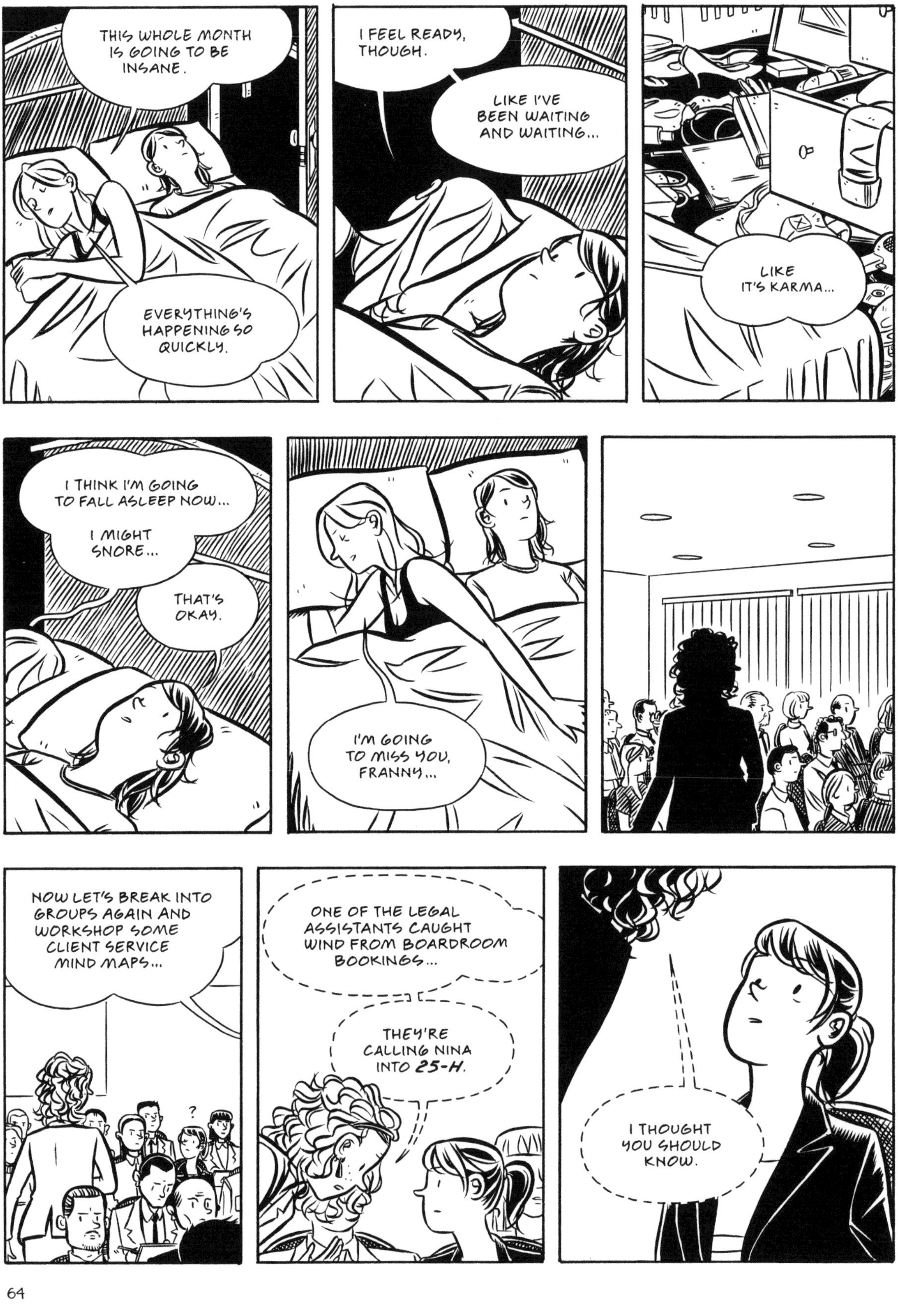
THIS WHOLE MONTH IS GOING TO BE INSANE.
EVERYTHING'S HAPPENING SO QUICKLY.
I FEEL READY, THOUGH.
LIKE I'VE BEEN WAITING AND WAITING...
LIKE IT'S KARMA...
I THINK I'M GOING TO FALL ASLEEP NOW...
I MIGHT SNORE...
THAT'S OKAY.
I'M GOING TO MISS YOU, FRANNY...
NOW LET'S BREAK INTO GROUPS AGAIN AND WORKSHOP SOME CLIENT SERVICE MIND MAPS...
?
ONE OF THE LEGAL ASSISTANTS CAUGHT WIND FROM BOARDROOM BOOKINGS...
THEY'RE CALLING NINA INTO 25-H.
I THOUGHT YOU SHOULD KNOW.

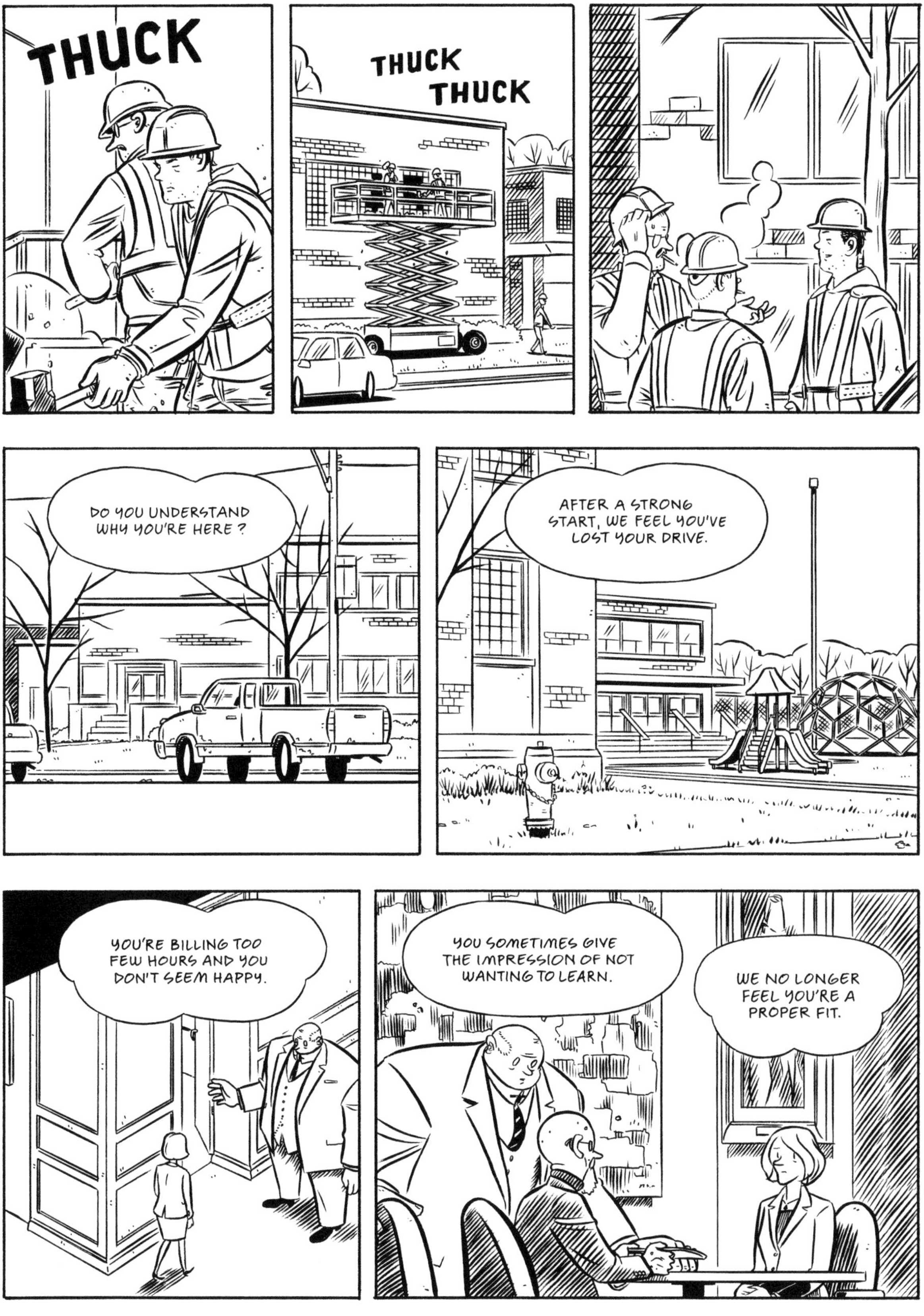
THUCK
THUCK
THUCK
DO YOU UNDERSTAND WHY YOU'RE HERE ?
AFTER A STRONG START, WE FEEL YOU'VE LOST YOUR DRIVE.
YOU'RE BILLING TOO FEW HOURS AND YOU DON'T SEEM HAPPY.
YOU SOMETIMES GIVE THE IMPRESSION OF NOT WANTING TO LEARN.
WE NO LONGER FEEL YOU'RE A PROPER FIT.

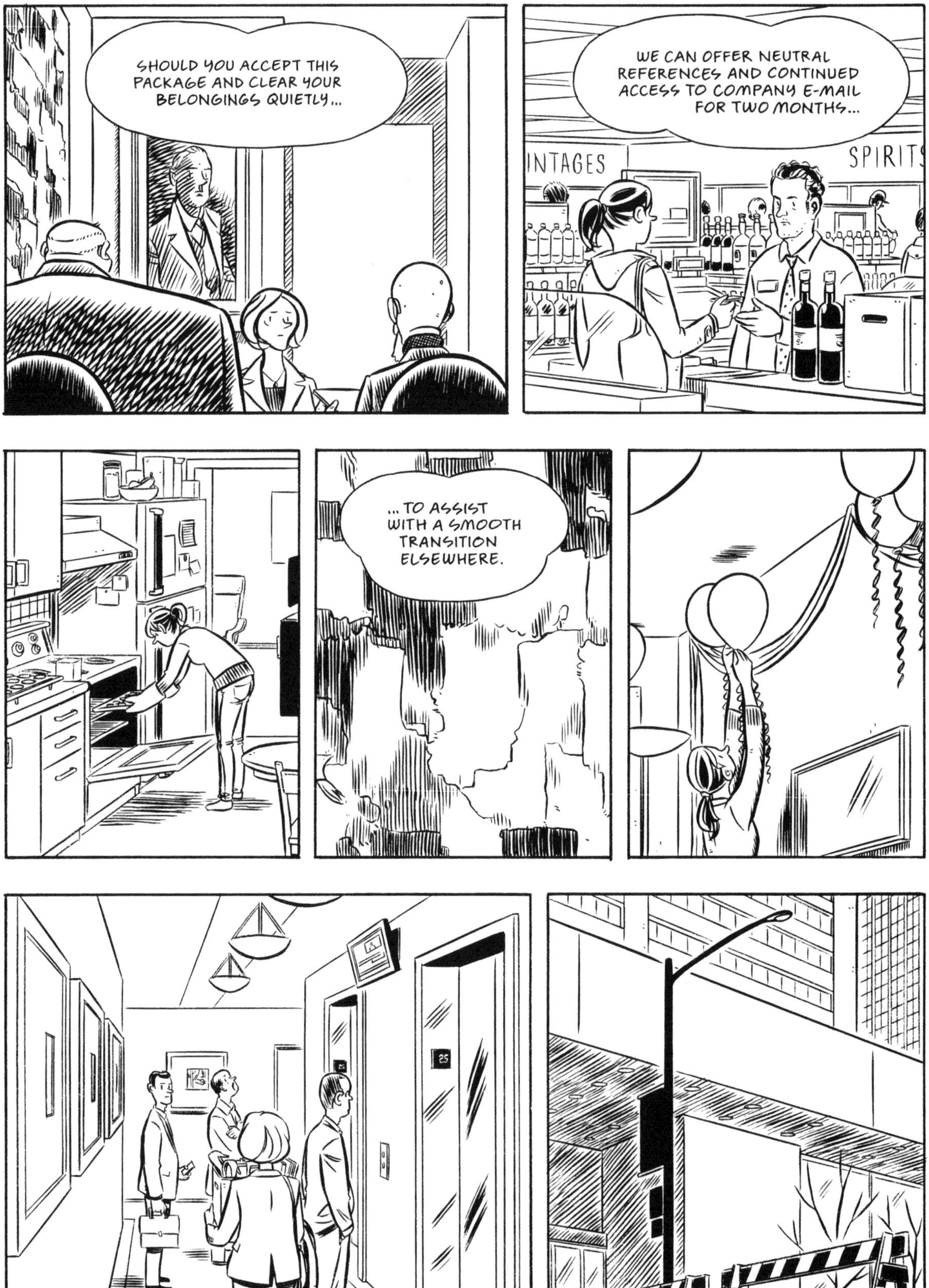
SHOULD YOU ACCEPT THIS PACKAGE AND CLEAR YOUR BELONGINGS QUIETLY...
WE CAN OFFER NEUTRAL REFERENCES AND CONTINUED ACCESS TO COMPANY E-MAIL FOR TWO MONTHS...
INTAGES
SPIRITS
...TO ASSIST WITH A SMOOTH TRANSITION ELSEWHERE.
25

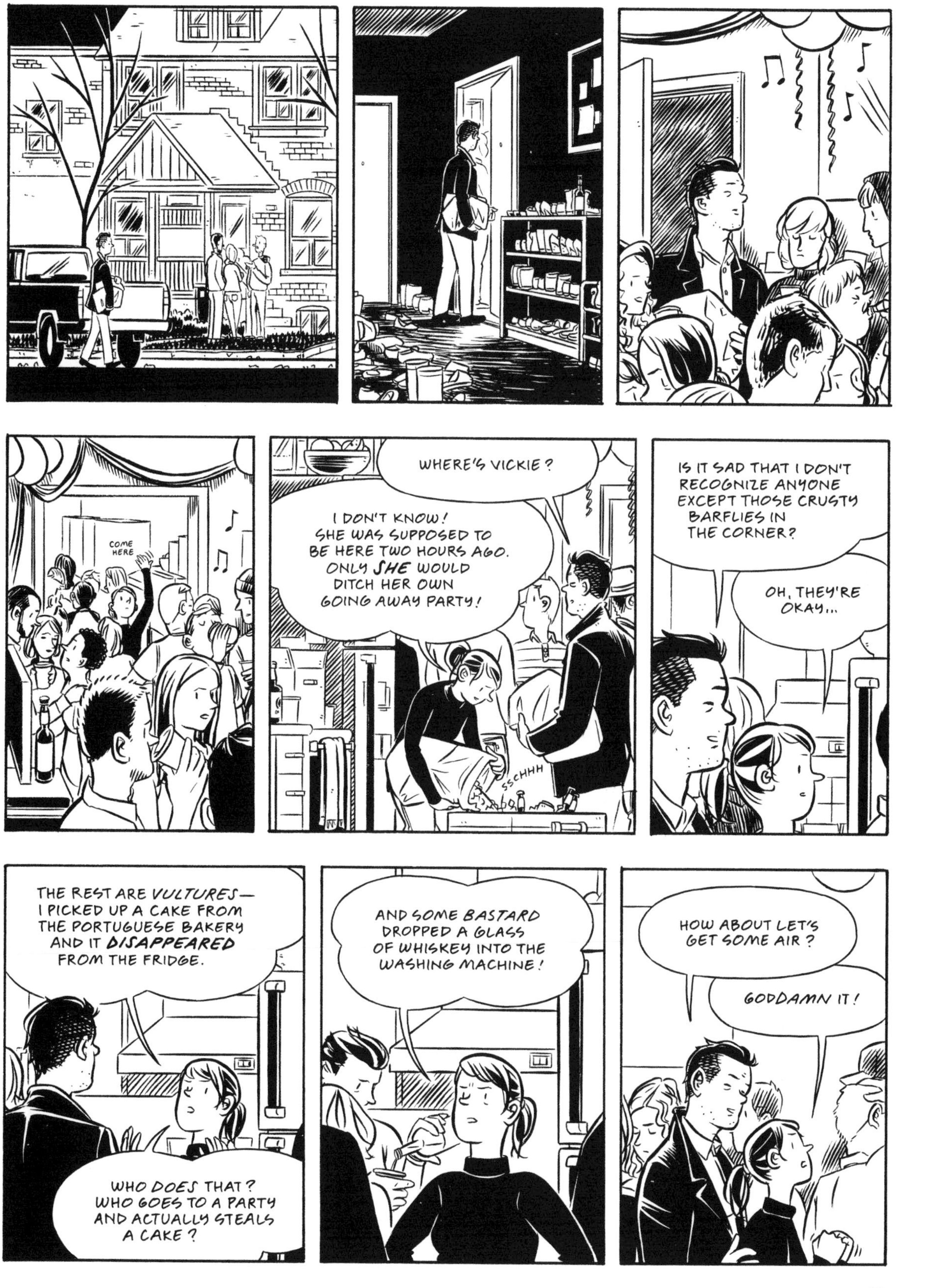
COME HERE
WHERE'S VICKIE?
I DON'T KNOW! SHE WAS SUPPOSED TO BE HERE TWO HOURS AGO. ONLY SHE WOULD DITCH HER OWN GOING AWAY PARTY!
SSCHHH
IS IT SAD THAT I DON'T RECOGNIZE ANYONE EXCEPT THOSE CRUSTY BARFLIES IN THE CORNER?
OH, THEY'RE OKAY...
THE REST ARE VULTURES— I PICKED UP A CAKE FROM THE PORTUGUESE BAKERY AND IT DISAPPEARED FROM THE FRIDGE.
WHO DOES THAT? WHO GOES TO A PARTY AND ACTUALLY STEALS A CAKE?
AND SOME BASTARD DROPPED A GLASS OF WHISKEY INTO THE WASHING MACHINE!
HOW ABOUT LET'S GET SOME AIR?
GODDAMN IT!

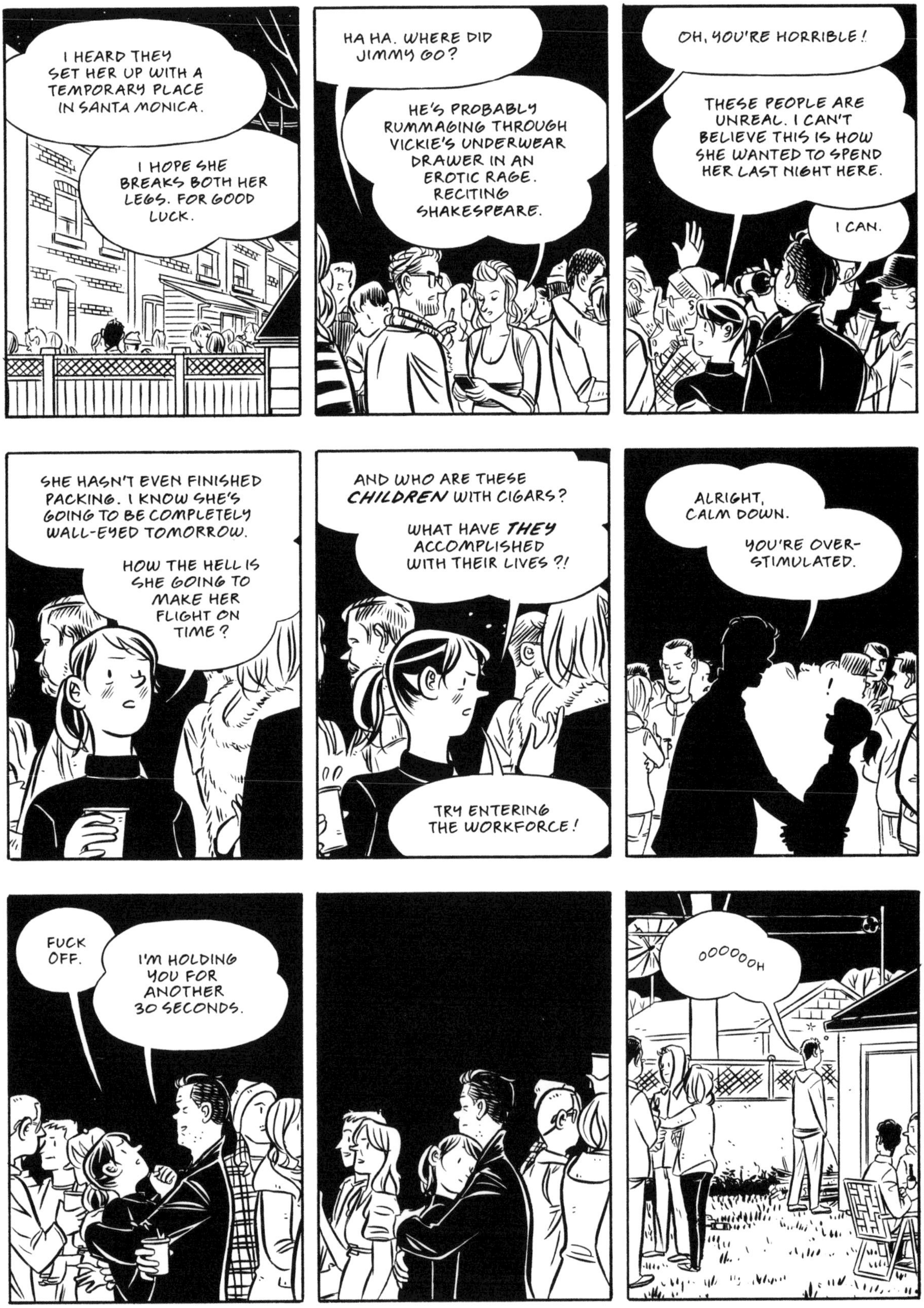
I HEARD THEY SET HER UP WITH A TEMPORARY PLACE IN SANTA MONICA.
I HOPE SHE BREAKS BOTH HER LEGS. FOR GOOD LUCK.
HA HA. WHERE DID JIMMY GO?
HE'S PROBABLY RUMMAGING THROUGH VICKIE'S UNDERWEAR DRAWER IN AN EROTIC RAGE. RECITING SHAKESPEARE.
OH, YOU'RE HORRIBLE!
THESE PEOPLE ARE UNREAL. I CAN'T BELIEVE THIS IS HOW SHE WANTED TO SPEND HER LAST NIGHT HERE.
I CAN.
SHE HASN'T EVEN FINISHED PACKING. I KNOW SHE'S GOING TO BE COMPLETELY WALL-EYED TOMORROW.
HOW THE HELL IS SHE GOING TO MAKE HER FLIGHT ON TIME?
AND WHO ARE THESE CHILDREN WITH CIGARS?
WHAT HAVE THEY ACCOMPLISHED WITH THEIR LIVES?!
TRY ENTERING THE WORKFORCE!
ALRIGHT, CALM DOWN.
YOU'RE OVER-STIMULATED.
!
FUCK OFF.
I'M HOLDING YOU FOR ANOTHER 30 SECONDS.
OOOOOOH

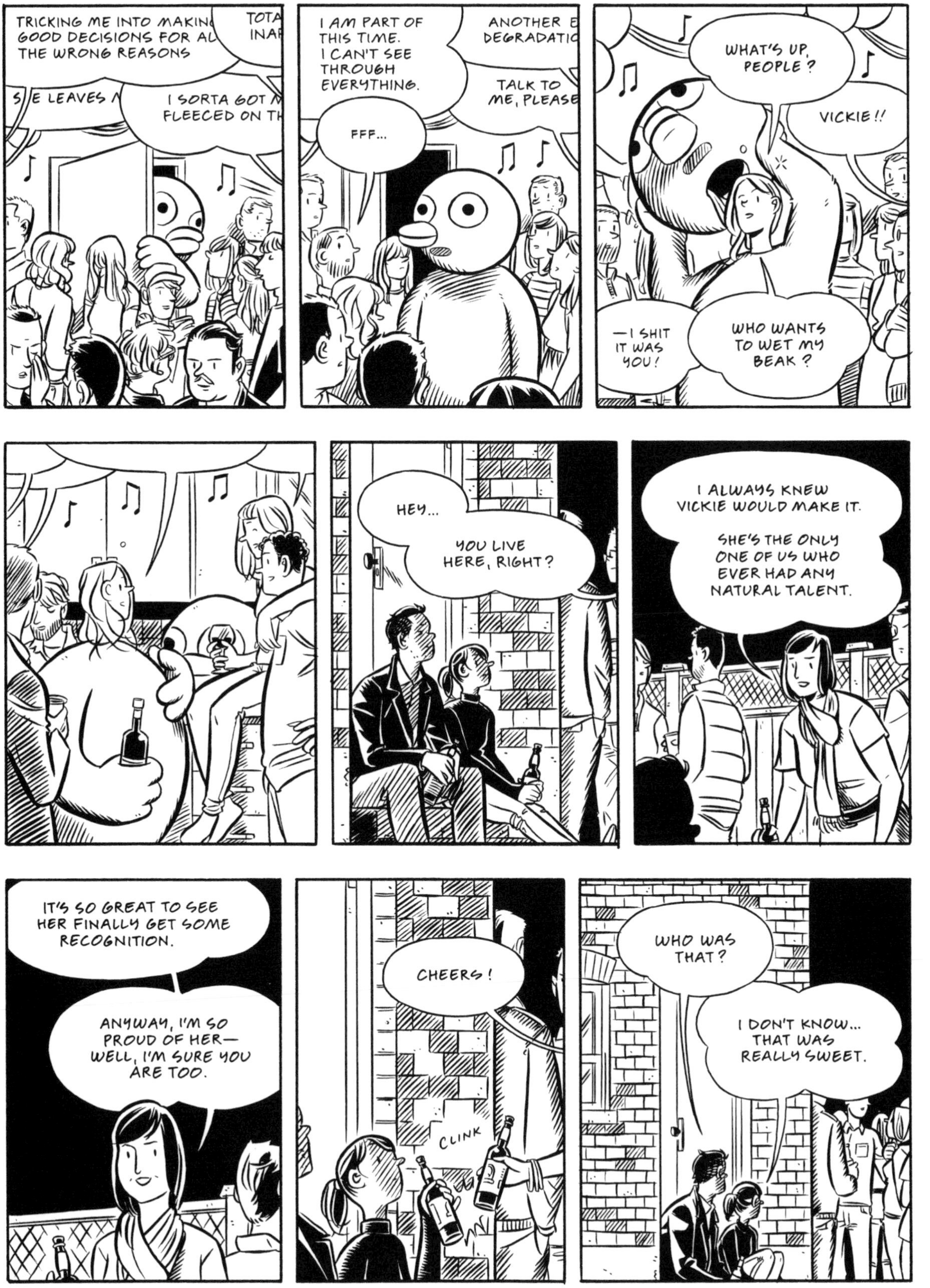

TRICKING ME INTO MAKING GOOD DECISIONS FOR AL THE WRONG REASONS
TOTA INAP
SHE LEAVES M
I SORTA GOT M FLEECED ON TH
I AM PART OF THIS TIME. I CAN'T SEE THROUGH EVERYTHING.
ANOTHER E DEGRADATIO
TALK TO ME, PLEASE
FFF...
WHAT'S UP, PEOPLE?
VICKIE!!
—I SHIT IT WAS YOU!
WHO WANTS TO WET MY BEAK?
HEY...
YOU LIVE HERE, RIGHT?
I ALWAYS KNEW VICKIE WOULD MAKE IT.
SHE'S THE ONLY ONE OF US WHO EVER HAD ANY NATURAL TALENT.
IT'S SO GREAT TO SEE HER FINALLY GET SOME RECOGNITION.
ANYWAY, I'M SO PROUD OF HER— WELL, I'M SURE YOU ARE TOO.
CHEERS!
CLINK
WHO WAS THAT?
I DON'T KNOW... THAT WAS REALLY SWEET.

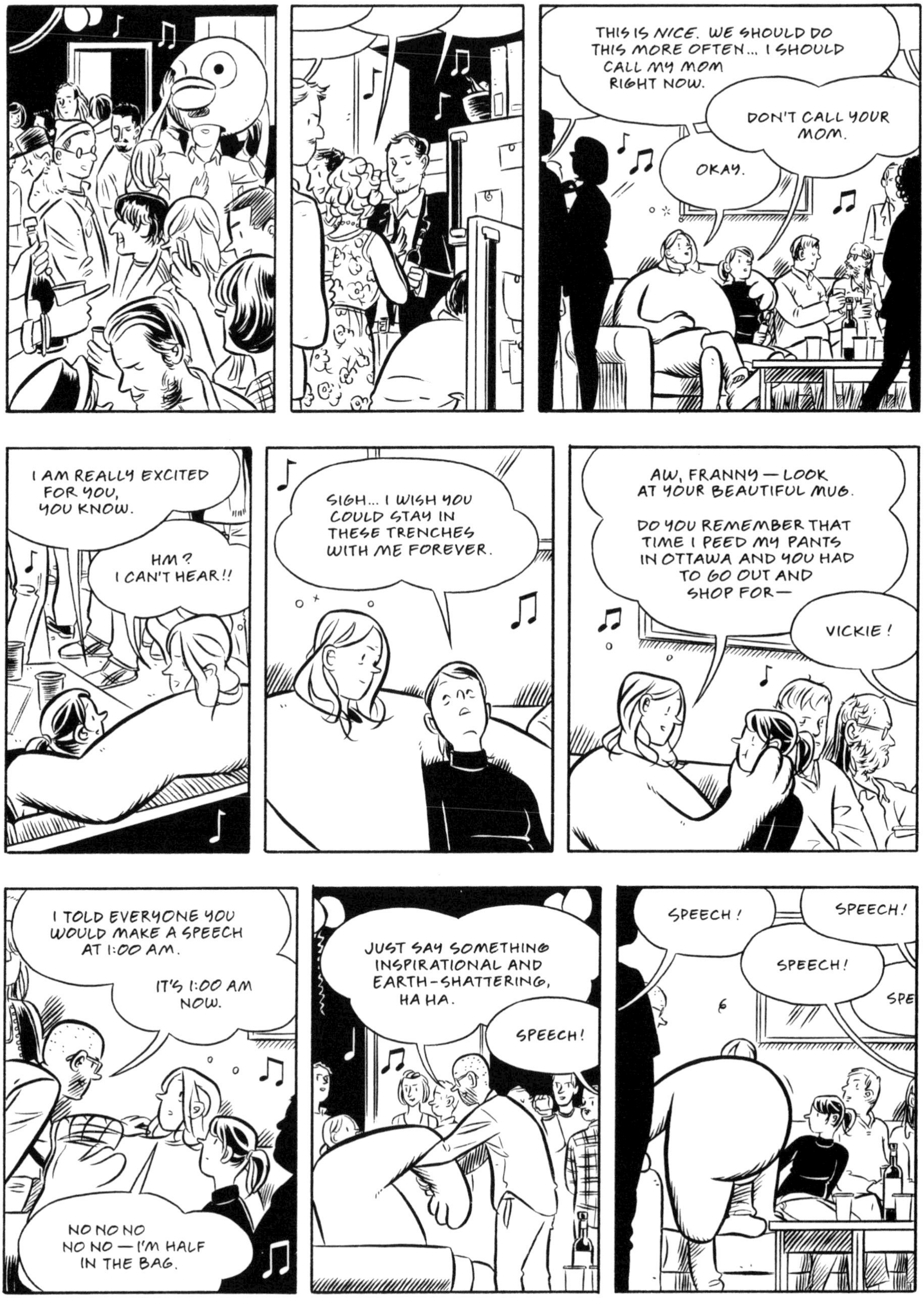
THIS IS *NICE*. WE SHOULD DO THIS MORE OFTEN... I SHOULD CALL MY MOM RIGHT NOW.
DON'T CALL YOUR MOM.
OKAY.
I AM REALLY EXCITED FOR YOU, YOU KNOW.
HM ? I CAN'T HEAR!!
SIGH... I WISH YOU COULD STAY IN THESE TRENCHES WITH ME FOREVER.
AW, FRANNY — LOOK AT YOUR BEAUTIFUL MUG.
DO YOU REMEMBER THAT TIME I PEED MY PANTS IN OTTAWA AND YOU HAD TO GO OUT AND SHOP FOR—
VICKIE !
I TOLD EVERYONE YOU WOULD MAKE A SPEECH AT 1:00 AM.
IT'S 1:00 AM NOW.
NO NO NO NO NO — I'M HALF IN THE BAG.
JUST SAY SOMETHING INSPIRATIONAL AND EARTH-SHATTERING, HA HA.
SPEECH!
SPEECH !
SPEECH!
SPEECH!

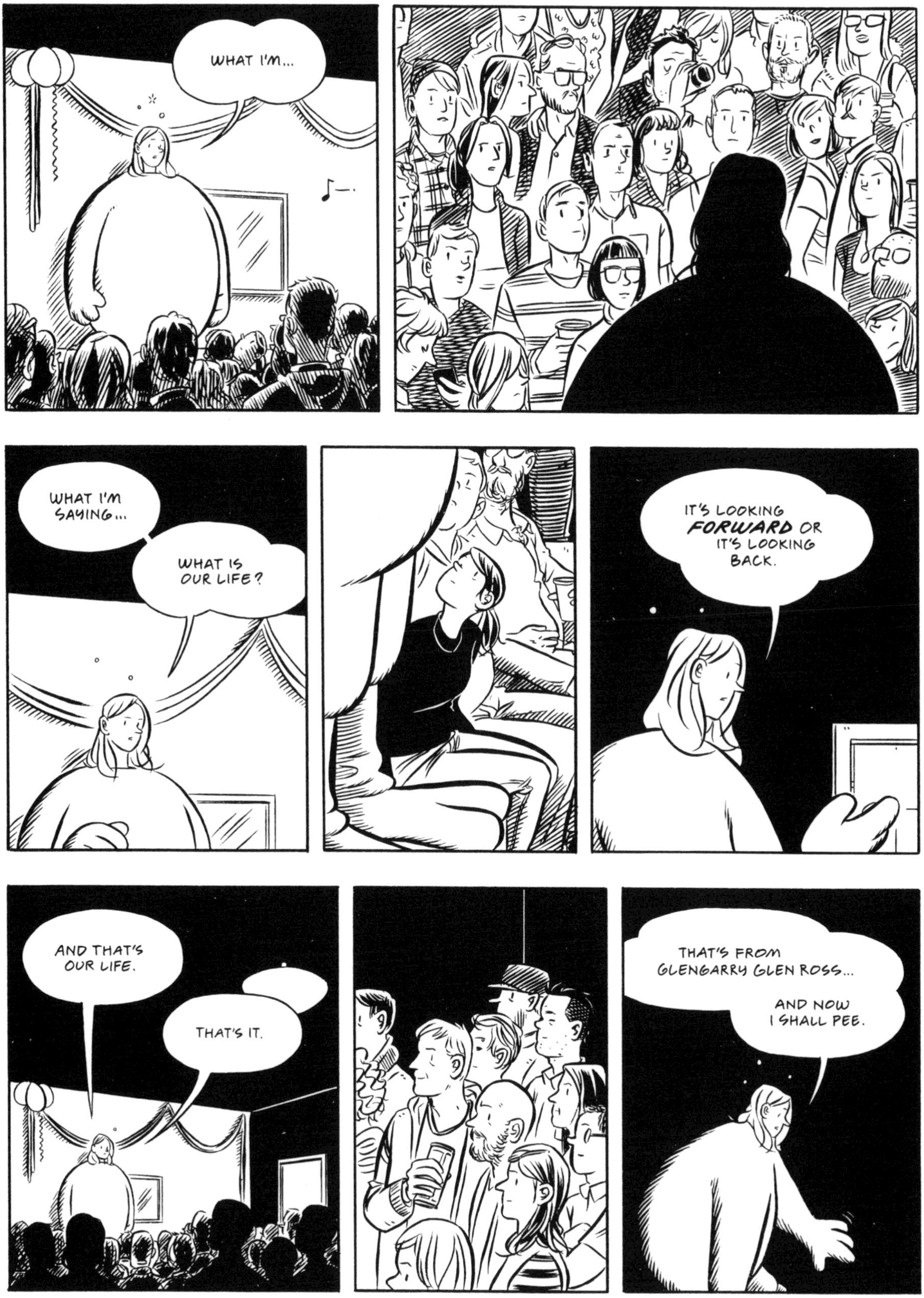
WHAT I'M...
WHAT I'M SAYING...
WHAT IS OUR LIFE?
IT'S LOOKING FORWARD OR IT'S LOOKING BACK.
AND THAT'S OUR LIFE.
THAT'S IT.
THAT'S FROM GLENGARRY GLEN ROSS...
AND NOW I SHALL PEE.

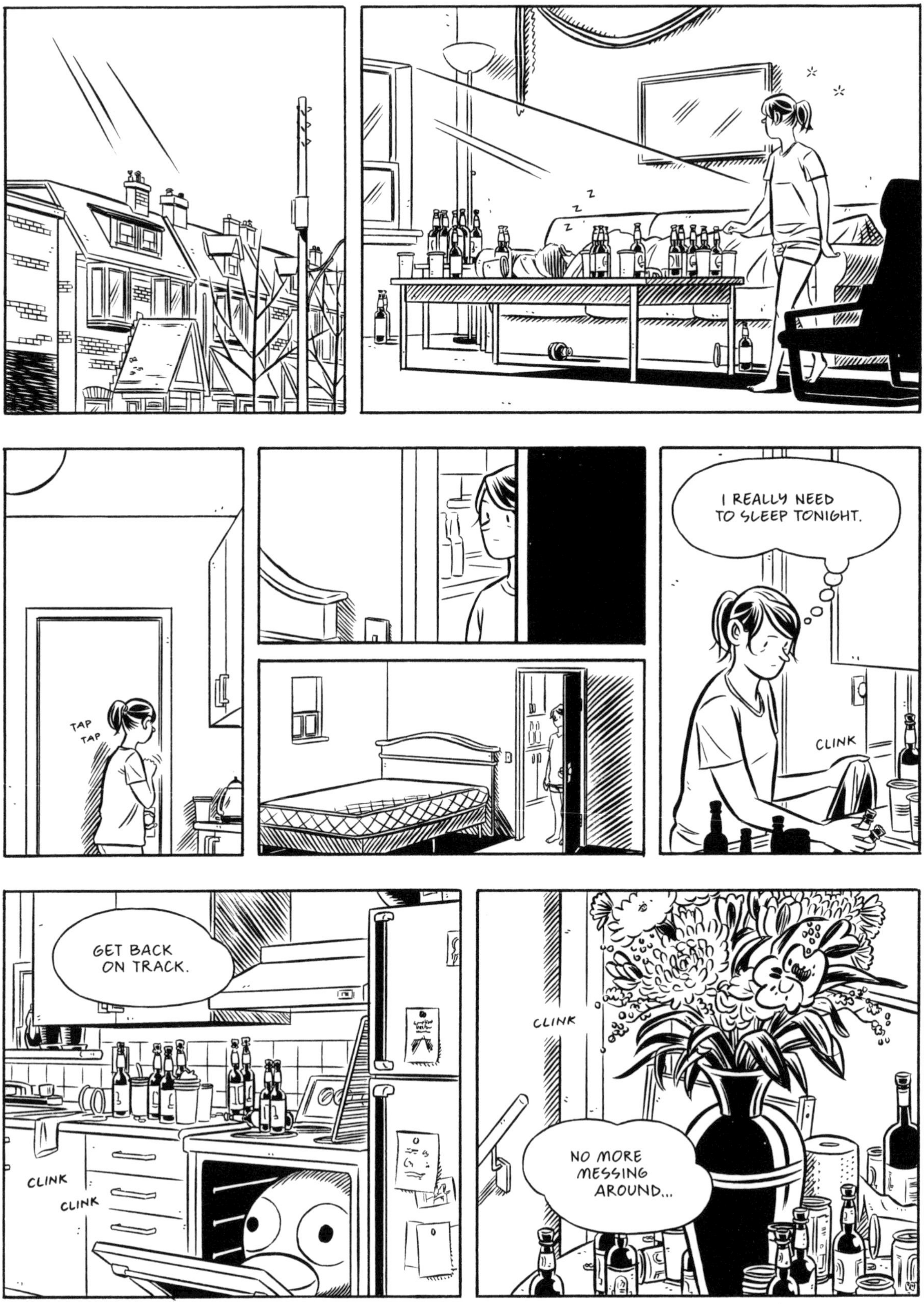
Z
Z
Z
TAP
TAP
I REALLY NEED TO SLEEP TONIGHT.
CLINK
GET BACK ON TRACK.
CLINK
CLINK
CLINK
NO MORE MESSING AROUND...

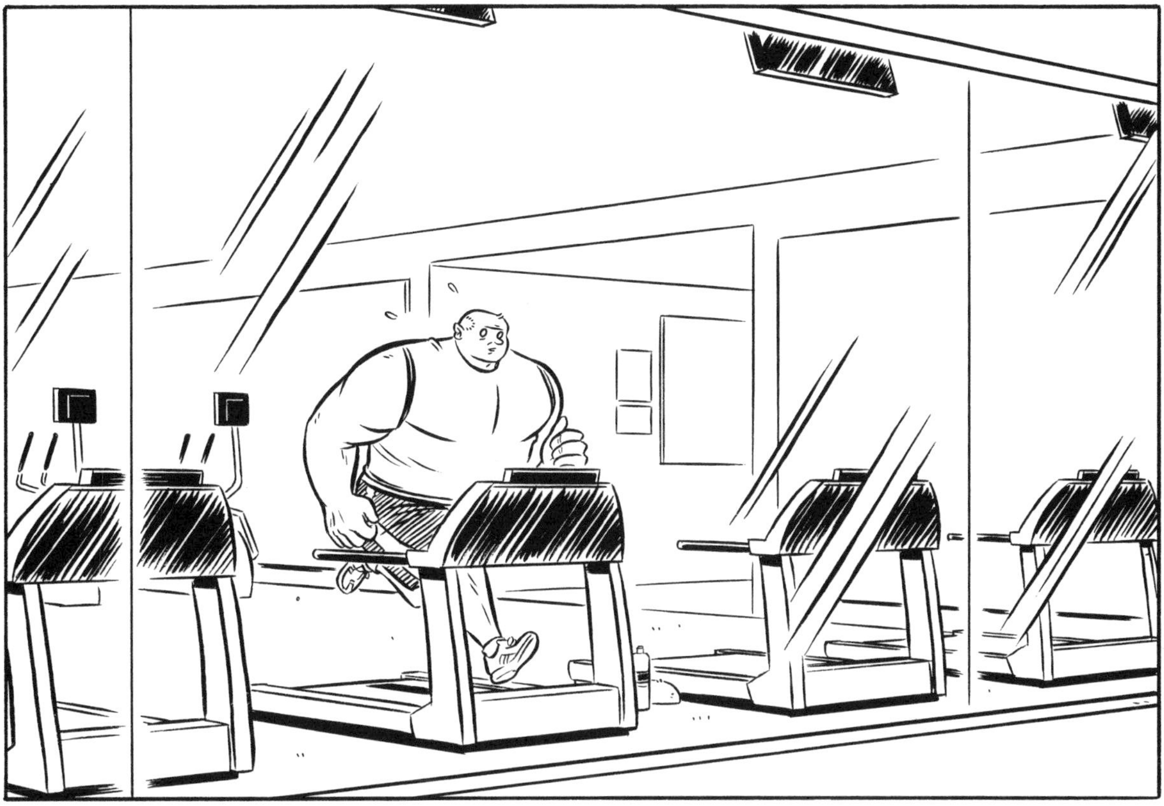

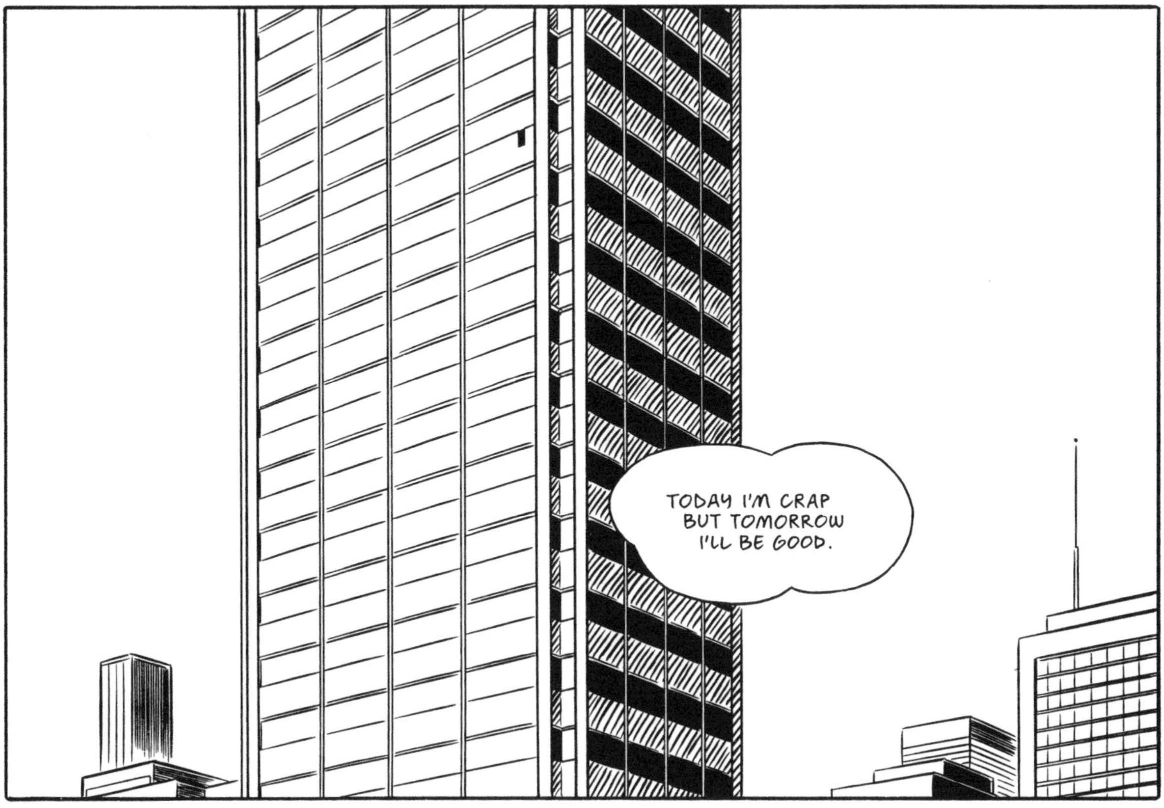
TODAY I'M CRAP BUT TOMORROW I'LL BE GOOD.

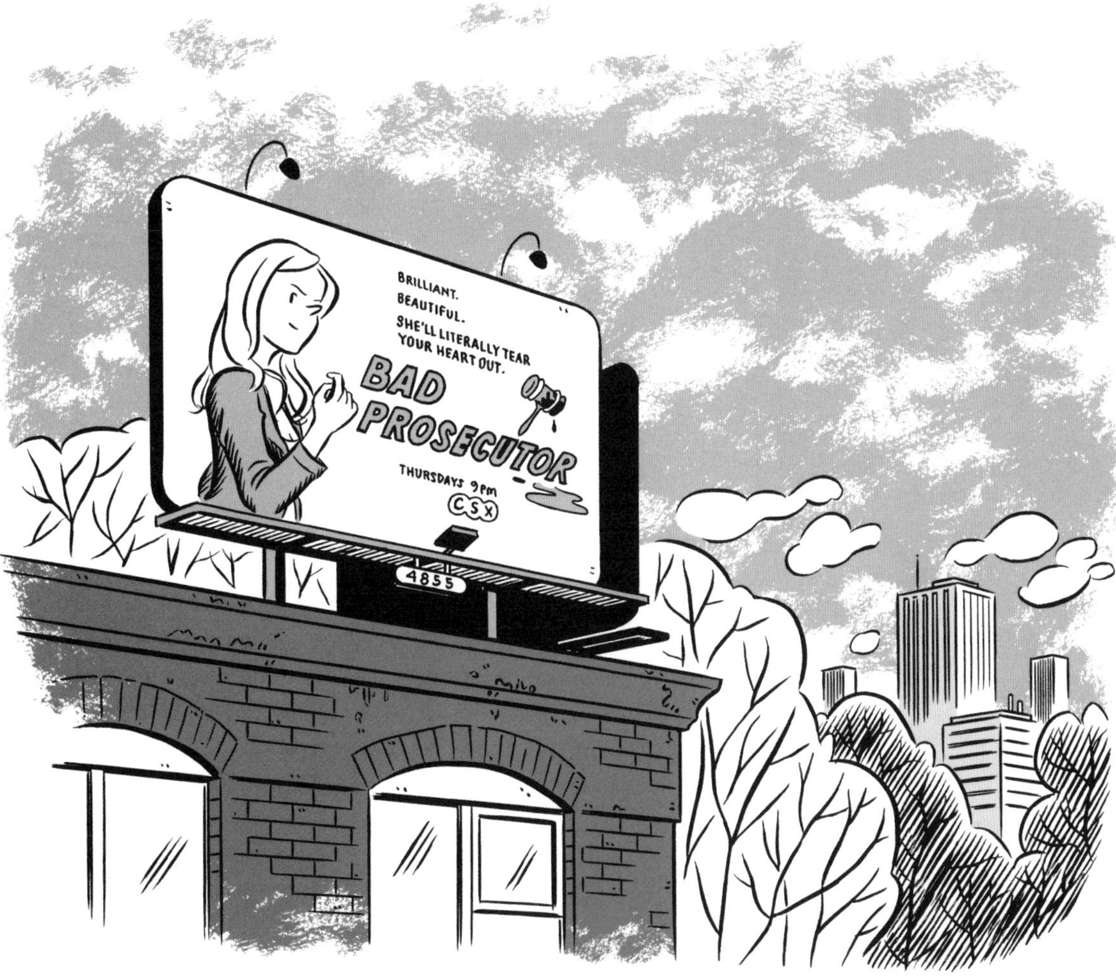
BRILLIANT.
BEAUTIFUL.
SHE'LL LITERALLY TEAR YOUR HEART OUT.
BAD PROSECUTOR
THURSDAYS 9pm
CSX
4855

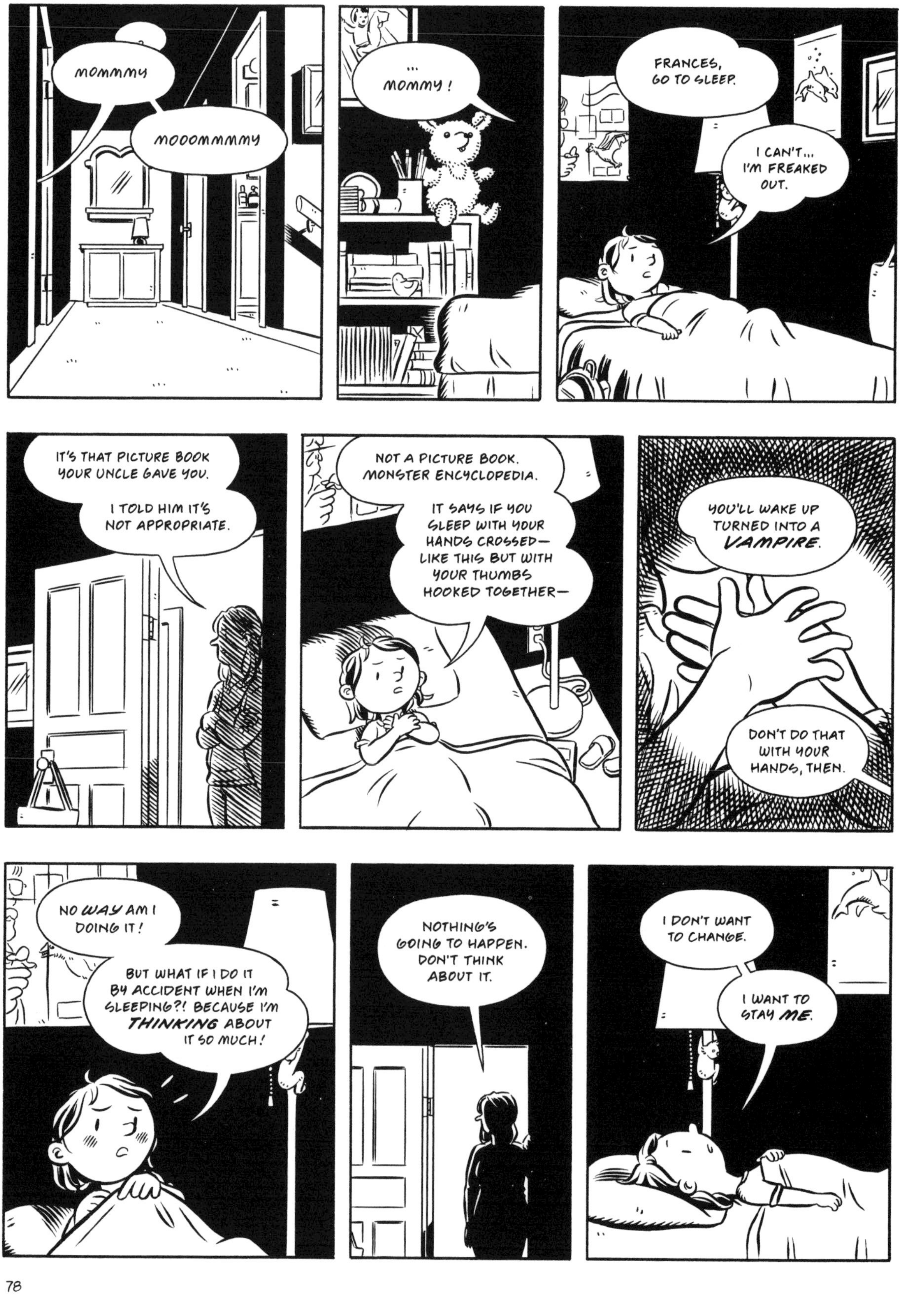
MOMMMY
MOOOMMMMY
... MOMMY!
FRANCES, GO TO SLEEP.
I CAN'T... I'M FREAKED OUT.
IT'S THAT PICTURE BOOK YOUR UNCLE GAVE YOU.
I TOLD HIM IT'S NOT APPROPRIATE.
NOT A PICTURE BOOK. MONSTER ENCYCLOPEDIA.
IT SAYS IF YOU SLEEP WITH YOUR HANDS CROSSED— LIKE THIS BUT WITH YOUR THUMBS HOOKED TOGETHER—
YOU'LL WAKE UP TURNED INTO A VAMPIRE.
DON'T DO THAT WITH YOUR HANDS, THEN.
NO WAY AM I DOING IT!
BUT WHAT IF I DO IT BY ACCIDENT WHEN I'M SLEEPING?! BECAUSE I'M THINKING ABOUT IT SO MUCH!
NOTHING'S GOING TO HAPPEN. DON'T THINK ABOUT IT.
I DON'T WANT TO CHANGE.
I WANT TO STAY ME.

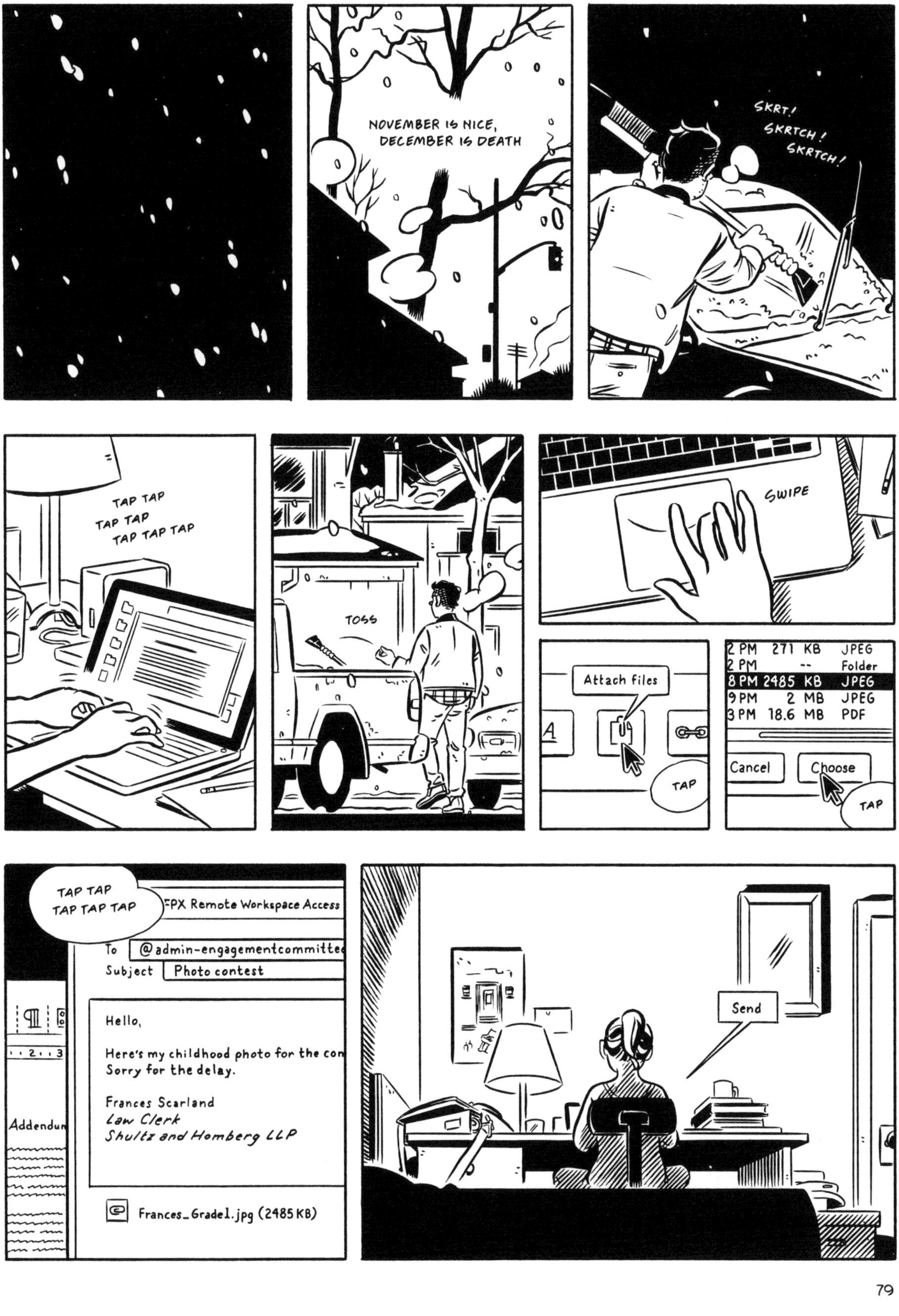

NOVEMBER IS NICE, DECEMBER IS DEATH
SKRT! SKRTCH! SKRTCH!
TAP TAP
TAP TAP
TAP TAP TAP
TOSS
SWIPE
Attach files
TAP
2 PM 271 KB JPEG
2 PM -- Folder
8 PM 2485 KB JPEG
9 PM 2 MB JPEG
3 PM 18.6 MB PDF
Cancel
Choose
TAP
TAP TAP
TAP TAP TAP
FPX Remote Workspace Access
To @admin-engagementcommittee
Subject Photo contest
Hello,
Here's my childhood photo for the con
Sorry for the delay.
Frances Scarland
Law Clerk
Shultz and Homberg LLP
Frances_Grade1.jpg (2485 KB)
Addendum
Send

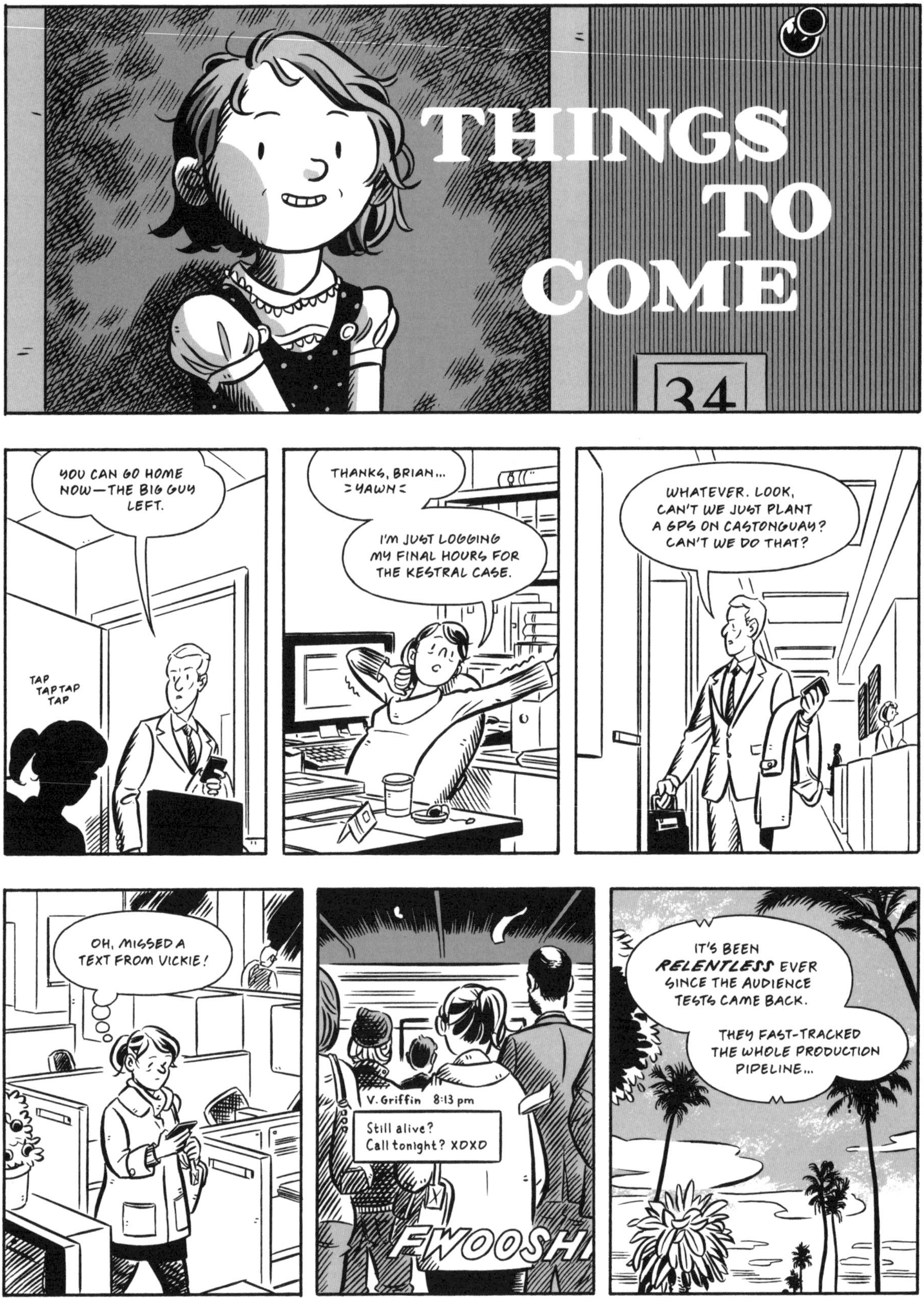
THINGS TO COME
34
YOU CAN GO HOME NOW—THE BIG GUY LEFT.
TAP TAP TAP TAP
THANKS, BRIAN... =YAWN=
I'M JUST LOGGING MY FINAL HOURS FOR THE KESTRAL CASE.
WHATEVER. LOOK, CAN'T WE JUST PLANT A GPS ON CASTONGUAY? CAN'T WE DO THAT?
OH, MISSED A TEXT FROM VICKIE!
V. Griffin 8:13 pm
Still alive? Call tonight? XOXO
FWOOSH!
IT'S BEEN RELENTLESS EVER SINCE THE AUDIENCE TESTS CAME BACK.
THEY FAST-TRACKED THE WHOLE PRODUCTION PIPELINE...

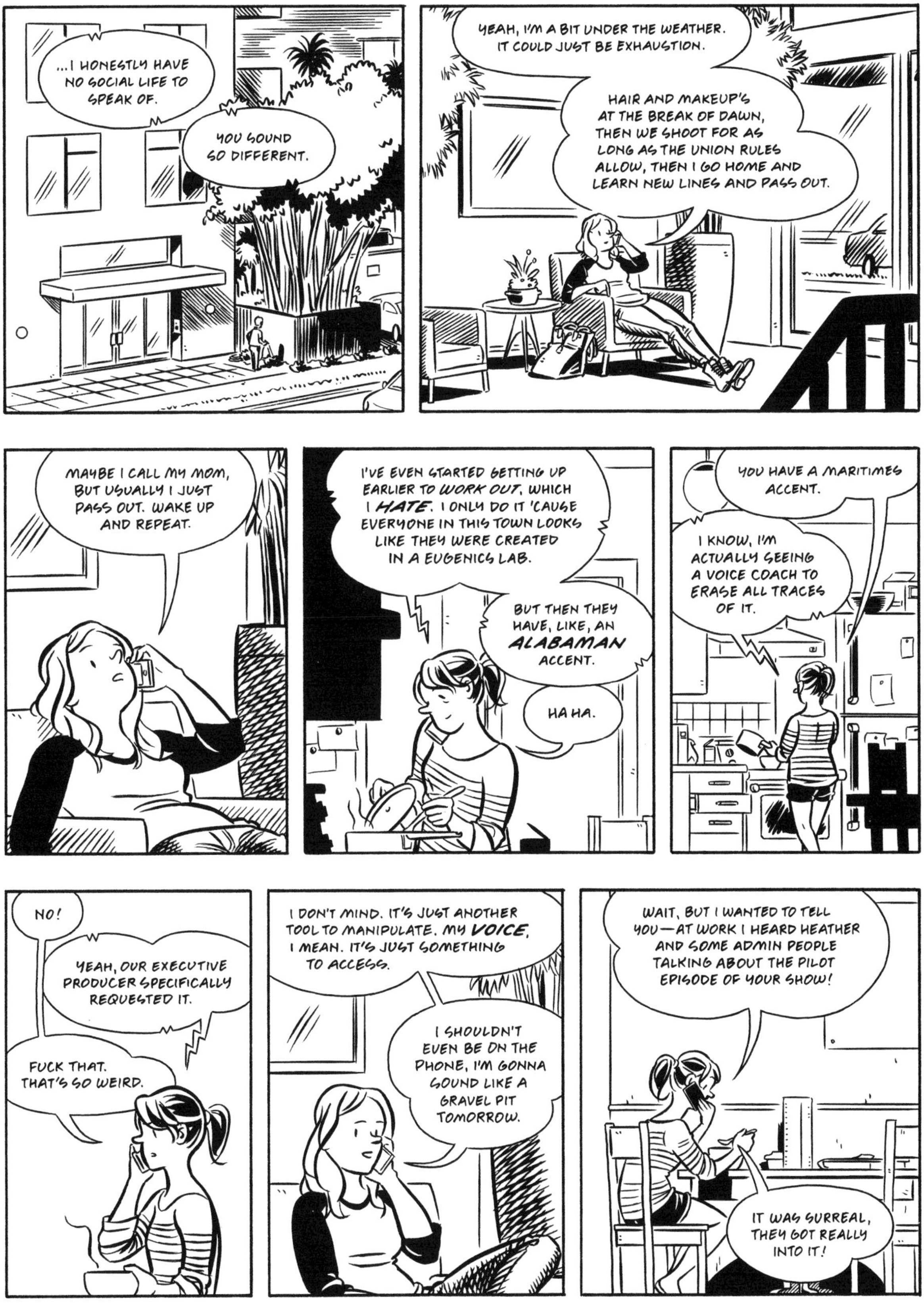
...I HONESTLY HAVE NO SOCIAL LIFE TO SPEAK OF.
YOU SOUND SO DIFFERENT.
YEAH, I'M A BIT UNDER THE WEATHER. IT COULD JUST BE EXHAUSTION.
HAIR AND MAKEUP'S AT THE BREAK OF DAWN, THEN WE SHOOT FOR AS LONG AS THE UNION RULES ALLOW, THEN I GO HOME AND LEARN NEW LINES AND PASS OUT.
MAYBE I CALL MY MOM, BUT USUALLY I JUST PASS OUT. WAKE UP AND REPEAT.
I'VE EVEN STARTED GETTING UP EARLIER TO WORK OUT, WHICH I HATE. I ONLY DO IT 'CAUSE EVERYONE IN THIS TOWN LOOKS LIKE THEY WERE CREATED IN A EUGENICS LAB.
BUT THEN THEY HAVE, LIKE, AN ALABAMAN ACCENT.
HA HA.
YOU HAVE A MARITIMES ACCENT.
I KNOW, I'M ACTUALLY SEEING A VOICE COACH TO ERASE ALL TRACES OF IT.
NO!
YEAH, OUR EXECUTIVE PRODUCER SPECIFICALLY REQUESTED IT.
FUCK THAT. THAT'S SO WEIRD.
I DON'T MIND. IT'S JUST ANOTHER TOOL TO MANIPULATE. MY VOICE, I MEAN. IT'S JUST SOMETHING TO ACCESS.
I SHOULDN'T EVEN BE ON THE PHONE, I'M GONNA SOUND LIKE A GRAVEL PIT TOMORROW.
WAIT, BUT I WANTED TO TELL YOU—AT WORK I HEARD HEATHER AND SOME ADMIN PEOPLE TALKING ABOUT THE PILOT EPISODE OF YOUR SHOW!
IT WAS SURREAL, THEY GOT REALLY INTO IT!

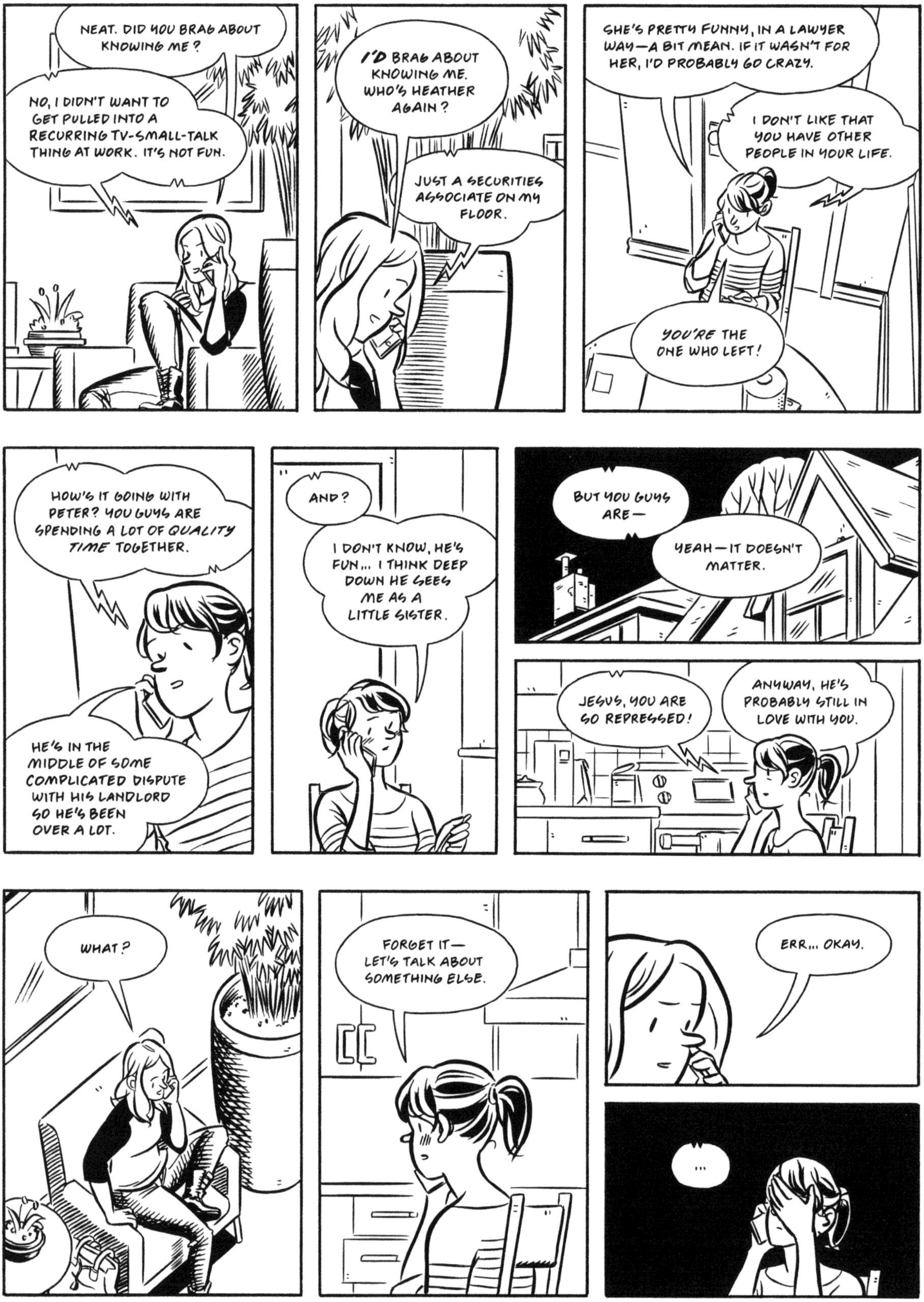
NEAT. DID YOU BRAG ABOUT KNOWING ME?
NO, I DIDN'T WANT TO GET PULLED INTO A RECURRING TV-SMALL-TALK THING AT WORK. IT'S NOT FUN.
I'D BRAG ABOUT KNOWING ME. WHO'S HEATHER AGAIN?
JUST A SECURITIES ASSOCIATE ON MY FLOOR.
SHE'S PRETTY FUNNY, IN A LAWYER WAY—A BIT MEAN. IF IT WASN'T FOR HER, I'D PROBABLY GO CRAZY.
I DON'T LIKE THAT YOU HAVE OTHER PEOPLE IN YOUR LIFE.
YOU'RE THE ONE WHO LEFT!
HOW'S IT GOING WITH PETER? YOU GUYS ARE SPENDING A LOT OF QUALITY TIME TOGETHER.
HE'S IN THE MIDDLE OF SOME COMPLICATED DISPUTE WITH HIS LANDLORD SO HE'S BEEN OVER A LOT.
AND?
I DON'T KNOW, HE'S FUN... I THINK DEEP DOWN HE SEES ME AS A LITTLE SISTER.
BUT YOU GUYS ARE—
YEAH—IT DOESN'T MATTER.
JESUS, YOU ARE SO REPRESSED!
ANYWAY, HE'S PROBABLY STILL IN LOVE WITH YOU.
WHAT?
FORGET IT—LET'S TALK ABOUT SOMETHING ELSE.
ERR... OKAY.
...

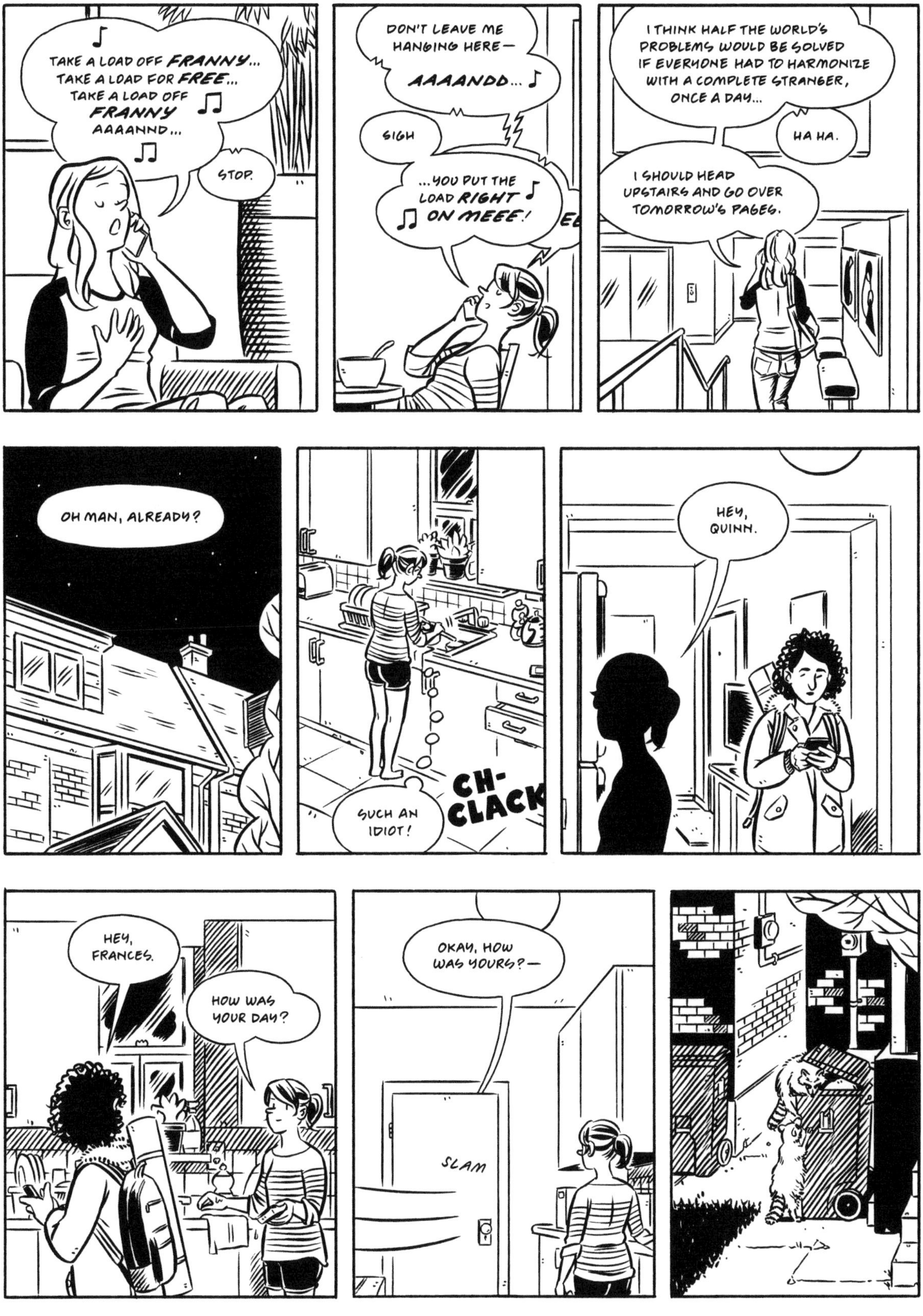
TAKE A LOAD OFF FRANNY... TAKE A LOAD FOR FREE... TAKE A LOAD OFF FRANNY AAAANND...
STOP.
DON'T LEAVE ME HANGING HERE— AAAANDD...
SIGH
...YOU PUT THE LOAD RIGHT ON MEEE!
I THINK HALF THE WORLD'S PROBLEMS WOULD BE SOLVED IF EVERYONE HAD TO HARMONIZE WITH A COMPLETE STRANGER, ONCE A DAY...
HA HA.
I SHOULD HEAD UPSTAIRS AND GO OVER TOMORROW'S PAGES.
OH MAN, ALREADY?
SUCH AN IDIOT!
CH-CLACK
HEY, QUINN.
HEY, FRANCES.
HOW WAS YOUR DAY?
OKAY, HOW WAS YOURS?—
SLAM

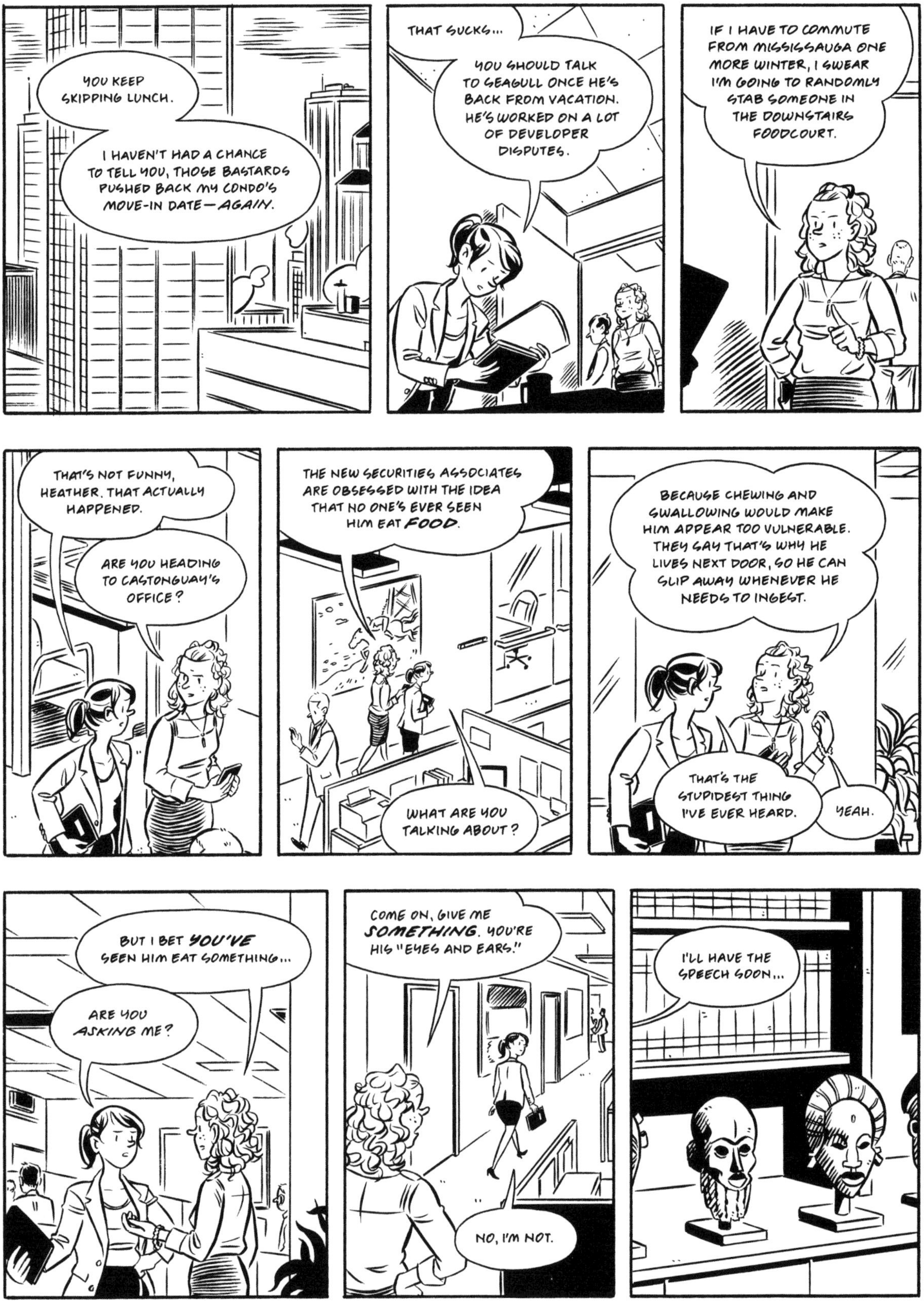

YOU KEEP SKIPPING LUNCH.
I HAVEN'T HAD A CHANCE TO TELL YOU, THOSE BASTARDS PUSHED BACK MY CONDO'S MOVE-IN DATE—AGAIN.
THAT SUCKS...
YOU SHOULD TALK TO SEAGULL ONCE HE'S BACK FROM VACATION. HE'S WORKED ON A LOT OF DEVELOPER DISPUTES.
IF I HAVE TO COMMUTE FROM MISSISSAUGA ONE MORE WINTER, I SWEAR I'M GOING TO RANDOMLY STAB SOMEONE IN THE DOWNSTAIRS FOODCOURT.
THAT'S NOT FUNNY, HEATHER. THAT ACTUALLY HAPPENED.
ARE YOU HEADING TO CASTONGUAY'S OFFICE?
THE NEW SECURITIES ASSOCIATES ARE OBSESSED WITH THE IDEA THAT NO ONE'S EVER SEEN HIM EAT FOOD.
WHAT ARE YOU TALKING ABOUT?
BECAUSE CHEWING AND SWALLOWING WOULD MAKE HIM APPEAR TOO VULNERABLE. THEY SAY THAT'S WHY HE LIVES NEXT DOOR, SO HE CAN SLIP AWAY WHENEVER HE NEEDS TO INGEST.
THAT'S THE STUPIDEST THING I'VE EVER HEARD.
YEAH.
BUT I BET YOU'VE SEEN HIM EAT SOMETHING...
ARE YOU ASKING ME?
COME ON, GIVE ME SOMETHING. YOU'RE HIS "EYES AND EARS."
NO, I'M NOT.
I'LL HAVE THE SPEECH SOON...

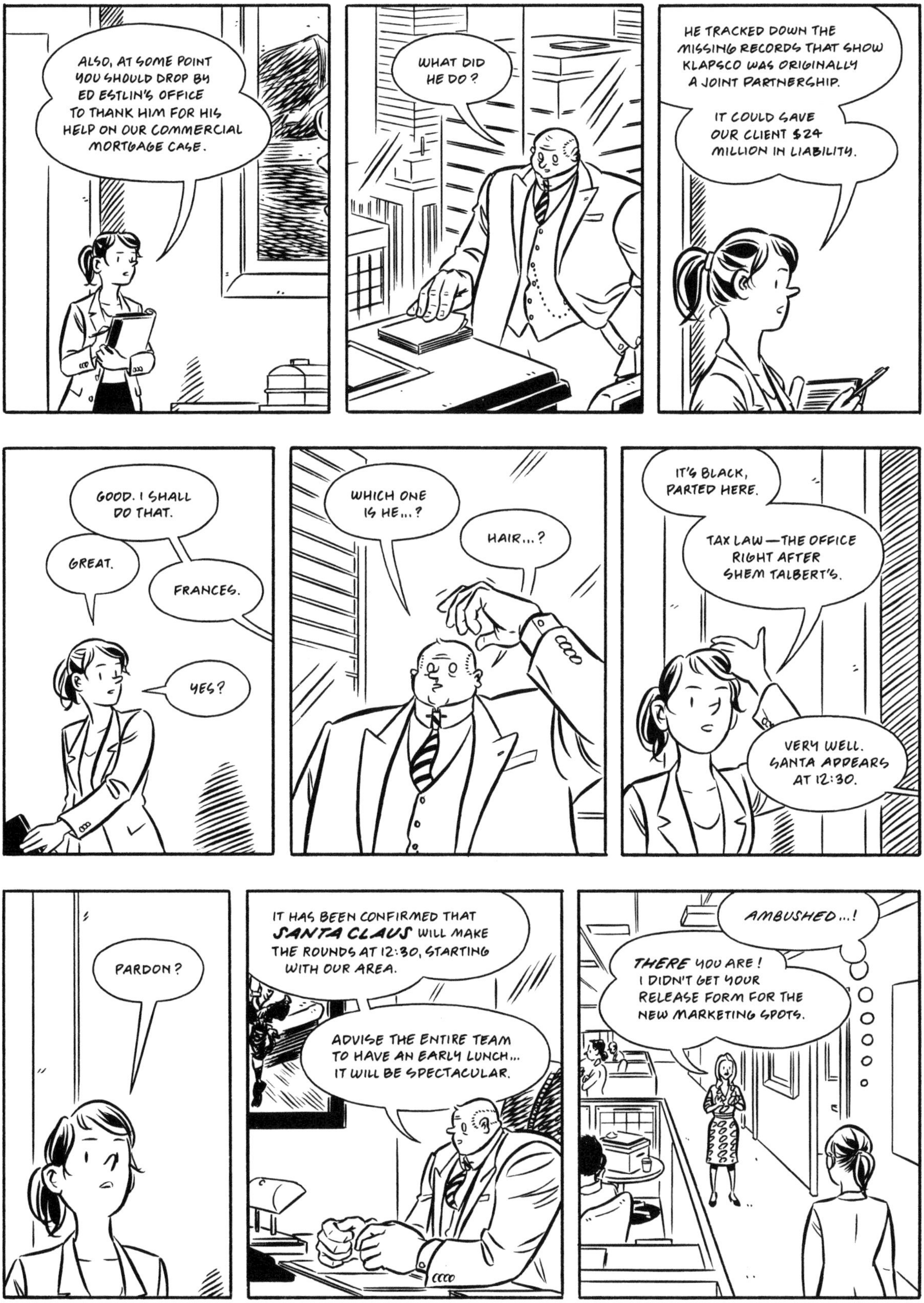
ALSO, AT SOME POINT YOU SHOULD DROP BY ED ESTLIN'S OFFICE TO THANK HIM FOR HIS HELP ON OUR COMMERCIAL MORTGAGE CASE.
WHAT DID HE DO?
HE TRACKED DOWN THE MISSING RECORDS THAT SHOW KLAPSCO WAS ORIGINALLY A JOINT PARTNERSHIP.
IT COULD SAVE OUR CLIENT $24 MILLION IN LIABILITY.
GOOD. I SHALL DO THAT.
GREAT.
FRANCES.
YES?
WHICH ONE IS HE...?
HAIR...?
IT'S BLACK, PARTED HERE.
TAX LAW—THE OFFICE RIGHT AFTER SHEM TALBERT'S.
VERY WELL. SANTA APPEARS AT 12:30.
PARDON?
IT HAS BEEN CONFIRMED THAT SANTA CLAUS WILL MAKE THE ROUNDS AT 12:30, STARTING WITH OUR AREA.
ADVISE THE ENTIRE TEAM TO HAVE AN EARLY LUNCH... IT WILL BE SPECTACULAR.
AMBUSHED...!
THERE YOU ARE! I DIDN'T GET YOUR RELEASE FORM FOR THE NEW MARKETING SPOTS.

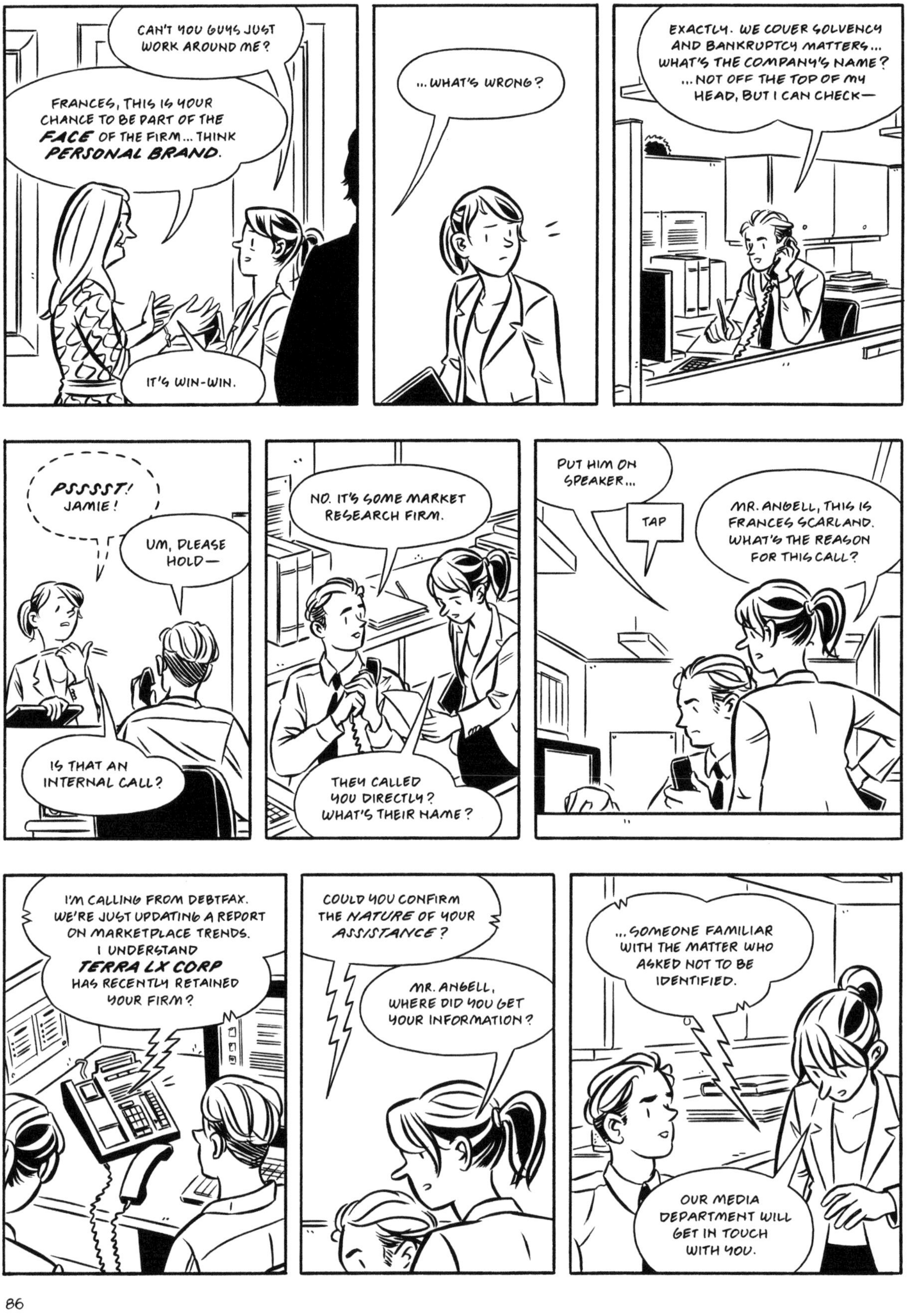

CAN'T YOU GUYS JUST WORK AROUND ME?
FRANCES, THIS IS YOUR CHANCE TO BE PART OF THE FACE OF THE FIRM... THINK PERSONAL BRAND.
IT'S WIN-WIN.
...WHAT'S WRONG?
EXACTLY. WE COVER SOLVENCY AND BANKRUPTCY MATTERS... WHAT'S THE COMPANY'S NAME? ...NOT OFF THE TOP OF MY HEAD, BUT I CAN CHECK—
PSSSST! JAMIE!
UM, PLEASE HOLD—
IS THAT AN INTERNAL CALL?
NO. IT'S SOME MARKET RESEARCH FIRM.
THEY CALLED YOU DIRECTLY? WHAT'S THEIR NAME?
PUT HIM ON SPEAKER...
TAP
MR. ANGELL, THIS IS FRANCES SCARLAND. WHAT'S THE REASON FOR THIS CALL?
I'M CALLING FROM DEBTFAX. WE'RE JUST UPDATING A REPORT ON MARKETPLACE TRENDS. I UNDERSTAND TERRA LX CORP HAS RECENTLY RETAINED YOUR FIRM?
COULD YOU CONFIRM THE NATURE OF YOUR ASSISTANCE?
MR. ANGELL, WHERE DID YOU GET YOUR INFORMATION?
...SOMEONE FAMILIAR WITH THE MATTER WHO ASKED NOT TO BE IDENTIFIED.
OUR MEDIA DEPARTMENT WILL GET IN TOUCH WITH YOU.

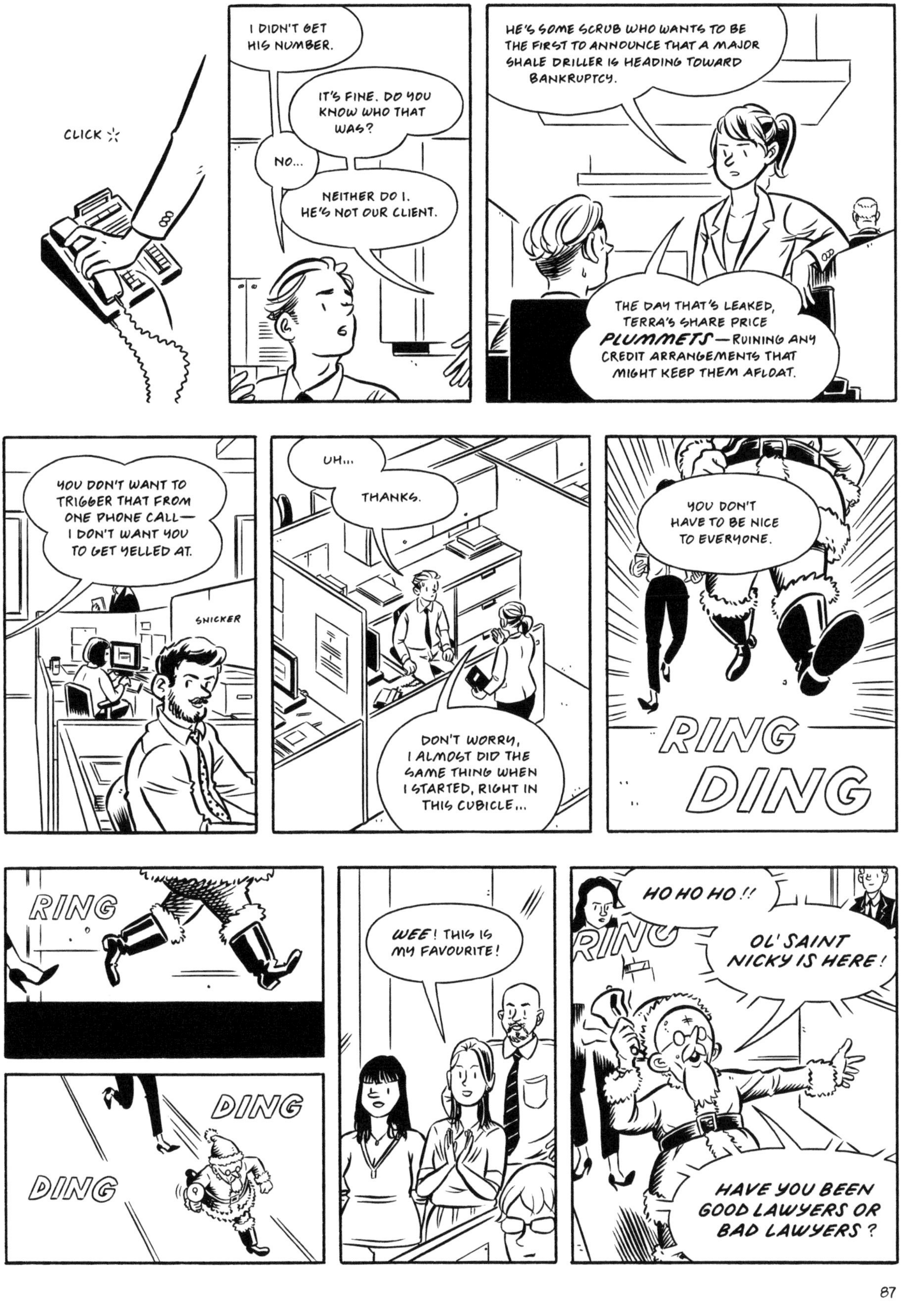
CLICK
I DIDN'T GET HIS NUMBER.
IT'S FINE. DO YOU KNOW WHO THAT WAS?
NO...
NEITHER DO I. HE'S NOT OUR CLIENT.
HE'S SOME SCRUB WHO WANTS TO BE THE FIRST TO ANNOUNCE THAT A MAJOR SHALE DRILLER IS HEADING TOWARD BANKRUPTCY.
THE DAY THAT'S LEAKED, TERRA'S SHARE PRICE PLUMMETS—RUINING ANY CREDIT ARRANGEMENTS THAT MIGHT KEEP THEM AFLOAT.
YOU DON'T WANT TO TRIGGER THAT FROM ONE PHONE CALL—I DON'T WANT YOU TO GET YELLED AT.
SNICKER
UH...
THANKS.
DON'T WORRY, I ALMOST DID THE SAME THING WHEN I STARTED, RIGHT IN THIS CUBICLE...
YOU DON'T HAVE TO BE NICE TO EVERYONE.
RING
DING
RING
DING
DING
WEE! THIS IS MY FAVOURITE!
HO HO HO!!
OL' SAINT NICKY IS HERE!
HAVE YOU BEEN GOOD LAWYERS OR BAD LAWYERS?

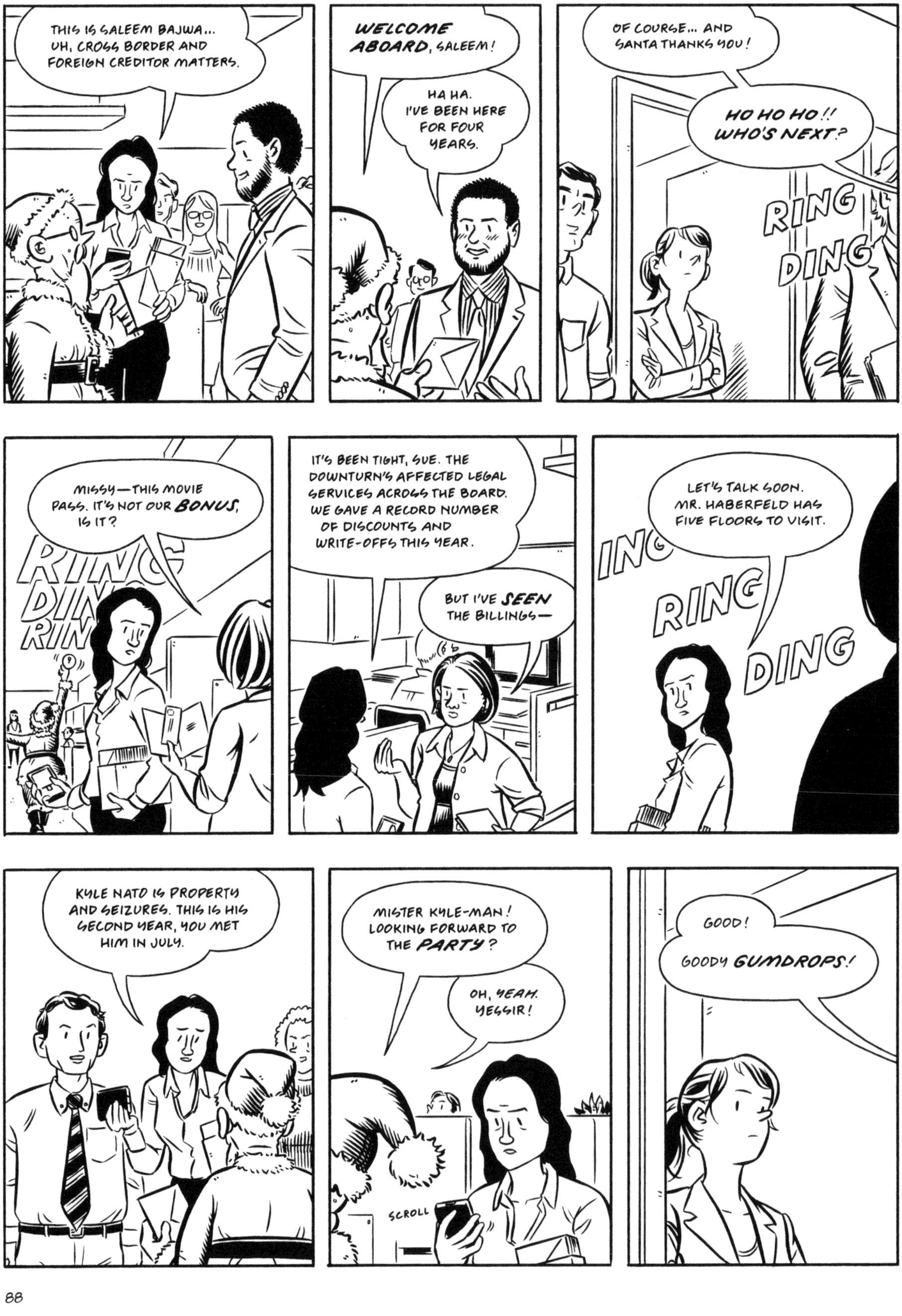
THIS IS SALEEM BAJWA... UH, CROSS BORDER AND FOREIGN CREDITOR MATTERS.
WELCOME ABOARD, SALEEM!
HA HA. I'VE BEEN HERE FOR FOUR YEARS.
OF COURSE... AND SANTA THANKS YOU!
HO HO HO!! WHO'S NEXT?
RING
DING
MISSY—THIS MOVIE PASS. IT'S NOT OUR BONUS, IS IT?
IT'S BEEN TIGHT, SUE. THE DOWNTURN'S AFFECTED LEGAL SERVICES ACROSS THE BOARD. WE GAVE A RECORD NUMBER OF DISCOUNTS AND WRITE-OFFS THIS YEAR.
BUT I'VE SEEN THE BILLINGS—
LET'S TALK SOON. MR. HABERFELD HAS FIVE FLOORS TO VISIT.
RING
DING
KYLE NATO IS PROPERTY AND SEIZURES. THIS IS HIS SECOND YEAR, YOU MET HIM IN JULY.
MISTER KYLE-MAN! LOOKING FORWARD TO THE PARTY?
OH, YEAH. YESSIR!
SCROLL
GOOD!
GOODY GUMDROPS!

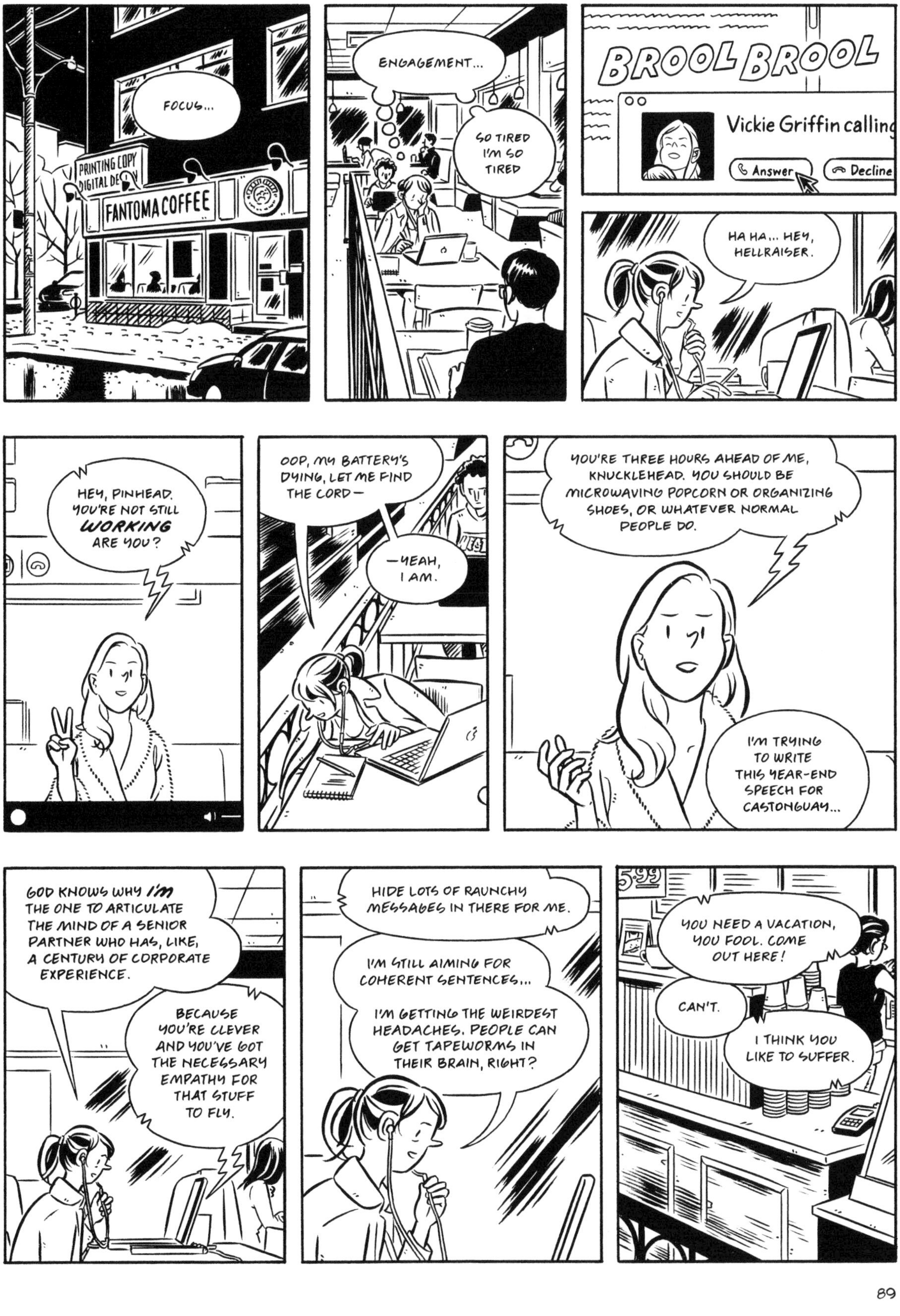
FOCUS...
PRINTING COPY
DIGITAL DE
FANTOMA COFFEE
ENGAGEMENT...
SO TIRED
I'M SO
TIRED
BROOL BROOL
Vickie Griffin calling
Answer
Decline
HA HA... HEY, HELLRAISER.
HEY, PINHEAD. YOU'RE NOT STILL WORKING ARE YOU?
OOP, MY BATTERY'S DYING, LET ME FIND THE CORD—
—YEAH, I AM.
YOU'RE THREE HOURS AHEAD OF ME, KNUCKLEHEAD. YOU SHOULD BE MICROWAVING POPCORN OR ORGANIZING SHOES, OR WHATEVER NORMAL PEOPLE DO.
I'M TRYING TO WRITE THIS YEAR-END SPEECH FOR CASTONGUAY...
GOD KNOWS WHY I'M THE ONE TO ARTICULATE THE MIND OF A SENIOR PARTNER WHO HAS, LIKE, A CENTURY OF CORPORATE EXPERIENCE.
BECAUSE YOU'RE CLEVER AND YOU'VE GOT THE NECESSARY EMPATHY FOR THAT STUFF TO FLY.
HIDE LOTS OF RAUNCHY MESSAGES IN THERE FOR ME.
I'M STILL AIMING FOR COHERENT SENTENCES...
I'M GETTING THE WEIRDEST HEADACHES. PEOPLE CAN GET TAPEWORMS IN THEIR BRAIN, RIGHT?
5.99
YOU NEED A VACATION, YOU FOOL. COME OUT HERE!
CAN'T.
I THINK YOU LIKE TO SUFFER.

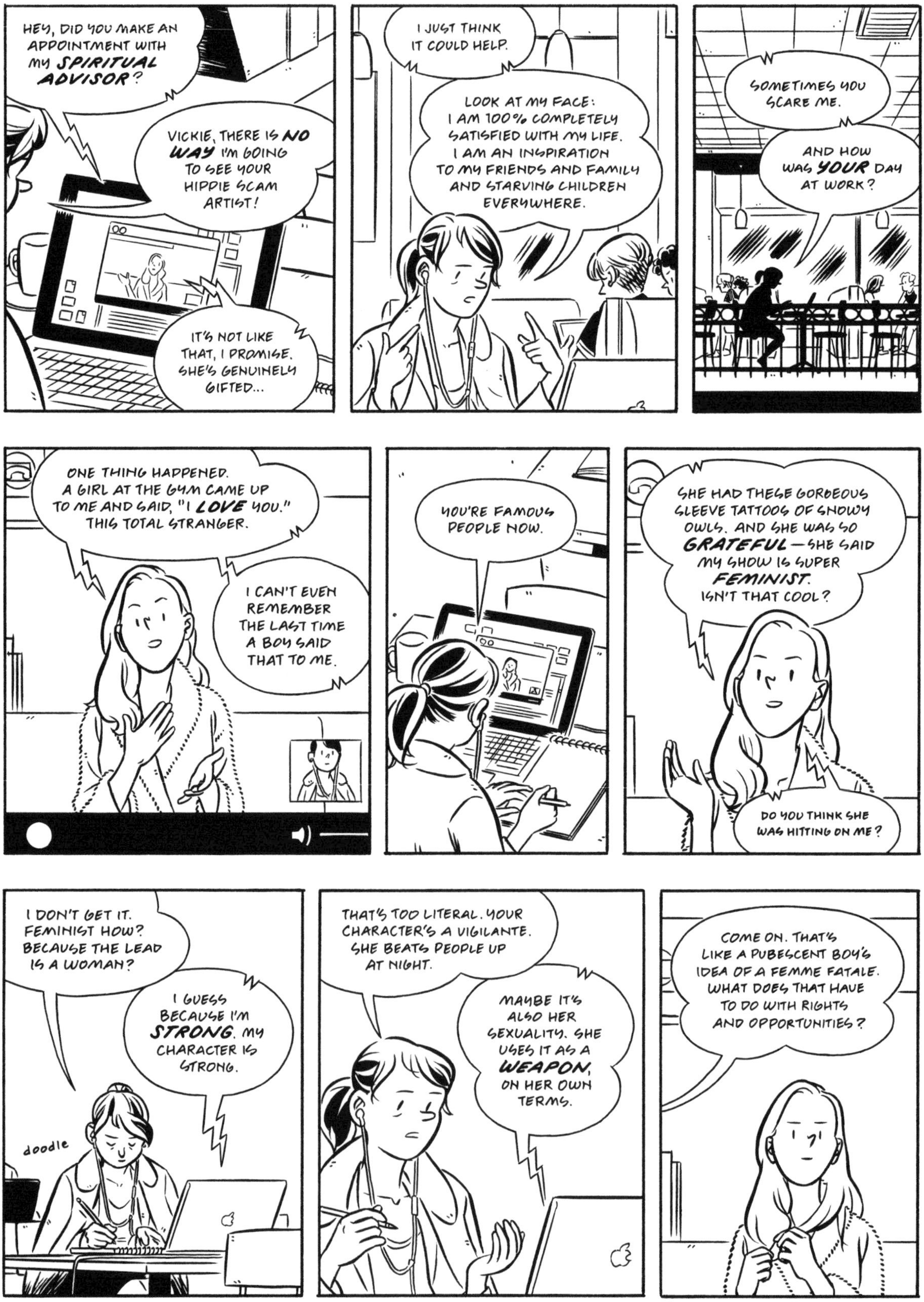
HEY, DID YOU MAKE AN APPOINTMENT WITH MY SPIRITUAL ADVISOR?
VICKIE, THERE IS NO WAY I'M GOING TO SEE YOUR HIPPIE SCAM ARTIST!
IT'S NOT LIKE THAT, I PROMISE. SHE'S GENUINELY GIFTED...
I JUST THINK IT COULD HELP.
LOOK AT MY FACE: I AM 100% COMPLETELY SATISFIED WITH MY LIFE. I AM AN INSPIRATION TO MY FRIENDS AND FAMILY AND STARVING CHILDREN EVERYWHERE.
SOMETIMES YOU SCARE ME.
AND HOW WAS YOUR DAY AT WORK?
ONE THING HAPPENED. A GIRL AT THE GYM CAME UP TO ME AND SAID, "I LOVE YOU." THIS TOTAL STRANGER.
I CAN'T EVEN REMEMBER THE LAST TIME A BOY SAID THAT TO ME.
YOU'RE FAMOUS PEOPLE NOW.
SHE HAD THESE GORGEOUS SLEEVE TATTOOS OF SNOWY OWLS. AND SHE WAS SO GRATEFUL—SHE SAID MY SHOW IS SUPER FEMINIST. ISN'T THAT COOL?
DO YOU THINK SHE WAS HITTING ON ME?
I DON'T GET IT. FEMINIST HOW? BECAUSE THE LEAD IS A WOMAN?
I GUESS BECAUSE I'M STRONG. MY CHARACTER IS STRONG.
doodle
THAT'S TOO LITERAL. YOUR CHARACTER'S A VIGILANTE. SHE BEATS PEOPLE UP AT NIGHT.
MAYBE IT'S ALSO HER SEXUALITY. SHE USES IT AS A WEAPON, ON HER OWN TERMS.
COME ON. THAT'S LIKE A PUBESCENT BOY'S IDEA OF A FEMME FATALE. WHAT DOES THAT HAVE TO DO WITH RIGHTS AND OPPORTUNITIES?

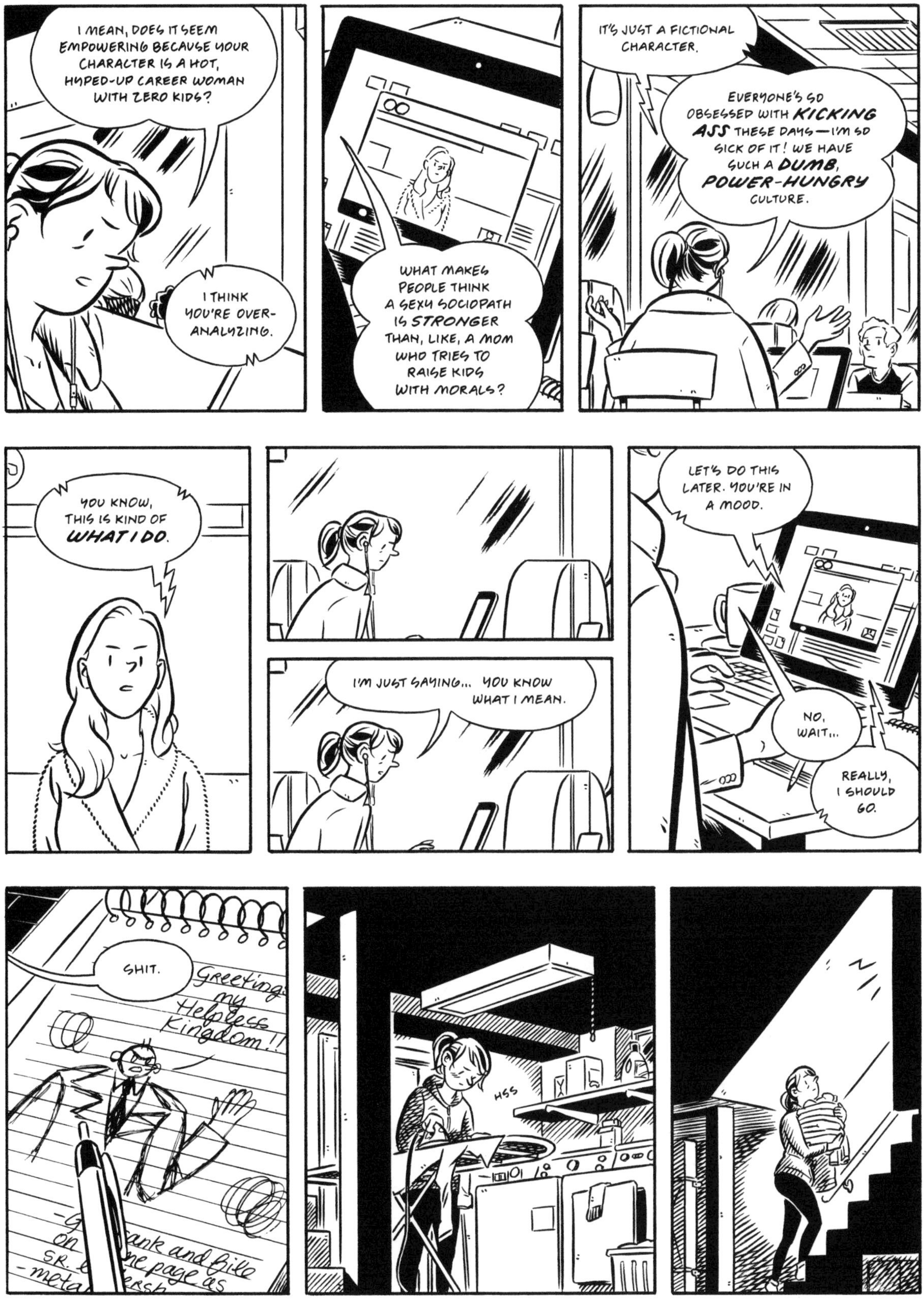
I MEAN, DOES IT SEEM EMPOWERING BECAUSE YOUR CHARACTER IS A HOT, HYPED-UP CAREER WOMAN WITH ZERO KIDS?
I THINK YOU'RE OVER-ANALYZING.
WHAT MAKES PEOPLE THINK A SEXY SOCIOPATH IS **STRONGER** THAN, LIKE, A MOM WHO TRIES TO RAISE KIDS WITH MORALS?
IT'S JUST A FICTIONAL CHARACTER.
EVERYONE'S SO OBSESSED WITH **KICKING ASS** THESE DAYS—I'M SO SICK OF IT! WE HAVE SUCH A **DUMB, POWER-HUNGRY** CULTURE.
YOU KNOW, THIS IS KIND OF ***WHAT I DO***.
I'M JUST SAYING... YOU KNOW WHAT I MEAN.
LET'S DO THIS LATER. YOU'RE IN A MOOD.
NO, WAIT...
REALLY, I SHOULD GO.
SHIT.
Greetings my Helpless Kingdom!!
HSS

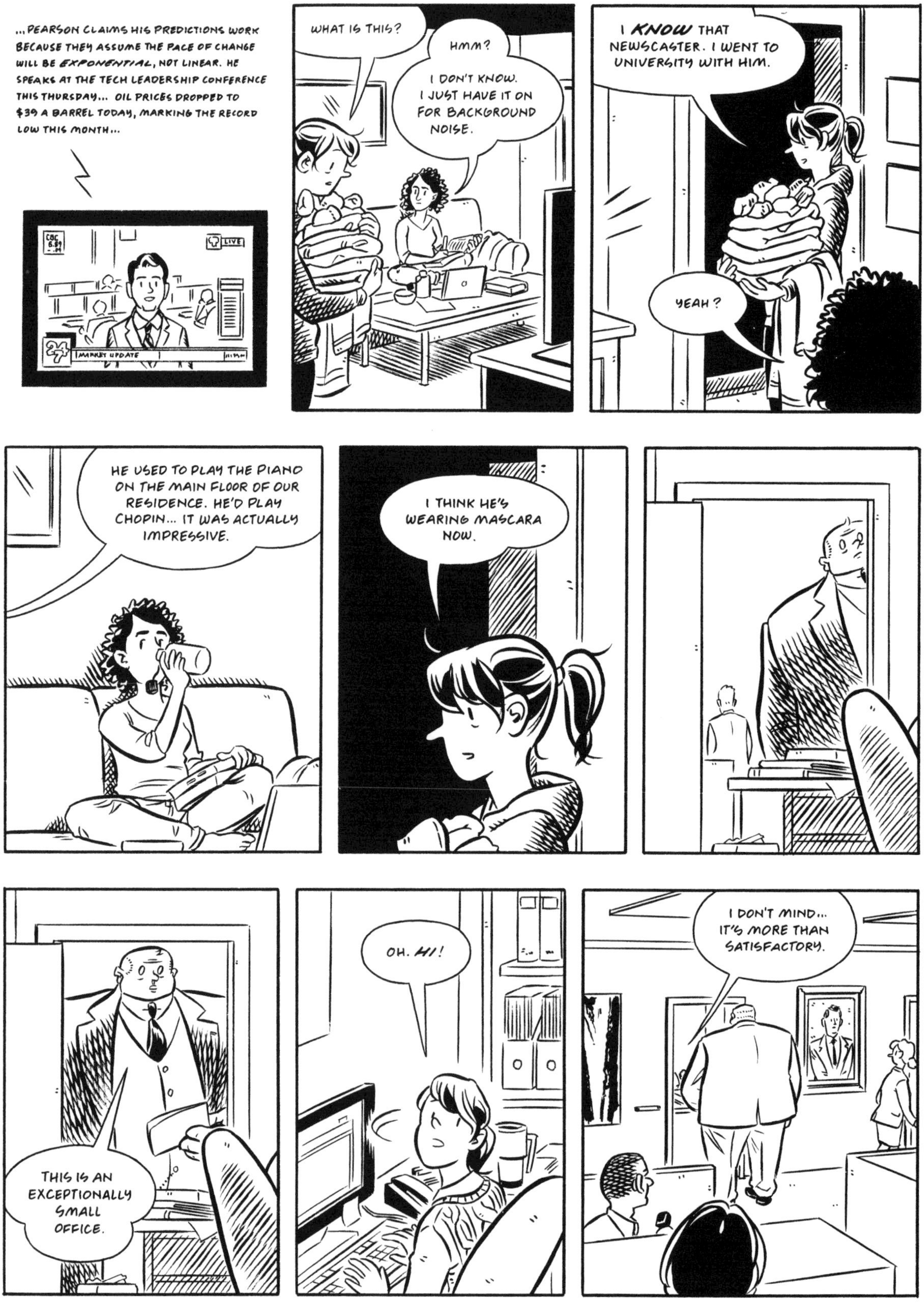
...PEARSON CLAIMS HIS PREDICTIONS WORK BECAUSE THEY ASSUME THE PACE OF CHANGE WILL BE EXPONENTIAL, NOT LINEAR. HE SPEAKS AT THE TECH LEADERSHIP CONFERENCE THIS THURSDAY... OIL PRICES DROPPED TO $39 A BARREL TODAY, MARKING THE RECORD LOW THIS MONTH...
WHAT IS THIS?
HMM?
I DON'T KNOW. I JUST HAVE IT ON FOR BACKGROUND NOISE.
I KNOW THAT NEWSCASTER. I WENT TO UNIVERSITY WITH HIM.
YEAH?
HE USED TO PLAY THE PIANO ON THE MAIN FLOOR OF OUR RESIDENCE. HE'D PLAY CHOPIN... IT WAS ACTUALLY IMPRESSIVE.
I THINK HE'S WEARING MASCARA NOW.
THIS IS AN EXCEPTIONALLY SMALL OFFICE.
OH. HI!
I DON'T MIND... IT'S MORE THAN SATISFACTORY.

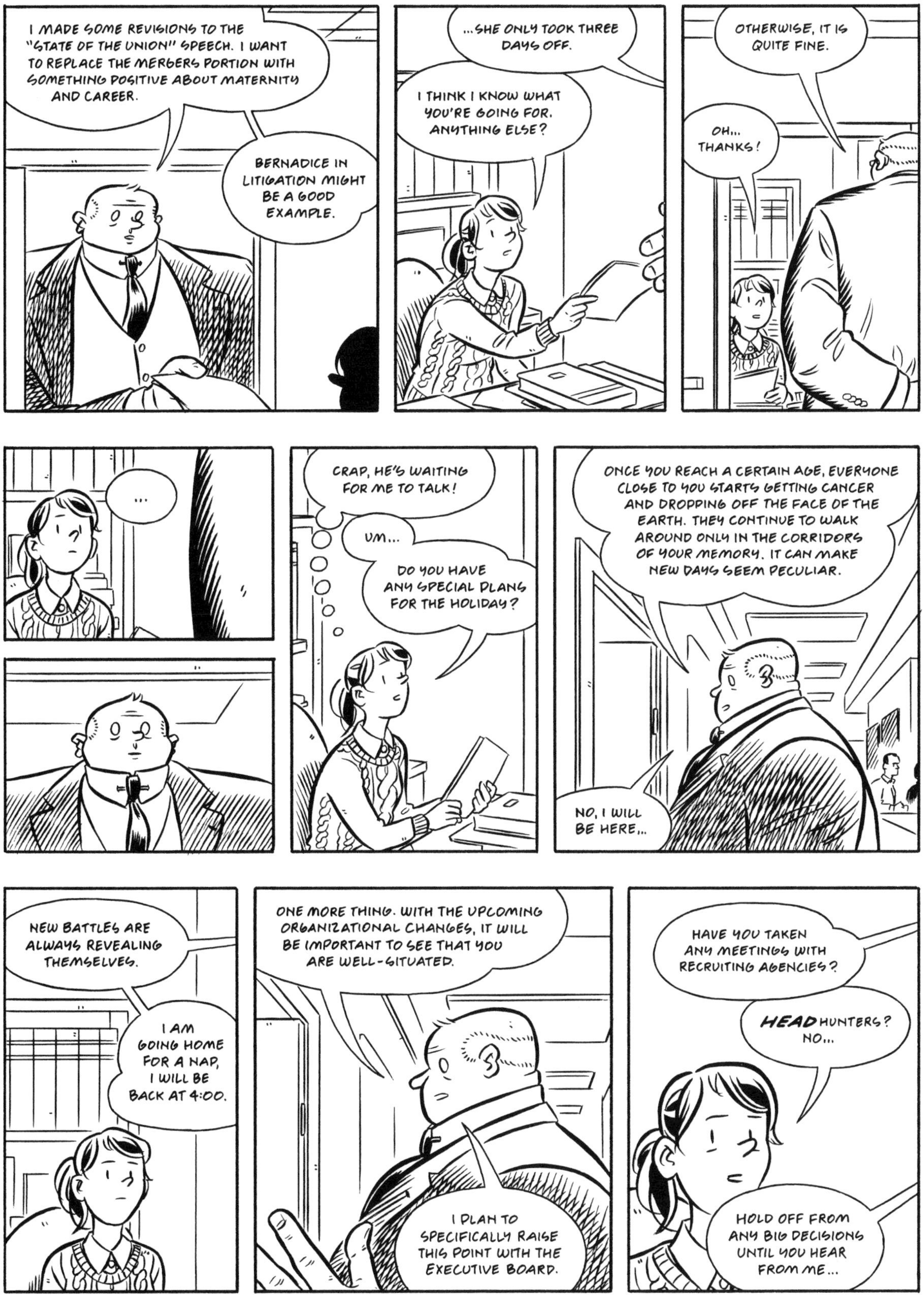
I MADE SOME REVISIONS TO THE "STATE OF THE UNION" SPEECH. I WANT TO REPLACE THE MERGERS PORTION WITH SOMETHING POSITIVE ABOUT MATERNITY AND CAREER.
BERNADICE IN LITIGATION MIGHT BE A GOOD EXAMPLE.
...SHE ONLY TOOK THREE DAYS OFF.
I THINK I KNOW WHAT YOU'RE GOING FOR. ANYTHING ELSE?
OTHERWISE, IT IS QUITE FINE.
OH... THANKS!
...
CRAP, HE'S WAITING FOR ME TO TALK!
UM...
DO YOU HAVE ANY SPECIAL PLANS FOR THE HOLIDAY?
ONCE YOU REACH A CERTAIN AGE, EVERYONE CLOSE TO YOU STARTS GETTING CANCER AND DROPPING OFF THE FACE OF THE EARTH. THEY CONTINUE TO WALK AROUND ONLY IN THE CORRIDORS OF YOUR MEMORY. IT CAN MAKE NEW DAYS SEEM PECULIAR.
NO, I WILL BE HERE...
NEW BATTLES ARE ALWAYS REVEALING THEMSELVES.
I AM GOING HOME FOR A NAP, I WILL BE BACK AT 4:00.
ONE MORE THING. WITH THE UPCOMING ORGANIZATIONAL CHANGES, IT WILL BE IMPORTANT TO SEE THAT YOU ARE WELL-SITUATED.
I PLAN TO SPECIFICALLY RAISE THIS POINT WITH THE EXECUTIVE BOARD.
HAVE YOU TAKEN ANY MEETINGS WITH RECRUITING AGENCIES?
HEAD HUNTERS? NO...
HOLD OFF FROM ANY BIG DECISIONS UNTIL YOU HEAR FROM ME...

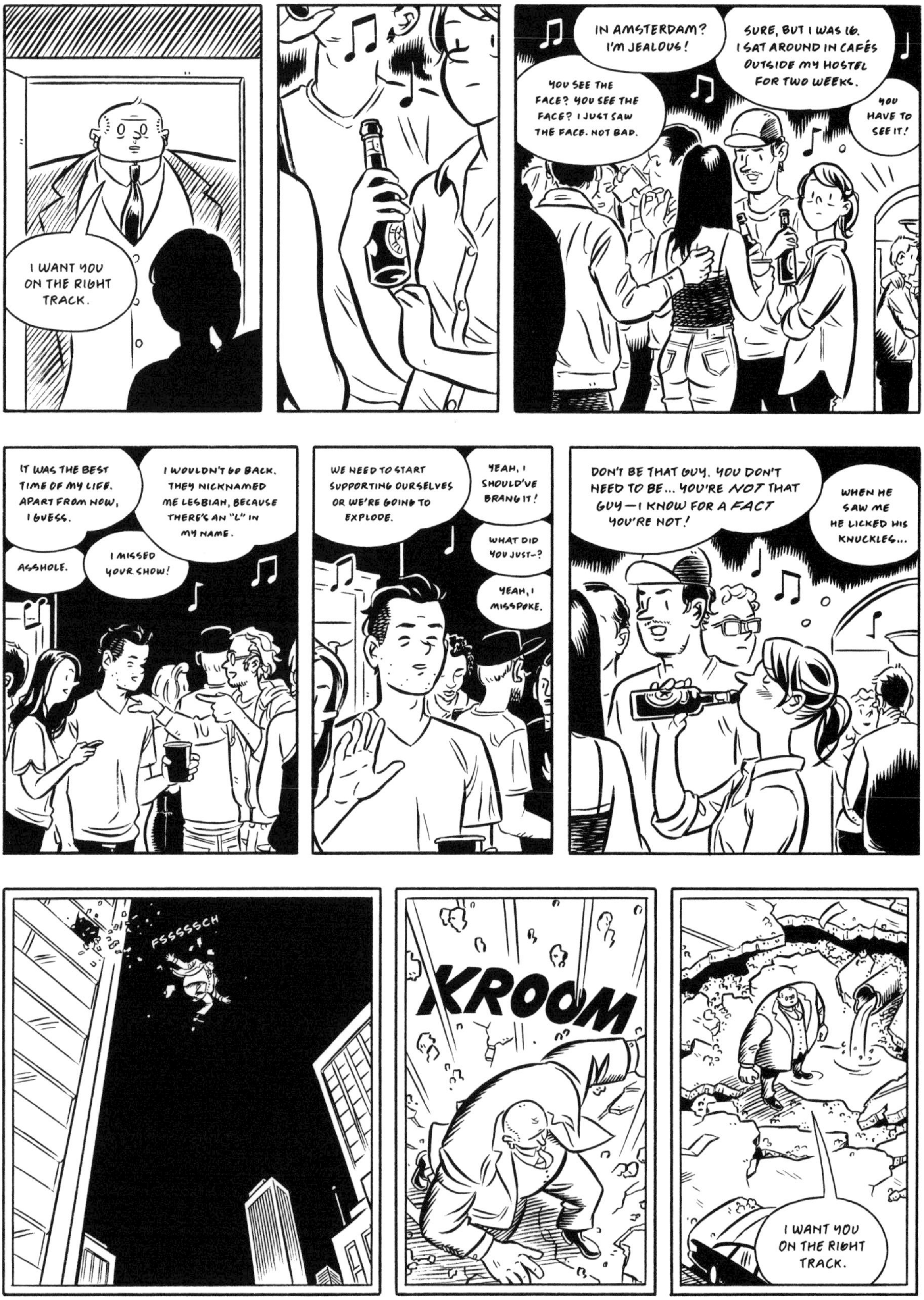
I WANT YOU ON THE RIGHT TRACK.
IN AMSTERDAM? I'M JEALOUS!
SURE, BUT I WAS 16. I SAT AROUND IN CAFÉS OUTSIDE MY HOSTEL FOR TWO WEEKS.
YOU SEE THE FACE? YOU SEE THE FACE? I JUST SAW THE FACE. NOT BAD.
YOU HAVE TO SEE IT!
IT WAS THE BEST TIME OF MY LIFE. APART FROM NOW, I GUESS.
I WOULDN'T GO BACK. THEY NICKNAMED ME LESBIAN, BECAUSE THERE'S AN "L" IN MY NAME.
ASSHOLE.
I MISSED YOUR SHOW!
WE NEED TO START SUPPORTING OURSELVES OR WE'RE GOING TO EXPLODE.
YEAH, I SHOULD'VE BRANG IT!
WHAT DID YOU JUST-?
YEAH, I MISSPOKE.
DON'T BE THAT GUY. YOU DON'T NEED TO BE... YOU'RE NOT THAT GUY—I KNOW FOR A FACT YOU'RE NOT!
WHEN HE SAW ME HE LICKED HIS KNUCKLES...
FSSSSSCH
KROOM
I WANT YOU ON THE RIGHT TRACK.

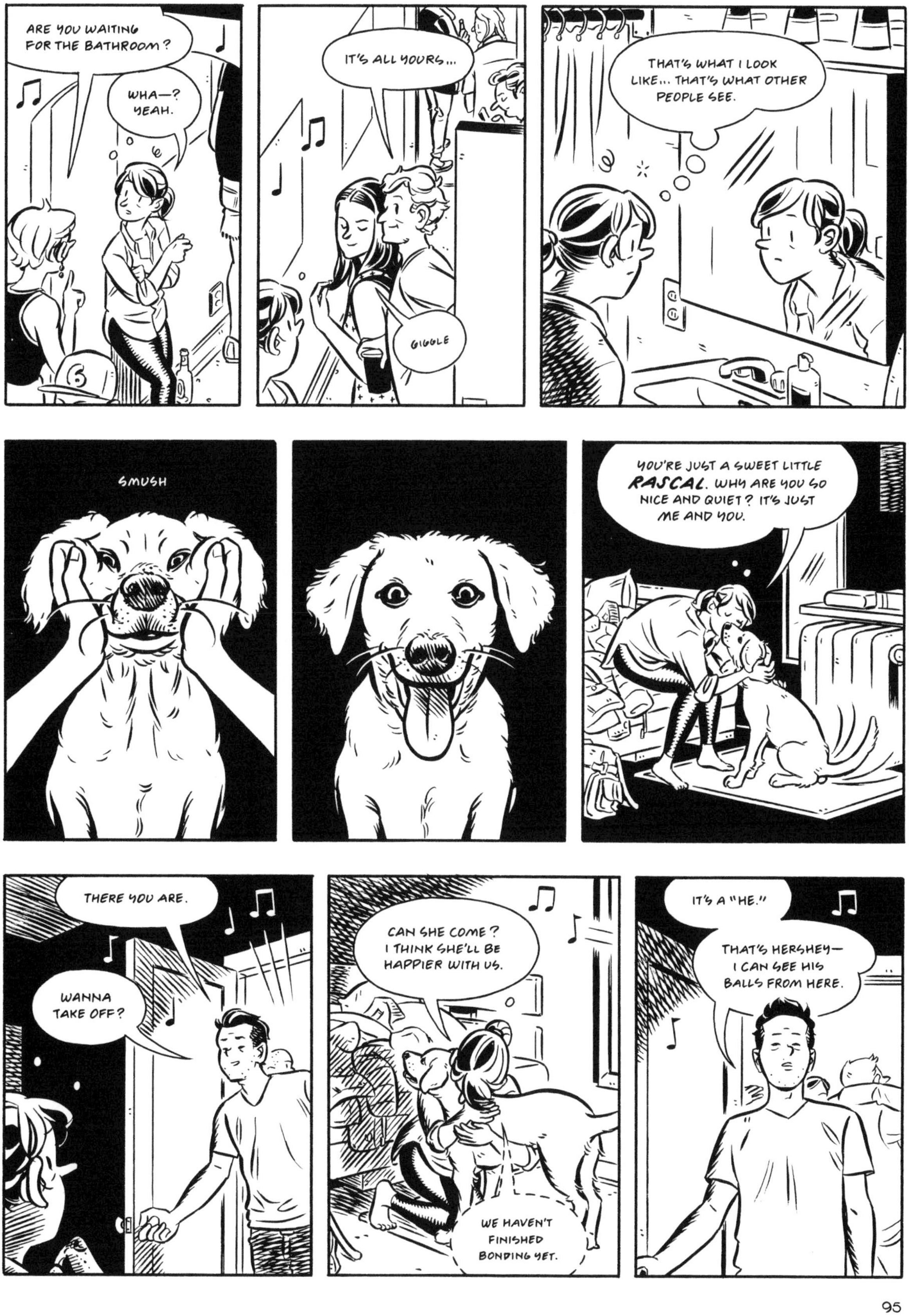
ARE YOU WAITING FOR THE BATHROOM?
WHA—? YEAH.
IT'S ALL YOURS...
GIGGLE
THAT'S WHAT I LOOK LIKE... THAT'S WHAT OTHER PEOPLE SEE.
SMUSH
YOU'RE JUST A SWEET LITTLE RASCAL. WHY ARE YOU SO NICE AND QUIET? IT'S JUST ME AND YOU.
THERE YOU ARE.
WANNA TAKE OFF?
CAN SHE COME? I THINK SHE'LL BE HAPPIER WITH US.
WE HAVEN'T FINISHED BONDING YET.
IT'S A "HE."
THAT'S HERSHEY— I CAN SEE HIS BALLS FROM HERE.

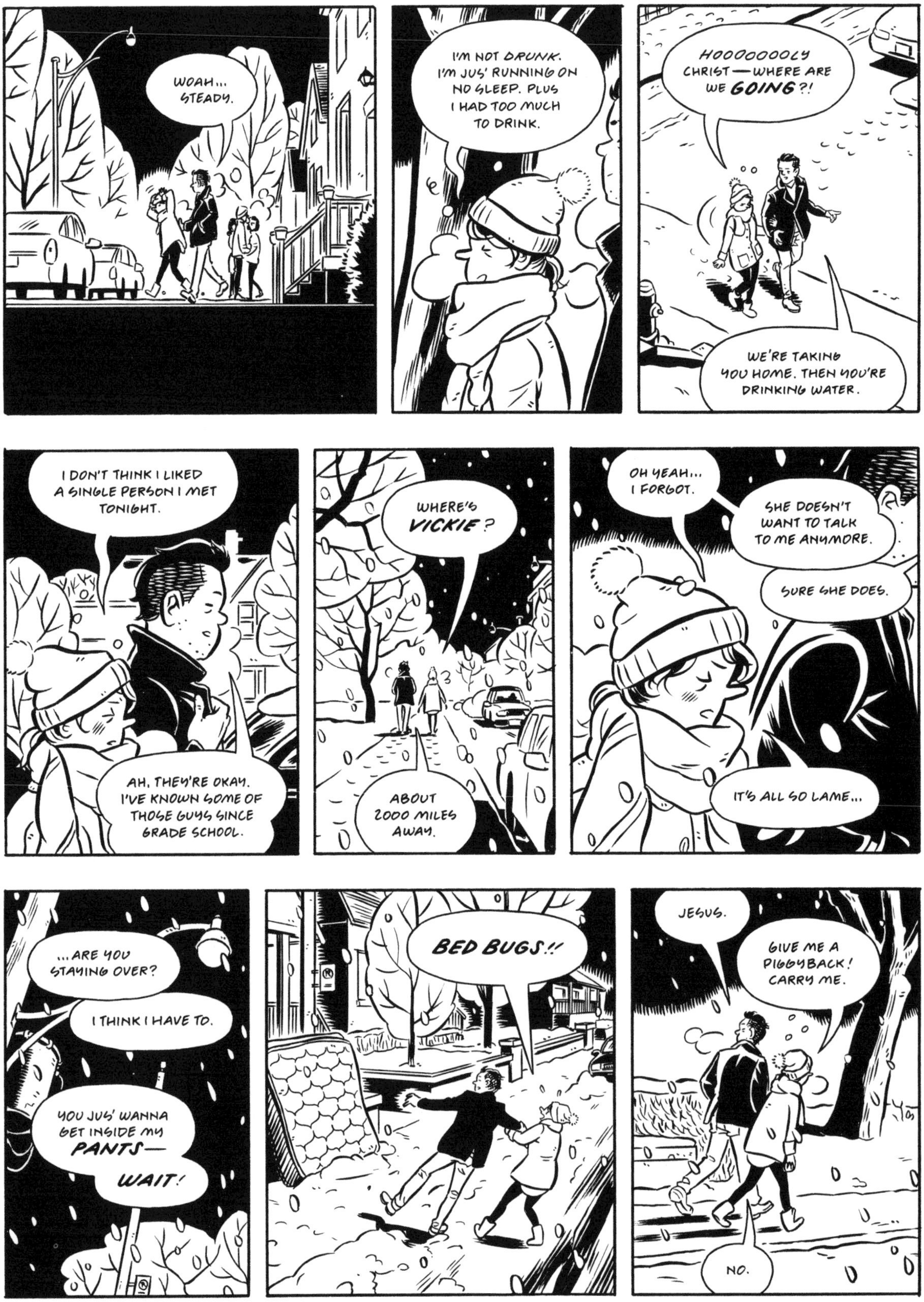
WOAH... STEADY.
I'M NOT DRUNK. I'M JUS' RUNNING ON NO SLEEP. PLUS I HAD TOO MUCH TO DRINK.
HOOOOOOOLY CHRIST — WHERE ARE WE GOING?!
WE'RE TAKING YOU HOME. THEN YOU'RE DRINKING WATER.
I DON'T THINK I LIKED A SINGLE PERSON I MET TONIGHT.
AH, THEY'RE OKAY. I'VE KNOWN SOME OF THOSE GUYS SINCE GRADE SCHOOL.
WHERE'S VICKIE?
ABOUT 2000 MILES AWAY.
OH YEAH... I FORGOT.
SHE DOESN'T WANT TO TALK TO ME ANYMORE.
SURE SHE DOES.
IT'S ALL SO LAME...
...ARE YOU STAYING OVER?
I THINK I HAVE TO.
YOU JUS' WANNA GET INSIDE MY PANTS—
WAIT!
BED BUGS!!
JESUS.
GIVE ME A PIGGYBACK! CARRY ME.
NO.

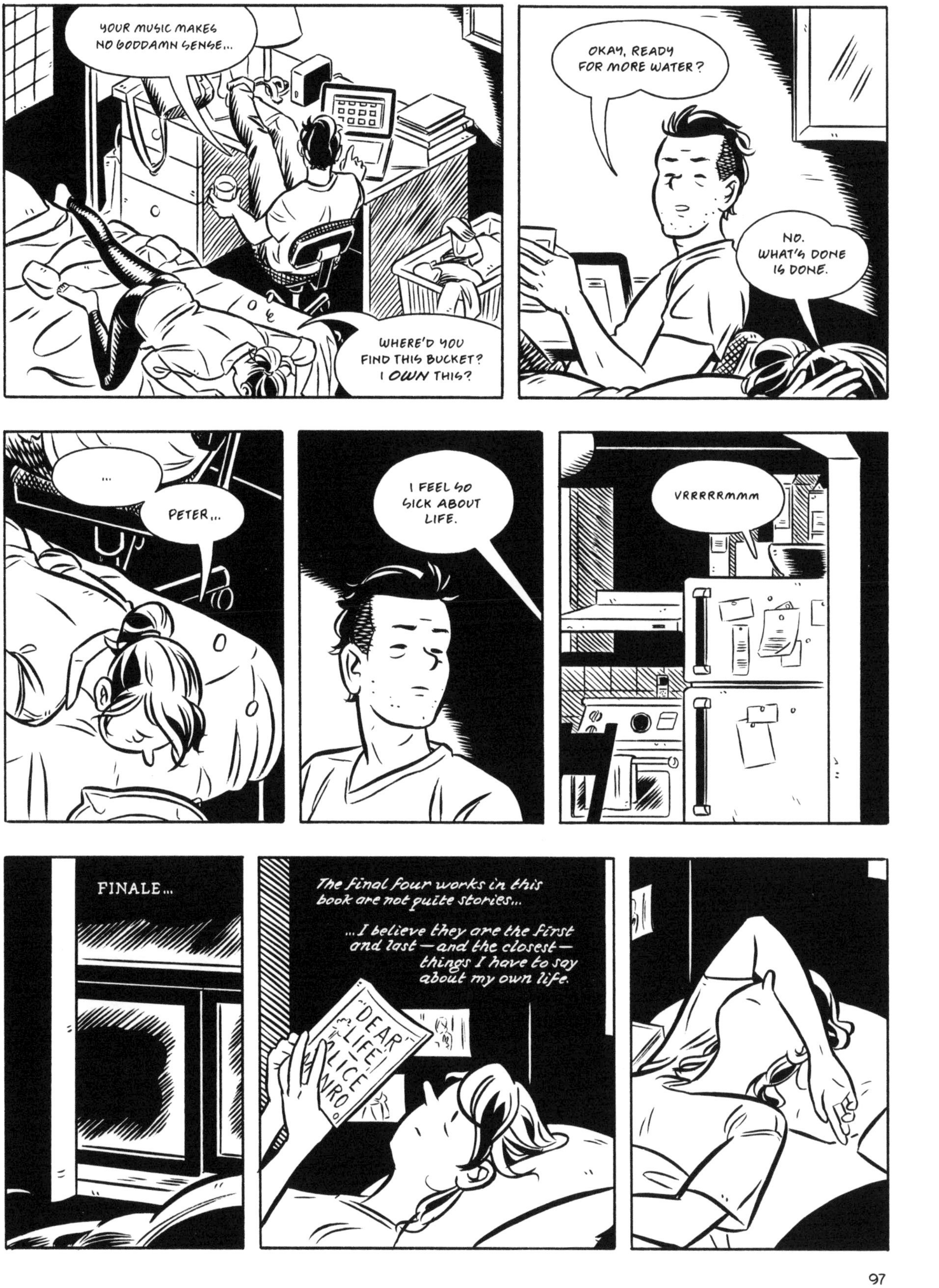
YOUR MUSIC MAKES NO GODDAMN SENSE...
WHERE'D YOU FIND THIS BUCKET? I OWN THIS?
OKAY, READY FOR MORE WATER?
NO. WHAT'S DONE IS DONE.
...
PETER...
I FEEL SO SICK ABOUT LIFE.
VRRRRRMMM
FINALE...
The final four works in this book are not quite stories...
...I believe they are the first and last—and the closest—things I have to say about my own life.
"DEAR LIFE" ALICE MUNRO

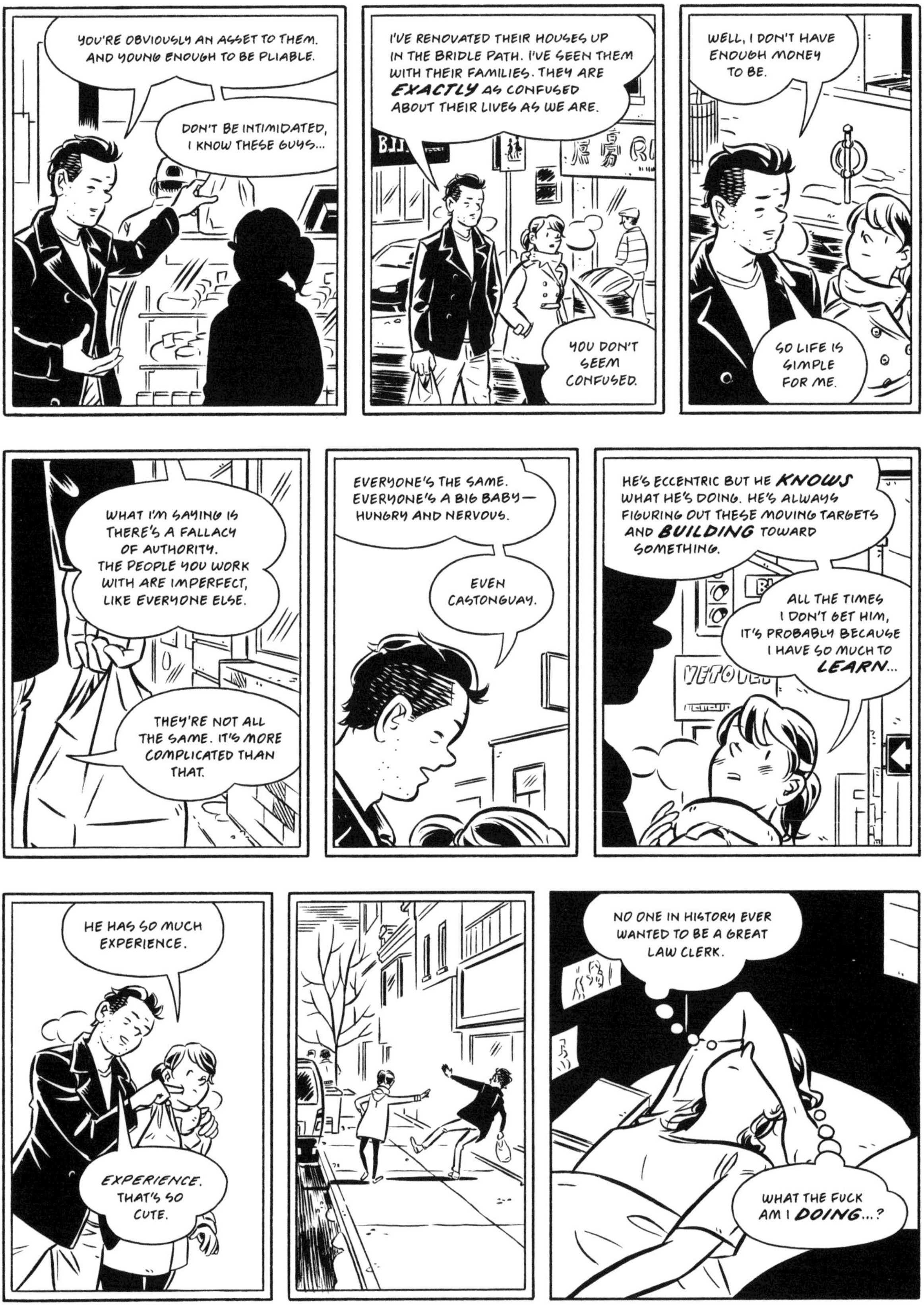
YOU'RE OBVIOUSLY AN ASSET TO THEM. AND YOUNG ENOUGH TO BE PLIABLE.
DON'T BE INTIMIDATED, I KNOW THESE GUYS...
I'VE RENOVATED THEIR HOUSES UP IN THE BRIDLE PATH. I'VE SEEN THEM WITH THEIR FAMILIES. THEY ARE EXACTLY AS CONFUSED ABOUT THEIR LIVES AS WE ARE.
YOU DON'T SEEM CONFUSED.
WELL, I DON'T HAVE ENOUGH MONEY TO BE.
SO LIFE IS SIMPLE FOR ME.
WHAT I'M SAYING IS THERE'S A FALLACY OF AUTHORITY. THE PEOPLE YOU WORK WITH ARE IMPERFECT, LIKE EVERYONE ELSE.
THEY'RE NOT ALL THE SAME. IT'S MORE COMPLICATED THAN THAT.
EVERYONE'S THE SAME. EVERYONE'S A BIG BABY— HUNGRY AND NERVOUS.
EVEN CASTONGUAY.
HE'S ECCENTRIC BUT HE KNOWS WHAT HE'S DOING. HE'S ALWAYS FIGURING OUT THESE MOVING TARGETS AND BUILDING TOWARD SOMETHING.
ALL THE TIMES I DON'T GET HIM, IT'S PROBABLY BECAUSE I HAVE SO MUCH TO LEARN...
HE HAS SO MUCH EXPERIENCE.
EXPERIENCE. THAT'S SO CUTE.
NO ONE IN HISTORY EVER WANTED TO BE A GREAT LAW CLERK.
WHAT THE FUCK AM I DOING...?

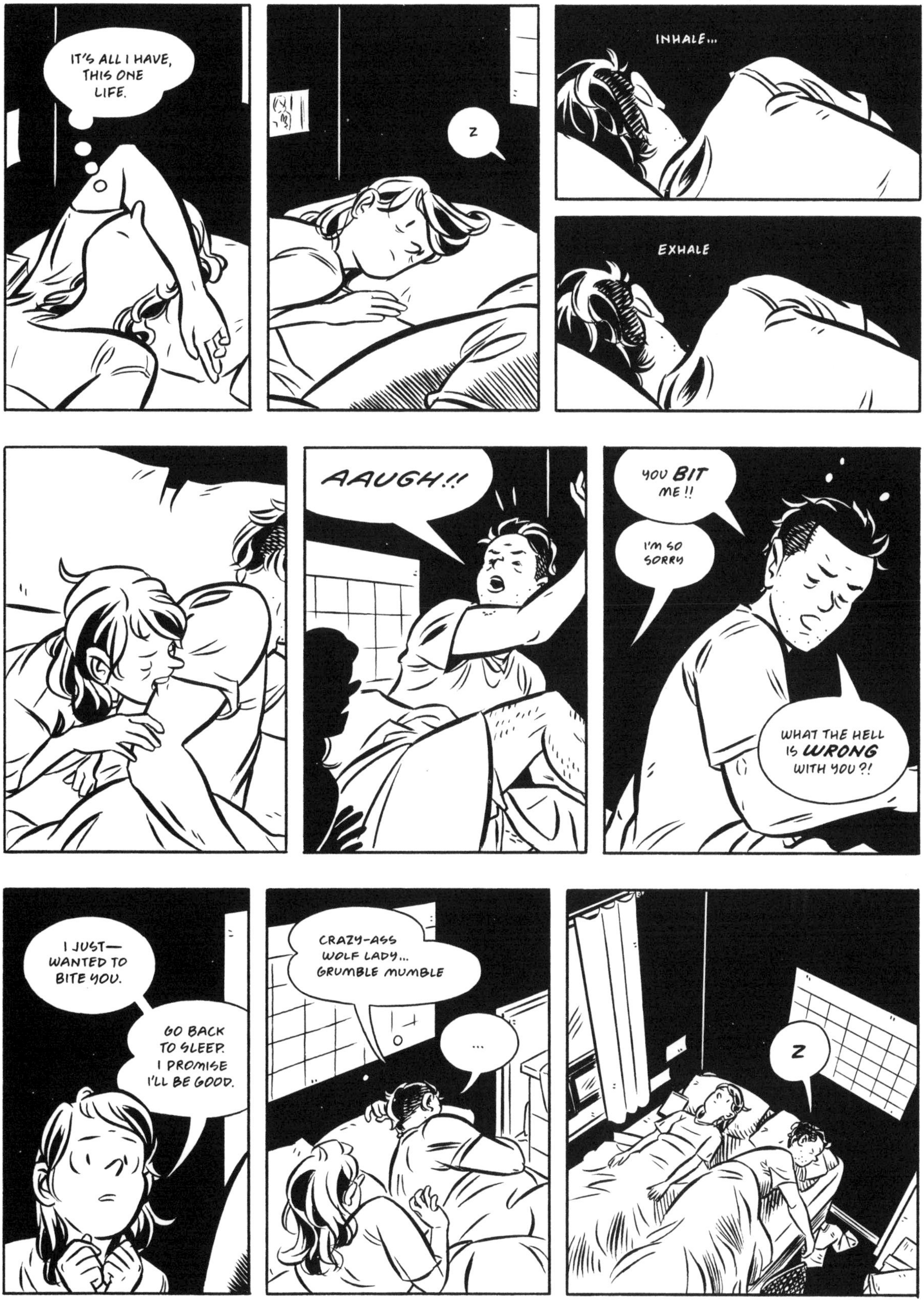
IT'S ALL I HAVE, THIS ONE LIFE.
Z
INHALE...
EXHALE
AAUGH!!
YOU BIT ME!!
I'M SO SORRY
WHAT THE HELL IS WRONG WITH YOU?!
I JUST— WANTED TO BITE YOU.
GO BACK TO SLEEP. I PROMISE I'LL BE GOOD.
CRAZY-ASS WOLF LADY... GRUMBLE MUMBLE
...
Z

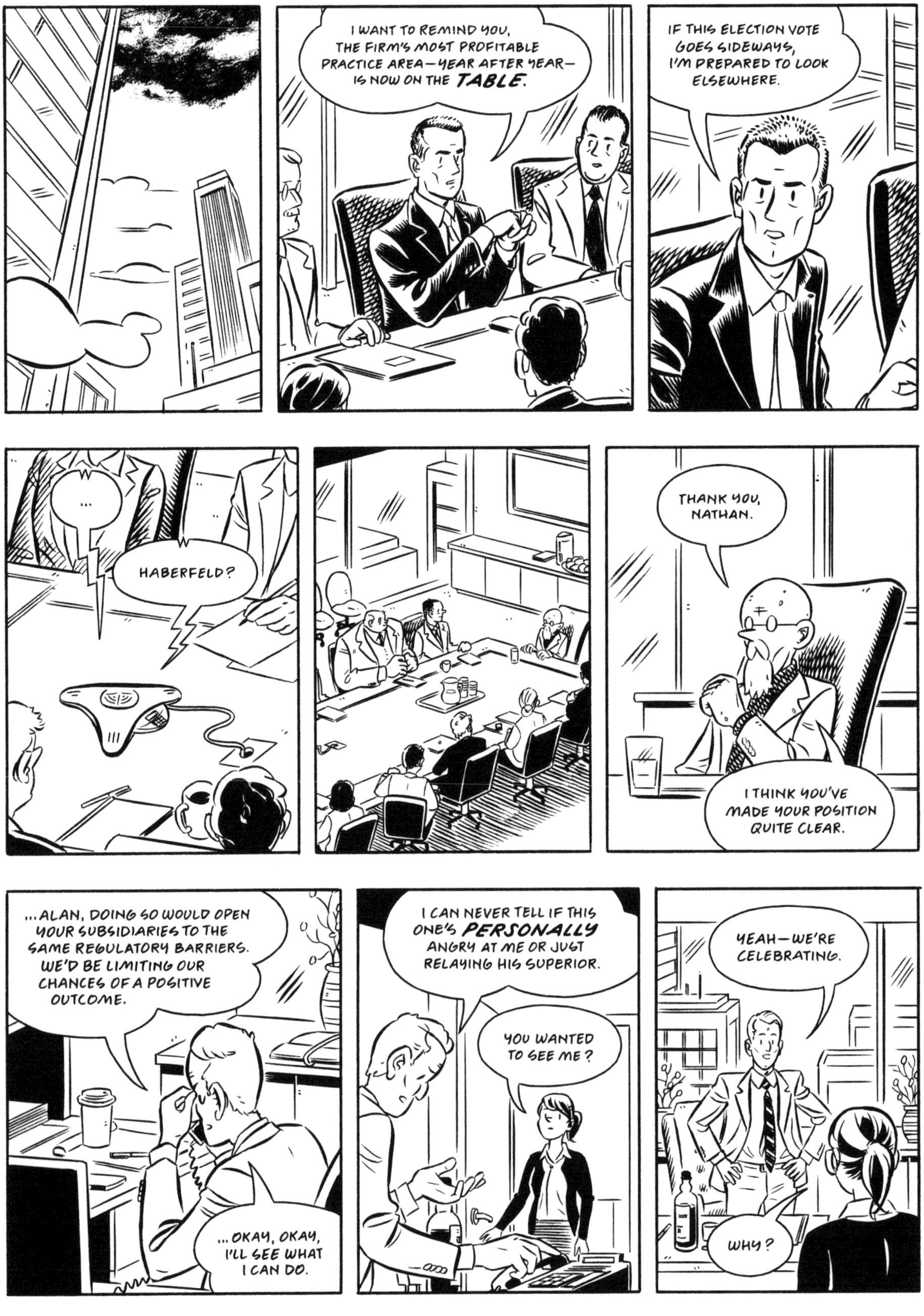
I WANT TO REMIND YOU, THE FIRM'S MOST PROFITABLE PRACTICE AREA—YEAR AFTER YEAR—IS NOW ON THE TABLE.
IF THIS ELECTION VOTE GOES SIDEWAYS, I'M PREPARED TO LOOK ELSEWHERE.
...
HABERFELD?
THANK YOU, NATHAN.
I THINK YOU'VE MADE YOUR POSITION QUITE CLEAR.
...ALAN, DOING SO WOULD OPEN YOUR SUBSIDIARIES TO THE SAME REGULATORY BARRIERS. WE'D BE LIMITING OUR CHANCES OF A POSITIVE OUTCOME.
...OKAY, OKAY, I'LL SEE WHAT I CAN DO.
I CAN NEVER TELL IF THIS ONE'S PERSONALLY ANGRY AT ME OR JUST RELAYING HIS SUPERIOR.
YOU WANTED TO SEE ME?
YEAH—WE'RE CELEBRATING.
WHY?

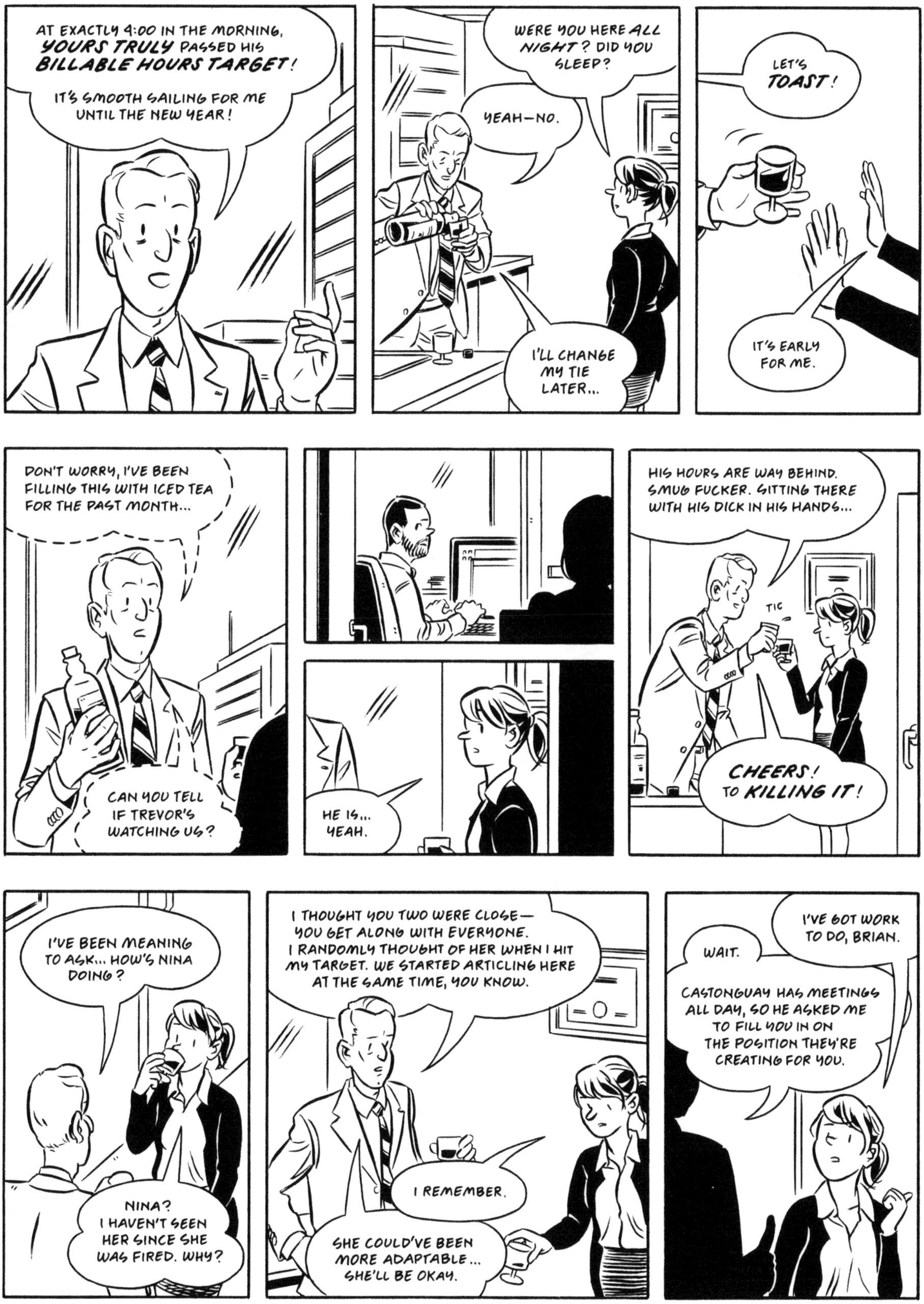

AT EXACTLY 4:00 IN THE MORNING, YOURS TRULY PASSED HIS BILLABLE HOURS TARGET!
IT'S SMOOTH SAILING FOR ME UNTIL THE NEW YEAR!
WERE YOU HERE ALL NIGHT? DID YOU SLEEP?
YEAH—NO.
I'LL CHANGE MY TIE LATER...
LET'S TOAST!
IT'S EARLY FOR ME.
DON'T WORRY, I'VE BEEN FILLING THIS WITH ICED TEA FOR THE PAST MONTH...
CAN YOU TELL IF TREVOR'S WATCHING US?
HE IS... YEAH.
HIS HOURS ARE WAY BEHIND. SMUG FUCKER. SITTING THERE WITH HIS DICK IN HIS HANDS...
TIC
CHEERS! TO KILLING IT!
I'VE BEEN MEANING TO ASK... HOW'S NINA DOING?
NINA? I HAVEN'T SEEN HER SINCE SHE WAS FIRED. WHY?
I THOUGHT YOU TWO WERE CLOSE— YOU GET ALONG WITH EVERYONE. I RANDOMLY THOUGHT OF HER WHEN I HIT MY TARGET. WE STARTED ARTICLING HERE AT THE SAME TIME, YOU KNOW.
I REMEMBER.
SHE COULD'VE BEEN MORE ADAPTABLE... SHE'LL BE OKAY.
I'VE GOT WORK TO DO, BRIAN.
WAIT.
CASTONGUAY HAS MEETINGS ALL DAY, SO HE ASKED ME TO FILL YOU IN ON THE POSITION THEY'RE CREATING FOR YOU.

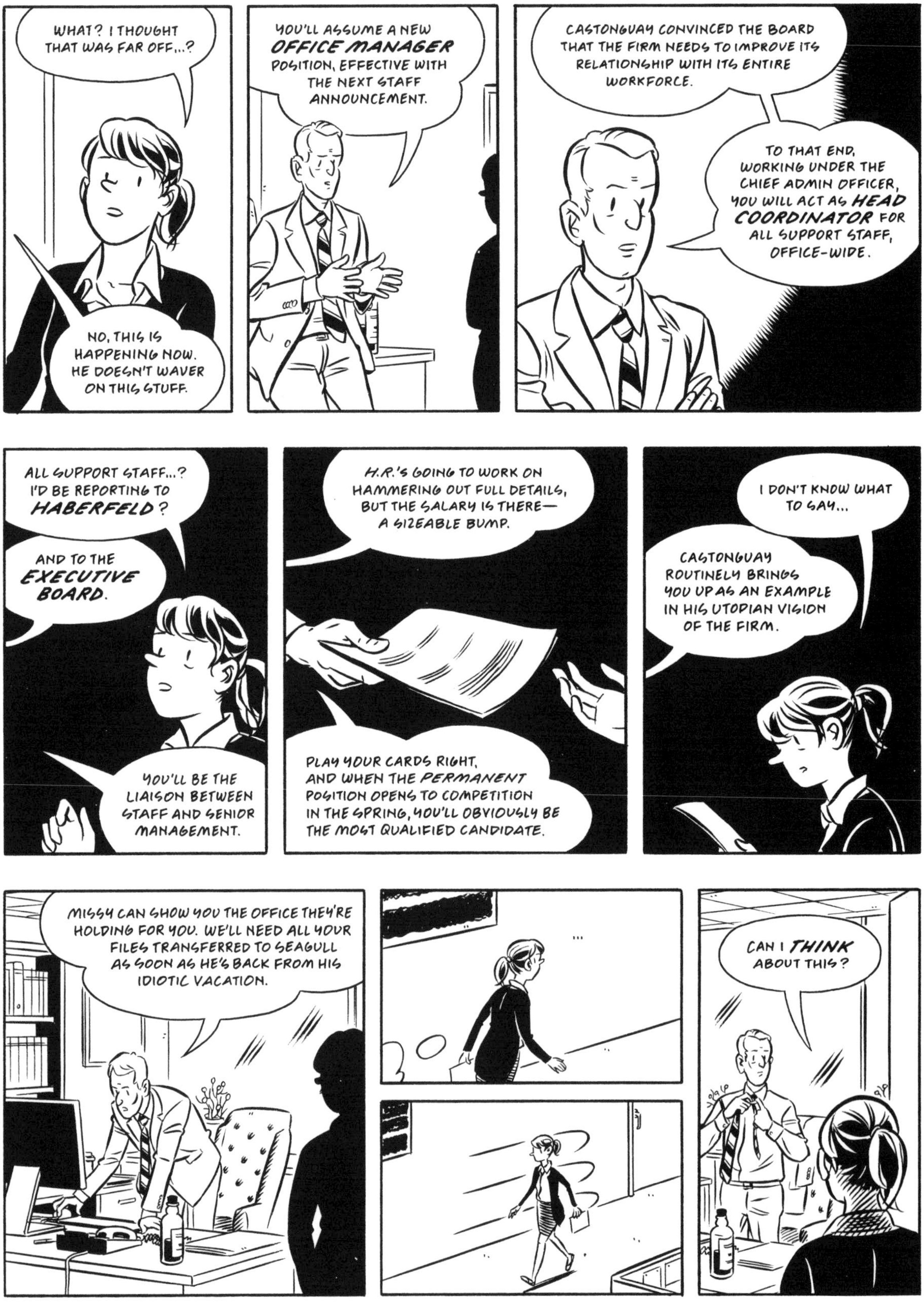
WHAT? I THOUGHT THAT WAS FAR OFF...?
NO, THIS IS HAPPENING NOW. HE DOESN'T WAVER ON THIS STUFF.
YOU'LL ASSUME A NEW OFFICE MANAGER POSITION, EFFECTIVE WITH THE NEXT STAFF ANNOUNCEMENT.
CASTONGUAY CONVINCED THE BOARD THAT THE FIRM NEEDS TO IMPROVE ITS RELATIONSHIP WITH ITS ENTIRE WORKFORCE.
TO THAT END, WORKING UNDER THE CHIEF ADMIN OFFICER, YOU WILL ACT AS HEAD COORDINATOR FOR ALL SUPPORT STAFF, OFFICE-WIDE.
ALL SUPPORT STAFF...? I'D BE REPORTING TO HABERFELD?
AND TO THE EXECUTIVE BOARD.
YOU'LL BE THE LIAISON BETWEEN STAFF AND SENIOR MANAGEMENT.
H.R.'S GOING TO WORK ON HAMMERING OUT FULL DETAILS, BUT THE SALARY IS THERE— A SIZEABLE BUMP.
PLAY YOUR CARDS RIGHT, AND WHEN THE PERMANENT POSITION OPENS TO COMPETITION IN THE SPRING, YOU'LL OBVIOUSLY BE THE MOST QUALIFIED CANDIDATE.
I DON'T KNOW WHAT TO SAY...
CASTONGUAY ROUTINELY BRINGS YOU UP AS AN EXAMPLE IN HIS UTOPIAN VISION OF THE FIRM.
MISSY CAN SHOW YOU THE OFFICE THEY'RE HOLDING FOR YOU. WE'LL NEED ALL YOUR FILES TRANSFERRED TO SEAGULL AS SOON AS HE'S BACK FROM HIS IDIOTIC VACATION.
...
CAN I THINK ABOUT THIS?

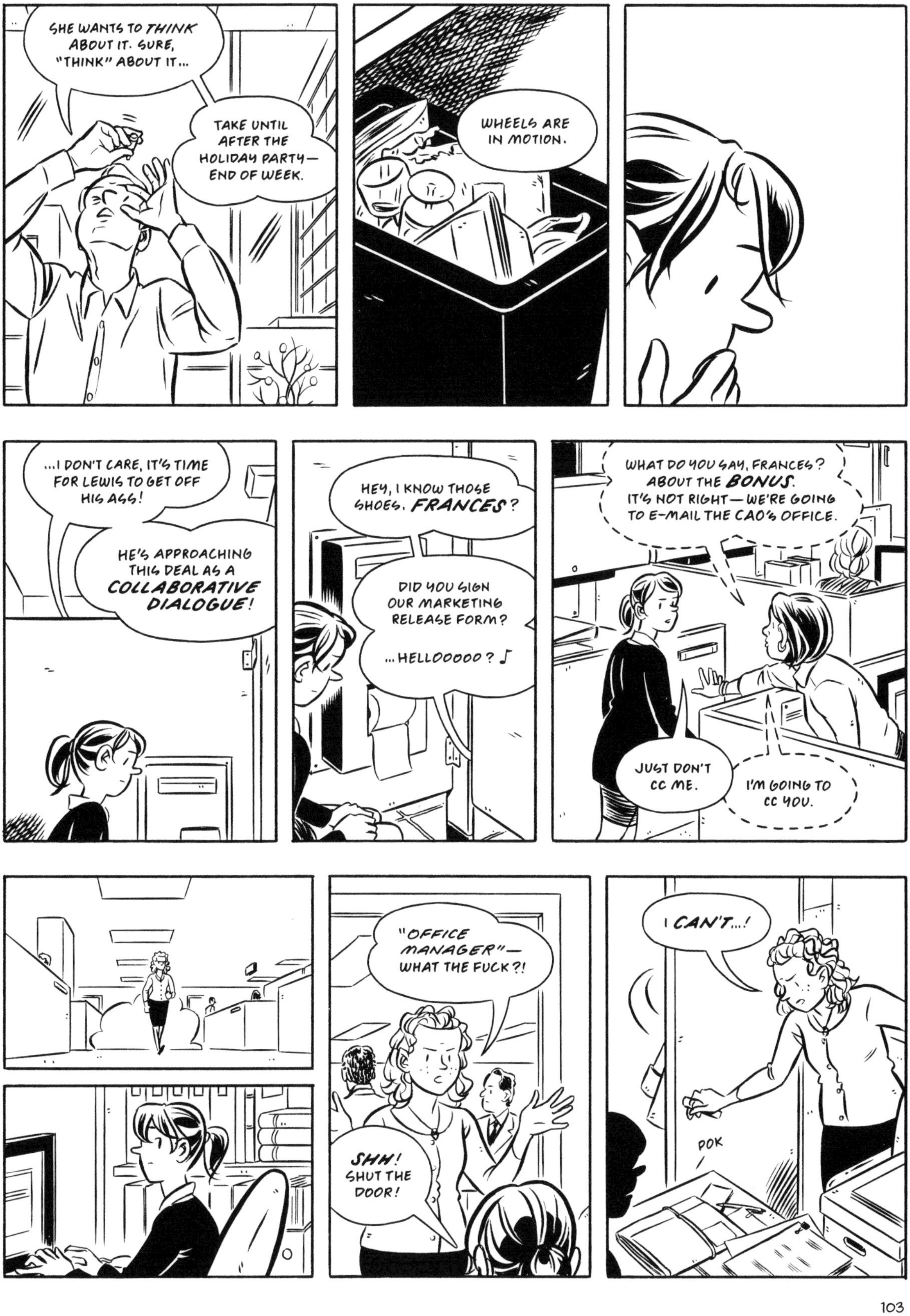

SHE WANTS TO *THINK* ABOUT IT. SURE, "THINK" ABOUT IT...
TAKE UNTIL AFTER THE HOLIDAY PARTY— END OF WEEK.
WHEELS ARE IN MOTION.
...I DON'T CARE, IT'S TIME FOR LEWIS TO GET OFF HIS ASS!
HE'S APPROACHING THIS DEAL AS A ***COLLABORATIVE DIALOGUE***!
HEY, I KNOW THOSE SHOES. ***FRANCES***?
DID YOU SIGN OUR MARKETING RELEASE FORM?
...HELLOOOOO? ♪
WHAT DO YOU SAY, FRANCES? ABOUT THE ***BONUS***. IT'S NOT RIGHT— WE'RE GOING TO E-MAIL THE CAO'S OFFICE.
JUST DON'T CC ME.
I'M GOING TO CC YOU.
"*OFFICE MANAGER*"— WHAT THE FUCK?!
SHH! SHUT THE DOOR!
I ***CAN'T***...!
POK

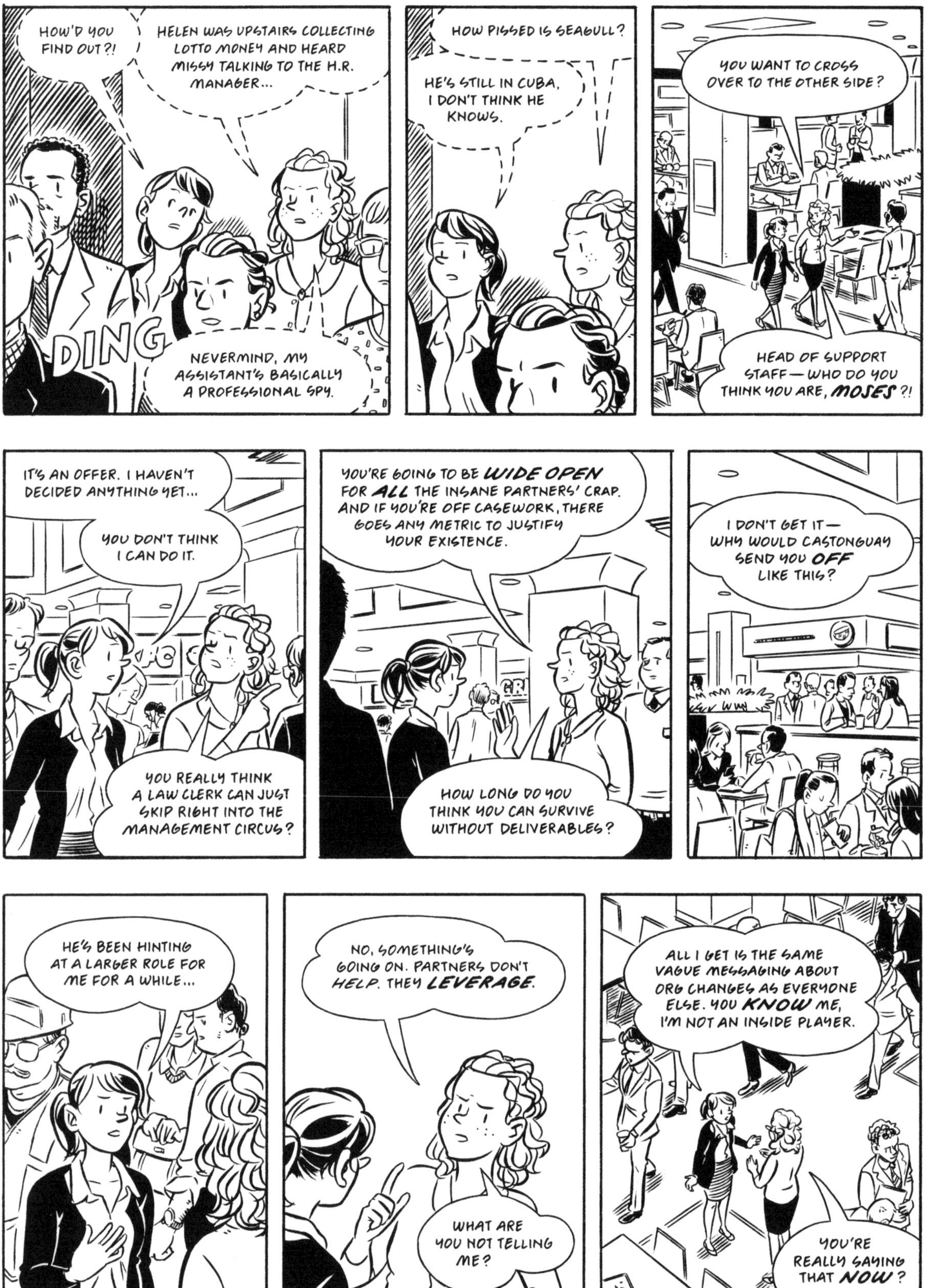
HOW'D YOU FIND OUT?!
HELEN WAS UPSTAIRS COLLECTING LOTTO MONEY AND HEARD MISSY TALKING TO THE H.R. MANAGER...
DING
NEVERMIND, MY ASSISTANT'S BASICALLY A PROFESSIONAL SPY.
HOW PISSED IS SEAGULL?
HE'S STILL IN CUBA, I DON'T THINK HE KNOWS.
YOU WANT TO CROSS OVER TO THE OTHER SIDE?
HEAD OF SUPPORT STAFF — WHO DO YOU THINK YOU ARE, MOSES?!
IT'S AN OFFER. I HAVEN'T DECIDED ANYTHING YET...
YOU DON'T THINK I CAN DO IT.
YOU REALLY THINK A LAW CLERK CAN JUST SKIP RIGHT INTO THE MANAGEMENT CIRCUS?
YOU'RE GOING TO BE WIDE OPEN FOR ALL THE INSANE PARTNERS' CRAP. AND IF YOU'RE OFF CASEWORK, THERE GOES ANY METRIC TO JUSTIFY YOUR EXISTENCE.
HOW LONG DO YOU THINK YOU CAN SURVIVE WITHOUT DELIVERABLES?
I DON'T GET IT — WHY WOULD CASTONGUAY SEND YOU OFF LIKE THIS?
HE'S BEEN HINTING AT A LARGER ROLE FOR ME FOR A WHILE...
NO, SOMETHING'S GOING ON. PARTNERS DON'T HELP. THEY LEVERAGE.
WHAT ARE YOU NOT TELLING ME?
ALL I GET IS THE SAME VAGUE MESSAGING ABOUT ORG CHANGES AS EVERYONE ELSE. YOU KNOW ME, I'M NOT AN INSIDE PLAYER.
YOU'RE REALLY SAYING THAT NOW?

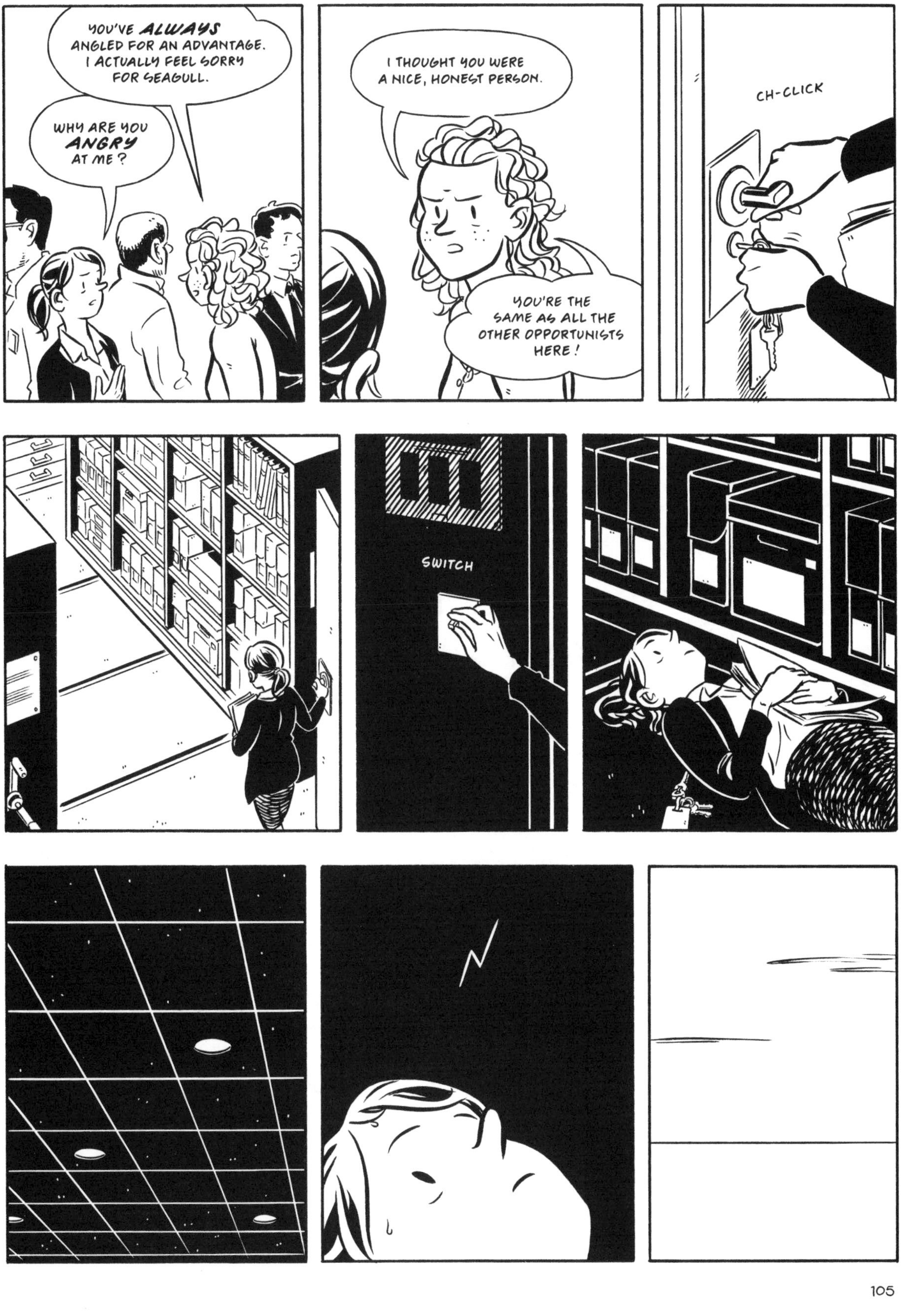
YOU'VE ALWAYS ANGLED FOR AN ADVANTAGE. I ACTUALLY FEEL SORRY FOR SEAGULL.
WHY ARE YOU ANGRY AT ME?
I THOUGHT YOU WERE A NICE, HONEST PERSON.
YOU'RE THE SAME AS ALL THE OTHER OPPORTUNISTS HERE!
CH-CLICK
SWITCH

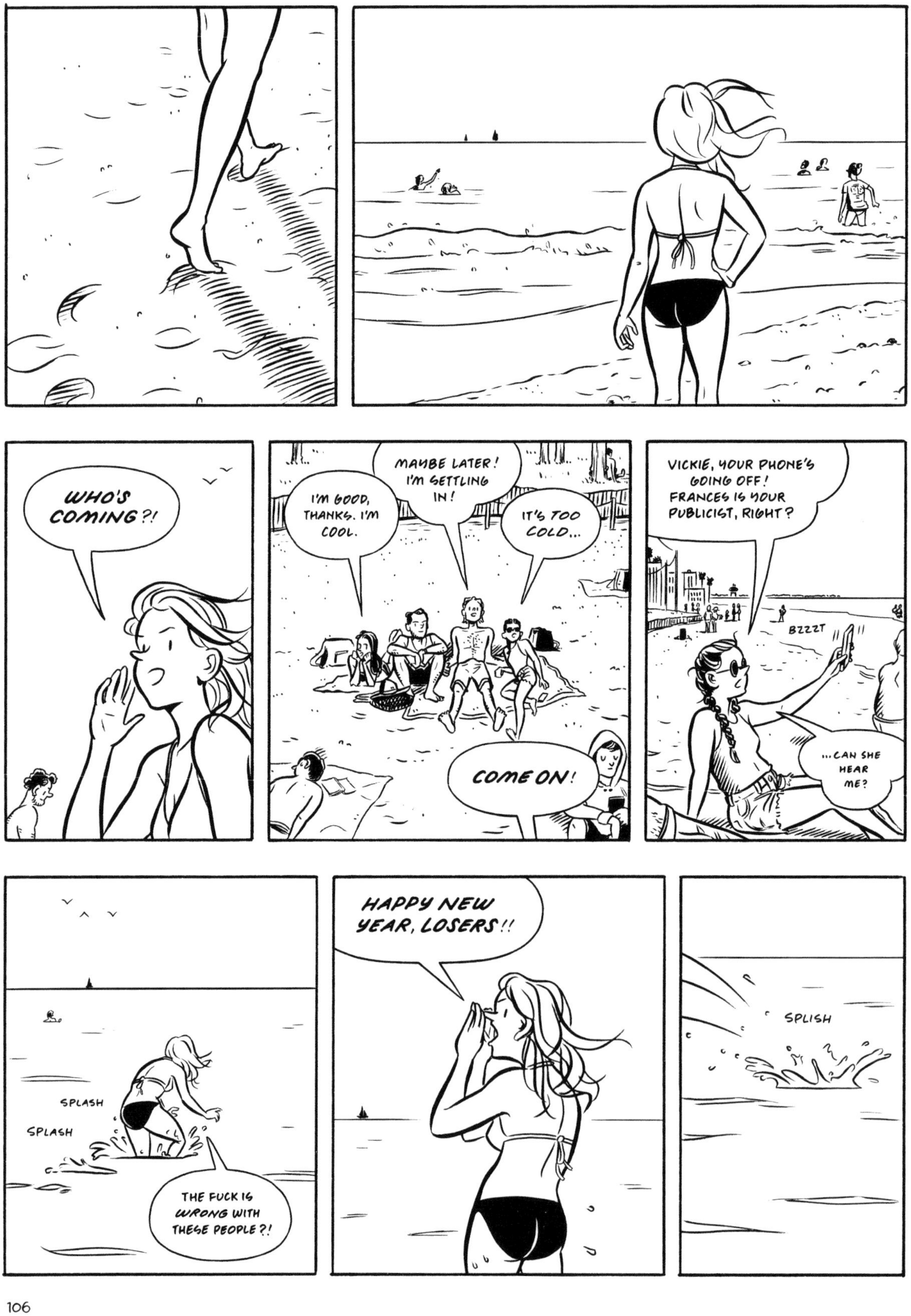
WHO'S COMING?!
I'M GOOD, THANKS. I'M COOL.
MAYBE LATER! I'M SETTLING IN!
IT'S TOO COLD...
COME ON!
VICKIE, YOUR PHONE'S GOING OFF! FRANCES IS YOUR PUBLICIST, RIGHT?
BZZZT
...CAN SHE HEAR ME?
SPLASH
SPLASH
THE FUCK IS WRONG WITH THESE PEOPLE?!
HAPPY NEW YEAR, LOSERS!!
SPLISH

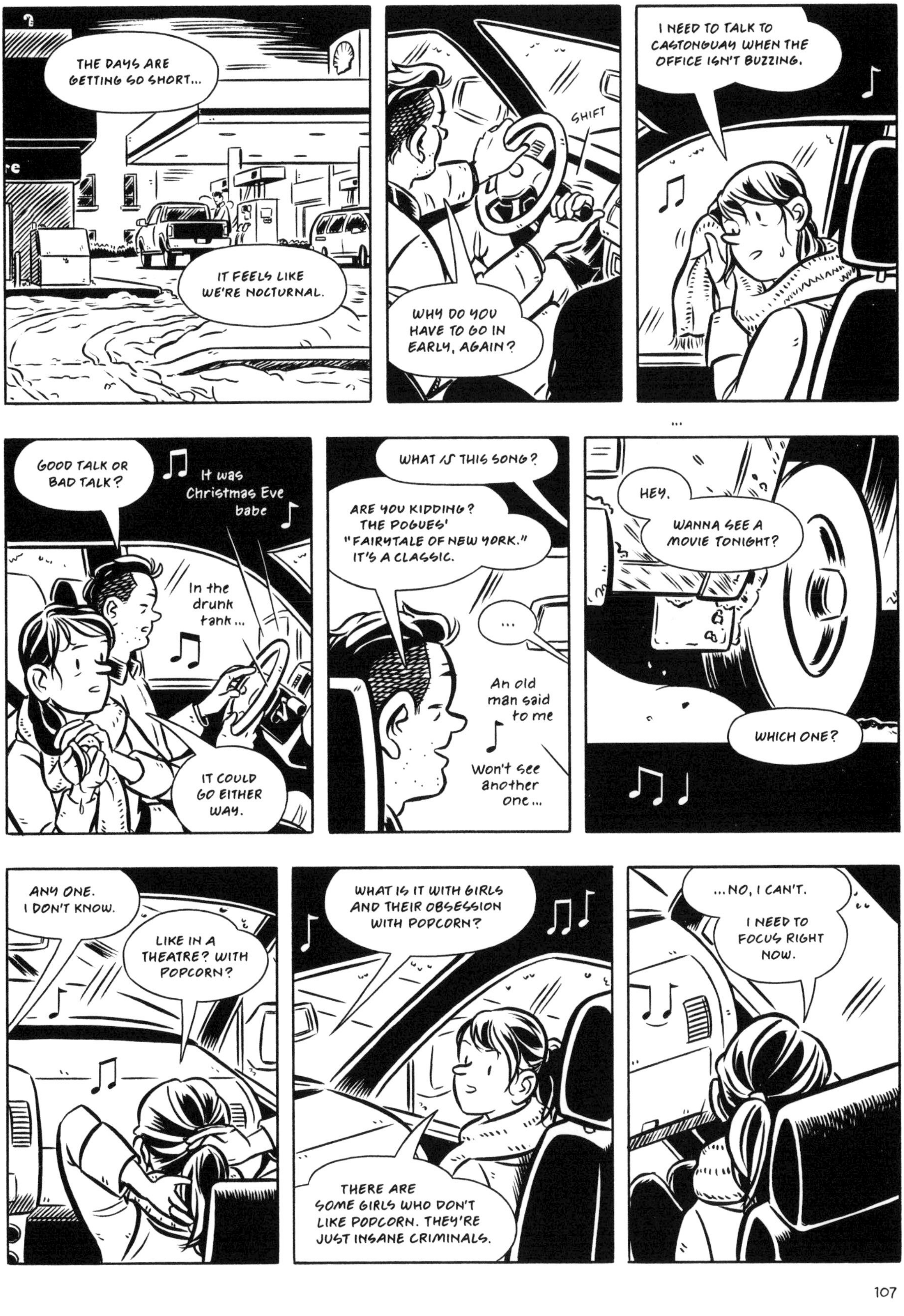
THE DAYS ARE GETTING SO SHORT...
IT FEELS LIKE WE'RE NOCTURNAL.
SHIFT
WHY DO YOU HAVE TO GO IN EARLY, AGAIN?
I NEED TO TALK TO CASTONGUAY WHEN THE OFFICE ISN'T BUZZING.
...
GOOD TALK OR BAD TALK?
It was Christmas Eve babe
In the drunk tank...
IT COULD GO EITHER WAY.
WHAT IS THIS SONG?
ARE YOU KIDDING? THE POGUES' "FAIRYTALE OF NEW YORK." IT'S A CLASSIC.
...
An old man said to me
Won't see another one...
HEY.
WANNA SEE A MOVIE TONIGHT?
WHICH ONE?
ANY ONE. I DON'T KNOW.
LIKE IN A THEATRE? WITH POPCORN?
WHAT IS IT WITH GIRLS AND THEIR OBSESSION WITH POPCORN?
THERE ARE SOME GIRLS WHO DON'T LIKE POPCORN. THEY'RE JUST INSANE CRIMINALS.
...NO, I CAN'T.
I NEED TO FOCUS RIGHT NOW.

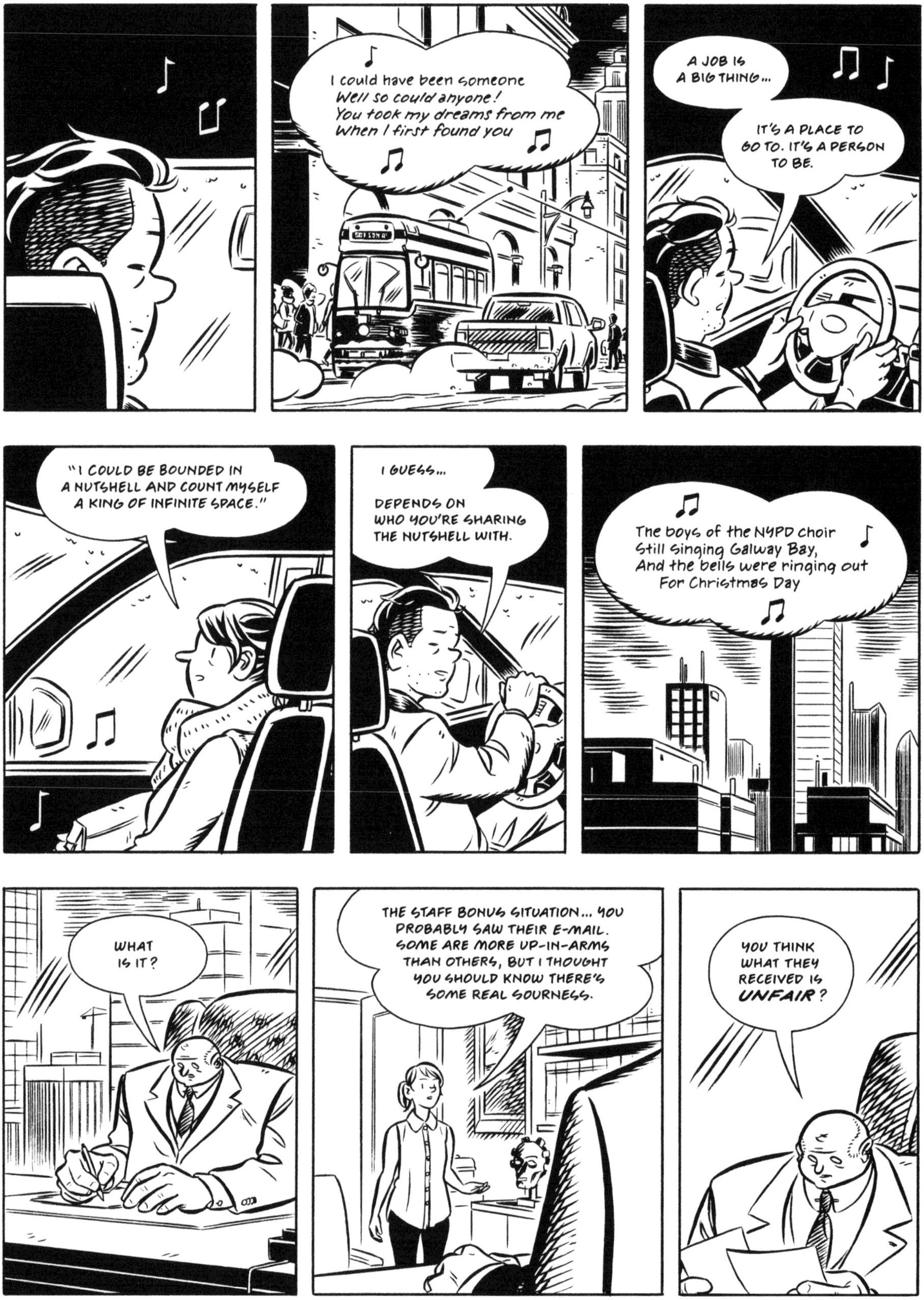
I could have been someone
Well so could anyone!
You took my dreams from me
When I first found you
A JOB IS A BIG THING...
IT'S A PLACE TO GO TO. IT'S A PERSON TO BE.
"I COULD BE BOUNDED IN A NUTSHELL AND COUNT MYSELF A KING OF INFINITE SPACE."
I GUESS...
DEPENDS ON WHO YOU'RE SHARING THE NUTSHELL WITH.
The boys of the NYPD choir
Still singing Galway Bay,
And the bells were ringing out
For Christmas Day
WHAT IS IT?
THE STAFF BONUS SITUATION... YOU PROBABLY SAW THEIR E-MAIL. SOME ARE MORE UP-IN-ARMS THAN OTHERS, BUT I THOUGHT YOU SHOULD KNOW THERE'S SOME REAL SOURNESS.
YOU THINK WHAT THEY RECEIVED IS **UNFAIR**?

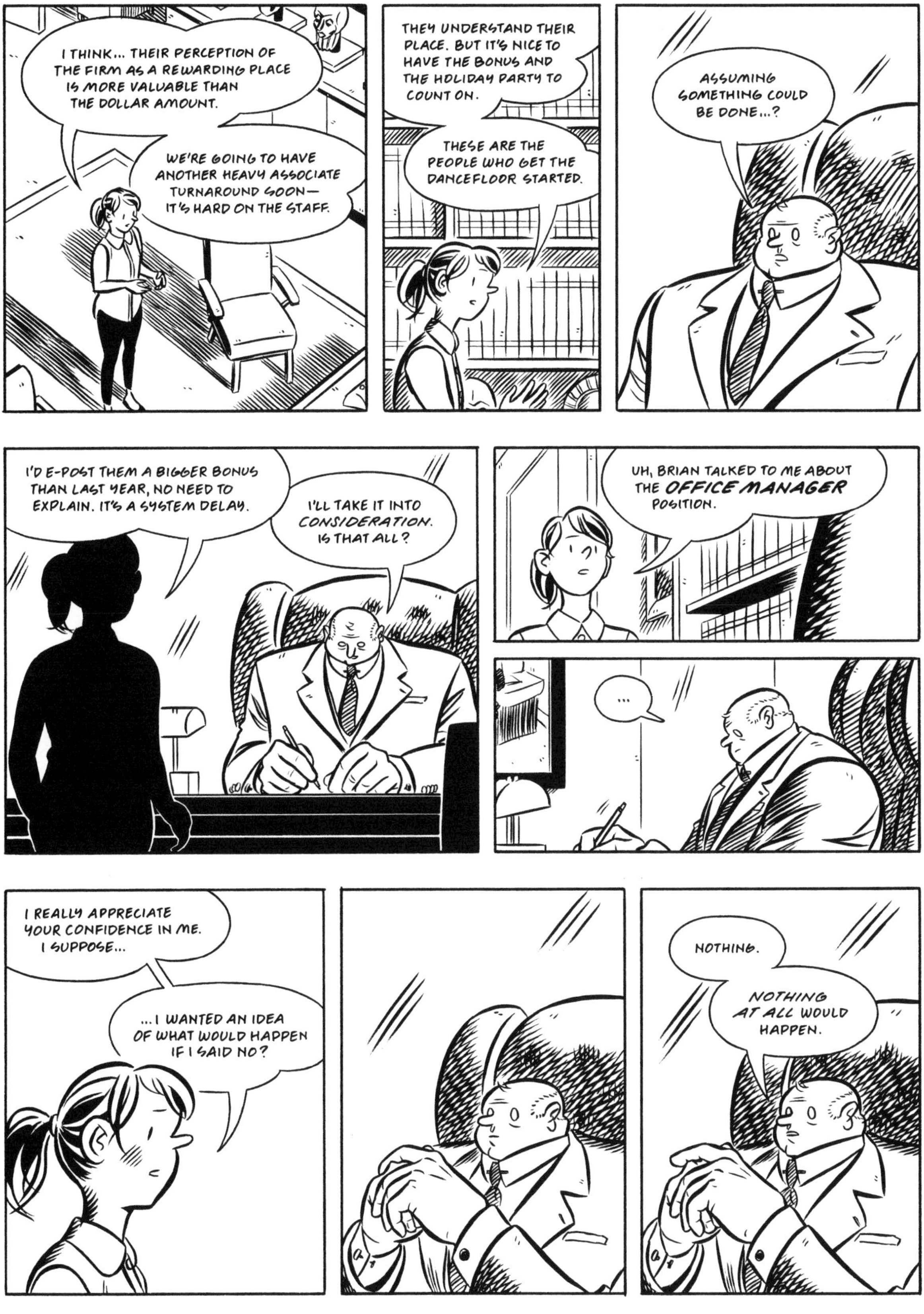
I THINK... THEIR PERCEPTION OF THE FIRM AS A REWARDING PLACE IS MORE VALUABLE THAN THE DOLLAR AMOUNT.
WE'RE GOING TO HAVE ANOTHER HEAVY ASSOCIATE TURNAROUND SOON— IT'S HARD ON THE STAFF.
THEY UNDERSTAND THEIR PLACE. BUT IT'S NICE TO HAVE THE BONUS AND THE HOLIDAY PARTY TO COUNT ON.
THESE ARE THE PEOPLE WHO GET THE DANCEFLOOR STARTED.
ASSUMING SOMETHING COULD BE DONE...?
I'D E-POST THEM A BIGGER BONUS THAN LAST YEAR, NO NEED TO EXPLAIN. IT'S A SYSTEM DELAY.
I'LL TAKE IT INTO CONSIDERATION. IS THAT ALL?
UH, BRIAN TALKED TO ME ABOUT THE OFFICE MANAGER POSITION.
...
I REALLY APPRECIATE YOUR CONFIDENCE IN ME. I SUPPOSE...
...I WANTED AN IDEA OF WHAT WOULD HAPPEN IF I SAID NO?
NOTHING.
NOTHING AT ALL WOULD HAPPEN.

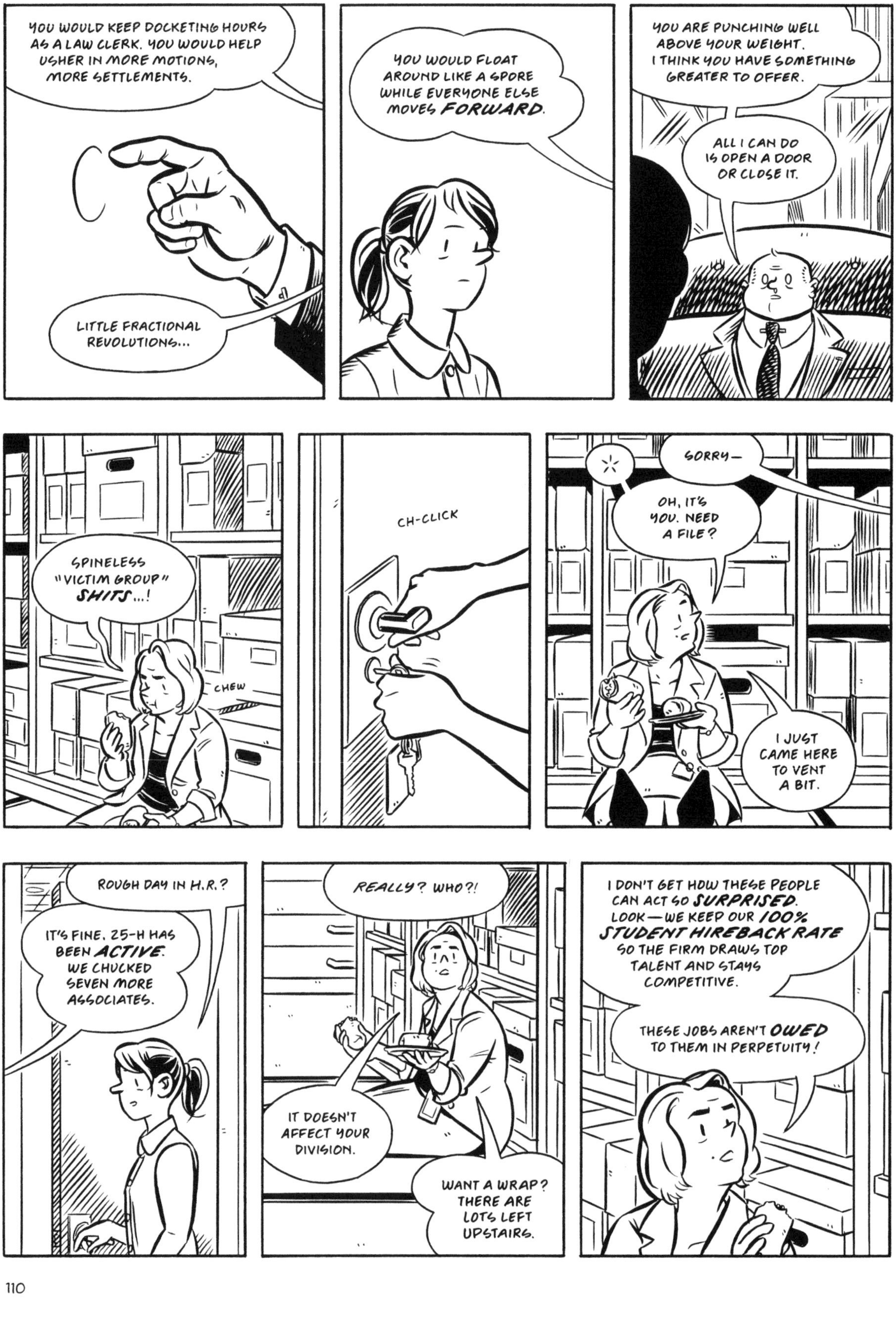
YOU WOULD KEEP DOCKETING HOURS AS A LAW CLERK. YOU WOULD HELP USHER IN MORE MOTIONS, MORE SETTLEMENTS.
LITTLE FRACTIONAL REVOLUTIONS...
YOU WOULD FLOAT AROUND LIKE A SPORE WHILE EVERYONE ELSE MOVES FORWARD.
YOU ARE PUNCHING WELL ABOVE YOUR WEIGHT. I THINK YOU HAVE SOMETHING GREATER TO OFFER.
ALL I CAN DO IS OPEN A DOOR OR CLOSE IT.
SPINELESS "VICTIM GROUP" SHITS...!
CHEW
CH-CLICK
SORRY—
OH, IT'S YOU. NEED A FILE?
I JUST CAME HERE TO VENT A BIT.
ROUGH DAY IN H.R.?
IT'S FINE. 25-H HAS BEEN ACTIVE. WE CHUCKED SEVEN MORE ASSOCIATES.
REALLY? WHO?!
IT DOESN'T AFFECT YOUR DIVISION.
WANT A WRAP? THERE ARE LOTS LEFT UPSTAIRS.
I DON'T GET HOW THESE PEOPLE CAN ACT SO SURPRISED. LOOK—WE KEEP OUR 100% STUDENT HIREBACK RATE SO THE FIRM DRAWS TOP TALENT AND STAYS COMPETITIVE.
THESE JOBS AREN'T OWED TO THEM IN PERPETUITY!

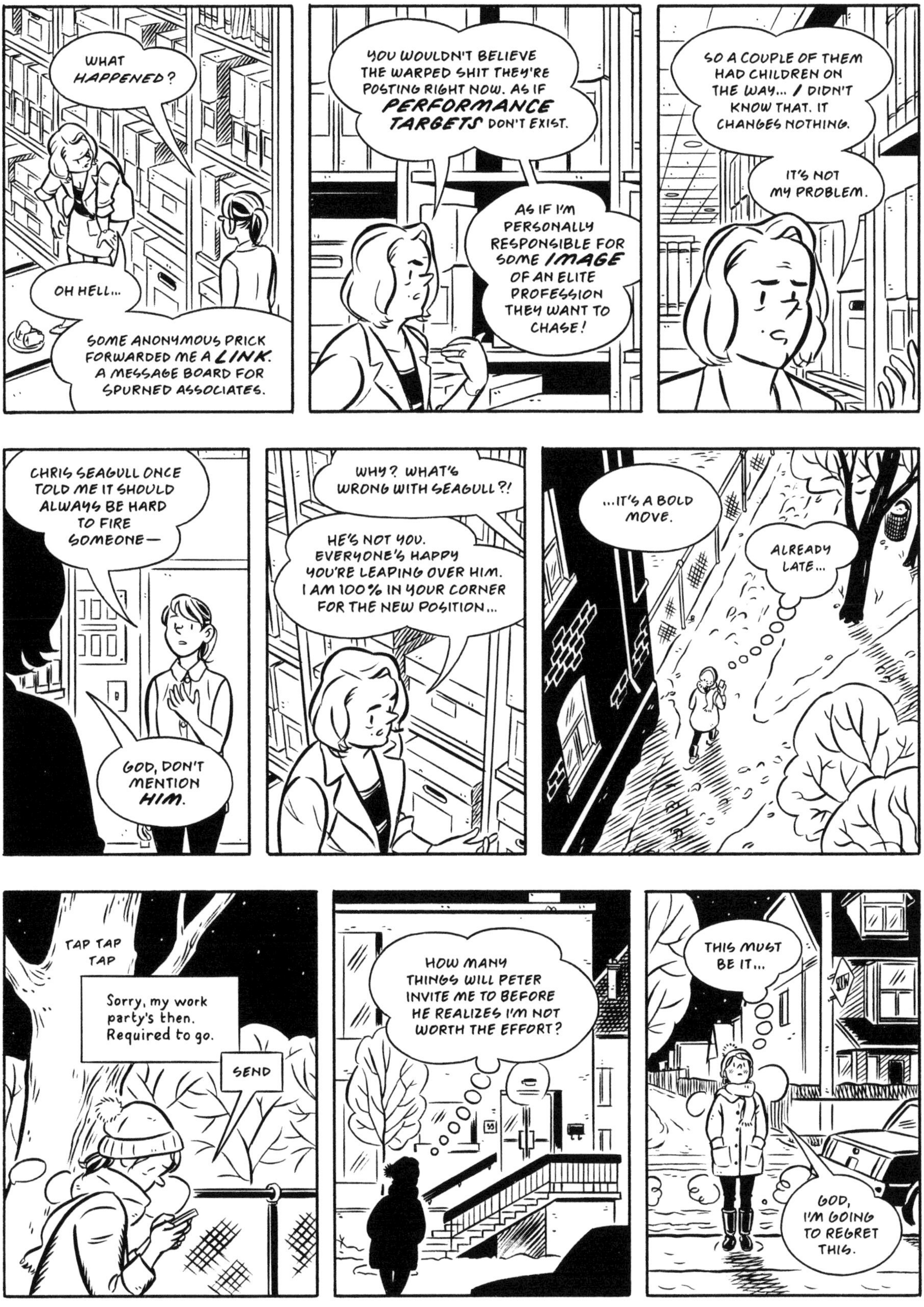
WHAT HAPPENED?
OH HELL...
SOME ANONYMOUS PRICK FORWARDED ME A LINK. A MESSAGE BOARD FOR SPURNED ASSOCIATES.
YOU WOULDN'T BELIEVE THE WARPED SHIT THEY'RE POSTING RIGHT NOW. AS IF PERFORMANCE TARGETS DON'T EXIST.
AS IF I'M PERSONALLY RESPONSIBLE FOR SOME IMAGE OF AN ELITE PROFESSION THEY WANT TO CHASE!
SO A COUPLE OF THEM HAD CHILDREN ON THE WAY... I DIDN'T KNOW THAT. IT CHANGES NOTHING.
IT'S NOT MY PROBLEM.
CHRIS SEAGULL ONCE TOLD ME IT SHOULD ALWAYS BE HARD TO FIRE SOMEONE—
GOD, DON'T MENTION HIM.
WHY? WHAT'S WRONG WITH SEAGULL?!
HE'S NOT YOU. EVERYONE'S HAPPY YOU'RE LEAPING OVER HIM. I AM 100% IN YOUR CORNER FOR THE NEW POSITION...
...IT'S A BOLD MOVE.
ALREADY LATE...
TAP TAP TAP
Sorry, my work party's then. Required to go.
SEND
HOW MANY THINGS WILL PETER INVITE ME TO BEFORE HE REALIZES I'M NOT WORTH THE EFFORT?
THIS MUST BE IT...
GOD, I'M GOING TO REGRET THIS.

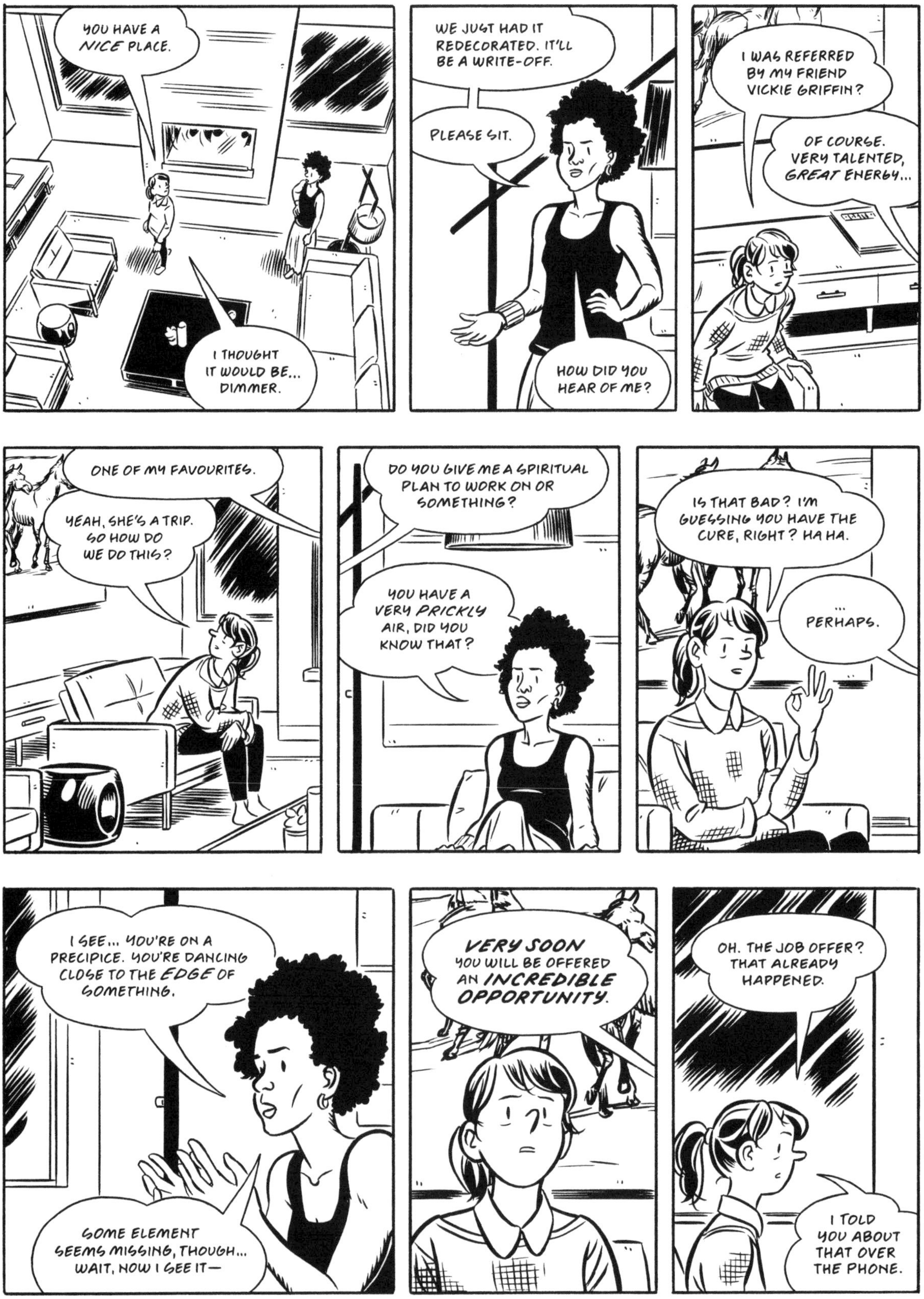
YOU HAVE A NICE PLACE.
I THOUGHT IT WOULD BE... DIMMER.
WE JUST HAD IT REDECORATED. IT'LL BE A WRITE-OFF.
PLEASE SIT.
HOW DID YOU HEAR OF ME?
I WAS REFERRED BY MY FRIEND VICKIE GRIFFIN?
OF COURSE. VERY TALENTED, GREAT ENERGY...
ONE OF MY FAVOURITES.
YEAH, SHE'S A TRIP. SO HOW DO WE DO THIS?
DO YOU GIVE ME A SPIRITUAL PLAN TO WORK ON OR SOMETHING?
YOU HAVE A VERY PRICKLY AIR, DID YOU KNOW THAT?
IS THAT BAD? I'M GUESSING YOU HAVE THE CURE, RIGHT? HA HA.
... PERHAPS.
I SEE... YOU'RE ON A PRECIPICE. YOU'RE DANCING CLOSE TO THE EDGE OF SOMETHING.
SOME ELEMENT SEEMS MISSING, THOUGH... WAIT, NOW I SEE IT—
VERY SOON YOU WILL BE OFFERED AN INCREDIBLE OPPORTUNITY.
OH. THE JOB OFFER? THAT ALREADY HAPPENED.
I TOLD YOU ABOUT THAT OVER THE PHONE.

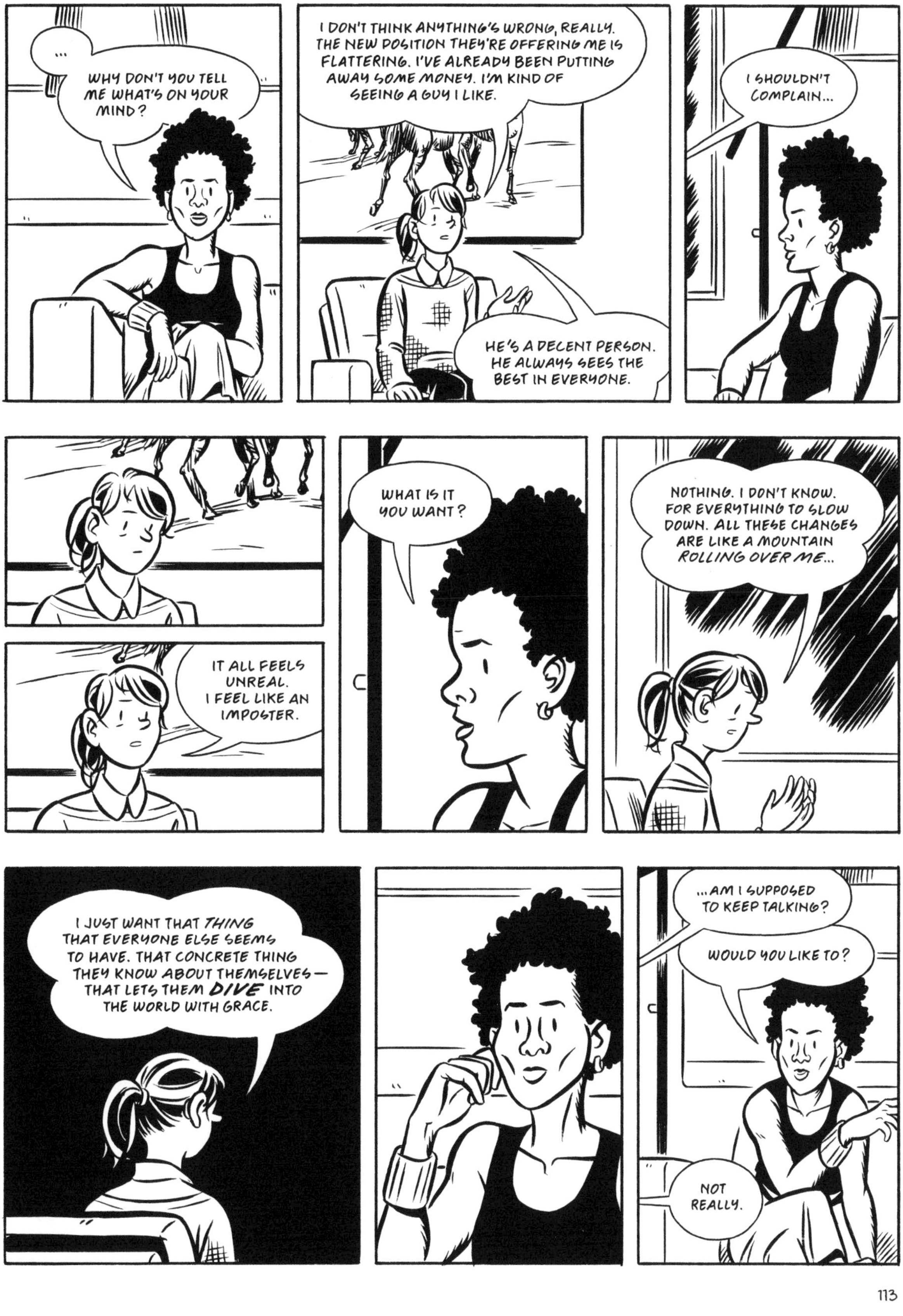
...
WHY DON'T YOU TELL ME WHAT'S ON YOUR MIND?
I DON'T THINK ANYTHING'S WRONG, REALLY. THE NEW POSITION THEY'RE OFFERING ME IS FLATTERING. I'VE ALREADY BEEN PUTTING AWAY SOME MONEY. I'M KIND OF SEEING A GUY I LIKE.
HE'S A DECENT PERSON. HE ALWAYS SEES THE BEST IN EVERYONE.
I SHOULDN'T COMPLAIN...
IT ALL FEELS UNREAL. I FEEL LIKE AN IMPOSTER.
WHAT IS IT YOU WANT?
NOTHING. I DON'T KNOW. FOR EVERYTHING TO SLOW DOWN. ALL THESE CHANGES ARE LIKE A MOUNTAIN ROLLING OVER ME...
I JUST WANT THAT THING THAT EVERYONE ELSE SEEMS TO HAVE. THAT CONCRETE THING THEY KNOW ABOUT THEMSELVES— THAT LETS THEM DIVE INTO THE WORLD WITH GRACE.
...AM I SUPPOSED TO KEEP TALKING?
WOULD YOU LIKE TO?
NOT REALLY.

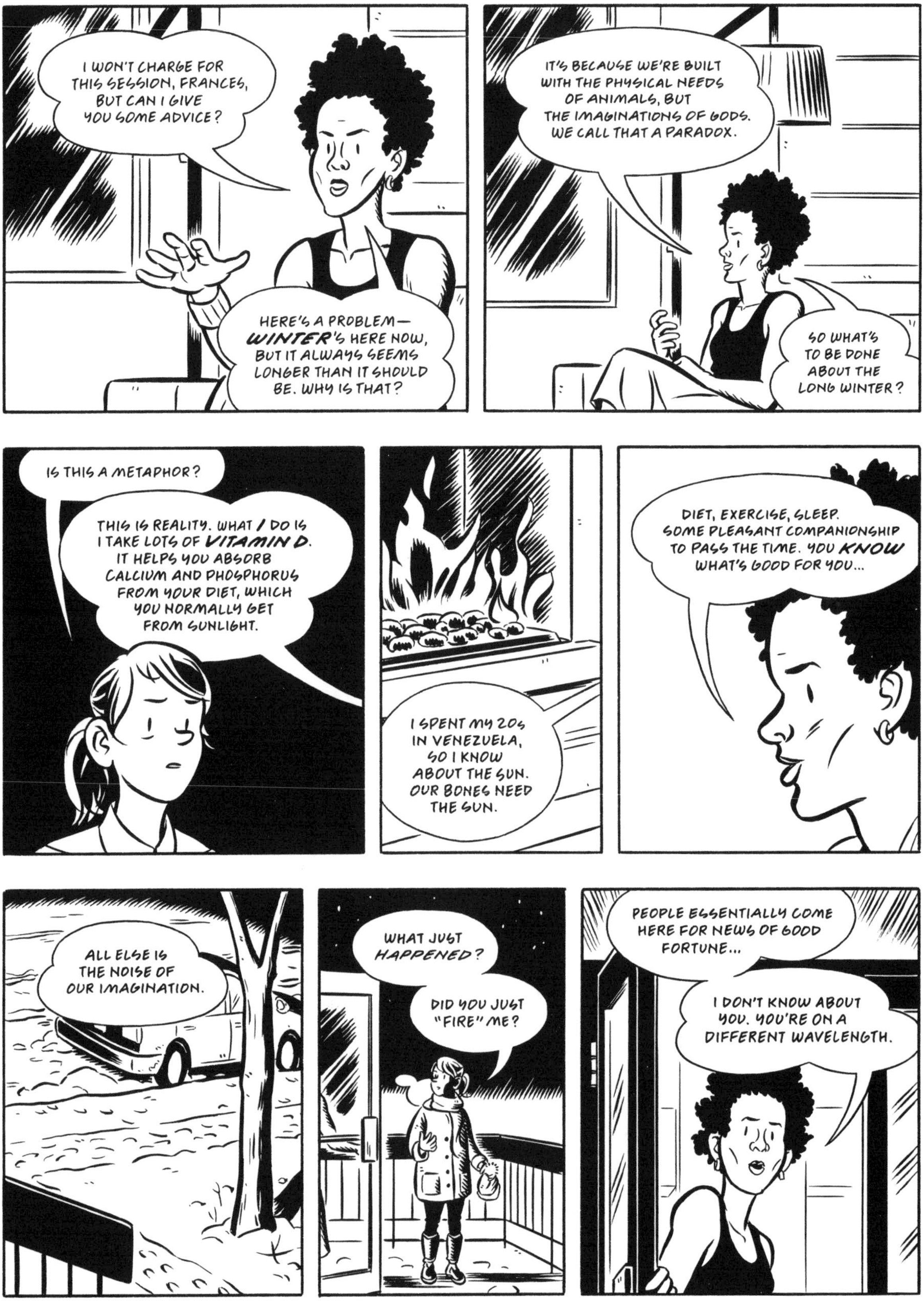
I WON'T CHARGE FOR THIS SESSION, FRANCES, BUT CAN I GIVE YOU SOME ADVICE?
HERE'S A PROBLEM— WINTER'S HERE NOW, BUT IT ALWAYS SEEMS LONGER THAN IT SHOULD BE. WHY IS THAT?
IT'S BECAUSE WE'RE BUILT WITH THE PHYSICAL NEEDS OF ANIMALS, BUT THE IMAGINATIONS OF GODS. WE CALL THAT A PARADOX.
SO WHAT'S TO BE DONE ABOUT THE LONG WINTER?
IS THIS A METAPHOR?
THIS IS REALITY. WHAT I DO IS I TAKE LOTS OF VITAMIN D. IT HELPS YOU ABSORB CALCIUM AND PHOSPHORUS FROM YOUR DIET, WHICH YOU NORMALLY GET FROM SUNLIGHT.
I SPENT MY 20s IN VENEZUELA, SO I KNOW ABOUT THE SUN. OUR BONES NEED THE SUN.
DIET, EXERCISE, SLEEP. SOME PLEASANT COMPANIONSHIP TO PASS THE TIME. YOU KNOW WHAT'S GOOD FOR YOU...
ALL ELSE IS THE NOISE OF OUR IMAGINATION.
WHAT JUST HAPPENED?
DID YOU JUST "FIRE" ME?
PEOPLE ESSENTIALLY COME HERE FOR NEWS OF GOOD FORTUNE...
I DON'T KNOW ABOUT YOU. YOU'RE ON A DIFFERENT WAVELENGTH.

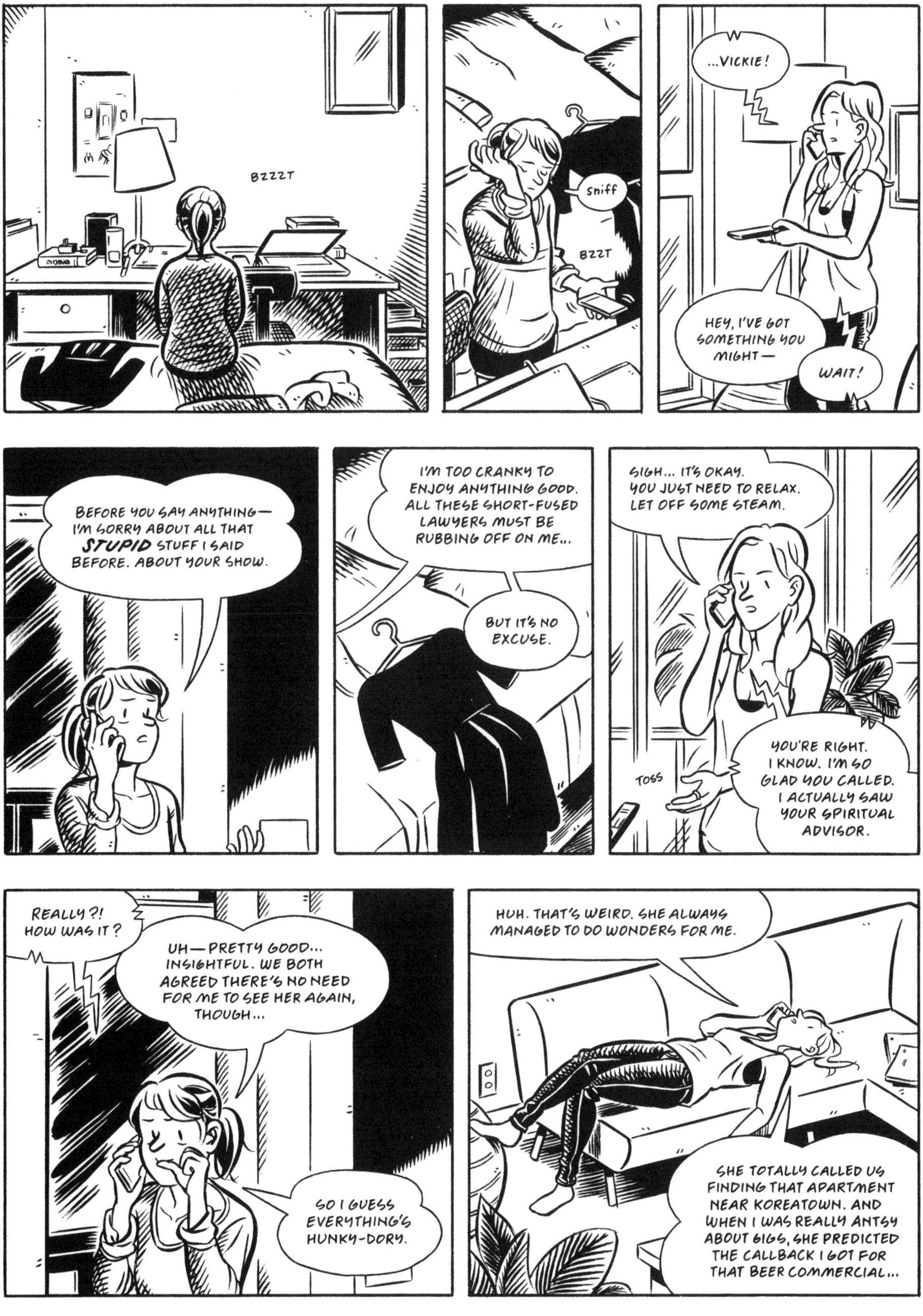
BZZZT
sniff
BZZT
...VICKIE!
HEY, I'VE GOT SOMETHING YOU MIGHT—
WAIT!
BEFORE YOU SAY ANYTHING— I'M SORRY ABOUT ALL THAT STUPID STUFF I SAID BEFORE. ABOUT YOUR SHOW.
I'M TOO CRANKY TO ENJOY ANYTHING GOOD. ALL THESE SHORT-FUSED LAWYERS MUST BE RUBBING OFF ON ME...
BUT IT'S NO EXCUSE.
SIGH... IT'S OKAY. YOU JUST NEED TO RELAX. LET OFF SOME STEAM.
TOSS
YOU'RE RIGHT. I KNOW. I'M SO GLAD YOU CALLED. I ACTUALLY SAW YOUR SPIRITUAL ADVISOR.
REALLY?! HOW WAS IT?
UH—PRETTY GOOD... INSIGHTFUL. WE BOTH AGREED THERE'S NO NEED FOR ME TO SEE HER AGAIN, THOUGH...
SO I GUESS EVERYTHING'S HUNKY-DORY.
HUH. THAT'S WEIRD. SHE ALWAYS MANAGED TO DO WONDERS FOR ME.
SHE TOTALLY CALLED US FINDING THAT APARTMENT NEAR KOREATOWN. AND WHEN I WAS REALLY ANTSY ABOUT GIGS, SHE PREDICTED THE CALLBACK I GOT FOR THAT BEER COMMERCIAL...

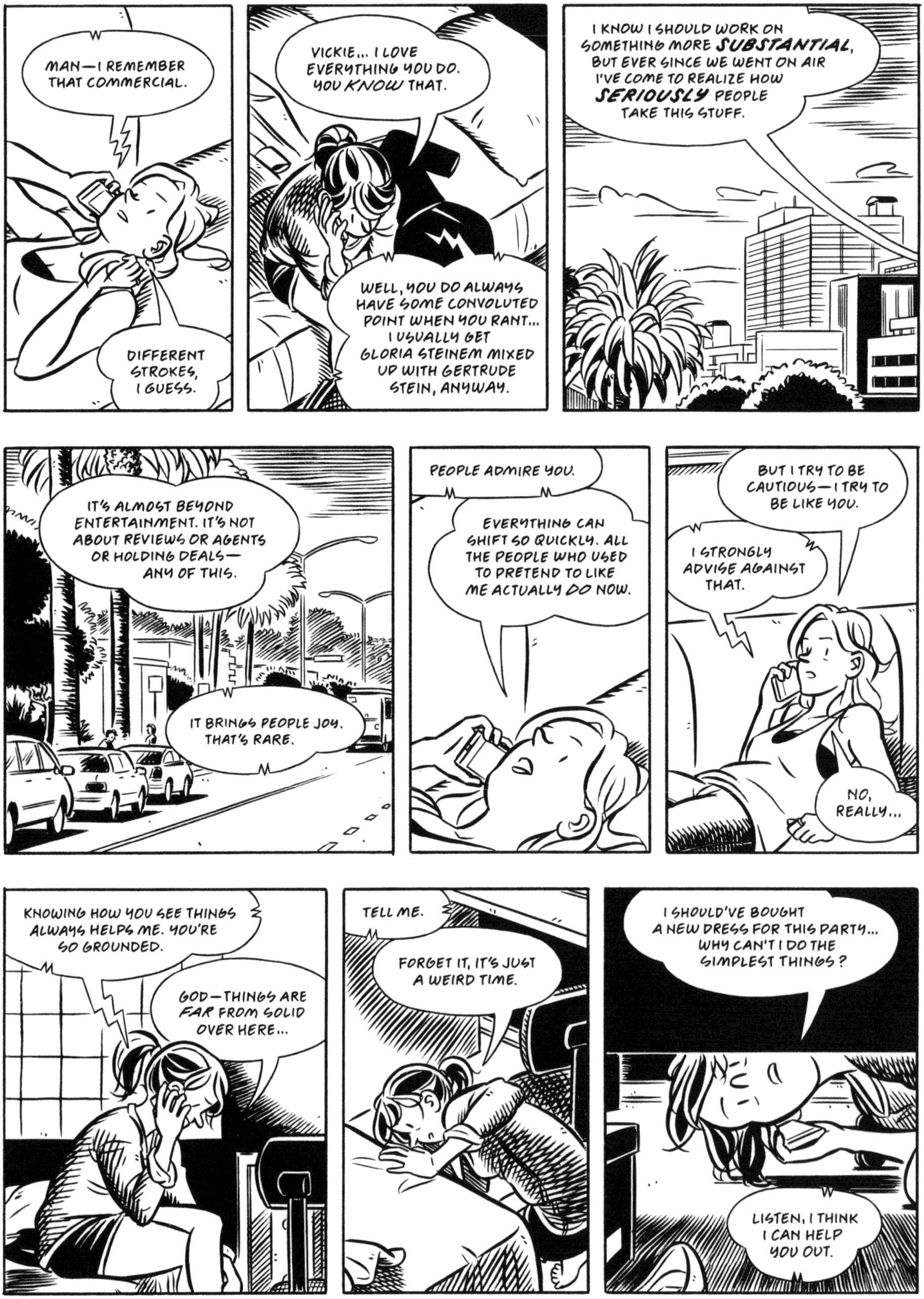
MAN—I REMEMBER THAT COMMERCIAL.
DIFFERENT STROKES, I GUESS.
VICKIE... I LOVE EVERYTHING YOU DO. YOU KNOW THAT.
WELL, YOU DO ALWAYS HAVE SOME CONVOLUTED POINT WHEN YOU RANT... I USUALLY GET GLORIA STEINEM MIXED UP WITH GERTRUDE STEIN, ANYWAY.
I KNOW I SHOULD WORK ON SOMETHING MORE SUBSTANTIAL, BUT EVER SINCE WE WENT ON AIR I'VE COME TO REALIZE HOW SERIOUSLY PEOPLE TAKE THIS STUFF.
IT'S ALMOST BEYOND ENTERTAINMENT. IT'S NOT ABOUT REVIEWS OR AGENTS OR HOLDING DEALS— ANY OF THIS.
IT BRINGS PEOPLE JOY. THAT'S RARE.
PEOPLE ADMIRE YOU.
EVERYTHING CAN SHIFT SO QUICKLY. ALL THE PEOPLE WHO USED TO PRETEND TO LIKE ME ACTUALLY DO NOW.
BUT I TRY TO BE CAUTIOUS—I TRY TO BE LIKE YOU.
I STRONGLY ADVISE AGAINST THAT.
NO, REALLY...
KNOWING HOW YOU SEE THINGS ALWAYS HELPS ME. YOU'RE SO GROUNDED.
GOD—THINGS ARE FAR FROM SOLID OVER HERE...
TELL ME.
FORGET IT, IT'S JUST A WEIRD TIME.
I SHOULD'VE BOUGHT A NEW DRESS FOR THIS PARTY... WHY CAN'T I DO THE SIMPLEST THINGS?
LISTEN, I THINK I CAN HELP YOU OUT.

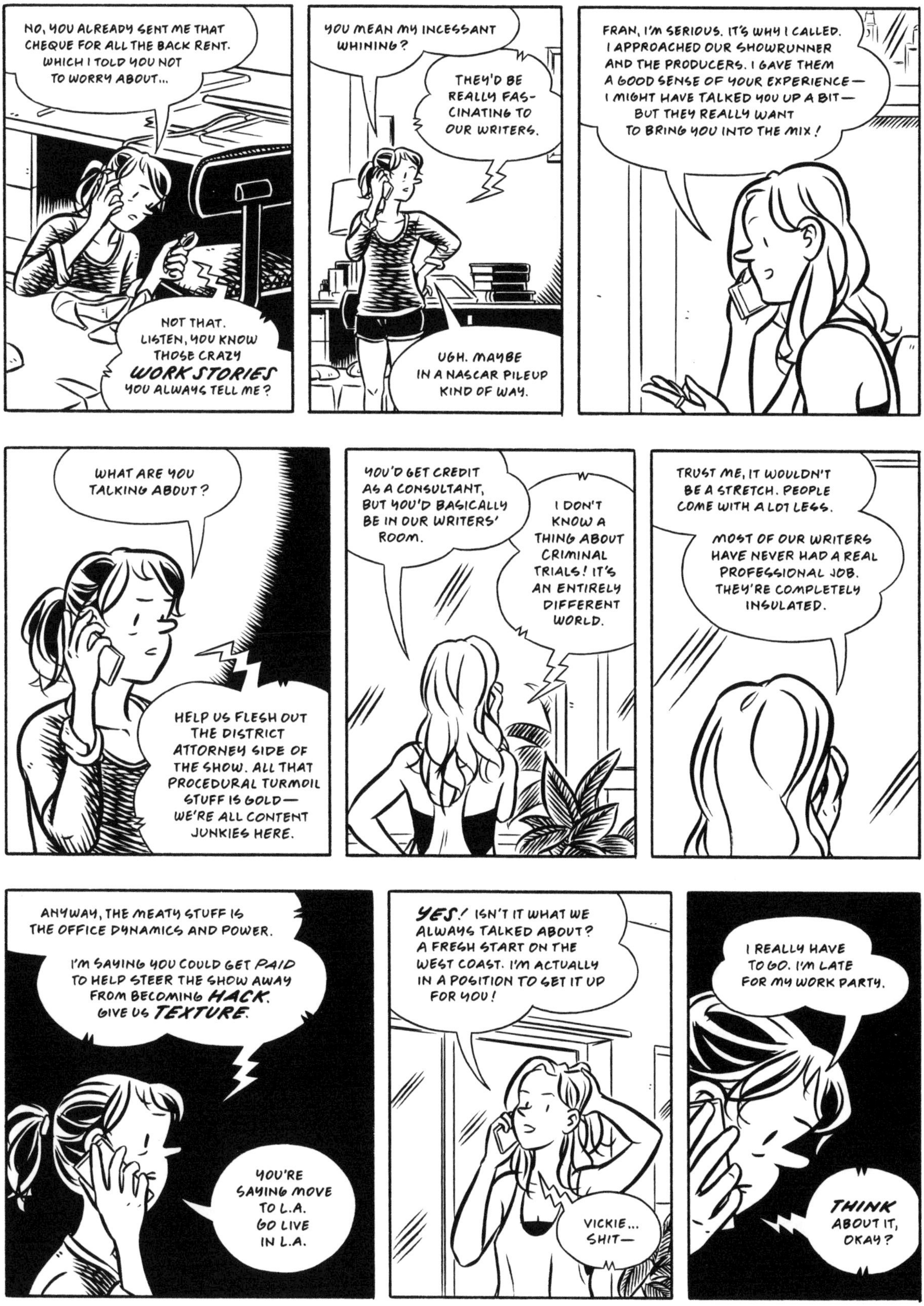
NO, YOU ALREADY SENT ME THAT CHEQUE FOR ALL THE BACK RENT. WHICH I TOLD YOU NOT TO WORRY ABOUT...
NOT THAT. LISTEN, YOU KNOW THOSE CRAZY WORK STORIES YOU ALWAYS TELL ME?
YOU MEAN MY INCESSANT WHINING?
THEY'D BE REALLY FAS-CINATING TO OUR WRITERS.
UGH. MAYBE IN A NASCAR PILEUP KIND OF WAY.
FRAN, I'M SERIOUS. IT'S WHY I CALLED. I APPROACHED OUR SHOWRUNNER AND THE PRODUCERS. I GAVE THEM A GOOD SENSE OF YOUR EXPERIENCE— I MIGHT HAVE TALKED YOU UP A BIT— BUT THEY REALLY WANT TO BRING YOU INTO THE MIX!
WHAT ARE YOU TALKING ABOUT?
HELP US FLESH OUT THE DISTRICT ATTORNEY SIDE OF THE SHOW. ALL THAT PROCEDURAL TURMOIL STUFF IS GOLD— WE'RE ALL CONTENT JUNKIES HERE.
YOU'D GET CREDIT AS A CONSULTANT, BUT YOU'D BASICALLY BE IN OUR WRITERS' ROOM.
I DON'T KNOW A THING ABOUT CRIMINAL TRIALS! IT'S AN ENTIRELY DIFFERENT WORLD.
TRUST ME, IT WOULDN'T BE A STRETCH. PEOPLE COME WITH A LOT LESS.
MOST OF OUR WRITERS HAVE NEVER HAD A REAL PROFESSIONAL JOB. THEY'RE COMPLETELY INSULATED.
ANYWAY, THE MEATY STUFF IS THE OFFICE DYNAMICS AND POWER.
I'M SAYING YOU COULD GET PAID TO HELP STEER THE SHOW AWAY FROM BECOMING HACK. GIVE US TEXTURE.
YOU'RE SAYING MOVE TO L.A. GO LIVE IN L.A.
YES! ISN'T IT WHAT WE ALWAYS TALKED ABOUT? A FRESH START ON THE WEST COAST. I'M ACTUALLY IN A POSITION TO GET IT UP FOR YOU!
VICKIE... SHIT—
I REALLY HAVE TO GO. I'M LATE FOR MY WORK PARTY.
THINK ABOUT IT, OKAY?

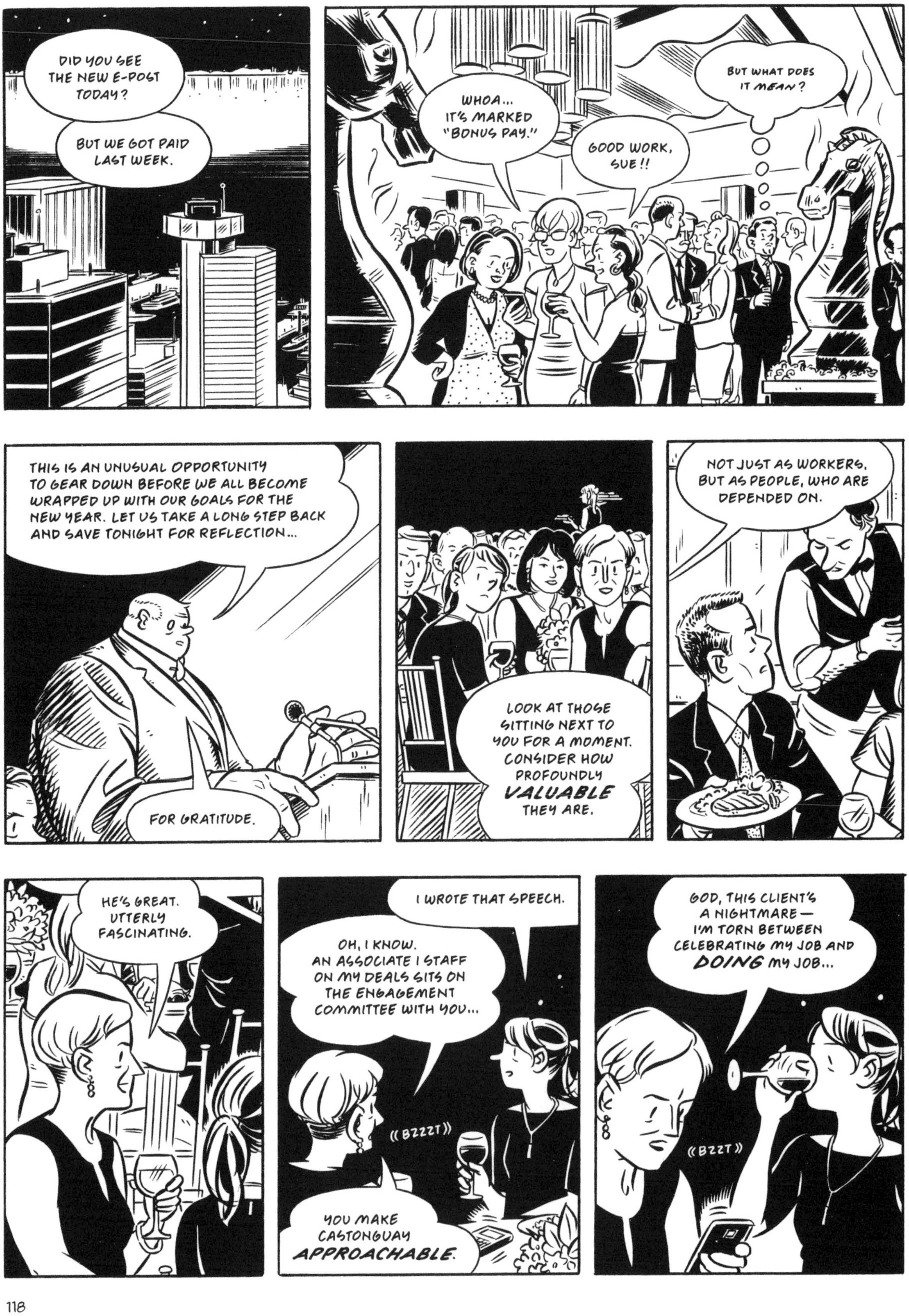
DID YOU SEE THE NEW E-POST TODAY?
BUT WE GOT PAID LAST WEEK.
WHOA... IT'S MARKED "BONUS PAY."
GOOD WORK, SUE!!
BUT WHAT DOES IT MEAN?
THIS IS AN UNUSUAL OPPORTUNITY TO GEAR DOWN BEFORE WE ALL BECOME WRAPPED UP WITH OUR GOALS FOR THE NEW YEAR. LET US TAKE A LONG STEP BACK AND SAVE TONIGHT FOR REFLECTION...
FOR GRATITUDE.
LOOK AT THOSE SITTING NEXT TO YOU FOR A MOMENT. CONSIDER HOW PROFOUNDLY VALUABLE THEY ARE.
NOT JUST AS WORKERS, BUT AS PEOPLE, WHO ARE DEPENDED ON.
HE'S GREAT. UTTERLY FASCINATING.
I WROTE THAT SPEECH.
OH, I KNOW. AN ASSOCIATE I STAFF ON MY DEALS SITS ON THE ENGAGEMENT COMMITTEE WITH YOU...
((BZZZT))
YOU MAKE CASTONGUAY APPROACHABLE.
GOD, THIS CLIENT'S A NIGHTMARE— I'M TORN BETWEEN CELEBRATING MY JOB AND DOING MY JOB...
((BZZZT))

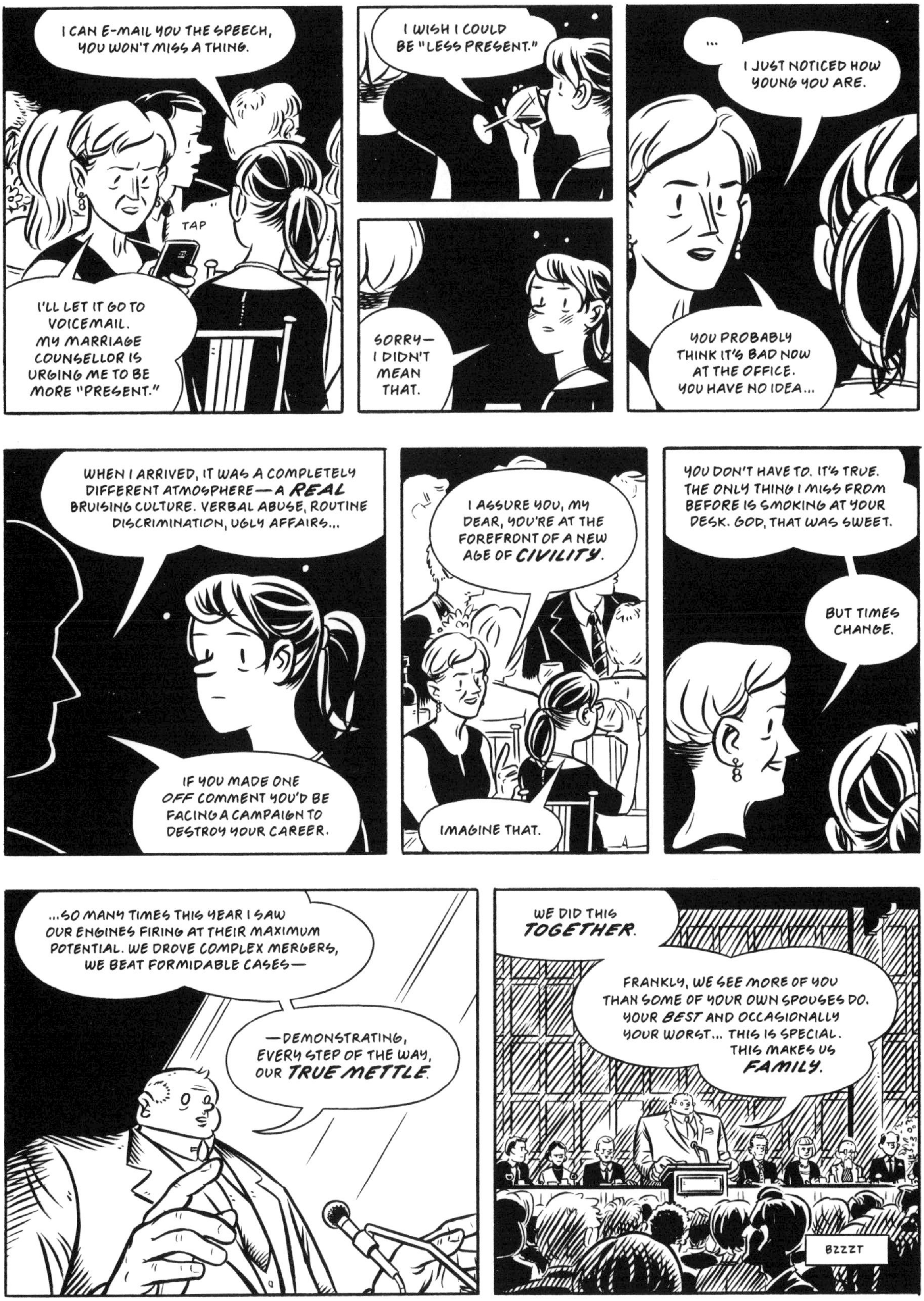
I CAN E-MAIL YOU THE SPEECH, YOU WON'T MISS A THING.
TAP
I'LL LET IT GO TO VOICEMAIL. MY MARRIAGE COUNSELLOR IS URGING ME TO BE MORE "PRESENT."
I WISH I COULD BE "LESS PRESENT."
SORRY— I DIDN'T MEAN THAT.
...
I JUST NOTICED HOW YOUNG YOU ARE.
YOU PROBABLY THINK IT'S BAD NOW AT THE OFFICE. YOU HAVE NO IDEA...
WHEN I ARRIVED, IT WAS A COMPLETELY DIFFERENT ATMOSPHERE—A REAL BRUISING CULTURE. VERBAL ABUSE, ROUTINE DISCRIMINATION, UGLY AFFAIRS...
IF YOU MADE ONE OFF COMMENT YOU'D BE FACING A CAMPAIGN TO DESTROY YOUR CAREER.
I ASSURE YOU, MY DEAR, YOU'RE AT THE FOREFRONT OF A NEW AGE OF CIVILITY.
IMAGINE THAT.
YOU DON'T HAVE TO. IT'S TRUE. THE ONLY THING I MISS FROM BEFORE IS SMOKING AT YOUR DESK. GOD, THAT WAS SWEET.
BUT TIMES CHANGE.
...SO MANY TIMES THIS YEAR I SAW OUR ENGINES FIRING AT THEIR MAXIMUM POTENTIAL. WE DROVE COMPLEX MERGERS, WE BEAT FORMIDABLE CASES—
—DEMONSTRATING, EVERY STEP OF THE WAY, OUR TRUE METTLE.
WE DID THIS TOGETHER.
FRANKLY, WE SEE MORE OF YOU THAN SOME OF YOUR OWN SPOUSES DO. YOUR BEST AND OCCASIONALLY YOUR WORST... THIS IS SPECIAL. THIS MAKES US FAMILY.
BZZZT

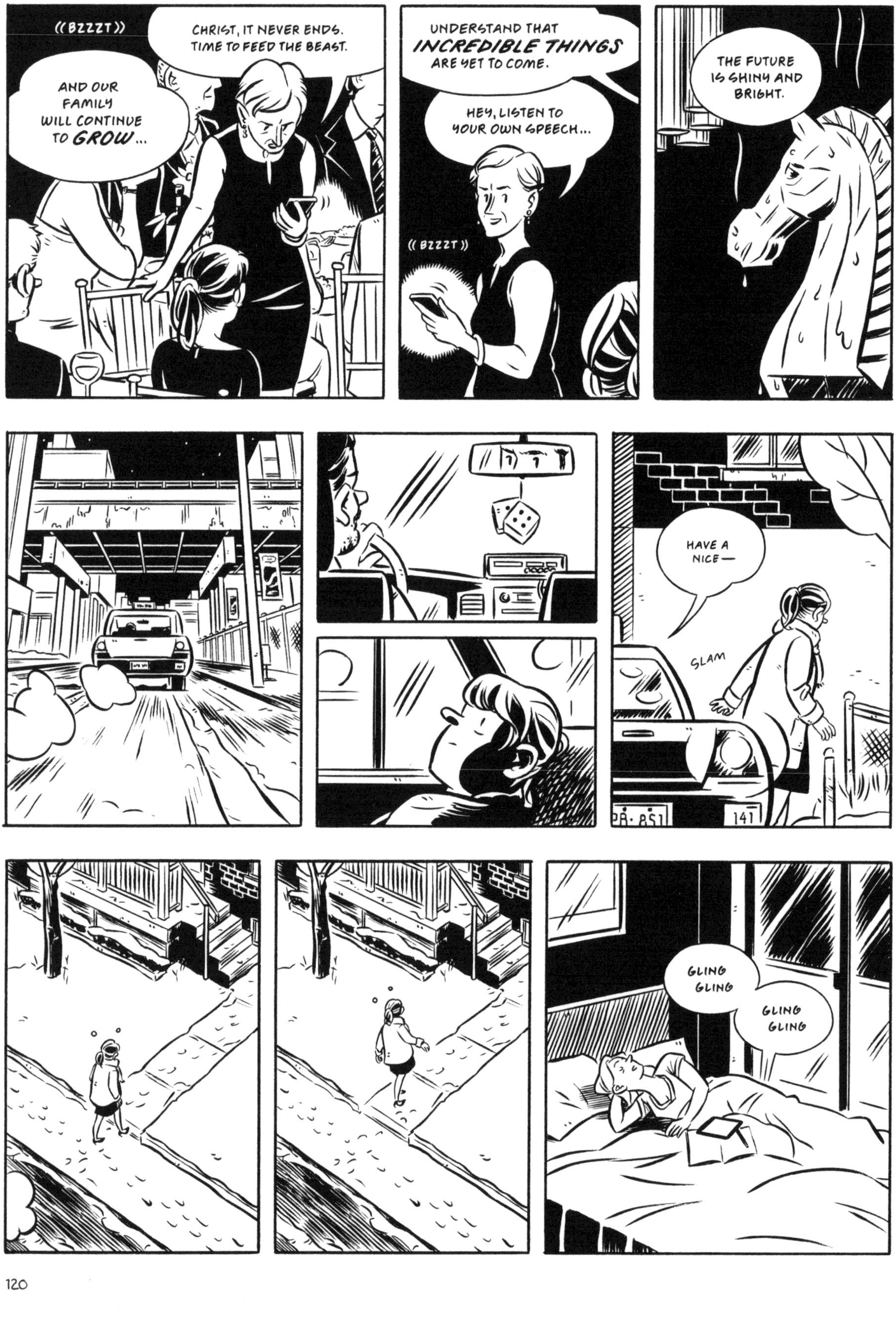
((BZZZT))
CHRIST, IT NEVER ENDS. TIME TO FEED THE BEAST.
AND OUR FAMILY WILL CONTINUE TO GROW...
UNDERSTAND THAT INCREDIBLE THINGS ARE YET TO COME.
HEY, LISTEN TO YOUR OWN SPEECH...
((BZZZT))
THE FUTURE IS SHINY AND BRIGHT.
HAVE A NICE—
SLAM
GLING GLING
GLING GLING

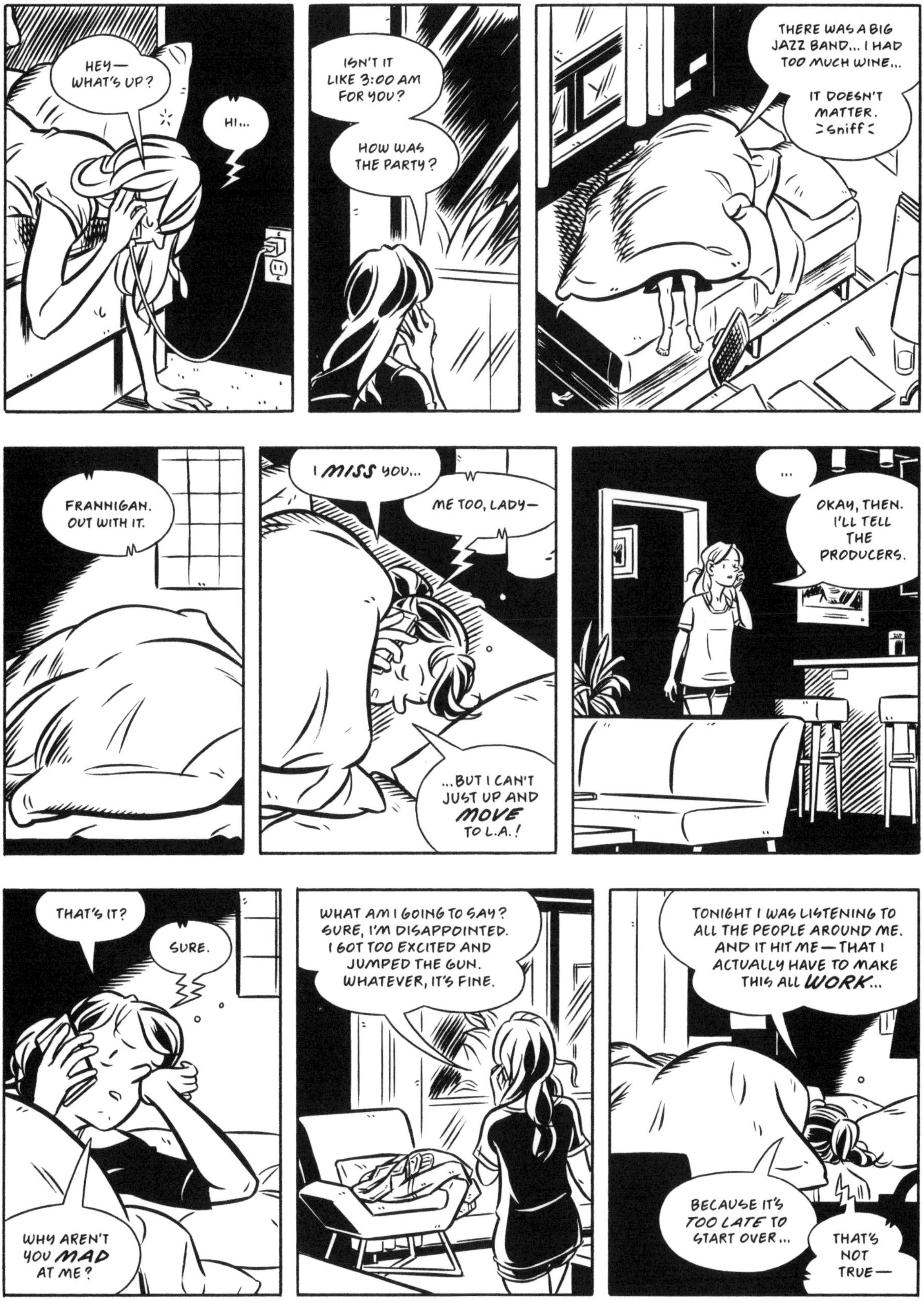
HEY— WHAT'S UP?
HI...
ISN'T IT LIKE 3:00 AM FOR YOU?
HOW WAS THE PARTY?
THERE WAS A BIG JAZZ BAND... I HAD TOO MUCH WINE...
IT DOESN'T MATTER.
sniff
FRANNIGAN. OUT WITH IT.
I MISS YOU...
ME TOO, LADY—
...BUT I CAN'T JUST UP AND MOVE TO L.A.!
...
OKAY, THEN. I'LL TELL THE PRODUCERS.
THAT'S IT?
SURE.
WHY AREN'T YOU MAD AT ME?
WHAT AM I GOING TO SAY? SURE, I'M DISAPPOINTED. I GOT TOO EXCITED AND JUMPED THE GUN. WHATEVER, IT'S FINE.
TONIGHT I WAS LISTENING TO ALL THE PEOPLE AROUND ME. AND IT HIT ME — THAT I ACTUALLY HAVE TO MAKE THIS ALL WORK...
BECAUSE IT'S TOO LATE TO START OVER...
THAT'S NOT TRUE—

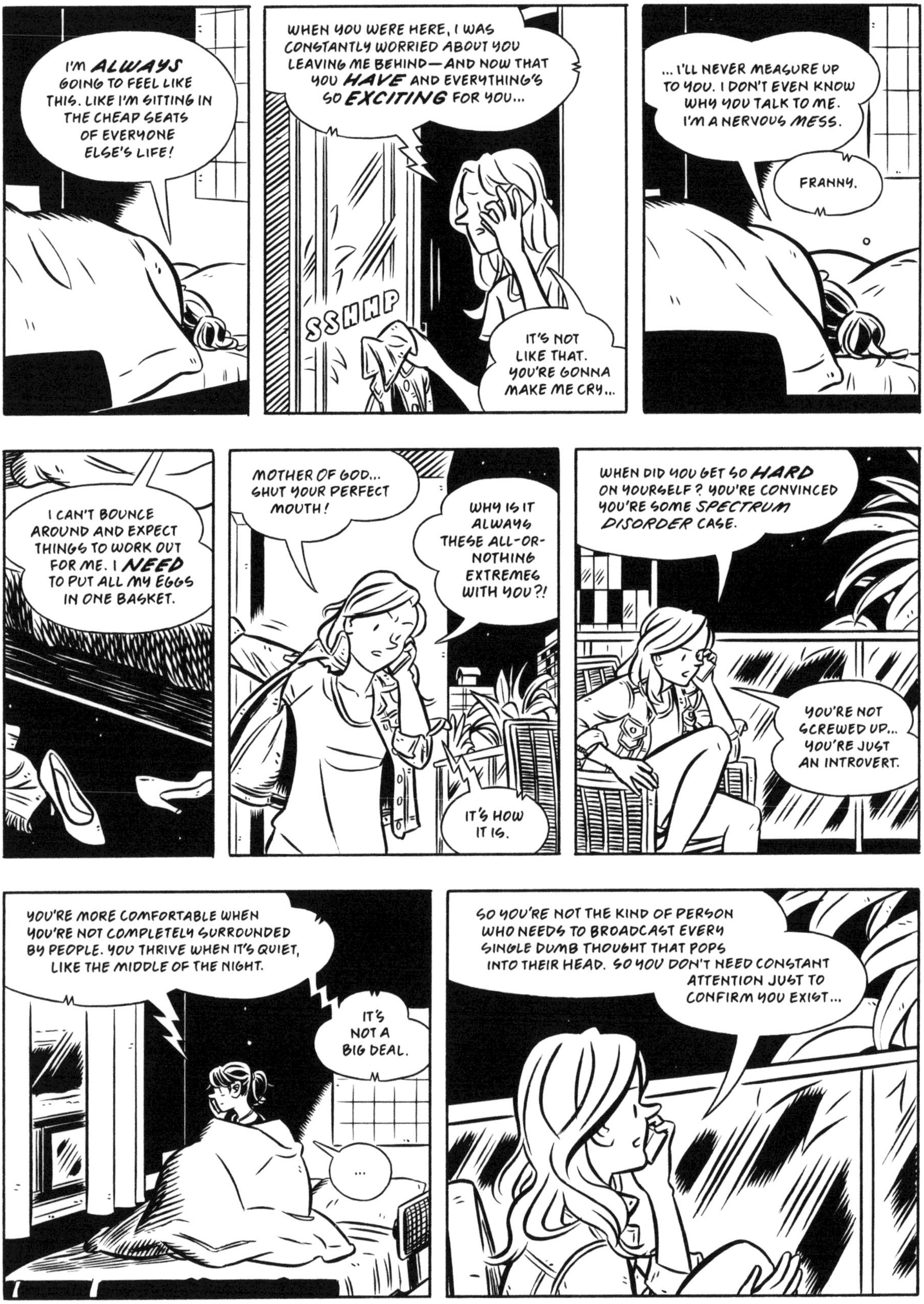
I'M ALWAYS GOING TO FEEL LIKE THIS. LIKE I'M SITTING IN THE CHEAP SEATS OF EVERYONE ELSE'S LIFE!
WHEN YOU WERE HERE, I WAS CONSTANTLY WORRIED ABOUT YOU LEAVING ME BEHIND—AND NOW THAT YOU HAVE AND EVERYTHING'S SO EXCITING FOR YOU...
SSHHP
IT'S NOT LIKE THAT. YOU'RE GONNA MAKE ME CRY...
...I'LL NEVER MEASURE UP TO YOU. I DON'T EVEN KNOW WHY YOU TALK TO ME. I'M A NERVOUS MESS.
FRANNY.
I CAN'T BOUNCE AROUND AND EXPECT THINGS TO WORK OUT FOR ME. I NEED TO PUT ALL MY EGGS IN ONE BASKET.
MOTHER OF GOD... SHUT YOUR PERFECT MOUTH!
WHY IS IT ALWAYS THESE ALL-OR-NOTHING EXTREMES WITH YOU?!
IT'S HOW IT IS.
WHEN DID YOU GET SO HARD ON YOURSELF? YOU'RE CONVINCED YOU'RE SOME SPECTRUM DISORDER CASE.
YOU'RE NOT SCREWED UP... YOU'RE JUST AN INTROVERT.
YOU'RE MORE COMFORTABLE WHEN YOU'RE NOT COMPLETELY SURROUNDED BY PEOPLE. YOU THRIVE WHEN IT'S QUIET, LIKE THE MIDDLE OF THE NIGHT.
IT'S NOT A BIG DEAL.
...
SO YOU'RE NOT THE KIND OF PERSON WHO NEEDS TO BROADCAST EVERY SINGLE DUMB THOUGHT THAT POPS INTO THEIR HEAD. SO YOU DON'T NEED CONSTANT ATTENTION JUST TO CONFIRM YOU EXIST...

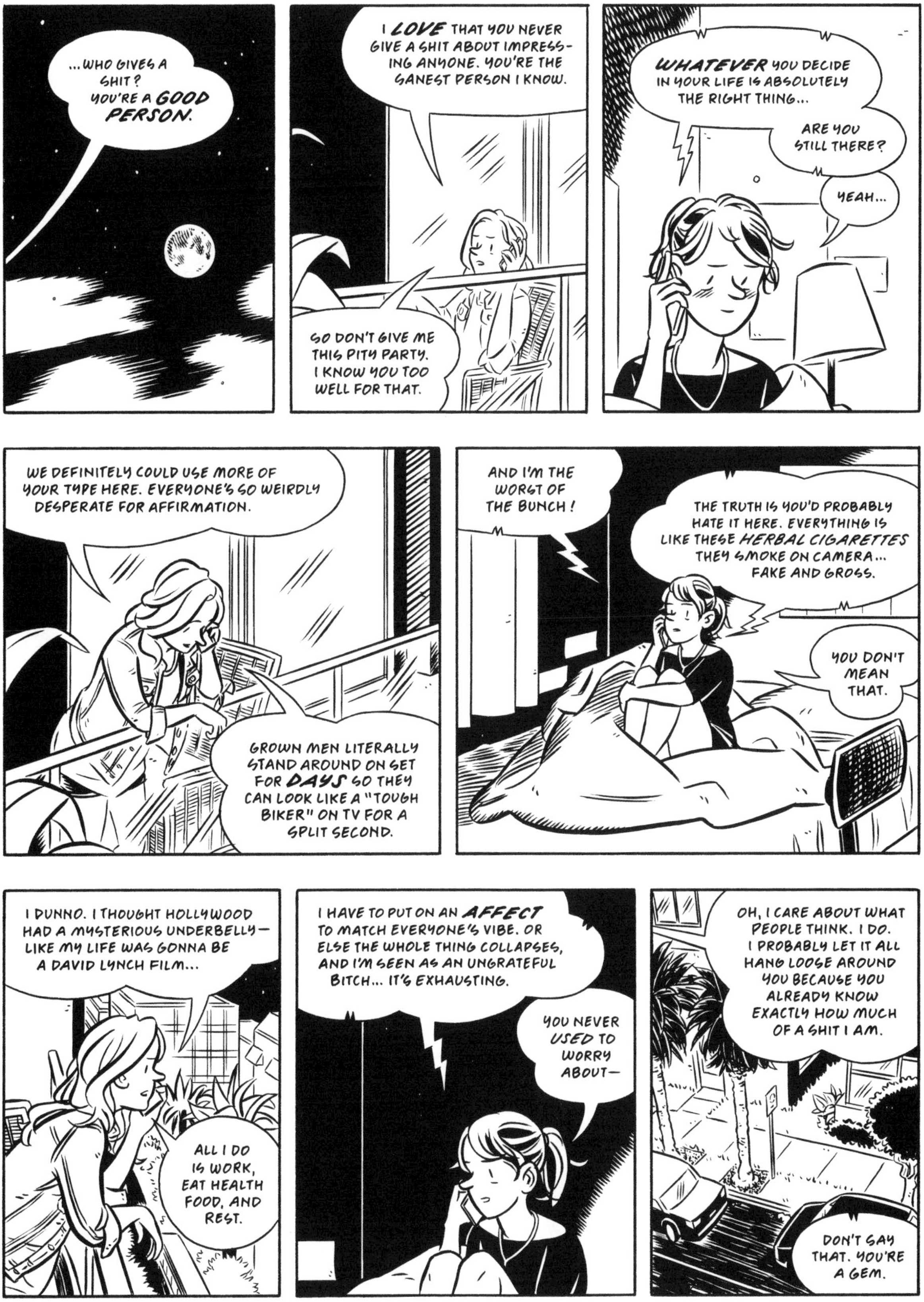
...WHO GIVES A SHIT? YOU'RE A GOOD PERSON.
I LOVE THAT YOU NEVER GIVE A SHIT ABOUT IMPRESSING ANYONE. YOU'RE THE SANEST PERSON I KNOW.
SO DON'T GIVE ME THIS PITY PARTY. I KNOW YOU TOO WELL FOR THAT.
WHATEVER YOU DECIDE IN YOUR LIFE IS ABSOLUTELY THE RIGHT THING...
ARE YOU STILL THERE?
YEAH...
WE DEFINITELY COULD USE MORE OF YOUR TYPE HERE. EVERYONE'S SO WEIRDLY DESPERATE FOR AFFIRMATION.
GROWN MEN LITERALLY STAND AROUND ON SET FOR DAYS SO THEY CAN LOOK LIKE A "TOUGH BIKER" ON TV FOR A SPLIT SECOND.
AND I'M THE WORST OF THE BUNCH!
THE TRUTH IS YOU'D PROBABLY HATE IT HERE. EVERYTHING IS LIKE THESE HERBAL CIGARETTES THEY SMOKE ON CAMERA... FAKE AND GROSS.
YOU DON'T MEAN THAT.
I DUNNO. I THOUGHT HOLLYWOOD HAD A MYSTERIOUS UNDERBELLY— LIKE MY LIFE WAS GONNA BE A DAVID LYNCH FILM...
ALL I DO IS WORK, EAT HEALTH FOOD, AND REST.
I HAVE TO PUT ON AN AFFECT TO MATCH EVERYONE'S VIBE. OR ELSE THE WHOLE THING COLLAPSES, AND I'M SEEN AS AN UNGRATEFUL BITCH... IT'S EXHAUSTING.
YOU NEVER USED TO WORRY ABOUT—
OH, I CARE ABOUT WHAT PEOPLE THINK. I DO. I PROBABLY LET IT ALL HANG LOOSE AROUND YOU BECAUSE YOU ALREADY KNOW EXACTLY HOW MUCH OF A SHIT I AM.
DON'T SAY THAT. YOU'RE A GEM.

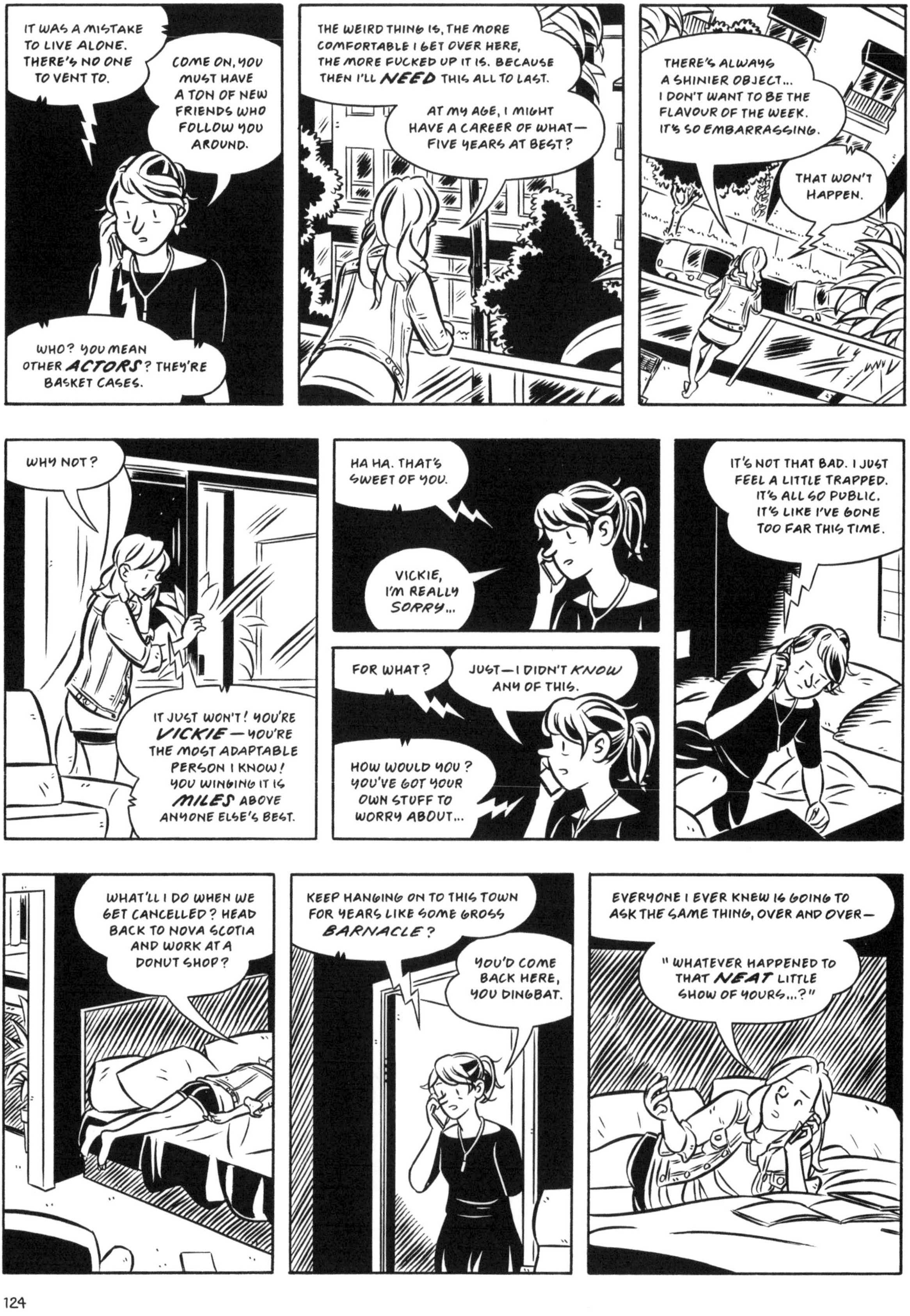

IT WAS A MISTAKE TO LIVE ALONE. THERE'S NO ONE TO VENT TO.
COME ON, YOU MUST HAVE A TON OF NEW FRIENDS WHO FOLLOW YOU AROUND.
WHO? YOU MEAN OTHER ACTORS? THEY'RE BASKET CASES.
THE WEIRD THING IS, THE MORE COMFORTABLE I GET OVER HERE, THE MORE FUCKED UP IT IS. BECAUSE THEN I'LL NEED THIS ALL TO LAST.
AT MY AGE, I MIGHT HAVE A CAREER OF WHAT— FIVE YEARS AT BEST?
THERE'S ALWAYS A SHINIER OBJECT... I DON'T WANT TO BE THE FLAVOUR OF THE WEEK. IT'S SO EMBARRASSING.
THAT WON'T HAPPEN.
WHY NOT?
IT JUST WON'T! YOU'RE VICKIE — YOU'RE THE MOST ADAPTABLE PERSON I KNOW! YOU WINGING IT IS MILES ABOVE ANYONE ELSE'S BEST.
HA HA. THAT'S SWEET OF YOU.
VICKIE, I'M REALLY SORRY...
FOR WHAT?
JUST—I DIDN'T KNOW ANY OF THIS.
HOW WOULD YOU? YOU'VE GOT YOUR OWN STUFF TO WORRY ABOUT...
IT'S NOT THAT BAD. I JUST FEEL A LITTLE TRAPPED. IT'S ALL SO PUBLIC. IT'S LIKE I'VE GONE TOO FAR THIS TIME.
WHAT'LL I DO WHEN WE GET CANCELLED? HEAD BACK TO NOVA SCOTIA AND WORK AT A DONUT SHOP?
KEEP HANGING ON TO THIS TOWN FOR YEARS LIKE SOME GROSS BARNACLE?
YOU'D COME BACK HERE, YOU DINGBAT.
EVERYONE I EVER KNEW IS GOING TO ASK THE SAME THING, OVER AND OVER—
"WHATEVER HAPPENED TO THAT NEAT LITTLE SHOW OF YOURS...?"

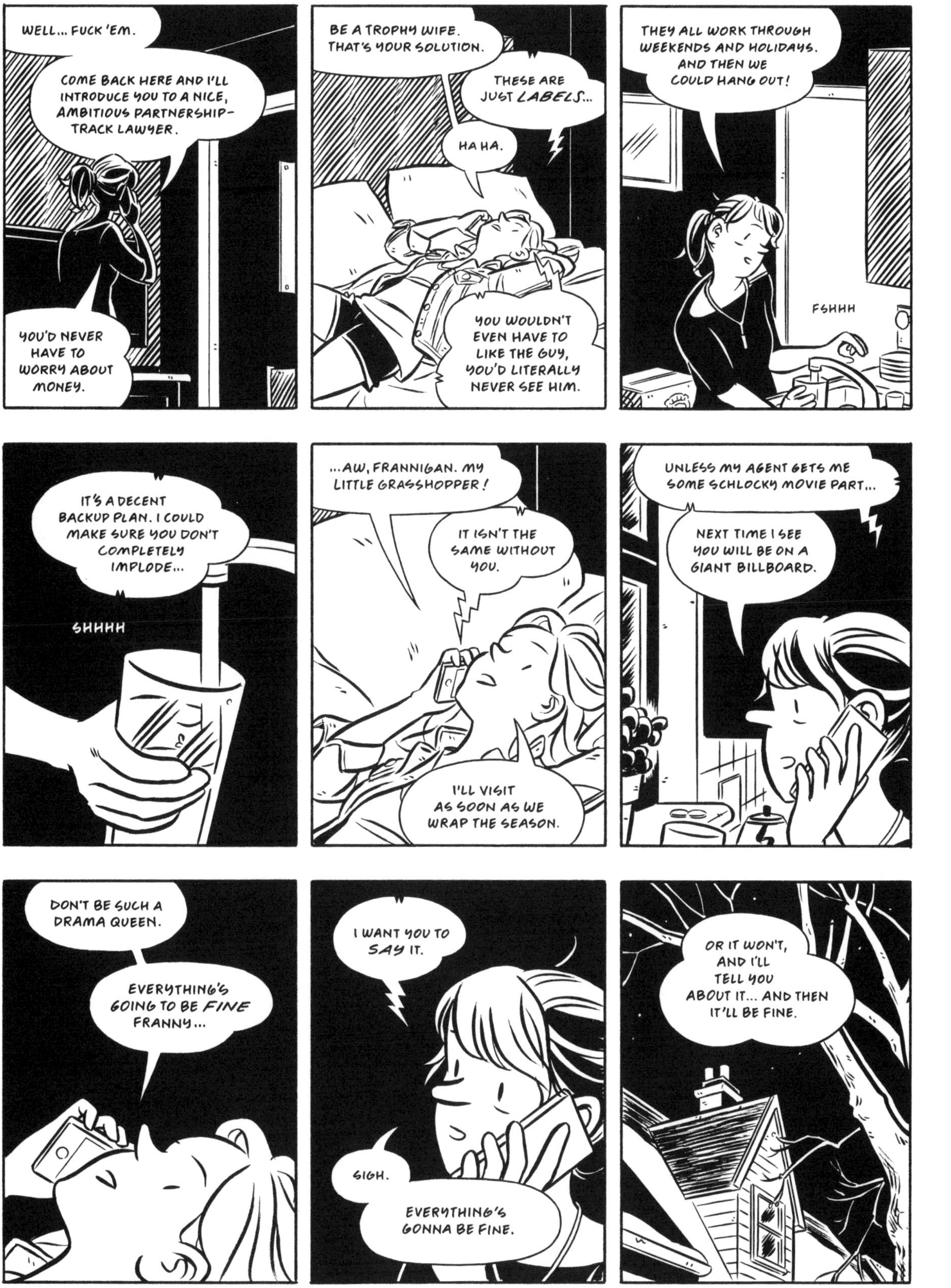
WELL... FUCK 'EM.
COME BACK HERE AND I'LL INTRODUCE YOU TO A NICE, AMBITIOUS PARTNERSHIP-TRACK LAWYER.
YOU'D NEVER HAVE TO WORRY ABOUT MONEY.
BE A TROPHY WIFE. THAT'S YOUR SOLUTION.
THESE ARE JUST LABELS...
HA HA.
YOU WOULDN'T EVEN HAVE TO LIKE THE GUY, YOU'D LITERALLY NEVER SEE HIM.
THEY ALL WORK THROUGH WEEKENDS AND HOLIDAYS. AND THEN WE COULD HANG OUT!
FSHHH
IT'S A DECENT BACKUP PLAN. I COULD MAKE SURE YOU DON'T COMPLETELY IMPLODE...
SHHHH
...AW, FRANNIGAN. MY LITTLE GRASSHOPPER!
IT ISN'T THE SAME WITHOUT YOU.
I'LL VISIT AS SOON AS WE WRAP THE SEASON.
UNLESS MY AGENT GETS ME SOME SCHLOCKY MOVIE PART...
NEXT TIME I SEE YOU WILL BE ON A GIANT BILLBOARD.
DON'T BE SUCH A DRAMA QUEEN.
EVERYTHING'S GOING TO BE FINE FRANNY...
I WANT YOU TO SAY IT.
SIGH.
EVERYTHING'S GONNA BE FINE.
OR IT WON'T, AND I'LL TELL YOU ABOUT IT... AND THEN IT'LL BE FINE.

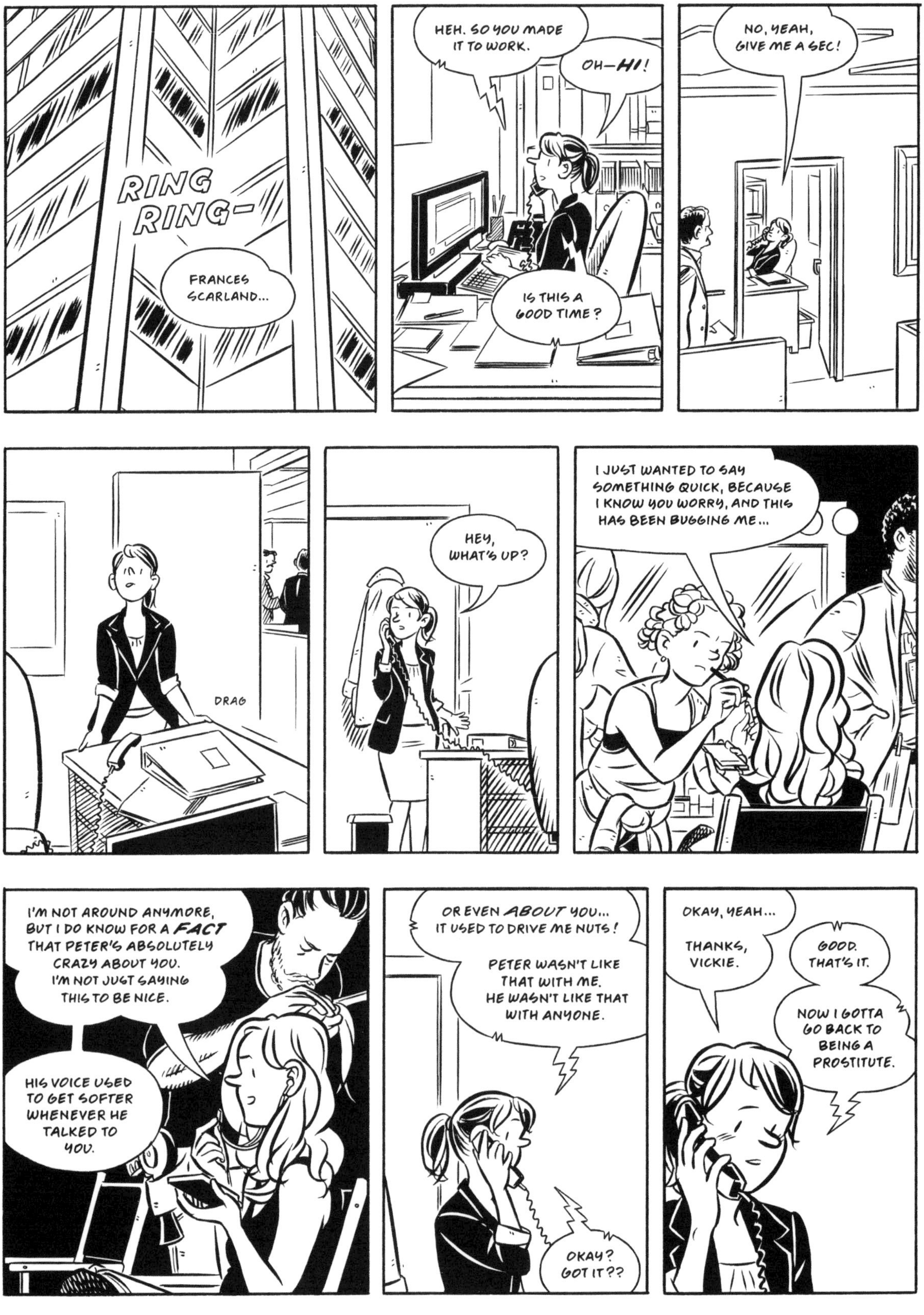
RING RING-
FRANCES SCARLAND...
HEH. SO YOU MADE IT TO WORK.
OH-HI!
IS THIS A GOOD TIME?
NO, YEAH, GIVE ME A SEC!
DRAG
HEY, WHAT'S UP?
I JUST WANTED TO SAY SOMETHING QUICK, BECAUSE I KNOW YOU WORRY, AND THIS HAS BEEN BUGGING ME...
I'M NOT AROUND ANYMORE, BUT I DO KNOW FOR A FACT THAT PETER'S ABSOLUTELY CRAZY ABOUT YOU. I'M NOT JUST SAYING THIS TO BE NICE.
HIS VOICE USED TO GET SOFTER WHENEVER HE TALKED TO YOU.
OR EVEN ABOUT YOU... IT USED TO DRIVE ME NUTS!
PETER WASN'T LIKE THAT WITH ME. HE WASN'T LIKE THAT WITH ANYONE.
OKAY? GOT IT??
OKAY, YEAH...
THANKS, VICKIE.
GOOD. THAT'S IT.
NOW I GOTTA GO BACK TO BEING A PROSTITUTE.

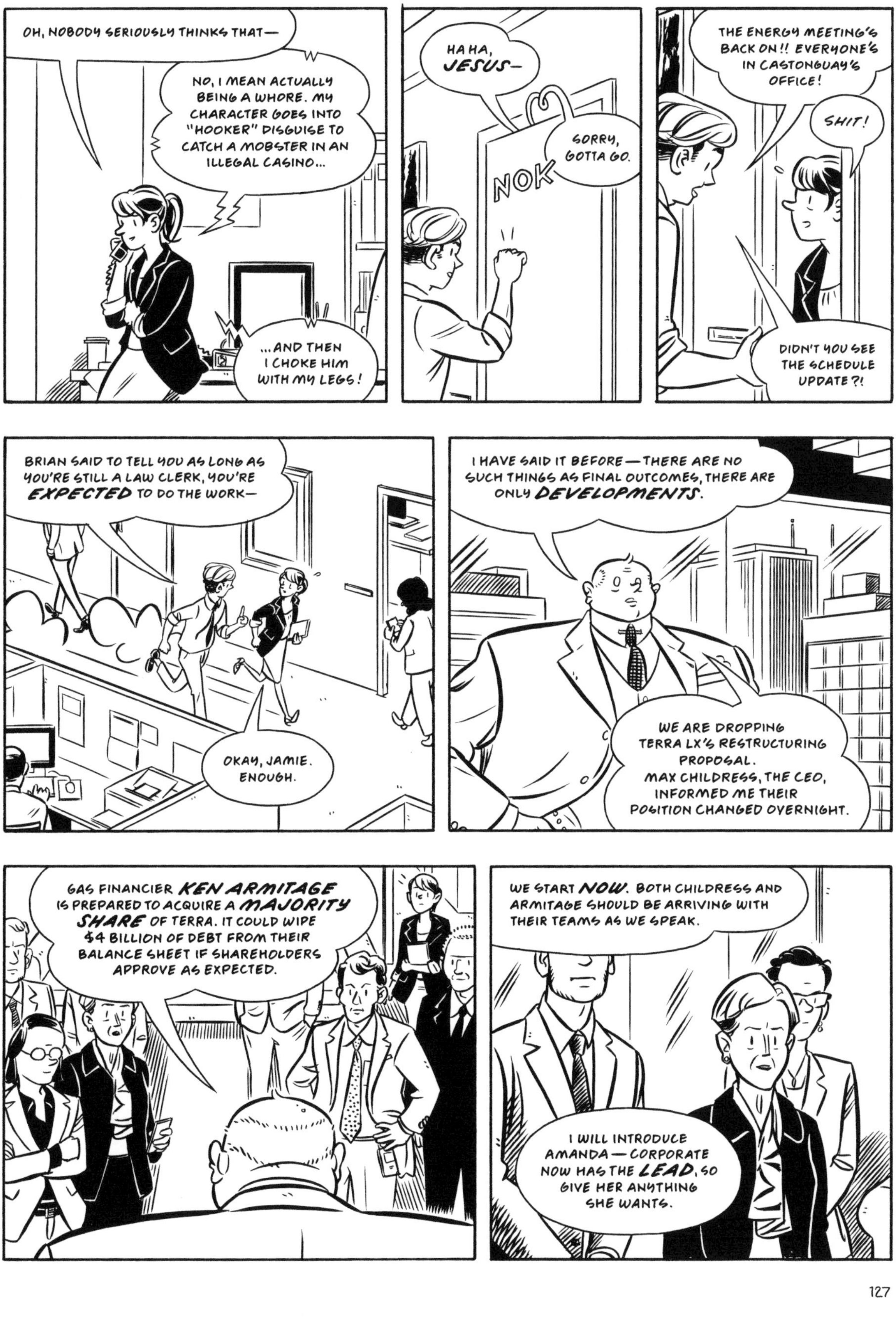
OH, NOBODY SERIOUSLY THINKS THAT—
NO, I MEAN ACTUALLY BEING A WHORE. MY CHARACTER GOES INTO "HOOKER" DISGUISE TO CATCH A MOBSTER IN AN ILLEGAL CASINO...
...AND THEN I CHOKE HIM WITH MY LEGS!
HA HA, JESUS—
NOK
SORRY, GOTTA GO.
THE ENERGY MEETING'S BACK ON!! EVERYONE'S IN CASTONGUAY'S OFFICE!
SHIT!
DIDN'T YOU SEE THE SCHEDULE UPDATE?!
BRIAN SAID TO TELL YOU AS LONG AS YOU'RE STILL A LAW CLERK, YOU'RE EXPECTED TO DO THE WORK—
OKAY, JAMIE. ENOUGH.
I HAVE SAID IT BEFORE—THERE ARE NO SUCH THINGS AS FINAL OUTCOMES, THERE ARE ONLY DEVELOPMENTS.
WE ARE DROPPING TERRA LX'S RESTRUCTURING PROPOSAL. MAX CHILDRESS, THE CEO, INFORMED ME THEIR POSITION CHANGED OVERNIGHT.
GAS FINANCIER KEN ARMITAGE IS PREPARED TO ACQUIRE A MAJORITY SHARE OF TERRA. IT COULD WIPE $4 BILLION OF DEBT FROM THEIR BALANCE SHEET IF SHAREHOLDERS APPROVE AS EXPECTED.
WE START NOW. BOTH CHILDRESS AND ARMITAGE SHOULD BE ARRIVING WITH THEIR TEAMS AS WE SPEAK.
I WILL INTRODUCE AMANDA—CORPORATE NOW HAS THE LEAD, SO GIVE HER ANYTHING SHE WANTS.

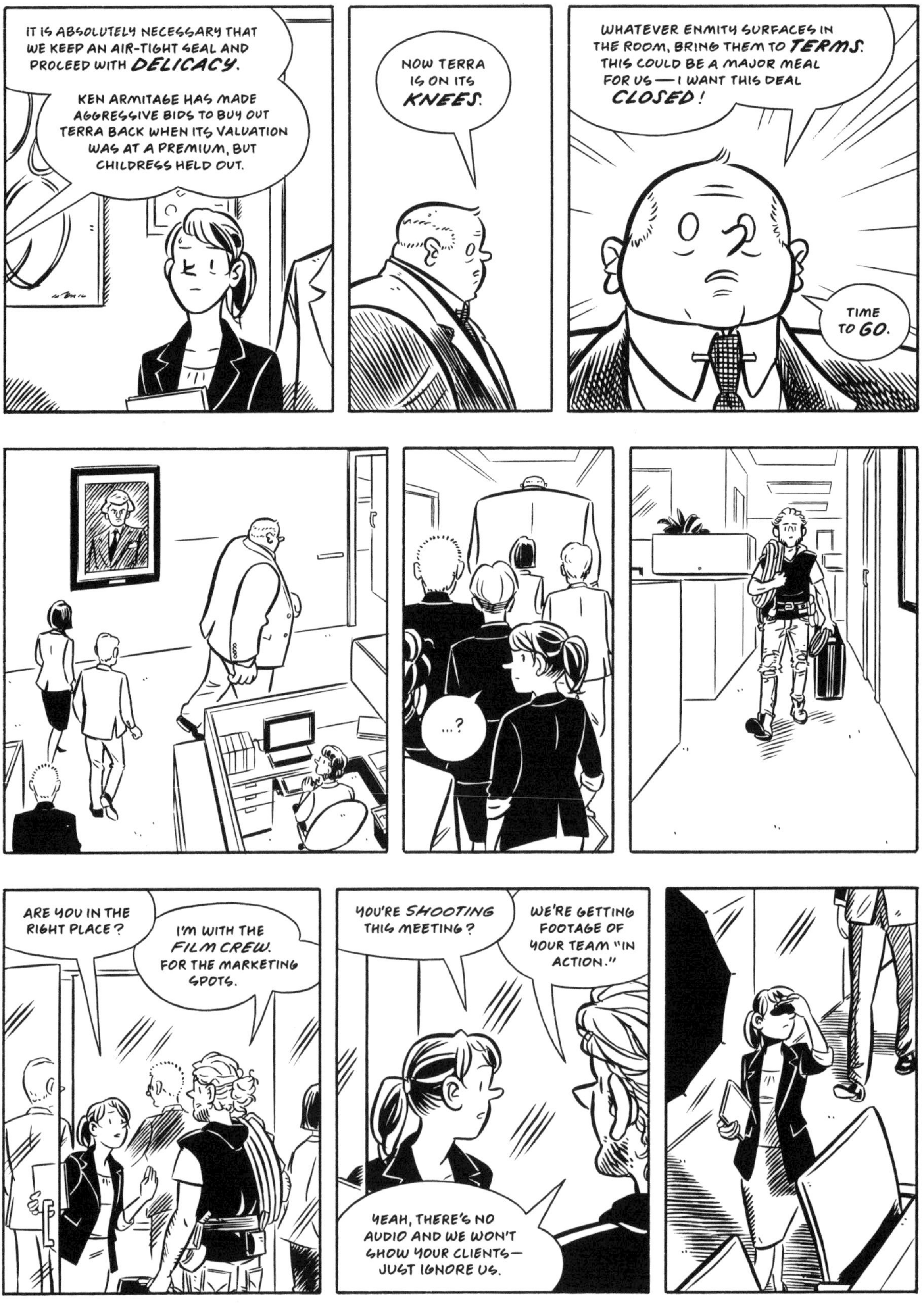
IT IS ABSOLUTELY NECESSARY THAT WE KEEP AN AIR-TIGHT SEAL AND PROCEED WITH DELICACY.
KEN ARMITAGE HAS MADE AGGRESSIVE BIDS TO BUY OUT TERRA BACK WHEN ITS VALUATION WAS AT A PREMIUM, BUT CHILDRESS HELD OUT.
NOW TERRA IS ON ITS KNEES.
WHATEVER ENMITY SURFACES IN THE ROOM, BRING THEM TO TERMS. THIS COULD BE A MAJOR MEAL FOR US — I WANT THIS DEAL CLOSED!
TIME TO GO.
...?
ARE YOU IN THE RIGHT PLACE?
I'M WITH THE FILM CREW. FOR THE MARKETING SPOTS.
YOU'RE SHOOTING THIS MEETING?
WE'RE GETTING FOOTAGE OF YOUR TEAM "IN ACTION."
YEAH, THERE'S NO AUDIO AND WE WON'T SHOW YOUR CLIENTS— JUST IGNORE US.

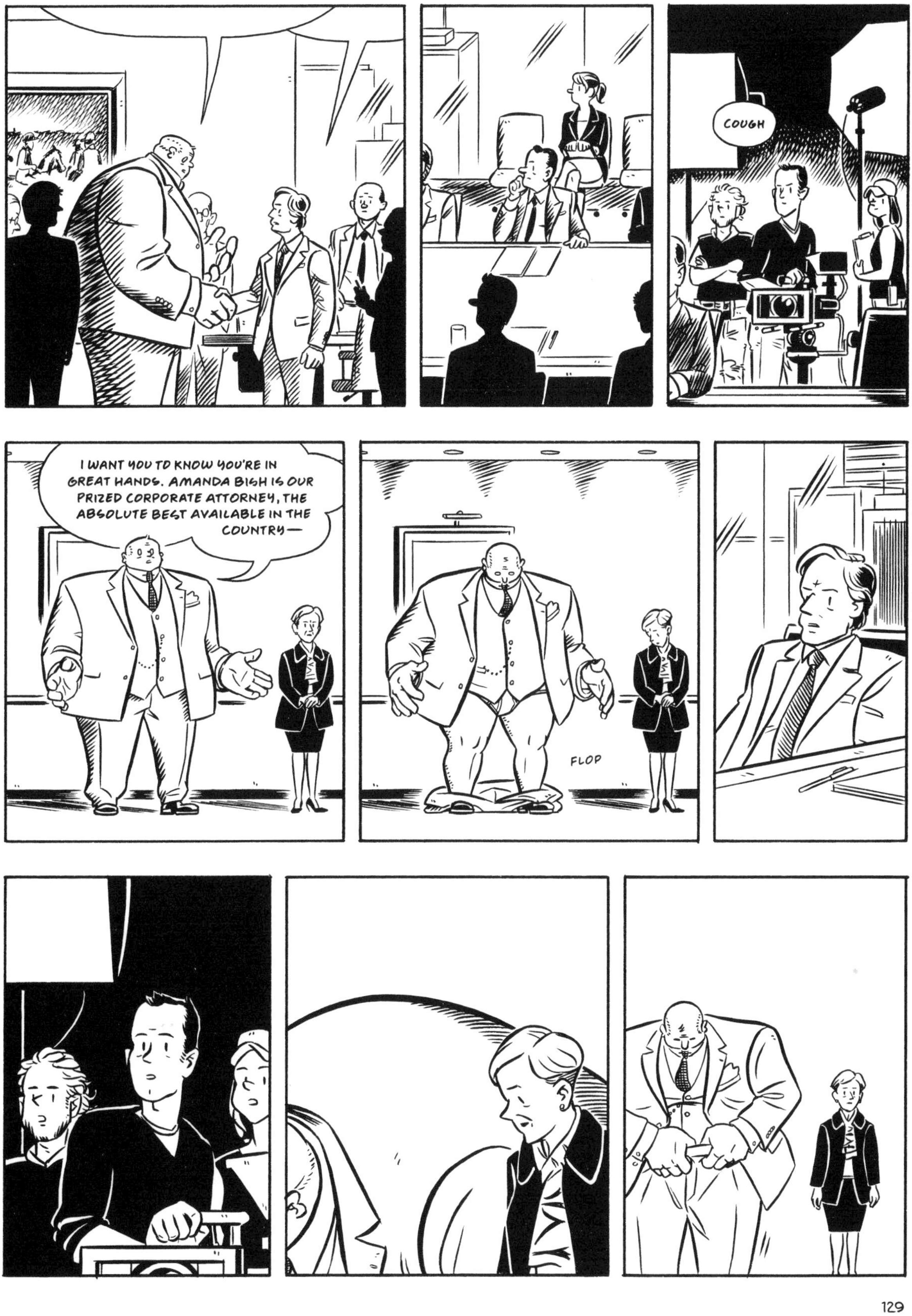
COUGH
I WANT YOU TO KNOW YOU'RE IN GREAT HANDS. AMANDA BISH IS OUR PRIZED CORPORATE ATTORNEY, THE ABSOLUTE BEST AVAILABLE IN THE COUNTRY—
FLOP

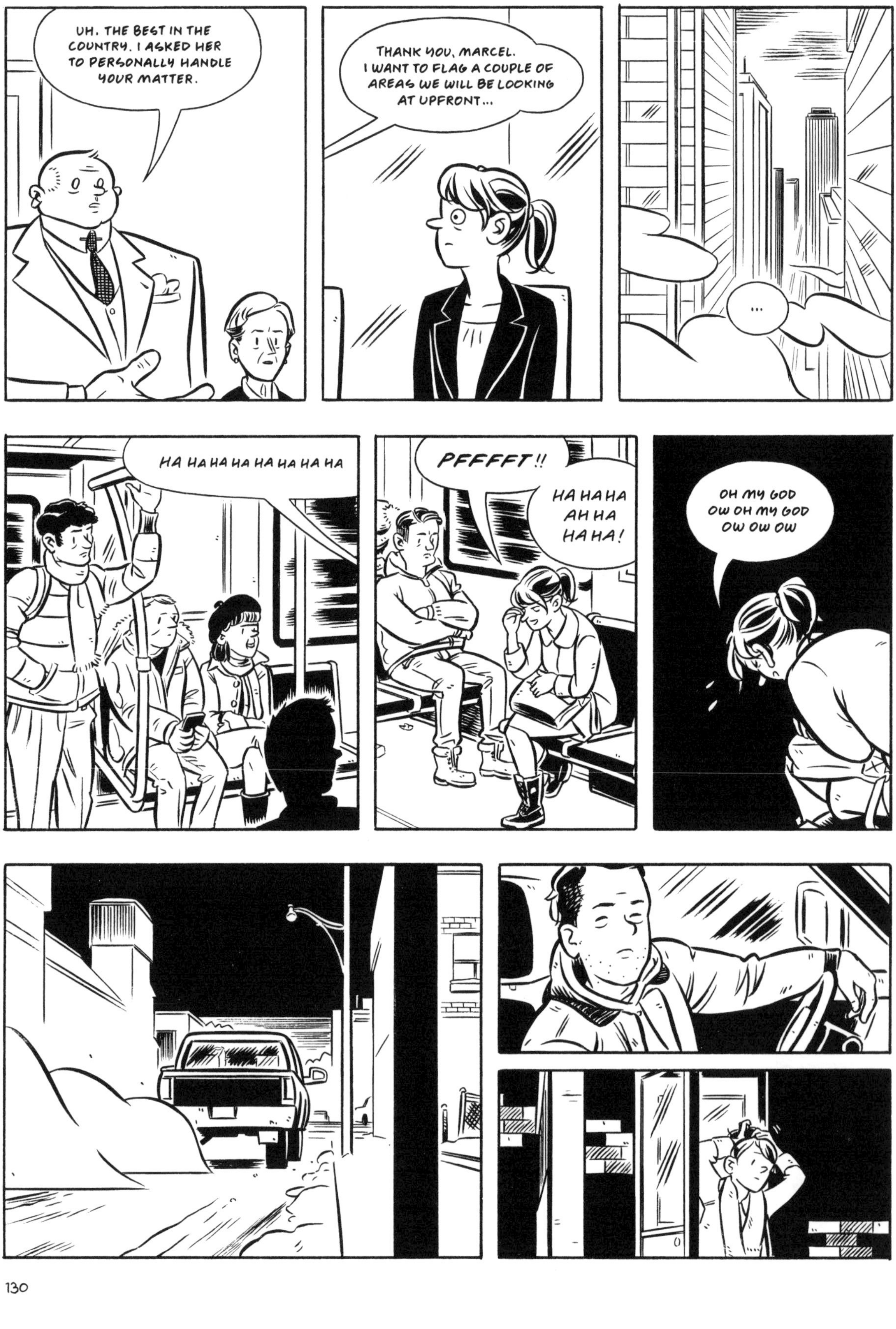
UH. THE BEST IN THE COUNTRY. I ASKED HER TO PERSONALLY HANDLE YOUR MATTER.
THANK YOU, MARCEL. I WANT TO FLAG A COUPLE OF AREAS WE WILL BE LOOKING AT UPFRONT...
...
HA HA HA HA HA HA HA HA HA
PFFFFT!!
HA HA HA AH HA HA HA!
OH MY GOD OW OH MY GOD OW OW OW

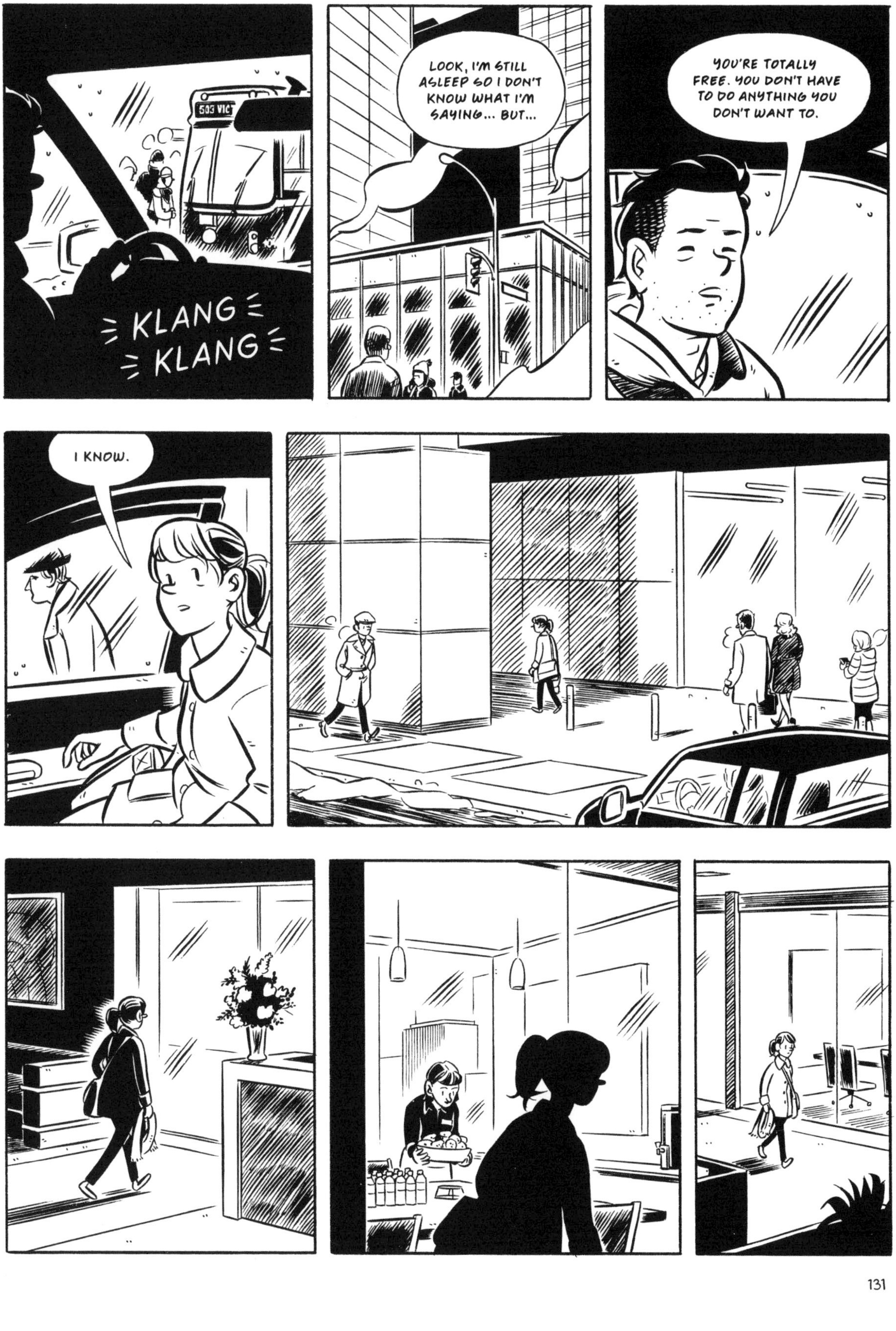
503 VIC
KLANG KLANG
LOOK, I'M STILL ASLEEP SO I DON'T KNOW WHAT I'M SAYING... BUT...
YOU'RE TOTALLY FREE. YOU DON'T HAVE TO DO ANYTHING YOU DON'T WANT TO.
I KNOW.

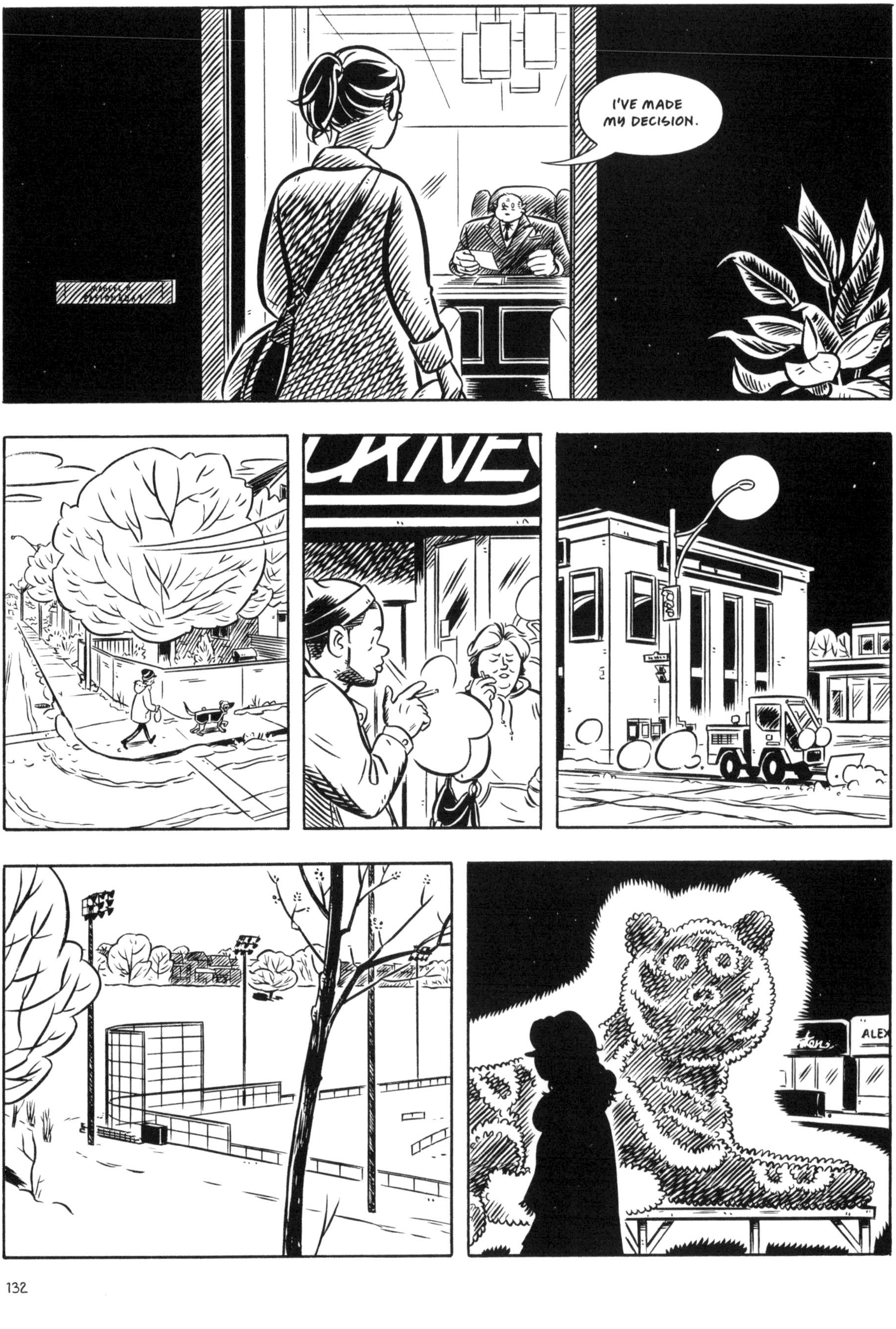
I'VE MADE MY DECISION.
ALEX

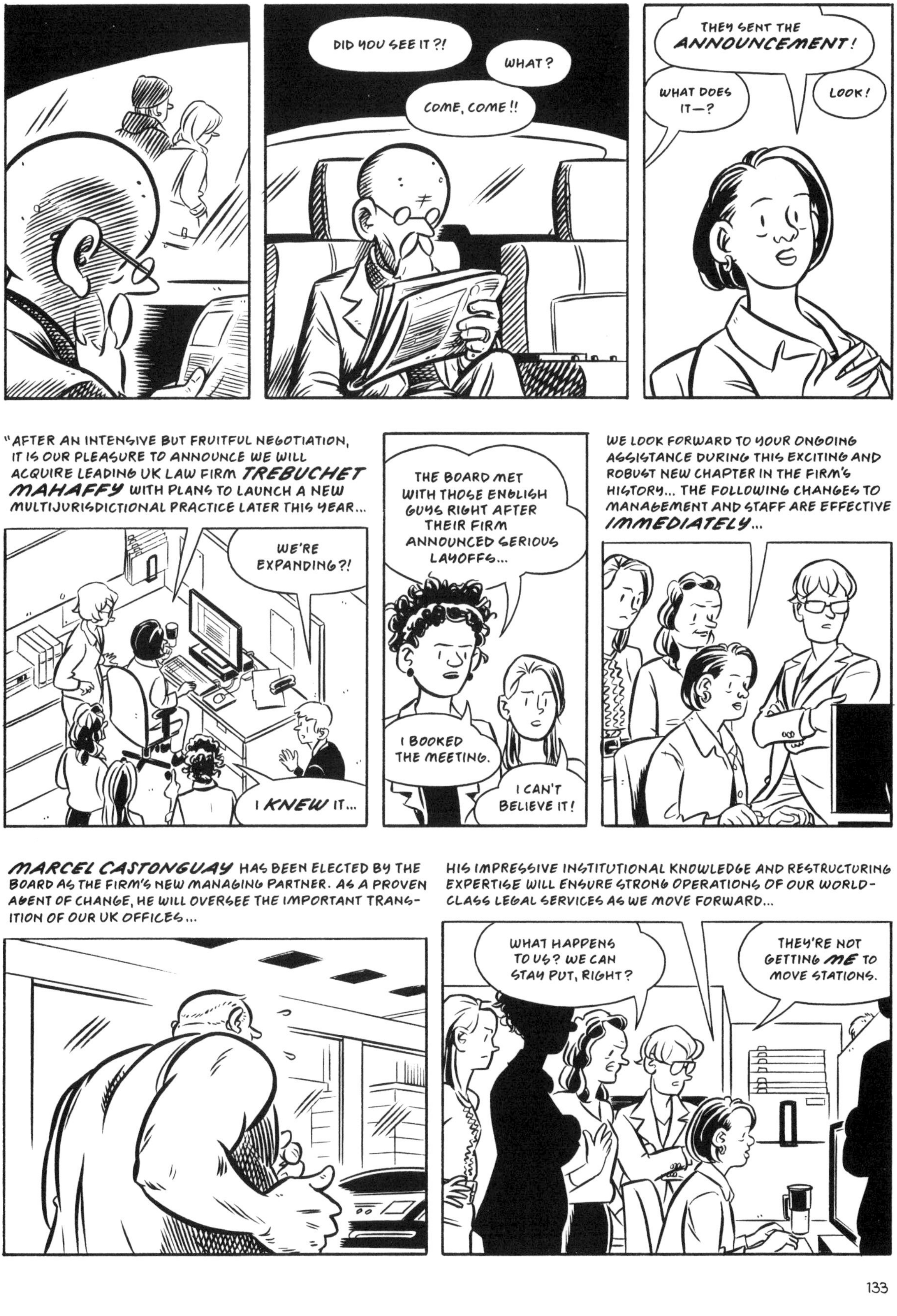
DID YOU SEE IT?!
WHAT?
COME, COME!!
THEY SENT THE ANNOUNCEMENT!
WHAT DOES IT—?
LOOK!
"AFTER AN INTENSIVE BUT FRUITFUL NEGOTIATION, IT IS OUR PLEASURE TO ANNOUNCE WE WILL ACQUIRE LEADING UK LAW FIRM TREBUCHET MAHAFFY WITH PLANS TO LAUNCH A NEW MULTIJURISDICTIONAL PRACTICE LATER THIS YEAR...
WE'RE EXPANDING?!
I KNEW IT...
THE BOARD MET WITH THOSE ENGLISH GUYS RIGHT AFTER THEIR FIRM ANNOUNCED SERIOUS LAYOFFS...
I BOOKED THE MEETING.
I CAN'T BELIEVE IT!
WE LOOK FORWARD TO YOUR ONGOING ASSISTANCE DURING THIS EXCITING AND ROBUST NEW CHAPTER IN THE FIRM'S HISTORY... THE FOLLOWING CHANGES TO MANAGEMENT AND STAFF ARE EFFECTIVE IMMEDIATELY...
MARCEL CASTONGUAY HAS BEEN ELECTED BY THE BOARD AS THE FIRM'S NEW MANAGING PARTNER. AS A PROVEN AGENT OF CHANGE, HE WILL OVERSEE THE IMPORTANT TRANSITION OF OUR UK OFFICES...
HIS IMPRESSIVE INSTITUTIONAL KNOWLEDGE AND RESTRUCTURING EXPERTISE WILL ENSURE STRONG OPERATIONS OF OUR WORLD-CLASS LEGAL SERVICES AS WE MOVE FORWARD...
WHAT HAPPENS TO US? WE CAN STAY PUT, RIGHT?
THEY'RE NOT GETTING ME TO MOVE STATIONS.

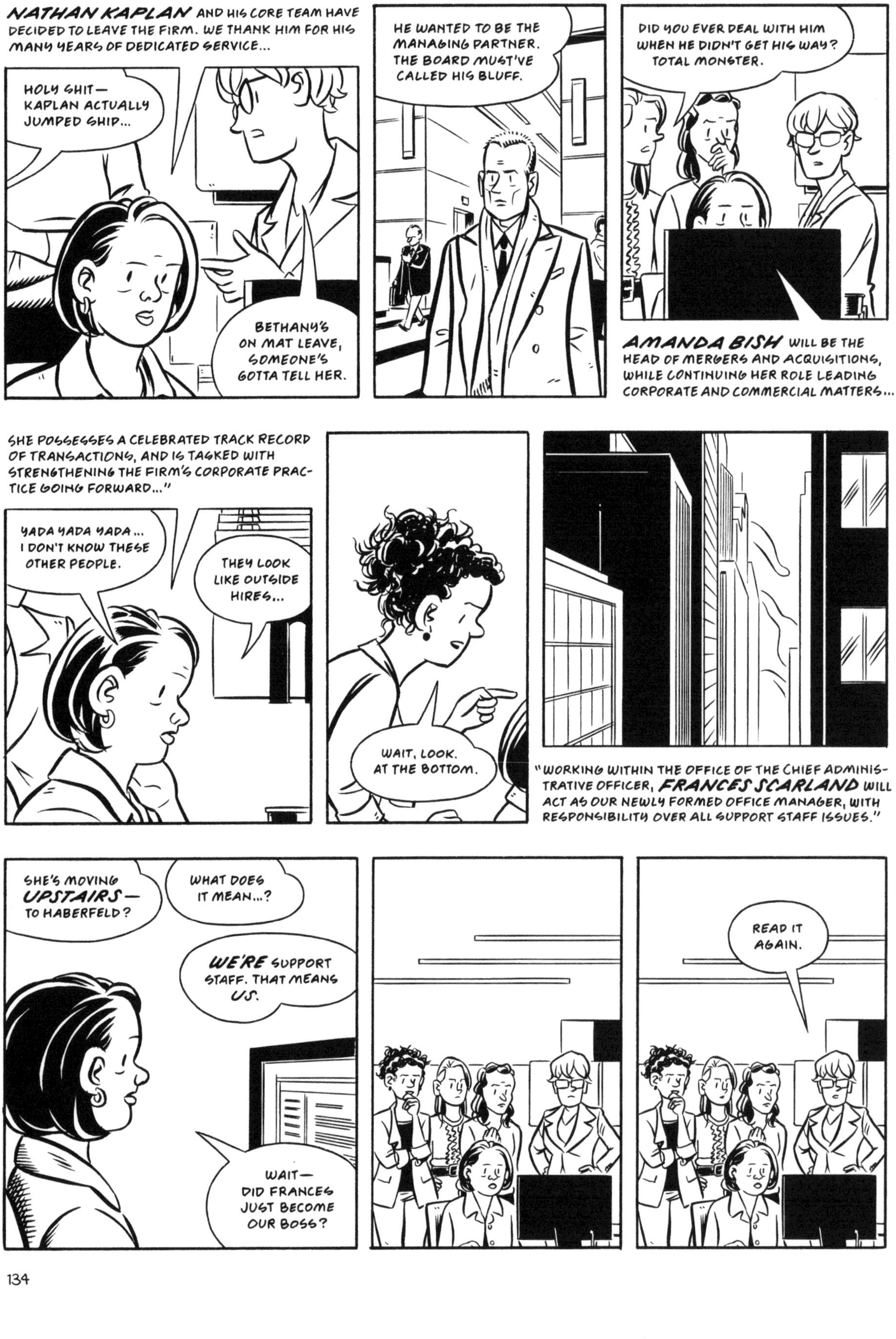
NATHAN KAPLAN AND HIS CORE TEAM HAVE DECIDED TO LEAVE THE FIRM. WE THANK HIM FOR HIS MANY YEARS OF DEDICATED SERVICE...
HOLY SHIT— KAPLAN ACTUALLY JUMPED SHIP...
BETHANY'S ON MAT LEAVE, SOMEONE'S GOTTA TELL HER.
HE WANTED TO BE THE MANAGING PARTNER. THE BOARD MUST'VE CALLED HIS BLUFF.
DID YOU EVER DEAL WITH HIM WHEN HE DIDN'T GET HIS WAY? TOTAL MONSTER.
AMANDA BISH WILL BE THE HEAD OF MERGERS AND ACQUISITIONS, WHILE CONTINUING HER ROLE LEADING CORPORATE AND COMMERCIAL MATTERS...
SHE POSSESSES A CELEBRATED TRACK RECORD OF TRANSACTIONS, AND IS TASKED WITH STRENGTHENING THE FIRM'S CORPORATE PRACTICE GOING FORWARD..."
YADA YADA YADA... I DON'T KNOW THESE OTHER PEOPLE.
THEY LOOK LIKE OUTSIDE HIRES...
WAIT, LOOK. AT THE BOTTOM.
"WORKING WITHIN THE OFFICE OF THE CHIEF ADMINISTRATIVE OFFICER, FRANCES SCARLAND WILL ACT AS OUR NEWLY FORMED OFFICE MANAGER, WITH RESPONSIBILITY OVER ALL SUPPORT STAFF ISSUES."
SHE'S MOVING UPSTAIRS— TO HABERFELD?
WHAT DOES IT MEAN...?
WE'RE SUPPORT STAFF. THAT MEANS US.
WAIT— DID FRANCES JUST BECOME OUR BOSS?
READ IT AGAIN.

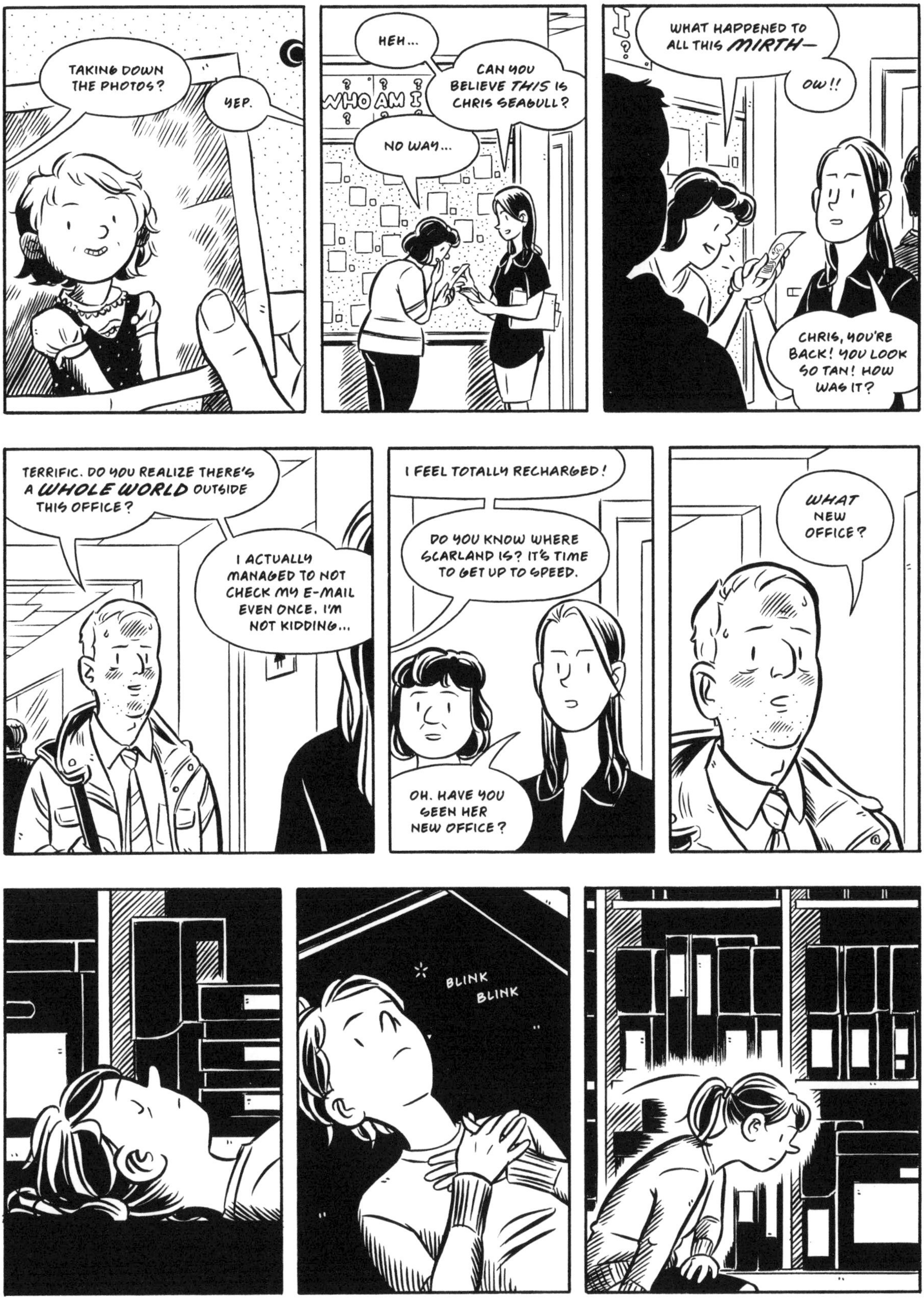
TAKING DOWN THE PHOTOS?
YEP.
HEH...
CAN YOU BELIEVE THIS IS CHRIS SEAGULL?
WHO AM I
NO WAY...
WHAT HAPPENED TO ALL THIS MIRTH—
OW!!
CHRIS, YOU'RE BACK! YOU LOOK SO TAN! HOW WAS IT?
TERRIFIC. DO YOU REALIZE THERE'S A WHOLE WORLD OUTSIDE THIS OFFICE?
I ACTUALLY MANAGED TO NOT CHECK MY E-MAIL EVEN ONCE. I'M NOT KIDDING...
I FEEL TOTALLY RECHARGED!
DO YOU KNOW WHERE SCARLAND IS? IT'S TIME TO GET UP TO SPEED.
OH. HAVE YOU SEEN HER NEW OFFICE?
WHAT NEW OFFICE?
BLINK
BLINK

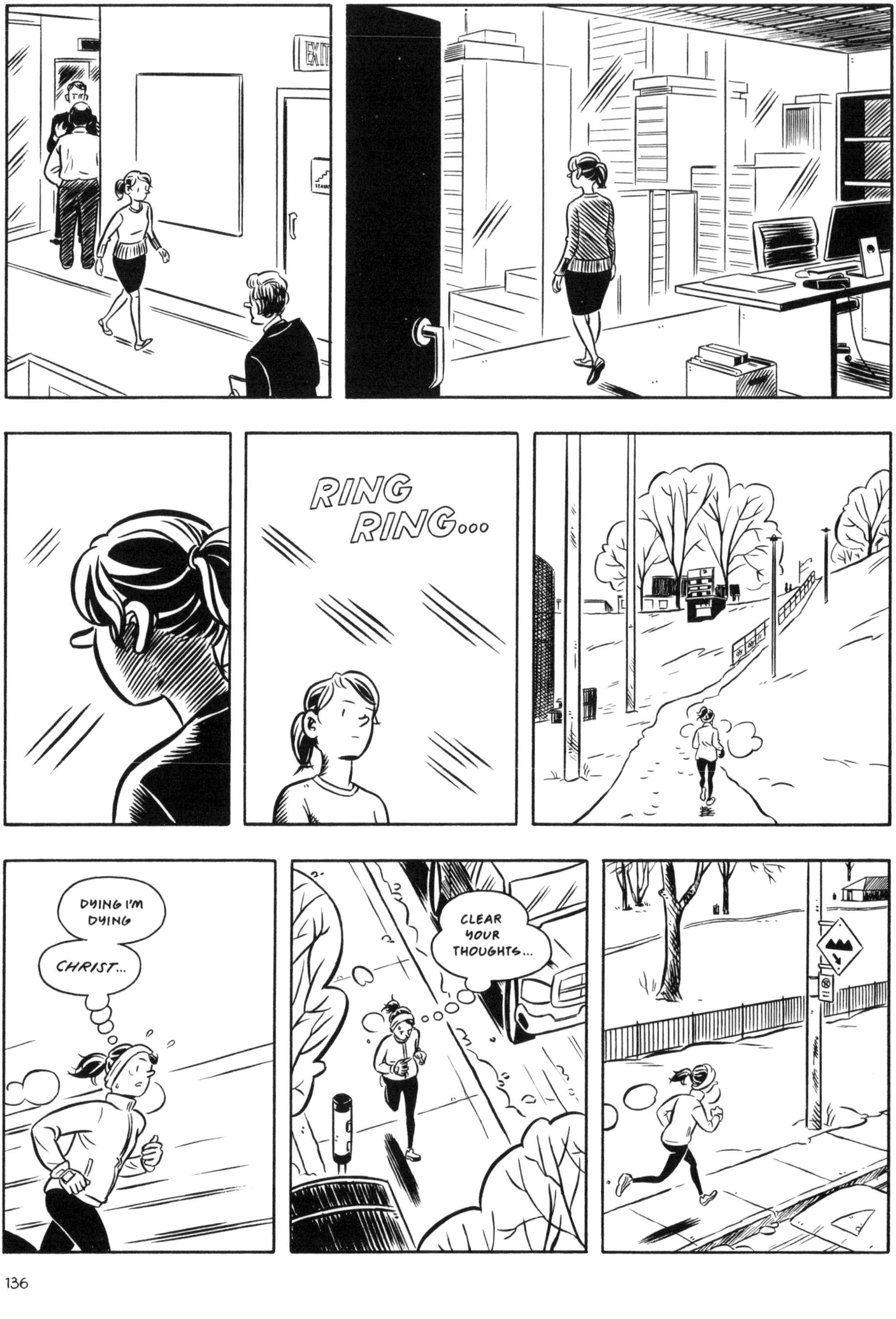
EXIT
RING RING...
DYING I'M DYING
CHRIST...
CLEAR YOUR THOUGHTS...

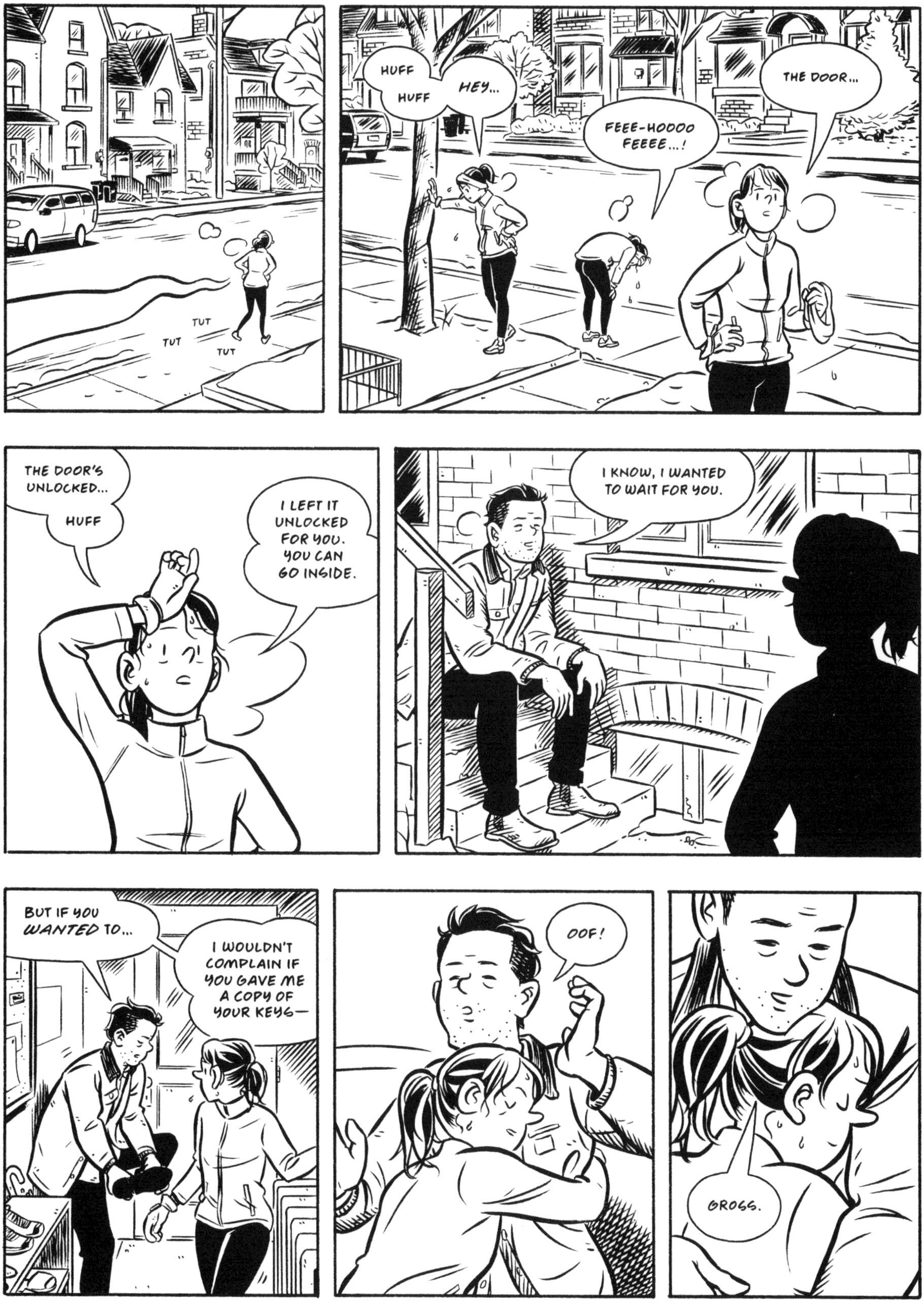
TUT
TUT
TUT
HUFF
HUFF
HEY...
FEEE-HOOOO
FEEEE...!
THE DOOR...
THE DOOR'S UNLOCKED...
HUFF
I LEFT IT UNLOCKED FOR YOU. YOU CAN GO INSIDE.
I KNOW, I WANTED TO WAIT FOR YOU.
BUT IF YOU WANTED TO...
I WOULDN'T COMPLAIN IF YOU GAVE ME A COPY OF YOUR KEYS—
OOF!
GROSS.

ACKNOWLEDGEMENTS

I'D LIKE TO THANK CHRIS PITZER FOR HIS CONSISTENT HELP, LEGWORK AND MORALE.

SARA ROZENBERG FOR HER SOBER PROOFREADING AND COPYEDITING, AND JENNY KAPICHEN FOR YEARS OF WEBSITE CARE.

ALL WHO WERE EXTREMELY GENEROUS IN SHARING TECHNICAL INFORMATION ABOUT THE LAW INDUSTRY OR OTHERWISE, INCLUDING MIKE BROWN, JENNIFER MARSTEN, JENNY KAPICHEN, JAMES RENIHAN AND RACHAEL WALISSER.

THANK YOU CHESTER BROWN, JASON KIEFFER, NICK MAANDAG, SETH, PETER BIRKEMOE, CONAN TOBIAS, CHRIS BUTCHER, MICHAEL DEFORGE, ANNIE KOYAMA, OLE DAMGAARD AND TOM SPURGEON. THANK YOU MARGARET S. LIN, DANIELLE KANGALEE, DAN BROWN, MICHAEL RABY, THE LING AND THE CARPIOS.

HOLLY GOLIGHTLY AND SALLY BROWN ARE TWO DOGS THAT DID NOT AID THIS BOOK IN THE SLIGHTEST, BUT THEY HAVE BEEN GOOD COMPANY.

THANKS TO THE FINANCIAL ASSISTANCE OF THE CANADA COUNCIL FOR THE ARTS, WHICH SIGNIFICANTLY HELPED THE COMPLETION OF THIS NOVEL.

FAIRYTALE OF NEW YORK

WORDS AND MUSIC BY JEREMY FINER AND SHANE MACGOWAN   PERFORMED BY THE POGUES
COPYRIGHT © 1987 BY UNIVERSAL MUSIC PUBLISHING MGB LTD. AND UNIVERSAL MUSIC PUBLISHING LTD.
ALL RIGHTS FOR UNIVERSAL MUSIC PUBLISHING MGB LTD. IN THE UNITED STATES AND CANADA
   ADMINISTERED BY UNIVERSAL MUSIC – MGB SONGS
ALL RIGHTS FOR UNIVERSAL MUSIC PUBLISHING LTD. IN THE UNITED STATES AND CANADA
   ADMINISTERED BY UNIVERSAL – POLYGRAM INTERNATIONAL PUBLISHING, INC.
INTERNATIONAL COPYRIGHT SECURED   ALL RIGHTS RESERVED
REPRINTED BY PERMISSION OF HAL LEONARD LLC

HARTLEY LIN WAS BORN IN 1981 IN TORONTO AND HE ATTENDED McGILL UNIVERSITY. HIS COMICS HAVE RECEIVED DOUG WRIGHT, IGNATZ, AND JOE SHUSTER AWARDS. HE LIVES IN MONTREAL WITH HIS WIFE, AND BROWN DOG OF UNDETERMINED STOCK. THIS IS HIS FIRST GRAPHIC NOVEL.

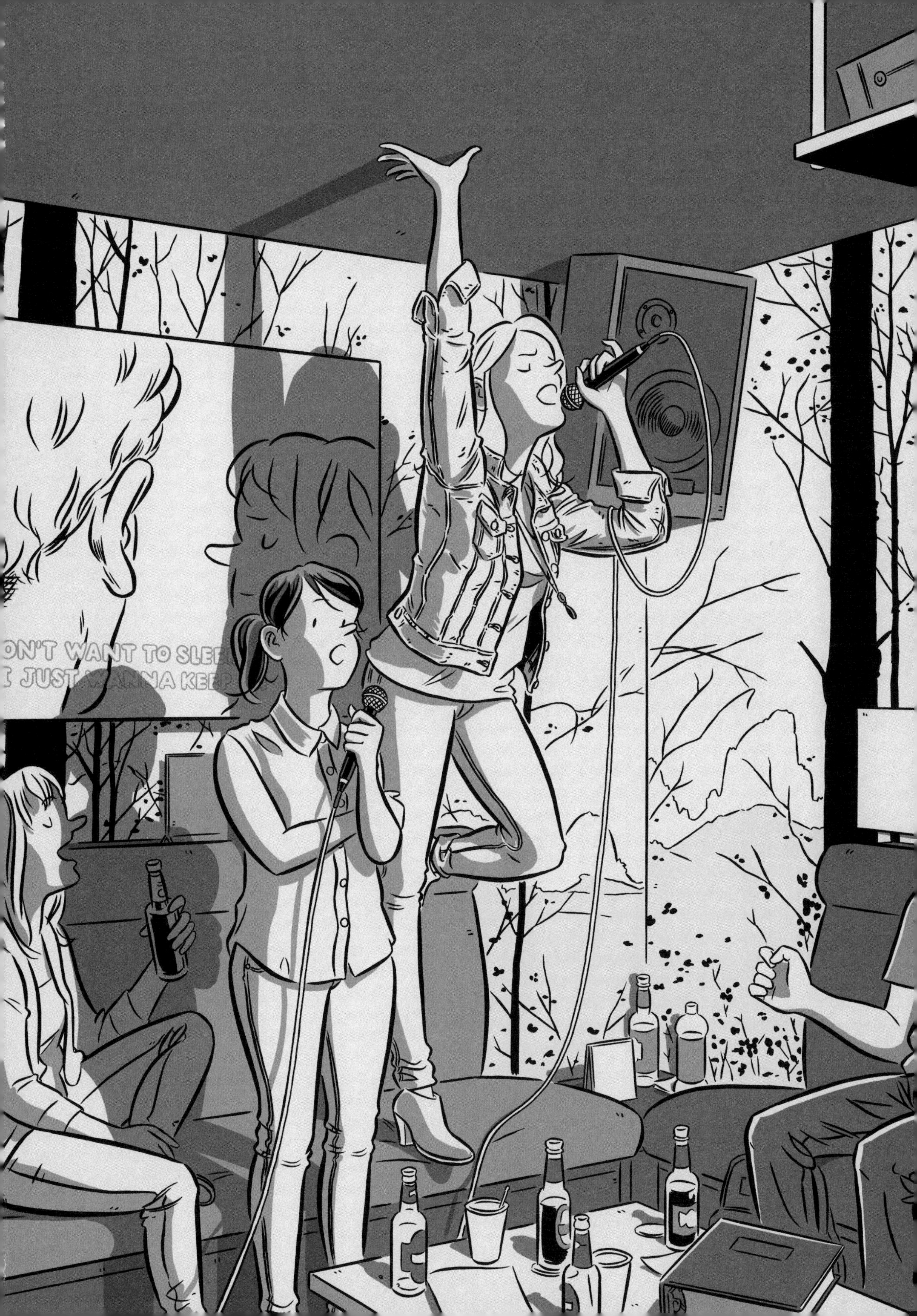
ON'T WANT TO SLEE
I JUST WANNA KEEP

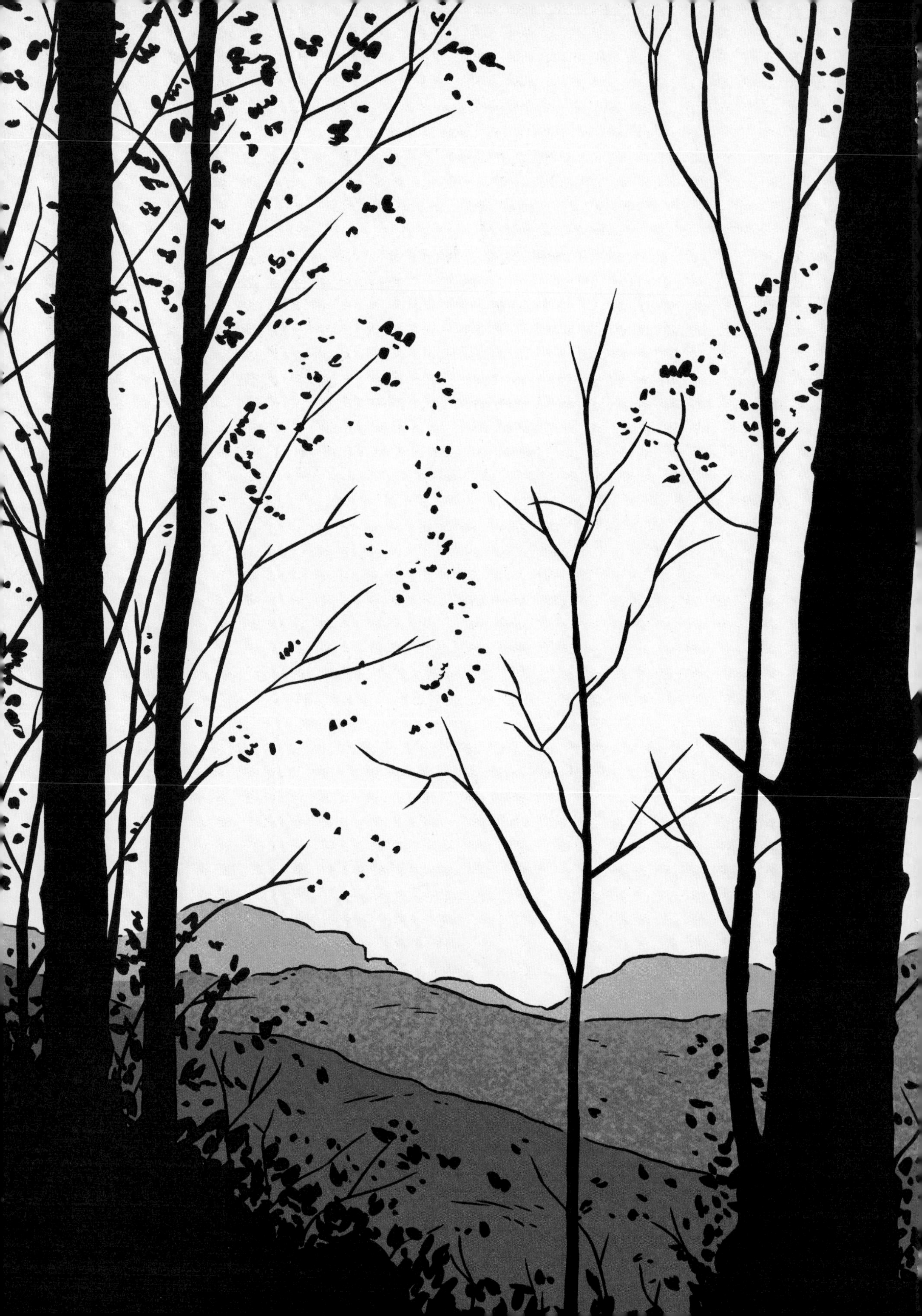